THE GRENADIER GUARDS IN THE WAR OF 1939-1945

Central Press Photos Ltd.

H.R.H. PRINCESS ELIZABETH

Colonel of the Regiment

THE GRENADIER GUARDS IN THE WAR OF 1939-1945

BY

CAPTAIN NIGEL NICOLSON, M.B.E.

AND

PATRICK FORBES

VOLUME II

BY

CAPTAIN NIGEL NICOLSON, M.B.E.

THE MEDITERRANEAN CAMPAIGNS

ALDERSHOT

GALE & POLDEN LIMITED

1949

FIRST EDITION APRIL, 1949

DEDICATED

BY GRACIOUS PERMISSION

TO

HIS MAJESTY

KING GEORGE VI

Colonel-in-Chief of the Regiment

THE GRENADIER GUARDS IN THE WAR OF 1939-1945

VOLUME II

THE MEDITERRANEAN CAMPAIGNS

Contents

PART II

THE ITALIAN CAMPAIGN, 1943-1945

APPENDICES

Illustrations

Maps

PART ONE

THE TUNISIAN CAMPAIGN 1942-43

CHAPTER I

THE EARLY STRUGGLE IN TUNISIA

3RD BATTALION

1

ALGIERS AND MEDJEZ-EL-BAB

Allied landing in North Africa—Original role of 1st Guards Brigade—Arrival and delay in Algiers—Move by road to Tunisia—An alarming situation at Beja—First clash with the Germans at Medjez—Occupation of Grenadier Hill—Strategy of the First Army—Attack on Longstop Hill on Christmas Day—Grenadiers in Medjez railway station—A successful raid in the mountains round Medjez—The appearance of the country and atmosphere of the campaign

ON the 8th of November, 1942, sixteen days after the opening of the **1942** Battle of El Alamein, the Allies forced a landing on the coasts of Algeria and Morocco. Within a few days they had secured the co-operation of the French troops in North Africa, and an Anglo-American force, amounting to little more than two divisions, and already called by the proud but deceptive title "The First Army," began to hurry eastwards to the Tunisian frontier.

The 1st Guards Brigade (Brigadier F. A. V. Copland Griffiths, *See Map p.* **294** D.S.O., M.C.) had had a key role in the original plan of invasion. They were to have landed at Bone and seized the harbour and the airfield. Once the French situation had been cleared up they would then have moved as quickly as possible into Tunisia, without waiting to link up with other Allied troops who had landed farther to the west. Months of hard staff work in London and Scotland had resulted in an elaborate plan for the capture of Bone and the advance to Tunis. The basic brigade of three infantry battalions (3rd Grenadiers, 2nd Coldstream and 2nd Hampshires) was reinforced by the 8th Argyll and Sutherland Highlanders, two Commando battalions, a squadron of tanks, and several specialized units, including a naval detachment whose sole task was to break the boom across the entrance to Bone harbour. The plan was based on the assumption that the French would defend themselves for a few days at least: but many months afterwards, when the Grenadiers found themselves fighting alongside a

1942 French unit in Tunisia, they met by chance the officer who had been in command of the Bone garrison. "We were waiting for you in November," he told them, "and I, for one, would have welcomed you with open arms." It is therefore no exaggeration to suggest that if the 1st Guards Brigade had been allowed to carry out their original role they would have been in a position to change the whole course of the campaign. With Bone in British hands on D Day, and with the French lending their support and perhaps their troops, the Brigade would have been released for their advance on Tunis before the Germans had had time to land more than a token force. A lorry can drive from Bone to Tunis in the course of a single day: a whole brigade could have covered the distance in two. There would certainly have been air attacks on their convoy, certainly a battle on the outskirts of Tunis, and the risks consequent on defeat would have been enormous. But had they been victorious, had they seized the harbour and airfield of Tunis, and been quickly reinforced by land, sea and air, the juncture of the First Army with the Eighth would have taken place in the deserts of Tripolitania instead of at Faid in Southern Tunisia; in January, perhaps, instead of April.

The landing of the 1st Guards Brigade at Bone was cancelled only a few weeks before the North African invasion. There were various reasons for this decision. There was a shortage of assault boats; there was the risk of a heavy bombardment on Bone by German aircraft based on Sicily, and later on Tunis itself; a long and anxious interval, perhaps of ten days or more, would elapse before the force at Algiers could link up with the force at Bone; and there was the political consideration, which governed much of the planning, that the Americans were thought to be more acceptable in North Africa than the British, on account of our overt support of General de Gaulle and our recent naval action against French battleships at Oran, and for this reason United States troops were placed in the lead wherever it was possible.

Nov. 14 Although the 1st Guards Brigade sailed from Gourock, in Scotland, only six days after the original landings, the leading brigade of the First Army were then already about to cross the Tunisian border, and the news of their progress was so startling that many Grenadiers feared that they would not be in time to witness the capture of Tunis, or even the juncture between the First and Eighth Armies. They were much mistaken.

The 3rd Battalion Grenadier Guards (Lieut.-Colonel A. G. W. Heber-Percy) sailed in company with some one thousand two hundred other troops on board the Belgian ship H.M.T. *Leopoldville*. She was uncomfortably crowded, and only good tempers and good discipline could make life tolerable for the men below. The deepest decks, far beneath the water-line, narrowed towards the bows and keel into 1942 wedge-shaped boxes, in each of which sixty or seventy Guardsmen would eat, sleep and take a perilous refuge during a ship's alert. The hammocks, which hung like clustering cocoons from the under-girders of the deck above, would be stowed away in the morning to reveal rows of white wooden tables, and when all was cleaned and scrubbed the men were mustered on deck to take exercise in whatever manner the limited space would allow. The weather throughout the voyage was calm, and the enemy made no attempt to interfere. Steaming in a wide circle round the north of Ireland and far out into the Atlantic, the convoy of a dozen ships approached Gibraltar on the Nov. 20 seventh day. A friendly flock of destroyers and shore-based aircraft emerged through the mist to escort them through the straits. At dusk they passed Gibraltar without stopping. Tarifa, on the Spanish shore, and Ceuta, to the south, threw out a blaze of neutral light across the water, and the Rock itself was visible as a dark hulk hung with lights as dim as glow-worms. In the morning they were safely inside the Mediterranean and within sight of the pink cliffs of Africa. The next day, nine days after leaving the Clyde, they docked in the harbour of Nov. 22 Algiers.

British, American and French flags were seen flying side by side in the city, and as the Battalion marched through the main streets and suburbs they were left in no doubt that the Allied invasion had now become extremely popular. A young Frenchman barred their path to exclaim with explanatory gestures: "Moi aussi, demain: en uniforme: combattant avec les Anglais. Compris?" It was understood. But there was no time to halt or sympathize. Algiers was labouring under its first air raid, and the Guardsmen had fourteen miles to march before they reached the open fields beyond Maison Carrée. Here they halted, and here they spent the next fortnight, encamped among the orange groves and French farms between the Atlas and the sea.

Badly as reinforcements were needed in Tunisia, the Brigade had no means of continuing their journey to the front. Bone harbour was temporarily blocked by sunken ships, the railway was already overloaded with supplies, and for the moment there were no troop-carrying lorries. The delay was most disappointing. Day after day definite orders were expected. The 2nd Hampshires were sent to Tunisia ahead of the remainder of the Brigade, but the Grenadiers and Coldstream only received instructions to provide detachments for a ceremonial parade in Algiers. The four most distinguished figures then associated with the North African operations—Eisenhower, Cunning- Dec. 2 ham, Giraud and Darlan—stood side by side at the foot of the war

1942 memorial to receive the salutes of the Allied contingents as they marched past. The Guardsmen made a great impression on the crowds ("Ils défilaient impeccablement," as the papers put it), difficult as it was for them to adapt their slow, swinging stride to the beat of a French band. Major A. C. Huntington, M.V.O., commanded the detachment, and Capt. D. V. Bonsor carried the British flag.

Dec. 3 This was the last day they spent at Algiers. The next morning the long-awaited lorries drew up between the eucalyptus trees on the road leading to the east, and the Brigade started on their five-hundred-mile journey to the front. They covered over a hundred miles each day, making up by speed across the plains the time which was lost in climbing the passes of the Lower Atlas, where the dusty road was draped fold upon fold across the steep hillsides, so that for an hour on end the progress of the column would be merely vertical. They had a warm welcome from the Arabs, to whom British troops and lorries were still a novelty. Dusky little children, with large eyes as brown and nervous as the eyes of a young fawn, and for clothing wearing nothing more than a patchwork of rags peeling like a scab from their bodies, would swarm round the men whenever they halted, holding up two grubby fingers in the V sign, and begging for the biscuits which had already become a form of international currency. In the evenings the Brigade bivouacked under olive trees, forming a close encampment round their lorries, and lit brushwood fires to scare away the children and
Dec. 5 the flies. They would be off again before dawn. On the third day they passed through Constantine, at that time the Headquarters of the First Army, and halted for the night just short of Souk Ahras. It was here that they received news of the disaster which had befallen the 2nd Hampshires.

> "We assembled in the back of a lorry," wrote one of the Battalion's officers, "let down the canvas flaps (for an air raid on Bone could be seen in progress far to the north), and by the light of a hurricane lamp Colonel Heber-Percy repeated to us the news of the Hampshires which he had just received. For most of us it was our first realization of what war means. People with whom we had talked and laughed a few days before were dead. Germans, angry and successful Germans, were waiting for *us* to follow behind the Hampshires. We must have looked a bit glum when we clambered out of the lorry, but for the moment we did not tell the men the reason why."

This, briefly, is what had occurred. Within a few days of their arrival at Tebourba, the Hampshires, much elated by the prospect of entering Tunis on the next day, had suddenly found themselves the target of an attack by the bulk of the German troops and tanks which had already landed. They fought back against unequal odds with such gallantry that the Battle of Tebourba remained a legend long **1942** after the Tunisian campaign was finished. The Hampshires eventually withdrew with no more than three officers and one hundred and seventy men. They were no longer an effective fighting force. The 1st Guards Brigade were therefore obliged to operate with only two of their three battalions from the very outset of their operations.

Beyond Souk Ahras the Brigade began to enter the zone which *See Map p.* **344** was within range of German fighter aircraft, and grim stories were heard of the destruction which the Messerschmitts had already caused. **Dec. 6** The canvas hoods of the lorries were stripped back, the Guardsmen held rifles and Bren guns at the ready, and the peaceful and almost indolent column suddenly acquired the appearance of a punitive expedition. They were undisturbed all that day. In the afternoon they crossed the Tunisian frontier near Ghardimao, and continued their journey by night, not only for greater security against air attack but because the situation ahead was too grave to allow of a moment's delay. The Germans were on the offensive, and the British line was dangerously thin.

As they approached Beja, the vehicle lights were switched off. It was difficult to know what was happening. American tanks lumbered past in the opposite direction. There was a great deal of confused shouting, but no definite orders. A staff officer thrust his head into the window of the Commanding Officer's car to say "Thank God you've arrived." No more: no explanation. The only course was to move slowly onwards, the drivers leaning forward with their noses pressed against the windscreens, their eyes boring through the darkness and the rain. At 3 a.m. Brigadier Copland Griffiths was found in a farmhouse four **Dec. 7** miles beyond Beja. On his map, which he held out silently to Colonel Heber-Percy, were marked the positions in which his two battalions had been ordered to fight the battle for Beja. The Germans, it seemed, had swept on from Tebourba to threaten the key town of Medjez-el-Bab. It had not yet fallen, for Allied troops were still astride the Medjerda Valley to the north-east, the 11th Brigade on Djebel el Ahmera (already known as "Longstop," a code name of more than usual aptness and permanence), and an American force, Combat Command "B," on the opposite side of the river round Djebel Bou Aoukaz ("The Bou"). The line was held so thinly that there was some doubt whether it would survive a determined attack, and preparations had reluctantly been made to abandon Medjez for a new line farther west. The obvious choice was an escarpment of hills which cut across the Medjez—Beja road eight miles east of the latter town, overlooking the valley of the Oued Zaaga. The Guards Brigade were ordered by the 78th Division (Major-General V. Evelegh) to dig positions on the

1942 escarpment. Here they would be temporarily in reserve, but they must be prepared to allow the forward troops to withdraw behind them at short notice. The safety of Beja would then depend entirely on their own efforts.

Although the battlefield was still many miles away, the distant thud of gun fire could clearly be heard, but as they filed across the hills to their positions and began to turn their first spadefuls of Tunisian soil the only movement discernible in the valley was that of Arab peasants ploughing unperturbed. In a short time the Coldstream, astride the road, and the Grenadiers slightly farther north among a group of sharply rising hillocks, had sketched out a series of trenches which gave them some security, but their flanks were unprotected, nobody seemed to have any idea where the nearest Allied troops were lying, and information from the front was so uncertain that the Battalion expected at any moment to see British troops swarming back over the ridge in front of them, and even German tanks in close pursuit. They had barely begun digging when a rainstorm of great violence burst upon them. It caved in the sides of the trenches, soaked their clothes and bedding, and turned the rough tracks into running streams. "It poured down," wrote the Battalion diarist, "in sliding sheets which whipped over our scanty cover and filled our beds of straw with pools three or four inches deep. Not many slept for more than a few hours, yet when the morning light filtered through the mist we all raised ourselves out of the water and stood around laughing at each other, each claiming to be the wettest and the most filthy. I have always noticed that there comes a point in really bad weather when even worse weather is just funny." The Oued Zaaga flood became a legend in the Battalion against which all subsequent discomfort would be measured. It was seldom even equalled.

One result of the rain was to halt the German attacks. Few aircraft could leave the ground, and no tanks could leave the road. Medjez remained in Allied hands. Brigadier Copland Griffiths went forward in an armoured car to report on the defences of the place, and gave it as his opinion that if it was essential to hold the town (a view which was held more strongly by the French commanders than the British), it would be wiser to economize in troops by withdrawing from Longstop, and hold a narrower perimeter based on the railway station and the group of hills to the south-east which soon afterwards became known as Grenadier Hill. On his return the Brigadier was ordered to move the Brigade into Medjez and take up the positions "which he had recommended." The Coldstream were allotted the station area, the Grenadiers the hill to which they gave their name. A scratch force of four French battalions, some British anti-tank guns, and a few

American tanks completed the garrison of a place which was already **1942** a familiar name in the newspapers of the world.

"He who holds Medjez," argued the French, "holds Tunisia." More accurately, he who does not hold Medjez can never hope to hold Tunisia. In peace time it had been a neat little market town, more French than Arab, deriving its prosperity from the same geographical features which gave it such tactical importance in war. It lies only *See Map* ***p.* 318** twenty miles from Tunis, at the point where the railway and two main roads leading from Tunis to the west converge at the crossing of the Medjerda River. Bounded by hills to the north and south, it blocks the narrow valley, leaving no alternative passage for many miles in either direction. It had already suffered heavily by the time the Grenadiers arrived. They found it deserted except for French troops, stamping mules and stray dogs and cats; the telephone wires trailed across the rooftops, shell holes pitted the streets and house walls, and the central span of the fine Roman bridge hung in the stream and had been replaced by the first Bailey bridge ever to be erected on active service. Before it was light the Grenadier Battalion Headquarters and No. 4 **Dec. 10** Company were already beyond the town, while the remainder of the Battalion were still struggling out of the mud of Oued Zaaga.

Later that morning the Germans attacked, and a Grenadier battalion found itself in action against the enemy for the first time since leaving the beaches at Dunkirk.

Before settling his dispositions on Grenadier Hill, Colonel Heber-Percy and a small party of officers had gone forward at about 8 a.m. to view the ground. As they stood there, looking around them with some dismay at the great size of the hill and the lack of any natural obstacles to tank attack, there was a sudden burst of firing from in front, and a column of American armoured cars appeared round a bend in the Tunis road, beating a hurried retreat towards Medjez.

> "We waited rather helplessly," reads the War Diary, "for some sign of the pursuers. Suddenly the French officers with us yelled: 'Tank Boche! Tank Boche!' pointing with rigid fingers at the plain. We saw four or five black shapes crawling like beetles over a rise in the ground, about fifty yards apart, and a quarter of a mile from where we stood. Shells began to explode on the ridge where the Americans were disappearing, and when they were out of sight the German tanks turned their attention to our own defenceless little group. I cannot pretend that the shells fell very thick or very close, but it did seem for the moment that we should all be cut off. We began to make our way back with affected calm in groups of twos and threes."

They reached the safety of the ridge without loss, and found that Capt. A. G. Way had already deployed No. 4 Company in makeshift positions round some Arab huts. The German tanks, of which ten or

1942 twelve had now appeared, unsupported by any infantry, remained five hundred yards away, and moved slowly from side to side of the road, wheeling round at intervals to shoot out a sudden tongue of flame; they were firing wildly along the whole length of the ridge. It was not an attack: it was a reconnaissance in force, a *Kraftprobe*. There was little our infantry could do with their rifles, but every heavier weapon was brought into action to give the enemy a false impression of our strength. Some French 75's, the anti-tank guns, and even the machine guns, began pumping back a stream of shells and bullets, and a squadron of American light tanks arrived in time to demonstrate effectively on the right flank. Two of the Grenadiers' 3-inch mortars were beginning to add their bombs to the display, when the Battalion suffered their only battle casualty of the day, their first of the campaign. Lieut. R. C. I. de Rougemont, who commanded the mortar platoon, was setting off to fetch more ammunition, when a shell exploded beside his motor-cycle. He died of his wounds the next day.

The Germans retreated after two hours, leaving on the plain five tanks. Three of them were a total loss, and yielded documents of much value, but the other two were repaired and driven away by German mechanics just as a Grenadier patrol led by Lieut. D. W. D. Bond was creeping forward to blow them up. The Battalion, now completed by the arrival of the remaining companies from Oued Zaaga, occupied the hills as originally intended, and scraped the first shallow trenches which developed month by month into the most complex system of defences on the whole Tunisian front. The total width of the series of rocky knolls which formed Grenadier Hill was over two thousand yards. Each company crowned with a circle of slit trenches the summit of their own knoll, from which they were able to keep the intervening gullies under observation until there was time to block them with mines and wire. One company was held in reserve on the Medjez side of the hill, and Battalion Headquarters occupied the shaft of an old lead mine which ran so deep under the highest hill that it was only after some days that they discovered a complete family of Arabs living in darkness at the far end.*

Once the fixed defences had been made fairly secure the Battalion's next task was to dominate No Man's Land by aggressive patrols. Night after night several independent parties of six to twelve men, usually under the command of an officer, would cross the stony plateau to investigate a farmhouse or a cactus grove, a prominent outcrop of rock or a cross-tracks, moving in ever-widening sweeps which often required every hour of darkness for their completion.

*In this shaft was produced the first copy of the *Cave Chronicle*, the 3rd Battalion's newspaper which retained its name throughout the African and Italian campaigns, long after most of the men had forgotten its original associations.

In this way, not only was Grenadier Hill protected by a screen of skirmishers and the enemy confined to his main line, but our officers and men gained invaluable knowledge of the ground, confidence in the patrolling methods which they had so often practised on training exercises, and the realization that the German troops were not, after all, the faultless automatons which they had supposed. 1942

Lieut. W. S. Dugdale's patrol was the first to draw blood in an encounter with five Germans near the bend in the Tunis road known as Peter's Corner: and a few days later Lieut. D. W. D. Bond earned for himself the Battalion's first Military Cross. The latter's patrol was of an unusual type. In addition to Bond's seven men, there were two 3-inch mortars under Lieut. J. F. Rowley, and a party of pioneers (under Lieut. The Lord Braybrooke), who carried the ammunition. Their object was to creep up to within range of a known enemy position, fire at it all their mortar bombs in as short a space of time as possible, and then seize a prisoner from the ensuing mêlée. At first all went well. The German sentries were spotted against the skyline, and, while Lieut. Bond went forward with a small covering force, Lieut. Rowley and his mortar crews fired one hundred and thirty-two high-explosive shells in three minutes. After the bombardment had ceased there were unmistakable cries of distress ahead, but Lieut. Bond had not moved more than fifty yards farther on when a fusillade of machine-gun fire poured from the German trenches. Lieut. Bond himself and three of his men were hit, one of them fatally, but rather than risk the capture of his entire force he ordered the mortars to withdraw without him. The three wounded men attempted to make their own way back. Lieut. Bond and Gdsm. Rigby crawled as far as their wounds would allow, but the third man, L./Cpl. Pollard, who had been hit in the foot, managed to struggle a mile farther to fetch a mule from a French farm. Returning with the animal, he mounted the other two upon it, and himself limped painfully back a third time along the track. On the main road they found Lieut. Rowley waiting for them with a car. Later that same night Major E. J. B. Nelson attacked the German position with a strong patrol and found that the enemy had fled. Dec. 16 Dec. 19

One further incident during these early days at Medjez illustrates the spirit of daring enterprise which animated all ranks of the Battalion. ("It is difficult," records the War Diary, "to keep a check on volunteers for the most hair-raising adventures.") Two lance-sergeants —Roberts and Cooper—went of their own accord to lie up upon a hillside and observe enemy movements at close range. Having hidden in a convenient cleft in the rocks, they found themselves the next morning in the middle of a German company, with a sentry pacing all

1942 day within twenty yards of where they were lying. This did not deter them from peering through cracks in the rocks and observing with great exactness the position of every post and gun within view. They returned with their invaluable information at nightfall, both wounded on their way back in an encounter with a chance patrol.

About a week before Christmas, rumours of an impending British offensive reached the cave on Grenadier Hill. The First Army was still a very meagre force, and no fresh troops could be drawn from the vast Anglo-American pool in Algeria and Morocco until communications were greatly improved between the base and the front line. There were still almost no reserve dumps of food and ammunition east of the Tunisian border. The field divisions were living from hand to mouth, from railhead direct to the most advanced supply points. The increased bombing of Bone harbour, the shortage of lorries and rolling stock, and the worsening state of the roads and rail tracks led to crisis after crisis in the organization of supply, and it was only through the untiring efforts and ingenuity of the lorry drivers and quartermasters' staffs that the fighting troops were never actually short. Of the appalling difficulties behind the front line the men remained happily unaware. What concerned them more was the consequence of the strain upon supplies, and the lack of fresh troops to relieve them in the front line and to fight at their side.

In mid-December the First Army consisted of little more than the Corps commanded by Lieutenant-General C. W. Allfrey. In it there was the 78th Division, of which the 1st Guards Brigade formed part, and which hitherto had borne the brunt of the infantry fighting: there were some regiments of the 6th Armoured Division which had formed the spearhead of the original advance; and there were a few American combat teams and a few French battalions. This force was mainly concentrated in the Medjerda Valley and in the Sedjenane-Mateur Valley farther north, with no more than armoured patrols, or "feelers," reaching out towards the southern deserts. The Germans, meanwhile, were pouring troops into the country by sea and air. The Commander of the First Army, General Anderson, considered that if he lost his chance to attack while he still had a slight superiority it would not recur for many months. Yet where was he to attack? General Eisenhower's proposal to cut the coastal road by a thrust to Sousse was ruled out by the shortage of troops and the risk of a German counter-thrust across our communications. The Mateur Valley was blocked by a narrow gorge, and led only to Bizerta. There remained Medjez-el-Bab. And it was at Medjez that General Anderson decided to make his second big effort of the campaign.

His objective was, once again, Tunis. His plan was to recapture Longstop, recapture Djebel Bou Aoukaz, and then use his tanks to complete the break-through. The 1st Guards Brigade, who were still considered the freshest infantry in the field, were ordered to carry out the initial phases. The 2nd Coldstream Guards would first take Longstop, hand it over on capture to an American battalion, and then regroup with the 3rd Grenadiers for the capture of Djebel Bou Aoukaz. The success of the plan depended entirely upon the condition of the ground. Unless there was fine weather for at least a week, the Medjerda Valley would never harden sufficiently to carry tanks: if the tanks were unable to move across country, the efforts of the infantry would be thrown away. The rain held off for six days, and it was decided to carry out at least the first phases of the operation. 1942

It was a wretched barrage of sixteen field guns and a few medium guns, firing for a quarter of an hour, which opened the attack on Longstop; but to most of the watchers on Grenadier Hill it was their first sight of massed artillery fire, and they were much impressed. The Grenadiers had detached No. 3 Company (Major E. J. B. Nelson) to occupy the village of Grich el Oued on the right bank of the Medjerda, both as a right-flank guard to the Coldstream and as a firm base for the later attack on the Bou. The village was said to be unoccupied except by the usual pack of half-wild dogs, but when the company reached it they saw a few figures flitting away in the moonlight after an exchange of shots. After Lieut. T. H. Faber had driven away an inquisitive German patrol, the enemy sat back on the higher ground and shelled the village methodically. The rain, on this all-important day, began to fall in sheets, reducing the flat water meadows to quagmires. In the morning two anti-tank guns were hauled up by bullocks harnessed to the trails, and three light tanks managed to struggle into the village, but soon afterwards the ground became too swampy even for mules. Not only was it very difficult to evacuate casualties, but the company found themselves cut off from all but a thin trickle of supplies, and on Christmas Day they put themselves on half-rations, supplemented by a few scraggy chickens boiled in the muddy water of the Medjerda. Dec. 23 Dec. 24 Dec. 25

The Coldstream meanwhile had found Longstop held more strongly than they had expected. They fought brilliantly to gain all but the final peak of this great complex of hills, but when the Americans relieved them the Germans launched strong counter-attacks, and the Coldstream were sent back to the assistance of their Allies. By this time the decision had been taken to cancel the bigger operation, and there now seemed no hope that even Longstop would be captured. Nos. 1 and 4 Companies of the Grenadiers were sent round to hold a

1942 firm line near the bottom of the hill to cover the withdrawal of the Coldstream and the Americans, and at the same time No. 3 Company withdrew unmolested from Grich el Oued.

It had been a most disheartening experience for the Brigade, particularly for the Coldstream. They had set out to capture Longstop without adequate information about the size or the configuration of the hill, or the strength in which it was held. It had been in Allied hands three weeks before, and voluntarily abandoned. And as they fought they knew that the rain, which poured down unceasingly, was making it impossible for the tanks to exploit any success which the infantry might gain. On the top of all this, it was Christmas. A German wireless operator chipped in on the British wave-length with this gloomy Christmas Eve message: "If any of you chaps have got a dry sock, I should hang it up. I haven't."

While the 8th Argyll and Sutherland Highlanders (now incorporated in the 1st Guards Brigade) took over the defence of Grenadier Hill, and the Coldstream moved into reserve, the Grenadiers reassembled in the area of Medjez railway station.

> "It is a collection of substantial sheds," wrote the Battalion's Intelligence Officer in the semi-official diary, "some of them of concrete, others of corrugated iron and white brick, and others are low, pink *abris* with shutters still hanging from the windows by one corner, until the next close miss brings them to the ground. There are no proper roads, but earth tracks link our various buildings, and these are cluttered up with bits of tile, stacks of railway sleepers, half-completed earth shelters, and hunks of clay thrown up from the shell craters. Inside the sheds is the abandoned equipment of three or four armies. The French, to whom these sheds represented Aldershot and Woolwich Arsenal rolled into one, have left stacks of ammunition and old guns. The Germans have left us a few helmets, leggings and sentimental scraps of letters hanging about their latrines. The Americans leave a great deal behind wherever they go, and many of us by this time have U.S. water-bottles and mess-tins, which the Americans eye with suspicious regret whenever they visit us. Finally, the Coldstream and ourselves have added a small British collection to the motley debris. In rain and mud, among shells and sudden moves and alarms, one cannot expect to have one's kit as permanently ready for inspection as at Wellington Barracks. The general effect of this station is one of untidiness and ruin and waste.
>
> "The most awful moment of the day is at 6 a.m., when the duty officer yells out 'Stand to!' We roll out of the wooden bunks in the command post, fully dressed as we always are, and the streaky stuffiness of sleep still clings to our hair and cheeks. We stand outside the sheds, stamping up and down in the starlight, and with the approach of dawn and prospect of breakfast we feel more prepared to address agreeable remarks to each other. About this time the four German guns behind Longstop begin their shelling programme. The sequence

> of noises is as follows: there is a dull distant boom; one waits a little 1942
> apprehensively: fifteen seconds later the shells begin to arrive with a
> rushing wind rising to a screech, followed by a shattering roar as they Dec. 26
> explode within our lines. Today the first shell landed on the road fifteen yards in front of the officers' mess. The next came only a few feet behind it, completely wrecking the outhouse which we use as a latrine. Nobody hurt so far, but, having been so skilfully bracketed, we await the next salvo with sinking hearts. But presumably, seeing the mess enveloped in a cloud of dust, the German gunners thought that it was fixed, for they put their next four rounds into the pioneer shed. Four men were hit, none badly, but the blast lifted the great steel rolling doors clean off their hinges and hurled them ten feet away, each one riddled with shrapnel holes like a cheese-grater. The next round was fortunately a dud ('fabriqué à Paris,' the French would murmur, in gratitude to their saboteurs at home), for it landed just outside our command post, and the remainder of that particular effort fell harmlessly in the field behind. It certainly makes life more interesting."

At night patrols began to master a new stretch of territory, reaching out from farm to farm until they were tapping the defences of Longstop itself. On one occasion only did a German patrol return the visit Dec. 27
to the station. They came shortly after dawn, halted in a ditch just short of our outposts, and sent three men forward to investigate the railway sheds. By the time they had discovered that the station was strongly held their comrades had been neatly outflanked by Lieuts. P. Maclean's and T. H. Faber's platoons, the latter supported by an American tank which pursued any Germans who attempted to escape across the plough. Four of the enemy were killed, including their officer, sixteen others wounded and taken prisoner, and the twenty-two who remained surrendered without further fight. This success had cost the Grenadiers not a single casualty. They were the first German prisoners whom the Battalion had seen face to face, and their appearance and the idiocy of their tactics gave our men much new confidence.

After twenty-two days in the front line the Battalion were with- 1943
drawn to a reserve area south of Medjez where the farms were un- Jan. 2
damaged and the hills already sprouting their first blades of wheat. Here they found not only rest but a change of clothing, warm water, letters from England, and the few luxuries which had been sent up for a belated Christmas.

While the remainder of the Battalion rested, No. 3 Company were Jan. 8
again detached for a special operation in the hills north of Medjez. Three battalions of Algerian troops under French officers had already extended the front in this direction, but there was need of men with better equipment and greater experience to exploit the opportunities offered. No. 3 Company had only one object: to capture a prisoner

1943 of war. On the information which could be extracted from him it would be decided whether it was possible to reopen the attack on Longstop from the north. To obtain his prisoner Major E. J. B. Nelson planned a raid which has been described as "a model company operation." Across a trough in the hills the French faced the Germans, the former on Djebel Ang, the latter on Djebel Tanngoucha, with less than five hundred yards between them. There was little activity on either side. As soon as the Grenadiers arrived they began to patrol into the valley, selecting the best approaches to Tanngoucha and taking the greatest care not to reveal the fact that French troops had been relieved by British. When their preparations were complete they attacked one morning just before first light. Two platoons under
Jan. 13 Lieuts. W. S. Dugdale, M.C., and R. A. Meyrick crept up to the base of the German position while a barrage from the 25-pounders fell on the peak and far slopes. Both platoons reached the summit before the Germans opened fire. Dugdale saw three men running towards a trench, and, outstripping his platoon by several yards, he reached it almost simultaneously with the Germans. Holding one of them down with his foot, he grappled with another, the third having run away. His own men then came up and the prisoners were secured. Meyrick meanwhile had worked his way up to the other side of the peak, and while he held the ridge with his platoon Major Nelson crawled forward to look down the reverse slope. The Germans were now thoroughly aroused, and the whole force withdrew through a hail of machine-gun bullets. Only a single Grenadier was slightly wounded, but one of the prisoners was killed while attempting to escape. The interrogation of the survivor provided all the necessary information on which was based a plan for the outflanking of Longstop by the whole Grenadier Battalion.

Let us, at this stage, pause in the narrative and consider the atmosphere of the Tunisian campaign, the conditions under which the Guardsmen lived and fought, their attitude to the Germans, and their own hopes and fears.

The 1st Guards Brigade had arrived in Tunisia after the careless rapture of the first advance had given place to disappointment and anxiety. The Battle of Tebourba had indeed been a bitter blow, but it was the failure to recapture Longstop in December which had shown them that the First Army were settled for a long campaign which could scarcely end before the Eighth arrived to their assistance. This was a humiliating situation, which the world's Press did not hesitate to point out. The First Army, compared with the Eighth, had sunk in the esteem of a public who naturally tended to measure fighting ability in terms of the number of miles gained and of prisoners 1943 captured. When the word "mud" was mentioned, derisive fingers were pointed at Rostov, where the Russians were making contemporary gains of great importance in similar conditions. Shortage of supplies? Surely the Eighth's Army's difficulties in the desert, where there was but one road, no railway and fewer ports, were at least equally severe? Mountains? But since when had any British army been halted by mere mountains? Shortage of troops? But you call yourselves a whole Army!—and security regulations forbade the explanation that an Army can sometimes be smaller than a Corps. The truth was that the First Army, alone of all the armies with which they were so disparagingly compared, faced all these difficulties simultaneously, and therefore they alone were halted.

The Guardsmen found themselves in a part of the country which did not closely correspond to their preconceived ideas of Africa: there was no desert, no jungle; a very few were heard to express their disappointment that there was no big game. Nor could the plain of Medjez-el-Bab be described as Mediterranean: there were no olive groves or orchards, and the soil, though fairly fertile, was not intensely cultivated: it was scratched with a primitive plough, allowed to lie waste for several years, and then hurriedly rescratched, so that it was often difficult to tell what land was under present cultivation, what was lying fallow, and what had never been ploughed. The basic colour of the country was tawny-brown, washed over with a film of grey. The seasons brought little change: the spindly stalks of corn were the same colour as the earth from which they sprang; the very flowers (except in the plain round Kairouan, which was a sheet of wild marigolds) hid themselves humbly beneath the surface dressing of loose stones. One had the impression that there was land in plenty and to spare; that man had bitten off only as much as he felt competent to chew, leaving the more awkward slopes and little hills uncultivated and unloved for many more centuries to come. The mountains, in contrast, were not brown but dark grey and speckled: seen from ground-level, they assumed the shape of a wavy serpent's back; seen from above (from an aeroplane or one of their own highest peaks) they were lumpy more than precipitous, as roundly moulded as a model in sand, and cut up by water courses etched in dark-green against the mountainside like the dried skeleton of a fern.

On this perennial background—the same Tunisia which Hannibal and Scipio Africanus had known—the French had imposed a few trappings of modern civilization. There was the railway, now cleanly cut by the demolition of a culvert in No Man's Land between Medjez and Longstop. There were the roads, of which a few reached Euro-

1943 pean standards, but the majority, especially in the south, were little more than levelled embankments of hard sand. There were telephones, local electricity plants, and here and there a chapel or an elementary school. Between the towns there were occasional French farms of pink-and-white stucco, and adjoining villas built in a neo-Palladian style, but these were far rarer than the native Arab hut-settlements of mud and wattle. The Arabs were part of the country: their very clothes and simple buildings merged with their dun background. But the French had brought with them a new element of strength and colour, a sense that Nature could and must be made to conform to their needs.

The invading armies of both sides, the one setting out from Tunis, the other from Algiers, remained locked together for six months among these mountains and thin fields. Finding few buildings to shelter them, little food to supplement their rations, and a scanty and mostly uncomprehending population, they impinged far less on the civilian life of Tunisia than they later did on the civilian life of Italy. The targets for their artillery were barren hill-tops and wadis; their tanks manœuvred over wide, stony plateaus for which man had never before found a use.

Well away from the roads and farms, the First Army dug or blasted slit trenches from the crumbling rock, and, having completed them, they sat in them, watching and waiting, alternately drenched in rain and scorched by the sun. They were well clothed (the British battle-dress, together with the bulldozer and the American jeep, were the infantryman's three great blessings of this war), and illness, apart from a mild form of dysentery, which attacked most fresh arrivals in Africa, was remarkably rare. They were well fed. The front-line ration was based on the "compo-box," a case of ready-cooked foods which was designed as a one-man load and contained sufficient to feed fourteen men for twenty-four hours. It could be eaten cold, or heated on petrol fires or tommy-cookers. A man might have tinned bacon, margarine, biscuits and jam for breakfast; and at midday and in the evening either bully beef, steak-and-kidney pudding or tinned meat and vegetables, with more biscuits and margarine; tea at frequent intervals, and seven cigarettes a day.

They were also well armed. Under the test of actual experience the weapons of the British battalion were sorted out into categories of usefulness. The basic weapon, the Bren gun, was at first criticized for its slow rate of fire compared with that of the German M.G.34 or M.G.42, and for the small capacity of its magazine; but in compensation it had great accuracy and reliability, and its design remained almost unchanged from the beginning of the war to the end. Of the other weapons, the British service rifle was supreme in the field: the 2-inch mortar was found to be less useful than its bigger brothers, the 3-inch and 4-inch. The anti-tank rifle was too heavy for a platoon to carry over long distances and was ineffective against all but the lightest German tanks: it was discarded early in the Tunisian campaign. For close fighting the bayonet and the No. 36 grenade were as valuable throughout this war as in the last. The 2-pounder anti-tank gun, later replaced by the 6-pounder, was never fully tested: the 3rd and 6th Battalions, in both the Tunisian and Italian campaigns, never had a single opportunity to use them; the 5th but very few. 1943

As for the enemy, none of the three Grenadier battalions came into close contact with the Italian divisions, which formed but a small and mostly contemptible part of both the Afrika Korps and von Arnim's army in the north. Their experience in battle was confined to the German Army. The effect on the British Army of the 1940 campaign in North-West Europe had never been entirely eradicated. The Germans were still regarded at the outset of the Tunisian campaign as possessing in some way a superiority in weapons, training, and even in morale. The panzer division was regarded as a weapon of war which neither the Americans nor ourselves had yet been able to forge. The first clashes in Tunisia, the astonishing speed with which the Germans reacted to the Allied invasion, their air superiority, the Battles of Tebourba and Longstop, tended to confirm the Guardsman in his worst fears. On the other hand, as the weeks passed, the Grenadiers began to realize that the Germans were by no means invincible, strategically or tactically. There had been Stalingrad; there had been Alamein; they had had their own successes at Medjez and Medenine. And they had found that when confronted with an actual German prisoner of war he was a small, ill-clad, overloaded young soldier who had less appetite than the Guardsman for extraordinary hardship and lacked his resilience in battle. In Tunisia the Germans were facing a losing battle, and they knew it. Their Commander-in-Chief, Field-Marshal Kesselring, had issued an order of the day in which he stated:

> "Every German soldier, destined to fight in Tunisia, must be clear in his own mind that he enters on a field of combat of vital importance to the fate of Germany and Italy.
>
> "I hereby give each soldier the irrevocable order that no step of ground once won is to be given up without authority."

The British soldier needed no such admonition. He was conscious, even in those dark days of December and January, that the tide was already beginning to turn.

2

BOU ARADA AND THE BATTLE OF DJEBEL MANSOUR

Extension of campaign into southern deserts—A successful tank action at Bou Arada—The object and course of the battle for Djebel Mansour—The Grenadiers fight alongside the Parachutists and French Foreign Legion—A gallant withdrawal

1943 Before the details had been settled the situation farther south led to the cancellation of the 3rd Battalion's attack on Longstop. Week by week, as more troops poured into the country to reinforce both Armies, the fighting in Tunisia, confined at first to the two northern valleys, began to spread farther and farther towards the southern desert. The armoured forces in particular were driven south in search of firmer and more open ground. The 6th Armoured Division had followed the German 10th Panzer Division to the valley between Bou Arada and Pont du Fahs, and a clash was expected at any moment. To support the tanks, the Grenadiers were detached from their
Jan 18 Brigade and sent round in lorries to Bou Arada. They came directly under the command of the 6th Armoured Division in an association which endured, with few breaks, until their entry into Austria more than two years later.

The expected German tank attack took place while the Battalion were still on their way from Medjez. Our own armour was not heavily engaged, perhaps fortunately, for at that time there was nothing heavier than the Valentine and Crusader tanks to meet the German Mark IVs. The latter soon found themselves adrift in the mud, and under the concentrated fire of the whole divisional artillery they could be seen writhing from side to side in their efforts to regain the road and a safe retreat. Colonel Heber-Percy and a small advance party watched the battle from a hill-top only a quarter of a mile away. "We were like spectators at a race meeting," one of them wrote, "field-glasses up to our eyes, grunting impatiently, and making aimless gestures with our free hands as though to direct the bursting shells from tank to tank." When the German survivors withdrew they left fifteen tanks behind them, and the first patrols which the Grenadiers sent out in this new sector took with them sappers and explosive charges to blow up all which were not already total losses.

Jan. 20 The Germans returned twice, the second time by night, when a dozen men, led by Lieut. D. I. Rollo, were obliged to flatten themselves on the open plain while a string of tanks and escorting infantry filed past in the moonlight a few hundred yards ahead. When the situation had eased, the Battalion were sent to occupy a group of low hills to the north of Bou Arada. They wasted no time in scouring the recent battlefield for documents and abandoned vehicles—the Battalion were already gaining a reputation in the First Army for acquiring for their own use the best equipment of all nations in the field. They soon settled down to their normal routine: in daylight sleeping and watching by turns; at night patrolling and improving their defences. There were inevitable casualties. There was the morning, for instance, when the enemy were spotted creeping forward to occupy a hill which our own men were in the habit of holding only at night time. No. 4 Company, led by Capt. A. G. Way, advanced in extended lines up the bare hillside, shelled and mortared as they went, and lost sixteen men before the Germans were halted. The next night Lieut. The Lord Braybrooke was killed. He had remained behind to make certain that his pioneers had laid a minefield correctly; stumbling in the darkness over one of his own mines, he was killed instantly.

1943 Jan. 21 **Jan. 22** **Jan. 23**

The Battalion returned for a few days to the reserve area south of Medjez and were preparing to occupy the station for a second time, when their orders were once again changed at the last moment. The whole Brigade was now to move to Bou Arada, and it was here that the 3rd Grenadiers fought their main battle of the Tunisian campaign —the Battle of Djebel Mansour.

Jan. 28-31

Although this battle began with a British attack, it had no other object than to relieve German pressure against a part of the line farther south. By thrusting down the valley leading from Pont du Fahs to Robaa with a force including the first Tiger tanks to be seen on any European front, the enemy had placed the 36th Brigade and some French battalions in a position of great danger. Brigadier Copland Griffiths was ordered to assist them by attacking over the mountains which separated the Bou Arada from the Robaa valleys, so threatening the northern flank of the German salient. If the Robaa road could be cut, even by patrols or observed artillery fire, the German offensive would be greatly hampered and probably halted. To carry out this task the Brigadier had the co-operation of the 1st Parachute Brigade (acting as infantry) and a few companies of the French Foreign Legion, but of the battalions in his own Brigade the 2nd Coldstream Guards were committed to a static position east of Bou Arada, and the Argylls could not be used without the permission of higher commanders. The Grenadiers were therefore the only troops immediately available. The parachutists and Foreign Legion were under separate command. There is little doubt that this dual control of a single operation and the limitations imposed on the Brigadier in the use of his own troops were very serious handicaps.

1943 The watershed between the two valleys at the point chosen for attack was formed by two mountains called Djebel Mansour and Djebel Alliliga. Mansour was slightly the higher of the two, separated from Alliliga by a deep gully: both were thickly wooded on the lower slopes, but the actual crests were for the most part devoid of cover and overlooked the approaches from every direction. The parachute battalion and the Foreign Legion had arrived at the site before the Grenadiers, and had decided to attack before the latter were prepared for a
Feb. 3 simultaneous assault. They captured Djebel Mansour without great difficulty, but Alliliga was still in enemy hands and the Germans were quick to move troops up to the threatened point. The parachutists were soon calling for support from the 1st Guards Brigade. No. 2 Company of the Grenadiers (Major K. E. M. Tufnell, M.C.) were sent up that evening and arrived at midnight to find the situation fairly quiet. They dug themselves in immediately below the western end of Mansour, slightly in rear of the parachutists. The remainder of the 3rd Grenadiers moved to the foot of Alliliga and lost no time in probing up the slope farthest removed from Mansour. No. 4 Company (Capt. G. H. Dixon) made two attempts that night to gain the western shoulder and found each time that, though they could advance to within about seventy yards of the summit, the hail of bullets and grenades which met them as soon as they emerged from the wood rendered further movement impossible.

The Commanding Officer (Major A. C. Huntington, M.V.O., acting in the absence of Lieut.-Colonel Heber-Percy) then decided to attempt the capture of Alliliga by simultaneous attacks at either end.
Feb. 4 No. 2 Company were to attack the eastern shoulder, moving from Mansour across the dividing ravine, while No. 1 Company approached the other shoulder by the same route which No. 4 Company had taken the night before. At 3 p.m. the artillery started to fire for an hour along the whole crest, and at 3.30 both companies moved forward. No. 2 Company had the greater success. Pushing their way upwards between the rocks and trees, they met little opposition until they were almost clear of the wood. Here they found that the Germans had cleared lanes through the undergrowth down which they poured the concentrated fire of several machine guns. Lieuts. A. M. Denny and P. Maclean worked their platoons for some distance along the far slope, while Lieut. C. O. M. Wills led his platoon forward with a hunting horn, and himself eagerly pressed onwards to attack almost single-handed one German machine gun after another. He had disposed of three when point-blank fire from a fourth killed him outright. Many months afterwards his body was found on the summit of Alliliga. The company had suffered almost fifty per cent. casualties,

including Lieut. Maclean, but the east shoulder was now in our hands, 1943 and complete success rested with the efforts of No. 1 Company at the farther end.

Once again the attempt on the western shoulder of Alliliga was halted by the devastating fire which raked the final stretch of open ground. For a short time part of a single platoon gained a foothold on the ridge, but, being unsupported, they were forced to return, and the platoon commander, Lieut. The Hon. E. R. H. Wills, was wounded. Soon afterwards the company commander, Capt. F. J. R. P. Needham, and Lieut. J. R. Bastard were also hit, and a fourth officer from the company, Lieut. D. I. Rollo, was wounded and taken prisoner.* This left the company under the command of the surviving officer, Capt. P. Lane, a Canadian who was temporarily attached to the Battalion. They were by now so weakened and the enemy so alert that there could be no question of renewing the assault. Capt. A. G. Way led a platoon of No. 4 Company round to their support, and the combined force dug in about half-way up the slope, sheltering under the meagre cover of the brushwood.

A new plan was at once devised. The Brigadier was allowed to use a single company of the Argylls which he placed in support of No. 1 Company, and Major Huntington ordered Nos. 3 and 4 Companies to reinforce No. 2 Company, hoping to widen the success which the latter had already gained. The move of the two companies was made by night, and Major Nelson (No. 3) relieved Major Tufnell (No. 2) just before dawn. Any move eastwards along the ridge was met by heavy Feb. 5 fire from a series of entrenched machine guns, while their shallow scrapings gave our men little cover from German snipers. They were not attacked, and Lieut. Faber easily beat back a small patrol which approached his platoon. So long as Djebel Mansour remained firmly in the hands of the parachutists there was great uncertainty but no immediate danger. The hopes of the Battalion were darkened when, looking over their shoulders, they saw the enemy beginning to sweep over Mansour from end to end. The Foreign Legion were the first to suffer, overwhelmed where they lay, and then the gallant parachutists, running short of ammunition at the critical moment, were forced to retire step by step from the summit of Mansour. The left flank was now wide open and the Grenadiers were in great danger of being surrounded. At 1 p.m. the Divisional Commander ordered their withdrawal. They moved back section by section down the ravine and across the strip of valley which separated them from the cover of friendly hills. A troop of tanks aided them by firing smoke shells on to

*Later in the year Lieut. Rollo escaped from a prisoner-of-war camp in Northern Italy and eventually rejoined the Battalion.

1943 the crest, but many casualties were suffered before all the companies were home. Grenadiers, parachutists, and a few Frenchmen intermingled, filed back in the dusk, while the carriers darted to and fro picking up the wounded.

The battle was lost, but its object gained. The Germans made no further advance to Robaa, for they had been forced to picket these remote heights with troops they could ill-afford.

3

SBIBA AND THE KASSERINE PASS

The wanderings of the 1st Guards Brigade—Rommel's offensive through Faid and Kasserine—The Brigade rushed down to save the situation at Sbiba—Churchills versus Tiger tanks—The Brigade switched to Thala in a great emergency—The Grenadiers reoccupy the Kasserine Pass

The Tunisian front had by now been extended to its widest limit, from the sea coast north of Sedjenane to the great salt lakes of the southern desert, a two-hundred-mile stretch which in parts was covered by no more than armoured-car patrols, in others, such as at Medjez and Bou Arada, Pichon and the Faid Pass, by as much as a whole division on either side. The British V Corps held the sector from the north coast as far as Djebel Mansour, the French XIX Corps from here to Pichon, and the American II Corps the southern sector. In the whole First Army the 1st Guards Brigade were almost the only mobile reserve, and they would be sent up and down the country to plug a gap wherever danger threatened, earning for themselves the nickname "The Plumbers."

Their wanderings during the months which followed the Battle of Djebel Mansour took them many hundreds of miles and into many engagements, each one of which was liable to prove decisive. They had undeniable good fortune. Their casualties were not heavy in comparison with those of many other formations, but there was the constant strain of long drives by night along indifferent and dusty roads, to arrive at dawn at yet another hill and face the chances of yet another battle, with too little time to prepare their defences and too few men to hold a solid line. It was an exciting period for those who were in a position to follow the ebb and flow of battle: for the Guardsmen it was so often no more than "a move," a march, more digging, more patrolling, weariness and apprehension. The dull security of Grenadier Hill had been far preferable.

Feb. 7 Their first journey took the Brigade to the area of Robaa, at the mouth of the same valley which they had attempted to enter from the

north. Here the Grenadiers were in reserve, near the dividing line 1943
between the French and the Americans. From their tented camp, which was bathed alternately in snow and brilliant sunshine, parties would reconnoitre for miles in all directions, planning the counter-attacks for which reserve battalions are always prepared but which they seldom execute. So it was on this occasion. The Robaa front remained quiet, but after ten days a serious situation developed farther south, and at a few hours' notice the Brigade were on their way to Sbiba.

The enemy had pooled the greater part of three armoured divisions to launch an attack on the southern sector of the First Army. They had surprised the Americans at Faid, captured or destroyed nearly a hundred tanks, and swept on to seize Sbeitla and Gafsa and cross the border into Algeria. The whole communication system on which the First Army depended was in sudden danger. If the Germans turned north from Sbeitla, as they were surely bound to do rather than allow the offensive to die away in the desert, there was little to prevent them striking for Le Kef or even Constantine. The damage already done must be sealed off without delay. The 6th Armoured Division, with the 1st Guards Brigade under command, moved to the edge of the desert, where they were joined by a few American battalions, and together they built two defensive positions covering the approaches Feb. 17
to the northern plain. One was on the pass at Kasserine; the other a few miles south of Sbiba, where the converging hills narrowed the plain to a strip about three miles wide. The Guards Brigade held the western part of the latter position, their right flank, for which the Grenadiers were responsible, resting on a steep escarpment, their left covered by the American 18th Combat Team on the floor of the valley.

To their surprise the Grenadiers had thirty-six hours' grace before the German advance guard approached. Their position was a strong one, inaccessible to any tanks and difficult for infantry, but the danger lay in the more open ground to the left, where a hard blow might have broken the crust of the American defences and hemmed in the Grenadiers against the hills. The Americans did not give way, and the Grenadiers were barely attacked. They watched from their hill-tops the onset of the victorious enemy columns—first the armoured cars, which halted to peer at them from half a mile away; then the Feb. 19
tanks, which approached closer to provoke their retaliation and estimate their strength; and finally the infantry, who left their lorries in the open, within view but beyond the maximum reach of the artillery, and began to advance in open formation to the crest of the opposing ridge. Both tanks and infantry halted about five hundred yards away

1943 and began to snipe and move about with every indication that they were about to attack. They were not allowed to complete their preparations in peace. The British and American artillery fired continuously, directed with splendid effect from observation posts on the higher ground, one of which was manned by Colonel Heber-Percy himself. A few German tanks waddled down the road to find it blocked by mines, another was knocked out by a Coldstream anti-tank gun, and when half a dozen more were set ablaze by shell fire the remainder veered off to the east to probe the American lines with no greater success. About a battalion of infantry stayed on the ridge. German officers were seen gazing through their field-glasses, and Arab peasants, whose neutrality had always been in doubt, were seen to point out to them the exact positions which we occupied. At night time German patrols filtered down into the valley and hid themselves among the cactus groves, but the opposing forces did not come to grips.

For two days the Germans hesitated. On the third a squadron of
Feb. 21 Churchills arrived at Sbiba—it was the first time that this type of tank had been used since the raid on Dieppe—and were sent up the road carrying a platoon of the Coldstream battalion to test German reactions on the ridge. At the same time a small force of Grenadiers under Capt. A. G. Way and Lieut. R. F. B. R. Clark demonstrated on the right flank. The latter reached the ridge with no great difficulty and only one casualty, but the tanks met serious trouble. From the higher ground in rear it was possible to watch the British and the German tanks crawling up the opposite slopes, for the moment blind to each other's approach, but certain to meet within a few minutes at point-blank range on the very crest. Each side was using its heaviest weapon in the field, the Churchill and the Tiger. As the latter mounted the bigger gun, there was little hope. Two Churchills were knocked out and after a confused mêlée lasting only a very short time the whole force, including the Grenadiers, withdrew under cover of smoke. The incident had little effect on the general situation.

While the enemy had suffered their first check at Sbiba, a second armoured column had cleared the Americans from the Kasserine Pass and engaged the light tanks of the 6th Armoured Division in an unequal battle between Kasserine and Thala. We suffered very heavily. The threat was now more serious than it had ever been, and even at the cost of withdrawing from Sbiba to a shorter line it was decided to switch the Guards Brigade to Thala. They withdrew by night, com-
Feb. 22 pany by company, without attracting attention, marched back in silence to the outskirts of Sbiba and drove by cross-country roads to face what seemed to be a desperate situation. Two miles north of

Carriers of the 3rd Battalion approaching the Kasserine Pass.

Thala the 2nd/5th Leicesters had already been overrun; the 2nd 1943
Hampshires had arrived; the 2nd Coldstream, the Grenadiers and a score of tanks completed the force. They awaited the German attack.
At that moment, when so much seemed within his grasp, Rommel Feb. 23
decided that the blow he had already dealt against the First Army would cripple them for long enough to enable him to turn his divisions about to meet the threat of the Eighth Army across the Tunisian border. He retired from Thala, from Sbiba, from Kasserine and Gafsa, left a rearguard at the Faid Pass and gathered his strength for the Battle of Medenine. The news of his withdrawal was so astonishing that many could scarcely credit it, until they began to move in complete security towards the widening V of the Kasserine Pass. The Germans had left behind many of their own derelict tanks and hundreds of mines embedded in the soft sand of the roadway. The mines caused interminable delays, and there were many casualties.
Major Nelson was wounded, and his driver killed, when his carrier Feb. 24
blew up, but the bulk of the Battalion, following slowly in their lorries, arrived intact at the entrance to the pass. After driving all night they were ordered to advance on foot and occupy, if necessary capture, the hills on the east side of the defile. The Americans were to attack simultaneously from the north-west.

At 6.30 a.m. the advance began. Three companies were strung out Feb. 25
between the plain and the highest peaks: No. 4 Company (Capt. G. H. Dixon) on the right nearest the valley; No. 1 Company (Capt. D. V. Bonsor) in the centre; and No. 2 Company (Capt. H. W. O. Bradley) one thousand feet up on the left flank. Battalion Headquarters and No. 3 Company (Capt. A. K. C. Nation) followed slightly in rear. The marching companies could move only in single file along the rough tracks, for the hill was too steep to allow them to deploy, while the carrier platoon (Lieut. J. G. C. Jameson) and the essential wireless vehicles with Battalion Headquarters were faced by a series of wadis, each pronounced at first to be impassable but overcome in turn by hard manual labour on the approaches. The total distance on the map was about eight miles. On the ground, owing to the rise and fall and the detours, it was nearer twelve. They covered the distance in six hours, so far ahead of the expected schedule that the Battalion, much to their amusement, were warned by the Americans that suspicious figures could be seen moving about on the objective long after the Grenadiers had in fact arrived. There was no opposition. All that they found on the summit of the pass were the corpses and the litter of the battle six days before, and, looking southwards beyond Kasserine and Sbeitla, they could distinguish not a single movement, not a puff of dust, to indicate how far the Germans had withdrawn.

4

THE END OF THE BEGINNING

German offensive continued in Northern Tunisia—The Brigade switched to El Aroussa, Beja, and once more to Medjez—Incorporation in the 6th Armoured Division—The Battle of the Fondouk Pass—Capture of Kairouan and link-up with the Eighth Army—The first and unsuccessful attempt to finish the campaign by the Goubellat offensive—The 3rd, 5th and 6th Battalions all concentrated near Grenadier Hill

1943 The pursuit was left to the Americans. No sooner had the Battalion
Feb. 26 returned from the hills than the whole Brigade was off once again on a night drive to the north, this time in response to a call for assistance at El Aroussa. It was one of the many places where the Germans had recently attacked, and with a small force of tanks and infantry they had cut the road from El Aroussa to Medjez. The Grenadiers were at first in reserve to a scratch force known as "Y" Division, and when they moved up into the front line just north of the village, it was to find that the enemy had withdrawn, leaving behind them a mass of equipment which the Grenadiers were not slow to pick over for their own benefit. "Not even the cold stare of the dead Germans," wrote the Adjutant, Capt. J. D. Buchanan, "could deter the hunters from their fair share of the plunder."

It was now quite clear that the enemy intended to pin down the First Army by continual attacks in the north while the Eighth Army were held away from the main Tunisian battlefield by the barrier of the Mareth Line. The affair at El Aroussa was insignificant compared with the violence of the German onslaughts in the northern valleys. At Sedjenane the situation was saved only by plugging the gap with battalion after battalion of the 46th Division and the 1st Parachute Brigade, while north of Medjez the Germans had swept through the hills to threaten the Oued Zaaga Line and even Beja. Medjez itself had held out at the head of a deep salient, but the situation had been so serious that the Quartermaster of the Grenadiers (Lieut. E. V. Philpott) had been ordered to collect all available men at "B" Echelon
Mar. 3 and hold a makeshift line. As a final reserve to both Sejenane and Oued Zaaga the 1st Guards Brigade were moved up to Beja.

The remarkably good fortune of the Brigade saved them once more from a desperate engagement. Time after time they had been sent to the most critical positions only to find on arrival that the situation had eased. It is true that the Coldstream Guards motored twice to the

Sejenane Valley and twice returned to Beja: it is also true that the 1943 Grenadiers were sent twice into the front line just short of Oued Zaaga. Yet neither battalion was seriously engaged. During the whole period since the end of the Battle of Djebel Mansour until the First Army passed to the offensive the Grenadiers had suffered no more than thirty casualties in battle, but they badly needed time to rest and reorganize. They had been promised both for many weeks past, but "the Plumbers" were still in too great demand. On leaving the Beja Mar. 14
area they moved back to Medjez with a sigh of sheer weariness, but not without a sense of returning home. The Grenadiers found themselves once more in the familiar caves and trenches of the hill to which they had given their name three months before.

The second period at Medjez was remarkable only for the quick ascendancy which the Battalion gained over No Man's Land. The tracks, the rocky outcrops, the shabby, humble mosques, dry wadis and whitened villages and farms, the barking of dogs and sudden scent of thyme—all these were landmarks not easily forgotten by those many officers and men who had patrolled night after night across the wide valley of the Medjerda, and they soon picked up the threads of the old routes. They found that in recent weeks the enemy had become more daring, and there were frequent clashes before the Germans were pressed back to their proper distance as the orbit of our patrols widened night by night. A prisoner was urgently required to give an indication of the intentions and grouping of the German forces opposite Medjez. Lieut. Faber was cheated of a fine prize when he crawled Mar. 19
with a daylight patrol towards a group of German officers and men only to be spotted and accurately shelled when less than three hundred yards away. The next night Lieut. Denny set out from Medjez with a Mar. 20
fighting patrol to Grich el Oued. As they approached the village four Germans came towards them fluttering white handkerchiefs and crying, "British Tommy! British Tommy!" They were deserters (a rare phenomenon in Tunisia) who were exhausted by rain and shell fire and were very willing to describe the exact strength and dispositions of the small garrison at Grich el Oued. On their information Sergt. Lovett led a raid on the village at dawn the next morning, and brought back two more prisoners, who completed the story to the satisfaction of the British Intelligence. Medjez, it appeared, was in no immediate danger of attack.

The time had now at last come for the 1st Guards Brigade to be Mar. 22
withdrawn for a prolonged rest. Since the advance to Kasserine the Brigade had been officially incorporated in the 6th Armoured Division, and the transformation necessitated certain changes in equip-

1943 ment—particularly in the signal platoon (Lieut. R. C. Riseley)—and some specialized training to fit them for close co-operation with tanks. For this purpose, and to exchange their light tanks for Shermans, the whole Division had assembled far behind the line among the wooded hills of Sidi Youssef on the Algerian border. For two or three days the Guards Brigade were left in peace. The security, the absence of gunfire, the silence of the field telephones and wirelesses, uninterrupted sleep, clean clothes and warm baths, soon revived their tired bodies, and when training started in earnest they felt that a new chapter had opened in their lives. Not only were they now part of one of the most distinguished and powerful divisions in any army in the world but the whole tone of their discussions and exercises suggested that the First Army would not long remain on the defensive and that the 6th Armoured Division had a leading role to play in the conclusion of the campaign. They were not disappointed.

By the end of March the Mareth Line was broken, Gabes captured and the First and Eighth Armies were combined under the operational command of General Alexander. The Germans were hurrying northwards, abandoning the whole plain which lies between Sfax and Enfidaville. To cover their retreat against a flank attack by the First Army they continued to picket the long range of hills which runs north and south parallel to the coast and about thirty miles inland. There were two main passes through the ridge. The first was at Faid; the second at Fondouk. If the German line could be broken at either point and the 6th Armoured Division unleashed into the plain beyond, there was a good chance that the bulk of the Afrika Korps might be cut off from the security of the mountains of Northern Tunisia. Plans were first made at Sidi Youssef for an attack on the Faid Pass, but these were changed when the German retreat was accelerated and a break-through at Fondouk promised better results. The whole Divi-
April 4 sion moved in great secrecy to an assembly area in the Kessera Forest, ten miles east of Fondouk.

The initial assault was made by the 128th Brigade (46th Division) on the northern side of the pass, and by the American 34th Division on the southern side. The 6th Armoured Division was held in reserve. The preparations for an attack on this scale were very difficult to conceal, especially in the later stages, when the whole Allied force was obliged to deploy over the plain, and not even a jeep could move without churning up a cloud of the soft dust which covered every track. The Germans were not deceived. A prisoner later described how they were appalled by the "unerhörte Masse von Panzer" (the incredible array of tanks) which assembled in the plain vainly attempting to hide their great bulk among scattered thickets of cactus. When

our infantry moved forward to attack at zero hour they were faced 1943
by five German battalions, strongly entrenched and with orders to April 8 5.30 a.m.
hold the Fondouk Pass to the last man. The air reconnaissance sent back constant and tantalizing reports of vast German convoys streaming northwards through Kairouan.

The attack by the 128th Brigade was very successful and the village of Pichon was captured within a few hours. But the Americans on the southern flank disappointed our hopes of an early break-through, and
to avoid further waste of time the 3rd Battalion Welsh Guards were April 9
ordered to seize a hill called Djebel el Rhorab, which lay on the right of the 128th Brigade in the very mouth of the pass. It was the first attack which this battalion had ever undertaken, and they succeeded brilliantly. By nightfall the hill was in our hands. The Grenadiers, led by No. 3 Company (Capt. J. G. Jameson), moved forward to close the gap between the Welsh Guards and the 128th Brigade. They had no fighting, suffering only one casualty (Drum-Major Watling), and rounded up about twenty-five prisoners of war before reaching the summit of the ridge to see the great plain spread beneath them. Early
the next morning the tanks found a way through the minefields, and April 10
against little opposition fanned out in all directions in search of German stragglers.

The 10th and 11th of April were great days in the history of the 6th Armoured Division. For the first time the tanks found the ideal conditions for which they had been designed—a firm, unbroken plain over which they could range at will, a mass of soft-skinned vehicles open to attack, fine weather and a clear run, with infantry and spare tanks behind them in case of difficulties. The delay at Fondouk, it is true, had allowed the bulk of the German convoys to escape, but about a hundred vehicles were destroyed and the Division had the satisfaction of entering Kairouan (after Mecca the second most holy city in the Mohammedan world) a few hours ahead of the Eighth Army. South of the city the armoured cars sealed the junction between the two Armies. The yellow cars and sun-burned men from Cairo, the black cars and paler faces from Algiers, ranged together over the sheets of marigold and poppy which coloured the plain and filled the air with the strong scent of spring.

In all these skirmishes and triumphs the Guards Brigade took little part. They were required to do no more than follow up three or four miles behind the tanks, hold for a few hours at a time the slight ridges which rose above the plain, and wait until the tanks found that they could make no further progress without the assistance of infantry. That moment never came. The Eighth Army claimed a priority over the 6th Armoured Division, and passed beyond them towards Enfida-

1943 ville. The Grenadiers were ordered to disperse into the fields on either April 12 side of the road. Generals Alexander and Montgomery shot past in a staff car, followed by the first tawny-yellow desert vehicles which the Grenadiers had ever seen, and at nightfall the two Armies once more took their separate paths.

There followed another short interval of rest in the same forest at Kessera, where the Division had hidden before the Fondouk attack. The opportunity was taken by several Grenadier officers to exchange visits with their sister battalions—the 6th at Sousse, the 5th near Medjez, the former on the morrow, the latter on the eve, of greater battles than the 3rd Battalion were ever fated to endure in Africa. At the same time, Brigadier Copland Griffiths, D.S.O., M.C., after more
April 14 than two years in command, handed over the 1st Guards Brigade to Brigadier S. A. Forster.

The stage was now set for a combined offensive by both Armies against the north-east corner of Tunisia, all that remained in Axis hands of the whole African littoral. The day had passed when the action of a single battalion represented the effort of an entire army, and when the Grenadiers could by themselves dominate a battlefield. They were but a small unit among the seventeen Allied divisions which were about to attack along the whole line between Sejenane and Enfidaville. The first offensive was not concentrated. It was, in Mr. Churchill's phrase, "a squeeze": if the squeeze failed it was to be followed by "a punch." The part of the squeeze which affected the 6th Armoured Division was confined to the plain between Bou Arada and Peter's Corner. Two other divisions, the 46th and 1st Armoured, were concentrated at the same point, and their object was not so much to make a decisive breach in the enemy line as to draw away the German tanks and aircraft from more vital sectors.

In this they were fully successful. The 46th Division opened the
April 23 attack by securing two hills on either side of the plain, and the German infantry, reeling back towards Pont du Fahs, were closely pursued by our tanks. Hurriedly the enemy brought down from Tunis a large part of their armoured reserves, and the battle, cramped uncomfortably between a lake and the encircling hills, became largely an affair of tank firing at tank at extreme range while the aircraft of both sides wheeled overhead like carrion crows. The Guards Brigade were not involved until the later stages. The Grenadiers mopped up behind the tanks, taking more than fifty prisoners, including three German officers, at little cost to themselves. Capt. A. A. A. D. Ramsay was badly wounded in the leg, which was later amputated, and Capt. S. E. Bolitho was wounded on the next day. The main engagement was fought by the Coldstream Guards, with only fair success, for a thick

mist which had concealed their opening deployment suddenly lifted 1943 to expose their vehicles to direct fire from a German tank. Two Grenadier patrols went out—under Sergt. Irons and Lieut. R. Neville respectively—the first to destroy the tank and the second its observation post, but both were repelled by German infantry before they gained their object.

The battle ended inconclusively with the withdrawal of the 6th April 25 Armoured Division to the neighbourhood of Goubellat, and the Grenadiers found themselves among the cornfields south of Grenadier Hill. Not ten miles away the 5th Battalion were at the height of their battle for Bou Aoukaz, and the 6th drove round from Enfidaville to join the 3rd. Thus all three Battalions of the Regiment which fought in Africa, having started their journeys at many months' interval and from points thousands of miles apart, having endured such widely differing adventures, now found themselves by the chance of war within sight of the same stony hill which bore their name.

CHAPTER II

THE MARETH LINE

6TH BATTALION

1

SYRIA

Journey to the Cape—Good diplomacy in Durban—Journey continued to Qatana, near Damascus—Showing the flag in the Lebanon and Syria—Two-thousand-two-hundred-mile desert journey from Syria to Southern Tunisia covered in three weeks—The 201st Guards Brigade join the Eighth Army

THE rise and fall in the fortunes of the First Army are reflected clearly
1942 enough in the stories of the 3rd and 5th Battalions of the Grenadiers; but it cannot be said that the African period of the 6th Battalion touches more than a small part of the history of the Eighth Army. They joined the 201st Guards Brigade, veterans of the desert campaigns, only in September, 1942. From that time onwards, for only a single day and a single night, at Medenine and a few days later on the approaches to the Mareth Line, did the Brigade play the key role on the Eighth Army's stage. These two violent battles were both of very great importance. But there was no Grenadier battalion at Alamein, indeed, no battalion from the whole of the Brigade of Guards; and none joined in the pursuit of Rommel's Afrika Korps until after the Eighth Army had crossed the Tunisian border. The story of the 6th Battalion in Africa falls into three distinct phases: the period of waiting, a thousand miles behind the battle front; the period of their long desert journey and sudden bloody engagement; and the aftermath, when, weakened by their losses, they could play but a minor part in the winding-up of the Tunisian campaign.

For a long time the 201st Guards Brigade had been asking for a third Guards battalion to join them in the Middle East. When the 6th Battalion (Lieut.-Colonel A. F. L. Clive, M.C.) was formed in October, 1941, they were trained from the start as a motor battalion, to be dispatched to the Middle East as soon as their basic training was completed. It was in this way that the youngest battalion of the Regiment was the first to go overseas after the evacuation from Dunkirk. They

were promised time to continue their training on arrival in the Middle 1942
East, where they would have the benefit of semi-active service conditions, and of association with the other two battalions of the Brigade (3rd Coldstream Guards and 2nd Scots Guards), who had already endured more than their fair share of campaigning, and had been withdrawn for rest after fighting their way out of Tobruk.

The Battalion embarked at Liverpool on H.T. *Strathmore*, a June 16
P. & O. liner of twenty-three thousand tons, and after calling at the Clyde to pick up the remainder of a small convoy they headed out into the Atlantic for the long journey round the Cape, the Mediterranean route to Egypt being closed at that time to all but the Malta convoys.
They left Scotland in a fog. The *Strathmore* was a modern ship, air- June 20
conditioned throughout, and, although the officers felt keenly the contrast between the comfort of their own accommodation and the discomfort of the men's (a contrast which recurs in every account of war-time voyages), the lower decks were not too disagreeable and the weather remained excellent. "Very few of us have been sick," wrote the Adjutant, Capt. The Master of Forbes, "but a good many are thoroughly sick of the sea." It was inevitable, in spite of all their efforts to keep the men occupied. They would train on deck, play games, and mount the necessary guards; the whole Battalion learned semaphore, half of them the Morse code; they shot with revolvers at tins dropped over the stern; they exercised their wits with the sun compass, with map reading and with brains trusts; they even manned their own 2-pounder anti-tank gun to strengthen the ship's defences against submarine attack, but there was no sign of the enemy in the sea or in the air. As the weather grew warmer they changed their battledress for tropical clothing, and crossed the Equator on the
twentieth day. A month after leaving Scotland they dropped anchor July 8
in the harbour at Durban.

On their arrival they found that the reputation for dress and discip- July 20
line of the thousands of British troops who had passed through on convoys had suffered owing to the great numbers of reinforcements who were without the personal control and *esprit de corps* of formed units. It was therefore not difficult for the Grenadiers to make, in contrast, a very favourable impression on the population of Durban, and this was maintained throughout their stay in the country. It was also fortunate that their Commanding Officer was already well acquainted with South Africa, its personalities and its problems, as he had worked with the British Military Mission to South Africa in 1941. Hence he was able both to prepare the Battalion *en route* for what they would meet in Durban, and also make highly advantageous arrangements for their accommodation, training and ceremonial

1942 occasions during the visit. It was only the delicate political situation which prevented General Smuts from allowing the Grenadiers to carry out a two-week good-will tour through the Union by special train. The Grenadiers resumed their journey refreshed in body and spirits, and with the knowledge that their first task, an act not of war but of appeasement, had been most admirably performed.

Aug. 15 The second half of their voyage, from Durban to Suez, was very disagreeable. The Battalion were carried in a small, crowded troopship called H.T. *Ascanius,* which would have been uncomfortable enough in a temperate zone, but as they recrossed the Equator and entered the Red Sea the temperature on the lower decks rose to over 100 degrees, and the sea became far rougher than at any stage of the
Sept. 8 voyage south. When they eventually docked at Suez they were taken immediately to a tented camp at Qassassin, between Ismailia and Cairo. The Eighth Army were standing at El Alamein, worried indeed, but not in such desperate straits as to make it necessary for every available man to be hurried into the line. The 201st Guards Brigade (Brigadier J. A. Gascoigne) were for the moment withdrawn entirely from the battle front, and as the situation grew easier they were removed even farther afield, to Syria. The Grenadiers followed, partly
Oct. 3 by rail but mainly by road across the Sinai Desert, and up the length
See Map p. 294 of Palestine, through Asluj, Gaza and Tiberias, to the camp at Qatana, eighteen miles south-west of Damascus.

Oct. '42-Feb. '43 Here they spent the next four months. The camp lay in a stretch of rough, open country at the foot of Mount Hermon. It was sand-blown and fly-blown, isolated and rather bleak, but for all that not too unpleasant. There was, from the start, a great deal to do. It was the period promised to the Battalion for the completion of their basic training, and for their initiation into the tactics of mountains and desert. There was a continual coming and going of officers and men, some on courses of instruction, some to and from hospital (for jaundice, dysentery and malaria removed from their ranks never fewer than sixty men at a time), some on tours of the Western Desert battlefields, and others on leave to Cairo and Beirut. The weather, which was usually good, was apt to play disconcerting tricks. From time to time the rain would reduce the parade ground to the consistency of greasy porridge, and on one of their first exercises a sudden storm stranded the trucks with water up to the wheel-tops, and the men had to wade six miles to fetch their food and six miles back to their vehicles.

There was one interlude for which fine weather was very important, and fine weather remained fortunately unbroken. This was the tour of the Lebanon and Northern Syria undertaken in November by the larger part of the Brigade. Its main object was political—to impress 1942 upon the inhabitants of the Syrian interior the fact of Anglo-French unity, and the existence of a body of first-class British troops within reach of the remotest parts of the country. It was also hoped that the Turks would be encouraged to resist Axis infiltration by the appearance of the Brigade on their southern frontiers. Few Allied soldiers had yet visited these regions, and the Guardsmen now set out to repeat the diplomatic triumph of Durban. At the same time the tour was exactly what was needed to revive waning enthusiasm, to give the men a memory of Syria which went beyond sandstorms and rows of military huts, and to practise their new skill in manœuvres over wide stretches of desert.

From Qatana they went first to Baalbek, detaching a company under Major A. J. E. Gordon to Beirut, where they paraded on Armistice Day before General Catroux. From Baalbek the Brigade went Nov. 11 through Homs and Hama to Aleppo, where all three battalions marched through the centre of the town. From Aleppo to Djerablus; Nov. 14 and here there was another ceremonial march which ended at the bridge over the Euphrates which divided Syria from Turkey. They Nov. 15 crossed one hundred and twenty miles of desert—their first, and a most successful, attempt at land navigation—to Deir ez Zor, where the Brigade cancelled their march as a precaution against a smallpox epidemic, and substituted a drive past the French commander. This Nov. 18 ended the flag-showing, the propaganda, part of their journey, and striking westwards across the desert the Brigade returned via Palmyra with a three-day exercise *en route*. The tour had been a great success, Nov. 20 judging not only by the reaction of the population but by the stream of happy letters which began to flow from Qatana to England after their return. Many of these survive in family dossiers to show that the Syrian tour was one of those opportunities for enlightenment and great enjoyment which are thrown up by war and eagerly grasped by the British soldier. It refreshed him for battle, and left him with memories which no battle could efface.

More than two months were still to pass before the Brigade were called into action. The wind howled off the slopes of Hermon, and they watched with growing dismay the snow-line creeping farther and farther down the mountain until all movement from the camp became impossible for a stretch of five days on end. The sickness, the measured discipline of camp life, the local expeditions in search of relaxation in Damascus or of new training grounds in mountain and desert —all this continued as before. At Christmas they held services which Dec. 25 gained new significance from their Biblical surroundings, and they amused themselves with donkey and camel races and a display by the

1943 local Circassian cavalry. For a short time in January Major P. G.
Evelyn took six officers and three hundred and fifty men to mount
guards in Syrian Tripoli. But still no orders came from the Eighth
Army. There were, of course, rumours—rumours of a return to
Durban, of a move farther east, even of a lone assault on some isolated
part of Europe. Then suddenly the distant battlefield claimed the
Brigade. They were to motor the two thousand two hundred miles
from Syria to the Tunisian border, and on arrival prepare themselves
for immediate action with the Eighth Army.

Feb. 7 The Brigade road convoy first retraced their tracks from Qatana to
the Nile Delta, and halted there for a few days before embarking on
the main part of their journey. Once again they were billeted in the
camp at Qassassin while they made good all their deficiencies in transport and other equipment. When they resumed the road they were in
the best of spirits: if not yet fully trained they were strong and fresh
and eager: if most of them had never yet heard a shot fired in anger
it made them all the more anxious to acquit themselves with distinction in the eyes of the Desert Army. It might be thought that the
tedium of the journey, the growing proximity of actual danger, would
have tempered their enthusiasm. But this was not so. There are few
who took part in the desert drive who do not retain of it an impression
of mounting excitement. The day's journey did not often exceed one
hundred and fifty miles, starting in the early morning and halting at
4 or 5 p.m. in a bivouac camp, usually on the outskirts of some coastal
Feb. 13- town whose name had become a legend—Mersah Matruh, Buq-Buq,
Mar. 2 Tobruk, Derna, Barce, Benghazi, Agedabia, Marble Arch, Sirte,
And so the days and the miles rolled past, bringing the long column
of yellow vehicles, now the Grenadiers, now the Coldstream, now the
Scots Guards, in the lead, nearer and nearer to their battlefield. The
Grenadiers, through their excellent driving and maintenance, lost
only one vehicle throughout the entire journey. There were few other
convoys on the road, no hostile aircraft, and few relics even of the
recent battles. The site of Alamein was indicated by nothing more
than huge minefields and a dump of shattered lorries by the roadside.
Thereafter it was mile after mile of swirling desert, and occasionally
a coastal strip of green: a day of steady progress, fifteen miles regularly in each hour; a night of undisturbed rest under a cloud of desert
stars.

At Sirte a message was received from the Eighth Army ordering the
Brigade to move on with maximum speed to Medenine, across the
Tunisian border. Only sixteen days after leaving Qatana they joined
Mar. 2 the leading troops of the Eighth Army, and leaguered that night just
behind the gun lines. Four days later the Battalion was engaged in the
first battle of its history.

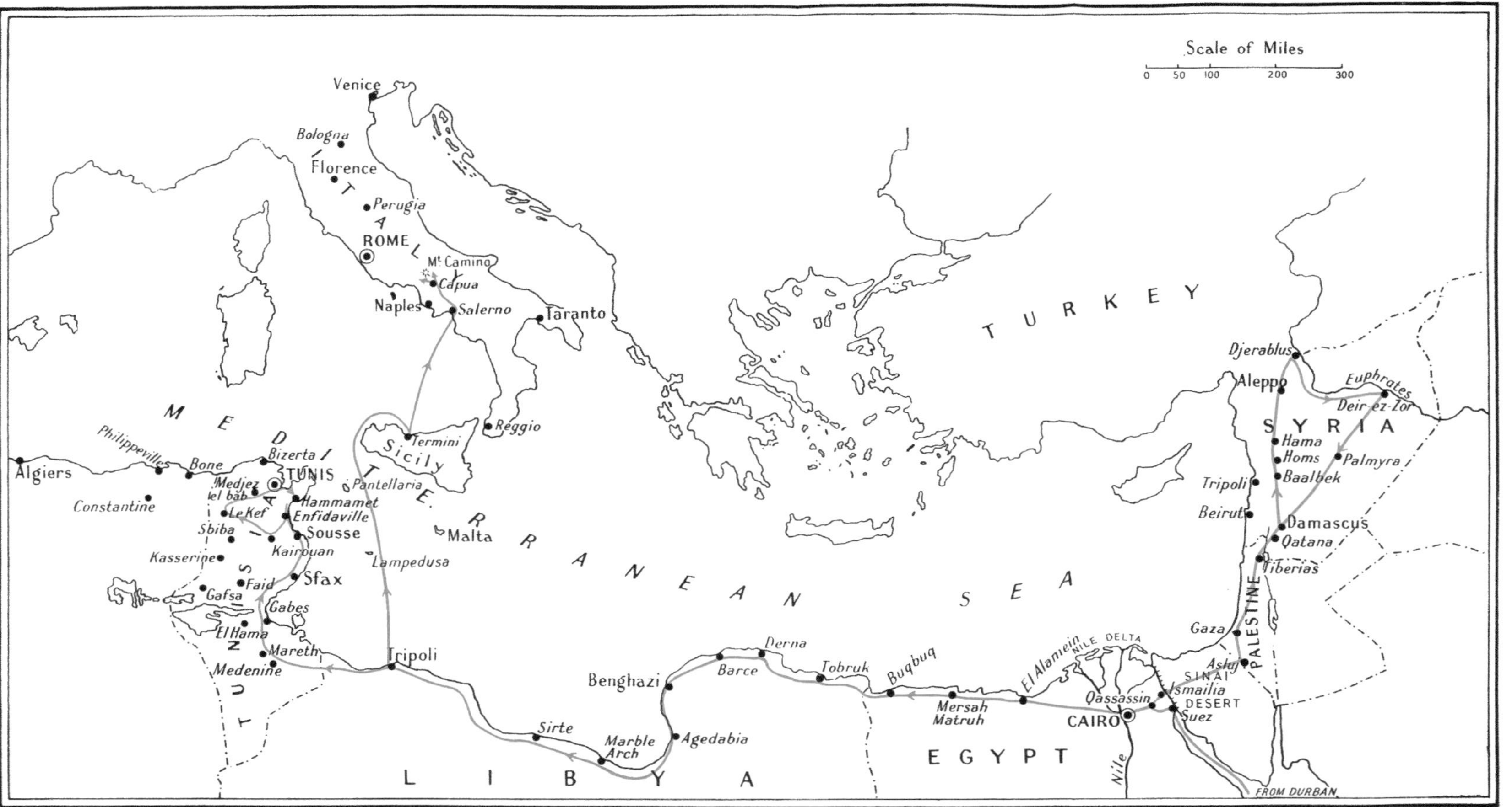

Face page 294

MEDITERRANEAN CAMPAIGNS OF THE 6th BATTALION

2

THE BATTLES OF MEDENINE AND THE HORSESHOE 1943

The strategy of Generals Montgomery and Rommel—The 6th Battalion first meet the enemy in the highly successful action at Medenine—Fifty-two German tanks destroyed almost without loss—General Montgomery orders the Brigade to attack an outpost of the Mareth Line—Planning for the attack—The Battle of the Horseshoe, 16th and 17th March, 1943—The enemy discover the British plans—The Battalion suffer very heavy casualties as they cross the wadi and the minefields—The three forward companies almost isolated—Desperate attempts to reach them with reinforcements—Brigade Commander withdraws the survivors at dawn—The battle summed up in the light of later knowledge

The pursuit by the Eighth Army had put a great strain on their communications, while the Germans had been continually withdrawing towards their own supply dumps and had been able to pool the resources of the Afrika Korps with those of von Arnim's army in Northern Tunisia. During the few weeks which elapsed between the juncture of the two German Armies and the juncture of the two Allied Armies, the enemy had an all-round advantage: now, if ever, was their opportunity to save themselves from disaster. Rommel's first move was to combine his three armoured divisions for the attack through the Faid Pass, with the intention of engaging in battle the armoured reserves of the First Army and inflicting upon them such a defeat that they would be in no position to intervene when he turned to confront the Eighth. His success was at first startling. With his heavier weapons he knocked out a large number of British and American tanks, and at one moment threatened the entire communication system of the First Army. How the situation was saved has already been described in the account of the 3rd Battalion's actions at Sbiba and the Kasserine Pass; but it was as much the onset of Montgomery's forces over the Libyan—Tunisian border as the exertions of the First Army in their self-defence which turned the scales at the last moment. Fairly content with his success in the north, Rommel wheeled his Feb. 23
tanks about and prepared to use the same troops for a knock-out blow against the few divisions of the Eighth Army which had advanced as far as Medenine, twenty miles south of the village of Mareth.

General Montgomery had planned his own attack on the Mareth Line for the 20th of March, allowing time for the repair of the harbour at Tripoli and for the assembly of the remainder of his divisions. Rommel's intentions, which were becoming more and more evident to the British Intelligence, made it essential to reinforce the Eighth

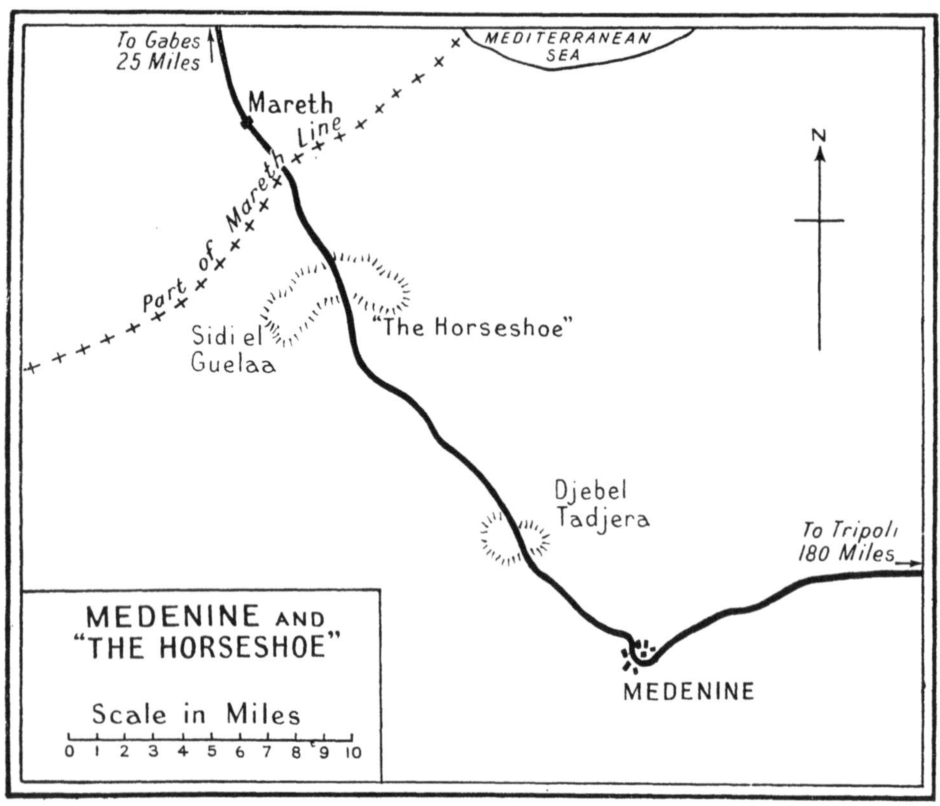

1943 Army ahead of their schedule. The New Zealanders and the 51st (Highland) Division were hurried up to Medenine to join the 7th Armoured Division. It was for the same reason that those urgent orders had reached the 201st Guards Brigade at Sirte. Our dispositions were complete by the morning of the 5th of March, the day on which the German attack was expected.

Mar. 6 It came at dawn on the 6th. The Guards Brigade had been stationed astride the main Medenine—Mareth road, firmly based on a circle of rocky hills, called Djebel Tadjera, which rose abruptly from the plain. The 6th Grenadiers held the basin through which passed the main Tripoli—Gabes coastal road, a position which would have borne the full weight of the German attack if they had chosen to approach from the north. The two other battalions of the Brigade lay farther to the west, overlooking a wide plain which seemed to afford the enemy better ground for the deployment of his tanks. Behind them—a formidable and a reassuring sight to the Grenadiers—lay the whole of the 7th Armoured Division, spaced out in desert formation and ready to intervene should the infantry find themselves in too great difficulties. The subsequent Battle of Medenine belongs more properly to the history of the 2nd Scots Guards. The Grenadiers were never directly attacked, and though they waited tensely not more than a few hundred yards away, the formation of the hills hid from them the actual battlefield, and not a single man of the Battalion claims to have fired a shot that day. **1943**

The enemy tanks took the obvious approach from the south-west, sheered away from a dummy minefield laid in front of the Coldstream Guards, and rode up to the crest of a ridge which was covered along its entire length by the 6-pounder anti-tank guns of the Scots Guards. It had seemed unlikely that the Germans would fall into so obvious a trap, or indeed ever attempt to attack in daylight a position which overlooked for miles the approach route which they chose to follow. In consequence, they lost sixteen tanks to the Scots Guards alone, seventeen more to the artillery, and with the successes of neighbouring brigades the total was brought up to fifty-two—without the intervention of a single unit of the 7th Armoured Division. By their knock-out blow the Germans had succeeded only in crippling their own striking power, and were obliged to fall back on the defences of the Mareth Line, leaving the Eighth Army intact and much elated. It was only after the battle that the Grenadiers suffered any severe loss. Two officers, Lieuts. H. J. Tufnell and B. J. D. Brooke, were killed outright **Mar. 11** when the jeep in which they were patrolling ran over a mine. Their bodies were recovered by Lieut. The Lord Brabourne and a party of volunteers.

General Montgomery adhered to his original plan to attack the Mareth Line on the 20th of March. It was a system of fortifications built by the French to guard the approaches into Southern Tunisia, backed by a range of high hills, and strengthened by concrete blockhouses and other paraphernalia of the Maginot type. In this line the Germans found the perfect position for a small army, and on it they based their last hopes of keeping the First and Eighth Armies apart. Montgomery had worked out his plan of attack many months before. The 51st (Highland) Division were to deliver a frontal assault between the main road and the sea while the New Zealanders took the long desert route round the left flank to seize El Hamma and so force a German withdrawal from the main defences.

A preliminary battle was necessary to clear the immediate approaches, to enable the Highlanders to confront the Mareth Line directly, without fear of any threat on either flank. On both sides of the road the Germans had not withdrawn into the main fortifications, but to an outpost position on a group of hills about three miles to the south. So long as these hills remained in enemy hands the High-

1943 landers would not be secure. The 201st Guards Brigade were given the task of capturing them. Though of great importance to the bigger plan, the operation was not expected to be very difficult, and in the words of General Leese, Commander of the XXX Corps, the Guards Brigade were deliberately selected "to give them a comparatively easy period of quiet operations in order to acclimatize the many newcomers to warfare," while the more experienced troops were reserved for the major assault. This idea was echoed by General Montgomery when he visited the Brigade shortly after the Battle of Medenine. "When I give a party," he said, "it is a good party. And this is going to be a good party." Certainly, from all the information then available, it appeared that the Brigade would have little trouble. It is true that the air photographs revealed a great many new trenches in addition to the defence works of the old French outpost, but the Germans were not believed to have sufficient troops to man them all, and there were even indications that they intended to abandon the hills entirely. No minefields were visible on the photographs, and shortage of time and troops would probably have prevented the enemy from laying mines thickly enough to impede our attack very seriously. In both these conclusions our Intelligence was at fault.

Mar. 13 When the Brigade moved forward to the front line they could clearly see their objectives. The sight was not reassuring. In general the country was changing from pure desert into the more broken
See plan p. 308 ground of the Tunisian Tell, and for vegetation there were already a few thin olive groves. The plain immediately in front was flat and cut up by dry water-courses (wadis), but, beyond, the ground began to swell into a group of bare, whale-backed hills which dominated the road in the vicinity: a mile or so farther north the black hulks of the Mareth Mountains closed the horizon. The nearer hills were the objectives of the attack. They spread out in horseshoe shape on either side of the road (from which was derived the name "The Battle of the Horseshoe," the most familiar title to those who took part in it), the larger and heavier group lying on the west side of the road, and rising to their highest point in Sidi el Guelaa (five hundred feet). It appeared from a distance that the hill-slopes were smooth and gentle enough to allow tracked vehicles to move over them at will, but the ground would clearly be too rocky for the quick excavation of trenches. The further study of the air photographs revealed an obstacle which was scarcely discernible from ground-level. This was a wadi of unusual size, known as the Wadi Zess, which ran along the foot of the hills on the British side. Its near bank was from five to thirty feet high, presenting to the infantry an awkward yet surmountable barrier, but to all types of vehicle an obstacle which they would be able to cross only after artifi-

General Montgomery visits the 6th Battalion after the Battle of Medenine.
Left to Right: Brig. J. A. Gascoigne, General Montgomery, Major-Gen. Erskine and Lt.-Col. A. F. L. Clive.

The Battle of the Horseshoe, Mareth Line.
Grenadier graves between the Wadi Zess and the Horseshoe.

cial entrances and exits had been constructed. The wadi lay too close under the enemy positions for the infantry attack to be delayed while such a crossing place was made. Their attack would have to be launched immediately with such equipment as each man could carry, and the heavier weapons brought up to them as soon as the wadi was made passable to vehicles. 1943

This was one of the first decisions taken. Another was that the attack should be made by night. Brigadier Gascoigne was at first in favour of a daylight attack, a simpler operation for inexperienced troops, but he reconsidered his plan when the artillery commanders told him that they could not guarantee to neutralize enemy fire while the Brigade were crossing the open plain in full view from the circle of hills. The moon, which was almost full, would not set until 3.30 a.m. and would illuminate the battlefield sufficiently for the men to distinguish their objectives without betraying their approach.

The next stage of the plan was to allot the various features as objectives to each battalion, and, within the battalions, to each of their companies. Brigadier Gascoigne decided that two battalions should attack side by side, the 6th Grenadier Guards on the right and the 3rd Coldstream Guards on the left, the dividing line between them running just east of Sidi el Guelaa, which therefore lay within the Coldstream sector. The Scots Guards, who had borne the brunt of the Medenine battle, would be in reserve at the start and would probably move up later to fill the gap which would open between the Grenadiers and the left of the Highland Division. The detailed objectives given by Colonel Clive to the Grenadier companies were as follows:

Right.—No. 3 Company (Capt. G. C. F. Gwyer): the hill on the right of the road known as B139.

Centre.—No. 1 Company (Major P. G. Evelyn): the hill on the left of the road known as Point 109.

Left.—No. 4 Company (Major T. P. Butler): the neck of land connecting Point 109 with Sidi el Guelaa.

No. 2 Company (anti-tank: Major A. J. E. Gordon, M.C.), together with the scout platoons, medium machine guns, mortars, wirelesses and medical stores, were to form the consolidation group, the group containing all the essential vehicles which were to follow the assaulting companies across the wadi. It was to be under the control of Major W. H. Kingsmill, M.C. From the very start the Battalion was therefore split into two halves, and the whole issue of the battle depended on the successful junction between them.

In considering his detailed plan for the 6th Battalion's attack, Colonel Clive was handicapped by several difficulties. His battalion had never been in action apart from the minor role which they had

1943 played at Medenine, and they were now embarking on one of the most difficult operations of war—a long advance by night over open country, the crossing of a big obstacle, and an assault uphill to capture ill-defined objectives. The 6th Battalion were not equipped and organized in a manner most suited to this type of operation. Technically speaking, they were a "motor battalion," designed for desert warfare in support of an armoured division: they had only three motor companies (instead of the four rifle companies of a normal infantry battalion), an anti-tank company, and a disproportionate number of carriers, forty-four in all, which were quite unusable in night attacks over rough country. Furthermore, the shortage of time and the necessity for concealment prevented detailed reconnaissance of the hills and
Mar. 14/15 the approaches to them. On the only two nights available many patrols
Mar. 15/16 were indeed taken out, but they added little to our knowledge. One, under Lieut. J. M. Strang-Steel, reached the near edge of the Wadi Zess, but saw no signs of mines. Another, which had occupied an outpost position under Lieut. J. K. W. Sloan, was surprised at dawn by an enemy raid covered by a box barrage, and lost several prisoners. Worse had already happened, unknown to the Battalion until long after the battle. An artillery officer of the Highland Division had been captured carrying a map on which were marked the successive lines of the intended artillery barrage, and the times at which they would be fired. This information was of vital importance to the enemy. He now knew when and where and by whom the attack was to be delivered, and was quick to take advantage of this knowledge.

Mar. 16 7.30 p.m. When the Battalion set off across the plain to their start line they still considered that they were about to attack a lightly held outpost, and their easy progress up to and across the Wadi Zess seemed to confirm this idea. The start line itself was marked in white tape by the Brigade and Battalion Intelligence Officers, Philipps and Vaughan, and for a few minutes the whole Battalion lay down behind it, grouped by their companies, and waiting for the zero hour. The Commanding Officer passed up and down the ranks, talking quietly to the men, and ordered them to fix their bayonets. Only one disconcerting incident had so far occurred, of which they of course did not realize the significance: a German aircraft flew overhead and dropped a flare. The whole Battalion lay still and no hostile shell fire followed. A few
8.45 p.m. minutes later our own artillery burst into sudden life,* and with this

*The artillery programme is of technical interest. In support of the Brigade there were three medium regiments and five field regiments. The mediums fired mainly counter-battery tasks. The 25-pounders fired a barrage on a two-thousand-yard front, lifting a hundred yards in every four minutes, to a depth of one thousand two hundred yards, and in addition were ready to supply on call ninety separate three-minute concentrations of a hundred and twenty shells each. In all, twenty-four thousand shells were fired during the battle.

signal the two battalions once more advanced towards the wadi. There 1943
were no more than a few isolated shots as they approached. The wadi was crossed, with few casualties, ahead of their timed programme, and the Battalion re-formed on the far bank ready to start their assault. While they were waiting, a thin wire was discovered close to the ground running for some distance parallel to the wadi and not more than fifty yards north of it. They cut the wire, thinking that it might be connected to a booby-trap. It was not a booby-trap. It marked the outer edge of the first minefield.

A German interrogator, questioning our prisoners after the battle, seemed amazed that even the infantry had managed to cross the minefields. He asked whether we did not have special appliances. But the only anti-mine devices which the Guardsmen were carrying were pieces of bent wire with which to feel for the prongs of shrapnel mines, and these were of little use. As they moved up the hillside the mines began to explode in every direction, and the heavy German mortars not only added to the casualties by their own explosion but touched off the big Teller mines which a man's weight alone would not have detonated. "At one moment," an officer wrote, "I thought that an Indian-file method of crossing the minefields would be best, but when several men following closely behind me were blown up I revised my views. Dispersal should be every man's aim, so that no mine caused more than a single casualty." The Grenadiers pressed on in spite of heavy losses, so eagerly that a few men were wounded by their own barrage. Among the officers Capt. G. C. F. Gwyer was badly wounded Mar. 16 9.45 p.m.
but insisted on being carried forward to his company objective, and died later in German hands; Lieut. E. M. Hovell, from the same company, was also hit but remained with his men for the greater part of the night. Both Lieuts. J. M. Strang-Steel and Hon. H. Trenchard were first wounded by mines, and shortly afterwards killed by mortar bombs. Lieut. N. S. T. Margetson set off to deal with an enemy machine gun and was never seen alive again. Colonel Clive, who was blown over and slightly wounded by the same mine which killed his orderly, remained in command. Lieuts. Lord Brabourne and E. B. M. Vaughan were wounded, but also stayed on the field.

After a few hundred yards the mines appeared to thin out, but then the Grenadiers came to a barbed-wire fence which marked the beginning of a second and yet thicker minefield. This too was crossed, and on reaching the far side the companies found themselves close to their objectives. It was not easy in the pale moonlight and smoke of battle to distinguish one hill from another, and each officer made a guess at the direction in which he should lead his platoon. No. 3 Company had the road to guide them, and covered the last few yards against little

1943 opposition, to find the deep German trenches for the most part un-
Mar. 16 10.30 p.m. occupied. They were the first to fire their red and green Very lights, a signal of their success to the watchers in the plain behind. The other two companies had become slightly confused. When Colonel Clive discovered their positions, he quickly switched their objectives, allotting Point 109 to No. 4 Company, and the left-hand spur to No. 1 Company, which he personally pointed out to Major Evelyn in the bright moonlight. It was the last time that he saw him alive. To the great credit of both company commanders, they managed to wheel their men directly towards their new objectives. Stumbling and shouting, bewildered by the thunder of a battle at its height but still very determined, the Guardsmen doubled forward over the final ridge and found the Germans lying terrified at the bottom of their circular entrenchments. Those who refused to surrender were killed by bayonets, and those trenches which were too deep for a bayonet to reach the bottom were plugged with grenades. Not more than ten prisoners were taken.

11.20 p.m. Silence, except for odd bursts of machine-gun fire, descended on the hills. To those in rear who had watched the three success signals rise from the three Grenadier objectives it seemed that all had gone extremely well. The signals were greeted by loud cheers. It is true that the Battalion had gained all that was demanded of them, and that for the moment there was little sign of a German counter-attack. But their situation was by no means a happy one. Each company was very much weakened. In No. 4 Company they had already suffered seventy per cent. casualties, they had only two Bren guns in working order, and were running low in ammunition. No. 1 Company, rallied on the objective to the sound of Major Evelyn's hunting horn (in peace time he was an M.F.H.), could now muster only thirty-five men. No. 3 Company were slightly better off. Each company was out of touch not only with its neighbours but also with Battalion Headquarters, for the light man-load wireless sets had not worked properly and communications were interrupted for hours on end. Hence they were unable to report their exact positions, unable to call for artillery support, and the gunners dared not fire blindly ahead. It soon became clear that many enemy pockets had been bypassed by our advance, as the two left-hand companies had swung wide of their true direction after leaving the wadi, and, though the Germans were at first stunned by the impact of the barrage, they now began to raise their heads and weapons to shoot into the rear of the company positions and at any reinforcements which attempted to make their way forward with supplies of ammunition. The main German pocket was on Point 117, a hillock which lay on the left flank of the Battalion's supply line, and was far more strongly defended than had been supposed. To add to their difficulties, a company of the Coldstream Guards, who had fought their way with great spirit to the top of Sidi el Guelaa, had been forced to withdraw to the foot of the hill, leaving a gap between themselves and the Grenadiers which the enemy were not slow to exploit. **1943**

These worries were nothing compared to the disasters which occurred when the carriers and the anti-tank guns attempted to cross the Wadi Zess and the minefields. The Commanding Officer considered that the Battalion could probably hold out if it were possible to reinforce them before dawn, and every effort was made to clear a passage through the series of obstacles which now lay between the two halves of the Battalion. There were four such obstacles: the wadi, which in its natural state was impassable to vehicles; the minefields; two artificial blocks across the road; and the enemy pockets which still remained behind the leading platoons. Each was tackled simultaneously. A track was dug out of the wadi bank (the earth of which it was composed being too crumbly for the use of explosives), and after an hour's work a few vehicles were able to descend into the wadi and mount the other side. But as the crossing place was under constant bombardment and under the fire of about ten machine guns from Point 117, it was not long before some of the towing lorries were set ablaze, illuminating the whole area, and silhouetting each vehicle which came up to the southern bank. Mines were also found in the wadi bed, and ten carriers were blown up before a way could be cleared. The road blocks gave less trouble, as they were constructed of loose stones in the manner of a Northumberland dry-wall, but as soon as any vehicle attempted to drive across country towards the companies it immediately blew up on a mine, and a tall column of black smoke rose from the wreckage and hung in the still air above. The casualties were very heavy, especially among the officers. The commanders of the scout platoons, who were in charge of the carriers, and the subalterns of the anti-tank company, who had gone forward with the assault companies to reconnoitre positions for their guns and had now returned to guide them into position, tried again and again to penetrate the minefields. Lieut. C. E. A. Trimmer-Thompson and Capt. R. J. V. Goss were killed immediately on mines. Capt. J. R. Allsopp, a master at Eton College, stepped from his demolished carrier only to be killed immediately by an "S" mine. Lieut. A. G. Buchanan, who had just returned across the minefield to collect his anti-tank guns, was wounded by a mine and killed soon afterwards by a mortar bomb. Lieut. R. C. Rowan was blown out of two carriers in succession before being wounded in the head. The commander of the anti-tank company, Major A. J. E. Gordon, M.C., **Mar. 17 Midnight-1 a.m.**

1943 Mar. 17 was wounded early on but continued not only with his reconnaissance on the right flank but organized a party to carry ammunition to No. 3 Company, before his wounds obliged him to retire. Of the troop of sappers from 21st Field Squadron, who worked all night at the wadi crossing, only two were left unharmed in the morning.

Casualties on this scale reduced the consolidation group to a state 1 a.m. even weaker than that of the assault companies, and it began to appear that even if a way could be found through the minefields there would be too few mortars, medium machine guns and anti-tank guns, and crews to man them, for the Battalion to be able to withstand a heavy counter-attack. The Germans were beginning to react more and more strongly: No. 3 Company, the only one which the Commanding Officer was able to visit, were already being attacked on their right flank; No. 4 Company were repelling with grenades the enemy who were creeping up on all sides; and No. 1 Company remained in comparative peace, but they could hear ominous sounds from the ridge in front, they were under machine-gun fire from Point 117 behind, and when Major Evelyn took a small patrol towards the assumed position of the Coldstream Guards he met Germans within a few hundred yards and was obliged to return. Even Advanced Battalion Headquarters, on the left of the road five hundred yards north of the wadi, were in great peril. Colonel Clive, Lieut. P. C. W. Alington, Major T. O'Brien Butler (a battery commander of the 2nd R.H.A., who were supporting the Battalion), Sergt. Bridges (the Intelligence Sergeant) and about four other ranks, made a sweep round the immediate area of the headquarters, collected five prisoners of war, but were able to gain but small relief from the pressing danger. This was an occasion when a reserve company would have been invaluable; but there was no reserve: the width of the front had made it necessary to employ at the start every man of the motor companies, and the platoons in front, weakened as they were, could not afford to abandon their hard-won 2.30 a.m. trenches to fight off the enemy who remained behind them. In this dilemma Colonel Clive appealed to the Brigade Commander to loan him two companies of the Scots Guards, who had not yet been engaged. In his report on the battle Brigadier Gascoigne gives this reason for refusing the Grenadiers' request: "It appeared to me that what was needed on their front was not so much men as weapons, and if in the end we were unable to hold the objective it would be difficult to withdraw the Battalion if the greater part of the Scots Guards were also involved, and if we had no firm base to withdraw through." In other words, the issue depended on the efforts of the consolidation group; if they were unable to force a passage before dawn no number of infantry reinforcements could possibly affect the decision to with-

draw, and by their employment the weakening of the reserve line 1943 Mar. 17
might turn the withdrawal into a major disaster.

In the few hours of darkness which remained a further attempt was 3 a.m.
made to bring relief to the forward companies. Major Kingsmill, the Second-in-Command, drew back from the edge of the wadi all the vehicles which remained on the southern bank, and Capt. Viscount Anson and the Adjutant, Capt. The Master of Forbes, formed a defensive flank to guard against an attack from the north-west. With the few carriers which survived on the enemy side of the wadi, Lieut. J. H. Wiggin attempted to find No. 1 Company, of whom nothing had been heard for several hours. Lieut. C. N. Grazebrook had returned earlier in the night with a message from Major Evelyn, but he had been killed by a mine as he set out to return. The exact position of the company was therefore in some doubt, and Wiggin set out into the unknown, across country which was mined and full of enemy troops. He had remarkably good fortune. For the first time that night his carriers struck a path which was clear of mines, and, having run the gauntlet of fire from Point 117, he took a branch track which led between Point 109 and the supposed position of No. 1 Company. Halting on the slopes of Point 109, he shouted for Major Evelyn, but, hearing no answer either from him or No. 4 Company, he continued round the front of No. 1 Company, past some of the Coldstream positions, and so back in a wide loop to Battalion Headquarters. Only one carrier was lost during the patrol. A few hours later Wiggin discovered that he had passed so close to Major Evelyn that the latter had heard his shouts but had been unable to attract his attention. This unhappy chance veiled an opportunity which, even at that late hour, might have saved the Battalion. Wiggin's patrol only added to the confusion: a way forward had been found, but the companies were lost. There was no object in sending blindly ahead the few vehicles which remained, through all the dangers of mine and bullet, in search of the men he had failed to find.

The Commanding Officer made his final dispositions. The Vickers 4.30 a.m.
machine guns of No. 4 Company, under Sergt. Smith, had already come into action near Battalion Headquarters, and knocked out four enemy machine guns before they themselves lost three out of four of their own weapons and two-thirds of the crews. The survivors of the consolidation group were divided into three parties: a platoon of four anti-tank guns under Capt. F. N. P. Osborne and Lieut. Vaughan; an infantry platoon under the Sergeant-Major, F. Dowling; and the four or five carriers which remained with Lieut. Wiggin. The wounded from those positions which could still be reached were brought to the wadi-bed, and from here they were ferried back by Capt. The Viscount

1943 Mar. 17 Anson and the Signals Officer, Lieut. R. A. Kennard, to the regimental aid post. The doctor, Capt. A. Winder, and the Padre, Capt. Rev. W. R. Leadbeater, tended them under a terrible rain of mortar bombs.

5.25 a.m. Just before dawn the Brigadier ordered the withdrawal of both the Grenadiers and the Coldstream. The withdrawal was to be covered by artillery smoke, but it seemed very doubtful whether the order would ever reach Nos. 1 and 4 Companies, and if it did, whether they would be able to fight their way back to safety. Communications with No. 3 Company were still intact, and to assist their withdrawal a scratch platoon under Lieut. W. C. Haden and Sergt. Delebecque was sent to their aid. Haden was killed by a sniper soon after he arrived. Of the officers in No. 3 Company, the acting commander, Lieut. T. G. Ridpath, who had been an inspiration to his men all night and had beaten off three separate German attacks, was killed just before the withdrawal, and Lieut. J. K. W. Sloan, the only survivor, was shot dead as he began to lead his men back. Sergts. Harrison and Delebecque
8.45 a.m. brought back the handful who remained. In spite of their terrible losses, No. 3 Company emerged stronger than either of the other two.

The fate of Nos. 4 and 1 Companies, which remained almost unknown for many months, can now be pieced together from the accounts of surviving prisoners of war.

The final stages of No. 4 Company's gallant resistance were described by the company commander, Major T. P. Butler, D.S.O., in these words:

> "Soon after dawn we receive a message over the air telling us to withdraw if we can, as nothing can get to our aid. There is a very close and ever-tightening ring round our position and a great number of machine guns and automatics pour a continuous stream of bullets just over our heads. In an effort to improve the situation I call for artillery fire all round our hill. This call is promptly answered, but doesn't appear to do a great deal of harm, in spite of shells bursting all round us. After a slight lull, during which a section of the company some seventy yards away is successfully withdrawn to the main position, the Germans start closing right in, and some bitter close-quarter fighting takes place with grenades. Lieut. Vivian does some good shooting. I decide that the time has come to try to fight our way out rather than be massacred in our trenches. In order to do so, it is first necessary to destroy a particularly troublesome machine gun very near our position. A few of us make the attempt, only to be shot down within a couple of yards of our trench. I find myself lying in the open with a bullet through my knee watching, fascinated, a grenade rolling towards me. It explodes almost in my face, and pieces paste my chest, knocking me out. Some time later I find myself being dragged back into the trench by German stretcher-bearers. It was only months later that I learnt that the remnants of the company were overwhelmed and captured. The German aid post to which I was carried was only a hundred and

fifty yards away at the bottom of the hill and in *rear* of our position. **1943**
Unknown to us, we must have penetrated right into the centre of the **Mar. 17**
German defences."

Major Butler and Lieuts. Vivian and The Lord Brabourne were taken prisoner.*

No. 1 Company never received the order to withdraw. Their wireless had been out of action for many hours, and in the final stages of the battle the aerial of the control set at Battalion Headquarters was shot away, and with it went the last hopes of restoring communications. No. 1 Company now had left three officers (Major Evelyn and Lieuts. M. R. Bonham-Carter and N. J. R. J. Durham) and about thirty men. When the dawn revealed no sign of the other companies and the Germans began to close in around them, Evelyn took the decision to withdraw, telling the men, for the sake of discipline and morale, that the company was about to attack Point 117 and regain touch with the remainder of the Battalion. They were forming up with this object when suddenly they saw four carriers coming towards them. It was Lieut. Wiggin. Once again, and this time in broad daylight, he had taken the hazardous route which he had discovered the night before, and had already lost one carrier to a German anti-tank gun. Wiggin records the delight with which he met Major Evelyn: "From a distance I saw three soldiers standing beside the track. I could not see at first who they were, but as I drew nearer I suddenly recognized one of them as Peter Evelyn. He came up to me and put both hands on my shoulders." They quickly loaded the carriers with as many men as they would bear and set off down the track under heavy fire from Points 117 and 109. One of the carriers was hit and caught fire; the three others escaped. But there had been no room on them for the four officers and about ten Guardsmen. They lay in the ditch in small isolated groups, waiting for the carriers to return and exposed to continuous rifle fire. Lieut. N. J. R. J. Durham was killed, although the others, lying prone beside him, did not know it for half an hour. Evelyn, shortly afterwards, was wounded very badly in the shoulder and the corner of his eye, and though his body was never found it is probable that he died of his wounds soon after capture. Wiggin, Bonham-Carter and the remaining Guardsmen were taken prisoner, **8.45 a.m.**
the carriers having failed to make their way back to their rescue.

The battle was almost over. The Commanding Officer was one of the last to withdraw across the wadi and, having survived risks as great as any to which his men had been exposed, he was wounded in the

*Brabourne and Vivian were both shot by the Germans in cold blood after they had been caught trying to jump the prisoner-of-war train on the German-Italian frontier. Major Butler and Lieut. Bonham-Carter (No. 1 Company) both successfully escaped to our own lines after the Italian armistice.

1943 Mar. 17 10 a.m. mouth as he set out to rejoin the remnants of his Battalion. They assembled under Major Kingsmill in the same position which they had left, so strong and so confident, sixteen hours before.

At the root of the trouble had been the failure of the British Intelligence to discover the existence of the huge minefields. This is not a matter on which opposing armies are usually well informed, as it is seldom possible to detect on air photographs the faint signs of minelaying, and the only other sources of information are prisoners of war, civilians and patrols. During the short time in which we were in contact with the El Guelaa position before the attack, no prisoners were taken, and the country was bare of Arab dwellings. Patrols across the Wadi Zess were ruled out by the even greater importance of concealing our preparations. The existence of mines in such large quantities seemed most unlikely. But we were wrong. Nothing, not even the warning given to the Germans of the impending attack, not even the lack of Battalion reserves, contributed so much to our ill-success. It was not the numbers of the enemy which overran the Brigade, for, although the whole of the German 90th Light Division were in a position to intervene in the battle, the Grenadiers had seized all their objectives and held every one against repeated counter-attacks until they were ordered to withdraw. It was the mines. The mines which were laid so close together that seven hundred and twenty had to be lifted after the battle before the bodies of sixty-nine Grenadiers could be recovered for burial. The mines which starved the assault companies of their ammuniton supplies and of the support of those heavier weapons without which no troops can fight for long. The mines which so weakened our ranks that we could no longer hold a solid front against the infiltration of the enemy, nor dominate even that part of the battlefield which had already been overrun.

The Battle of the Horseshoe was one of the greatest and most terrible fought by the Grenadier Guards in the Second World War. The fact that they were eventually forced to withdraw from the positions which they had captured should not be allowed to obscure the achievement of the 6th Battalion, nor to encourage the idea that the task, as originally conceived, was too great for a single brigade, the plan a bad one, or the officers and men in any way deficient in their duty. As regards the last point, the Commanding Officer wrote afterwards: "I only found one man who showed the fear we all felt, and he came on when encouraged"; and of Colonel Clive himself a brother-officer wrote: "I cannot tell you how marvellous he was in the battle: he was quite oblivious to all danger. All the men would follow him straight into the jaws of hell if he asked them, and they are continually

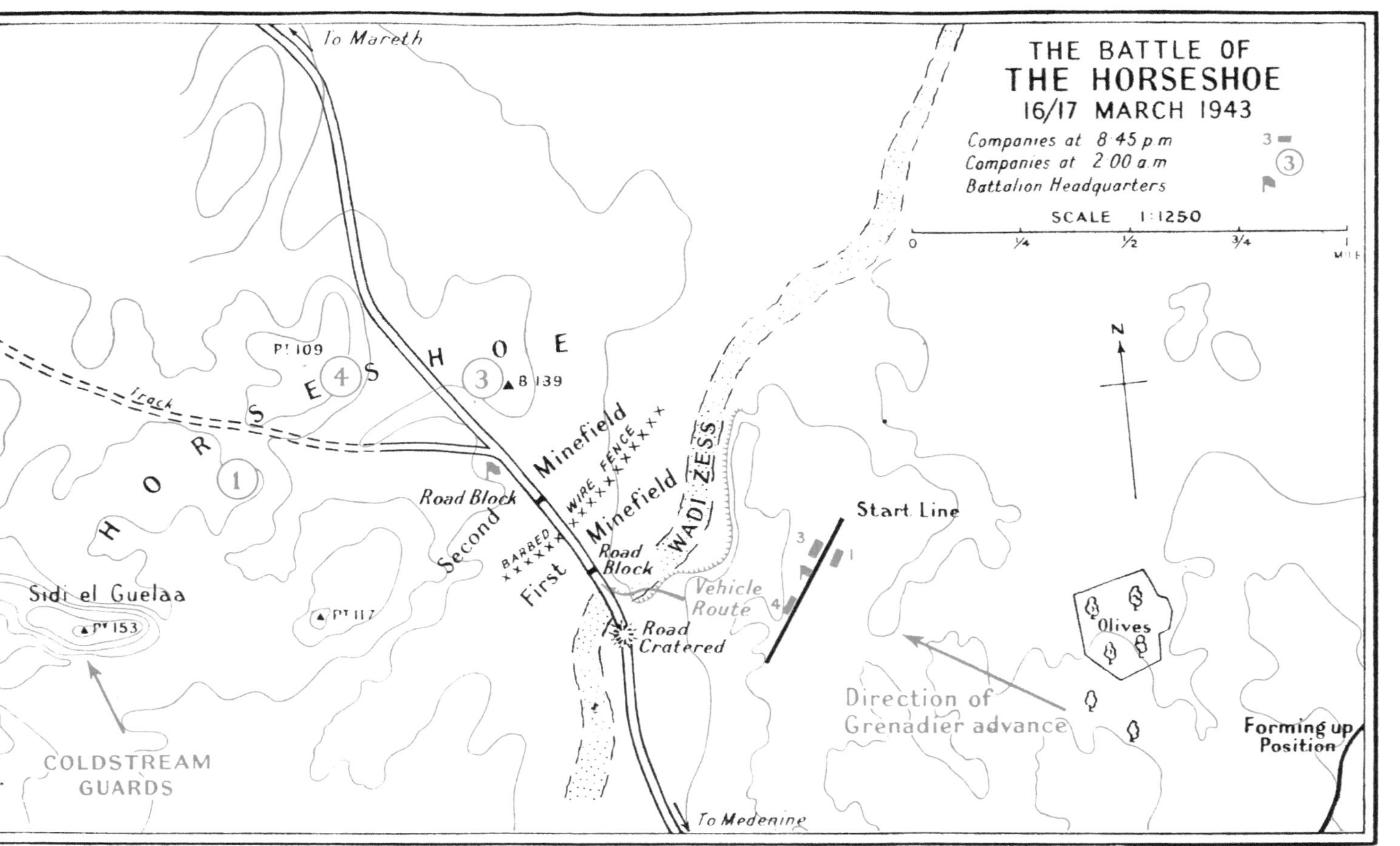

THE BATTLE OF THE HORSESHOE (MARETH LINE)

talking about him and what he did." General Leese said that the only **1943**
fault he found was that the young officers exposed themselves too much in their eagerness to cheer on the men by their own example. To these tributes General Montgomery added a note on the tactical results of the battle: "The operations on 16th/17th March," he wrote, "were on the whole a great success. We got all the identifications we needed. Your operations that night definitely helped the Army plan. Tell the men this." In effect, the Germans came to regard the Horseshoe area as the key to the defence of the Mareth Line. They reinforced it before, during and after the battle with troops which they could ill spare when the New Zealand Division marched round their
right flank to El Hamma. **Mar. 20**

The casualties suffered by the 6th Battalion during the Horseshoe battle were as follows: sixty-three other ranks were killed, eighty-eight wounded and a hundred and four taken prisoner. Among the officers, fourteen were killed, five wounded and five taken prisoner, of whom two were wounded before capture.

3

MARETH TO ENFIDAVILLE

The Wadi Akarit—The Eighth Army pursue the Germans through Sousse to Enfidaville—The 201st Guards Brigade switched to the First Army

The Battalion were re-formed into three weak companies under the handful of officers who survived unhurt, and were not engaged in another serious battle during the remainder of the Tunisian campaign. Major W. H. Kingsmill, M.C., was in temporary command; Major P. W. Marsham, M.B.E., Major A. J. E. Gordon, M.C., and Capt. A. Thorne commanded the companies.

They moved up the coastal road past Gabes to the Wadi Akarit, **April 1**
where the Germans held their last delaying position before retreating to the northern hills, and here the Battalion were placed in the forward line close to the sea while preparations were made for the main assault on the left flank. The 6th Battalion merely feigned an attack by firing smoke bombs and machine guns into the wadi. It was a process known in the Eighth Army as "leaning on the enemy," a process designed to pin down a large number of enemy troops with the minimum expenditure of our own. There were not more than a few casualties, among them Lieut. C. C. B. Oldfield, who took a carrier patrol towards the

1943 April 6 wadi and was wounded by a burst of mortar fire. The Akarit Line fell,
and from here for many miles to the north our pursuit across the olive
groves of Sfax and Sousse was almost unopposed. The 6th Battalion
had little share in the excitements of that chase. They followed up a
long way behind the armoured cars; they mounted a ceremonial guard
April 15 under Major Marsham for General Montgomery's entry into the ruins
of Sousse: that same evening they met officers of the 3rd Battalion,
who drove over from the First Army; and they spent their days either
resting or bathing, or edging slowly up the dusty by-roads to the north.

From a ridge just north of Sousse one caught a first glimpse of the
mountains of Tunisia, rising with astonishing abruptness from the
plain into a series of peaks and high escarpments. Somewhere behind
these mountains lay the common objectives of both Armies—Tunis:
Tunis and Bizerta, the terminal points of the Mediterranean crossing,
the airfields on which, even at this late stage, the Germans were daily
landing reinforcements to cram still tighter the patch of ground which
remained their only foothold in Africa. So small it seemed, yet almost
unconquerable. Looking up from the olive groves and cornfields
round Enfidaville, by day hardly able to stir a foot without attracting
the attention of enemy aircraft or of their infantry in the hills above,
by night scarcely able to sleep for the plagues of mosquitoes, the 6th
Battalion felt as though a portcullis had dropped down to hold them
from the inner keep. They continued to advance, cautiously. Their
April 20 carrier platoon, under Sergt. Pollard, were the first Allied troops to
enter Enfidaville, and, just beyond, they found themselves climbing
the lower foothills. An attack by the Brigade on the summits nearest
the coast road was planned and twice postponed until further progress
could be made on the left flank. Then came an unexpected reprieve.
The whole weight of the attack was to be thrown in on the First
Army's front, and the 201st Guards Brigade moved round in a slow
May 3 and secret convoy, by Kairouan and Le Kef, to lie up with the 1st
Guards Brigade a few miles south of Medjez el Bab.

CHAPTER III

BREAKING THE TUNISIAN DEADLOCK

5TH BATTALION

1

OUED ZAAGA AND MEDJEZ EL BAB

Arrival of the 5th Battalion in Tunisia—A sudden change of orders—First patrols at Oued Zaaga—Move to Medjez and the occupation of Grenadier Hill—Operation "Lilac Blossom"—German attempt to isolate Medjez outmanœuvred

THE relations between the battalions of a regiment are seldom very 1943
intimate during war time. Each one is cut off from the others by distance and the need for secrecy, for months or even years on end. Private and semi-official letters did something to keep the far-flung battalions of the Grenadiers informed of each other's activities, and throughout the war the London headquarters of the Regiment distributed to all battalions and the families of serving officers a news-letter which gave casualty lists and hinted at the location of each unit. The news was necessarily very out of date, and of impending moves there could be no mention at all. The 3rd Battalion, for example, though they were fighting in the same operational theatre as the 6th, heard only vague rumours of the battle on the Mareth Line, and it was not until they joined up at Sousse that they heard any details of the action, or of the deaths of friends or even of brothers. Yet the interest which one battalion felt in the activities of another was always very great. A casual hint at the end of a letter would arouse a flurry of discussion, and their first meeting would be an occasion for an interchange of news and opinions lasting far into the night.

So it was with the arrival of the 5th Battalion in North Africa—the third unit of Grenadiers to be mobilized for the Tunisian victory. To those already in the field the sight of their paler but familiar faces, their neat, unmuddied battledress, their map-cases fresh from the Army and Navy Stores, came as a most welcome surprise. There had

1943 long been talk of the arrival of the 24th Guards Brigade, but here they were in fact—at Medjez el Bab, on Grenadier Hill.

For some time before leaving the United Kingdom the 24th Guards Brigade (Brigadier R. B. R. Colvin) had been kept in readiness for an operation to hold open the Straits of Gibraltar in case of sudden Spanish intervention in the war. The details of the plan cannot yet be revealed. All that can be said is that the few officers who shared the secret viewed with many misgivings the prospect of steaming through the straits under fire of hostile guns from either shore. The Spaniards
Mar. 1 did not intervene, and when the Brigade at last sailed from the Clyde they formed part of a normal convoy of reinforcements, which included the bulk of the 1st Infantry Division. That their ultimate destination was Tunisia seemed hardly in doubt, but the sealed orders, opened with ceremony when they were three days out into the Atlantic, contained little more information than they already possessed. There were some small-scale maps of the country, a few notes on the course of the campaign up to date, an order of battle of the Allied forces, and some words of advice on behaviour—how to distinguish a Berber from a Moor, the likely effects on the troops of Algerian wine, how to have dinner with an Arab. The crew of the ship, s.s. *Samaria,* were most guarded with their information, and it was not until twenty-four hours beforehand that the Commanding Officer (Lieut.-Colonel R. H. Bushman) learned that the Battalion were to dock at Algiers.

The voyage was uneventful. Sixty per cent. of the men were sea-sick by the first morning, but recovered so quickly that one and a half million cigarettes were smoked during the ten days at sea. There were U-boat alarms and hostile-aircraft alarms, but no attacks. Every man slept, stuffily, in his clothes. They passed through the straits in daylight escorted by a screen of white destroyers flung out in a wide circle
Mar. 9 ahead and on either side. They arrived at Algiers in the middle of an air raid, disembarked in darkness, and were led off to a brick factory outside the city, where as best they could they settled down for their first night on African soil. Their future was extremely obscure.

The Battalion remained in Algiers only long enough to eat their fill of tangerines and to discover that they had no desire to stay there a day longer than was necessary. The brick factory had no panes in the windows, no furniture except stacks of bricks, and the officers' mess was a stable, shared with three mules and two horses. A base like Algiers is often more uncomfortable than the line of battle.

The 5th Battalion made the second stage of their journey in a manner which heightened their sense of adventure. They went by
Mar. 13-14 sea from Algiers to Bone in two destroyers and two cross-Channel steamers, slipping as fast as they could along the lee of that inhospit-

able shore. They were not spotted by the enemy until they were within 1943
half an hour of Bone harbour. Three Italian aircraft then attacked the convoy, each launching a torpedo. One passed within a few yards of a steamer; the others went wide of their mark and the aircraft made off through fountains of anti-aircraft fire. The Brigade landed peacefully at Bone. By a curious chance the 5th Battalion found themselves bivouacked in a camp which lay among those very sand-dunes where the 3rd Battalion were to have landed in the invasion of Africa four months before.

While they waited at Bone the men bathed in the sea and tested their guns and rifles on the wide expanses of sand. The commanders, in conference at Brigade Headquarters, heard from day to day that a further move eastwards was postponed. For this they were grateful. The vehicles of all three battalions had barely started on their long overland journey from Algiers, the Brigade were now separated from the remainder of the 1st Division, and a period of reassembly and preparation was very necessary before they were ready for battle. When the orders arrived, there appeared to be no change in plan. The whole Brigade were to concentrate at Ghardimao, just over the Tunisian border, where the different units of the Division and all the transport would join them. There seemed to be little hurry: it was merely the normal but complicated process involved in moving ten thousand men towards a battlefield five hundred miles from their base.

The Brigade never reached Ghardimao. Early one morning the Mar. 18
long column of borrowed vehicles left Bone by the coast road, and by *See Map* p. 344
midday was swinging slowly up into the pine-clad hills beyond La Calle. The Grenadiers were in the lead. They halted at the roadside just north of Fernana to give time for the remainder of the convoy to catch them up, and during those few minutes a liaison officer from Headquarters, First Army, drove up to them from the south. He sprang from his car in a state of great excitement, and handed Colonel Bushman a written message. The Germans, it said, had attacked heavily in the north: the French had withdrawn, and a battalion of the Foresters had been surrounded: the 24th Guards Brigade were to be diverted from Ghardimao, and the leading battalion were to go into the line fifteen miles east of Beja that very night. This was the type of situation which was continually occurring in the days when the First Army was hard pressed for reinforcements: the arrival of the 1st Guards Brigade at Beja at the end of 1942 had met with much the same reception, and since then they had come to accept these sudden moves and sudden counter-orders with a sigh but no surprise. But to the 24th Guards Brigade, and in particular to the Grenadiers, whom it most affected, the order was most disturbing. Their transport

1943 and most of their heavy weapons were somewhere on the road between Algiers and the frontier; two days' rations and all the blankets had already been sent ahead with the advance party to Ghardimao: the Battalion would not reach the new rendezvous until after dark, and then only to face what was pictured as a desperate situation. In the military jargon of the day, it seemed that they would be launched into their first battle on very much the wrong foot.

The parallel with the experience of the 1st Guards Brigade does not end there. On arrival at Beja with his Adjutant (Capt. T. A. Gore-Browne) Colonel Bushman was told that he was to relieve a battalion of the King's Own Yorkshire Light Infantry in those same hills overlooking the Oued Zaaga where the 3rd Battalion had taken up their first tactical positions in December. Like them, the 5th expected to be engaged in almost immediate battle. Like them, they found that the danger had become much exaggerated at rear headquarters, and that the enemy's activity on this particular part of the front was negligible. The relief did not take place that night—that much the commander of
Mar. 19 the 46th Division had been willing to concede—but early the next morning. The Guardsmen arrived sleepless and almost unfed, and filed into trenches already sodden with rain. They gazed across the valley towards the German-occupied hills, and could see three derelict tanks lying there in the valley bottom; it was their first glimpse of the German Army. There was no shelling: they could discern no movement among the fields and gullies opposite, and between the two lines the ploughmen of the native farms calmly continued with their work; to them it was not No Man's Land: it was their own.

Though there seemed to be no immediate danger once the K.O.Y.L.I. had withdrawn, the Battalion found themselves holding a frontage which differed widely from conventional ideas. It was over two miles long from end to end, and the few tracks were so muddy that it would take even a jeep half an hour to reach the companies at either extremity. On their left there was a gap of two miles; on their right a gap of fifteen. The other battalions of the 24th Guards Brigade had been sent to lie alongside their comrades of the 1st Guards Brigade at Medjez el Bab,* so that the 5th Battalion found themselves flanked, commanded, and supported by strangers of the 46th Division.

On the very first night they began to take the initiative with patrols to the far side of the Oued Zaaga Valley. Let the description of one of these patrols stand as an example of many others. Close to the road

*It is worthy of record that during these few days at Medjez all five Regiments of Foot Guards were represented side by side in the line. From right to left they lay in this order: 3rd Grenadiers, 2nd Coldstream, 3rd Welsh, 1st Scots and 1st Irish Guards.

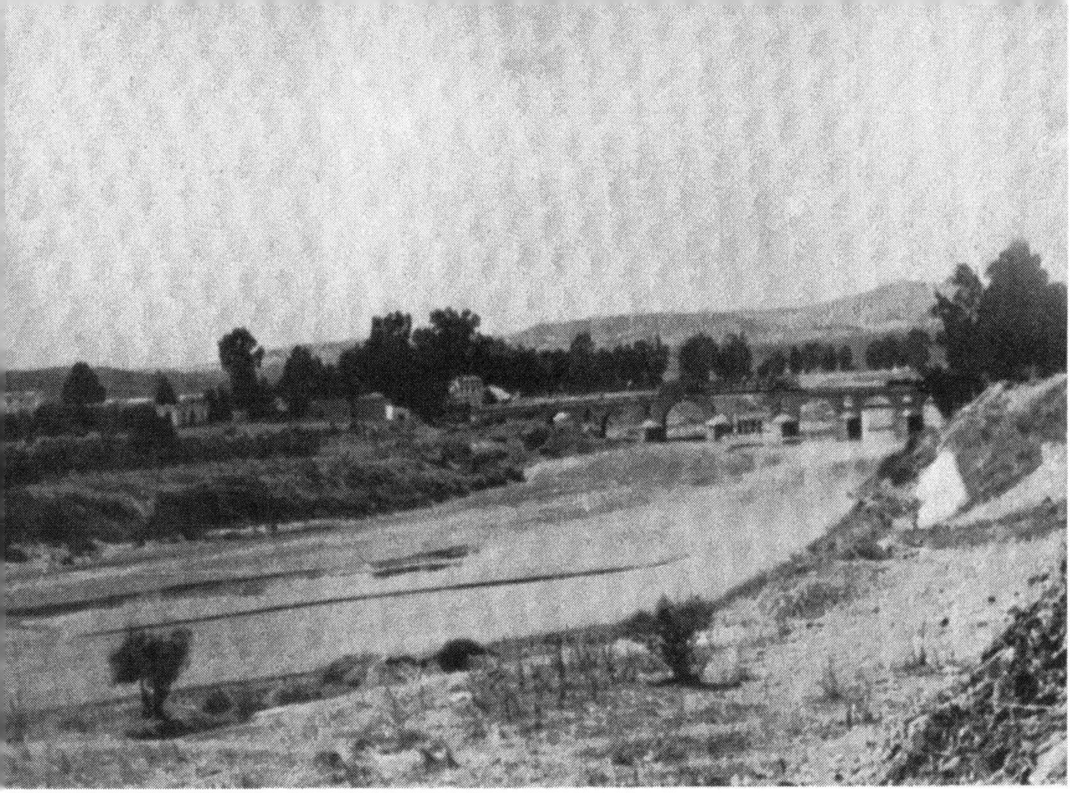

Photo: Dr. Epps

Medjez-el-Bab

The River Medjerda and the Roman bridge, spanned by the first Bailey Bridge to be built on active service.

Medjez-el-Bab

Churchill tanks moving under shell fire along the slopes of Grenadier Hill.

Crown Copyright

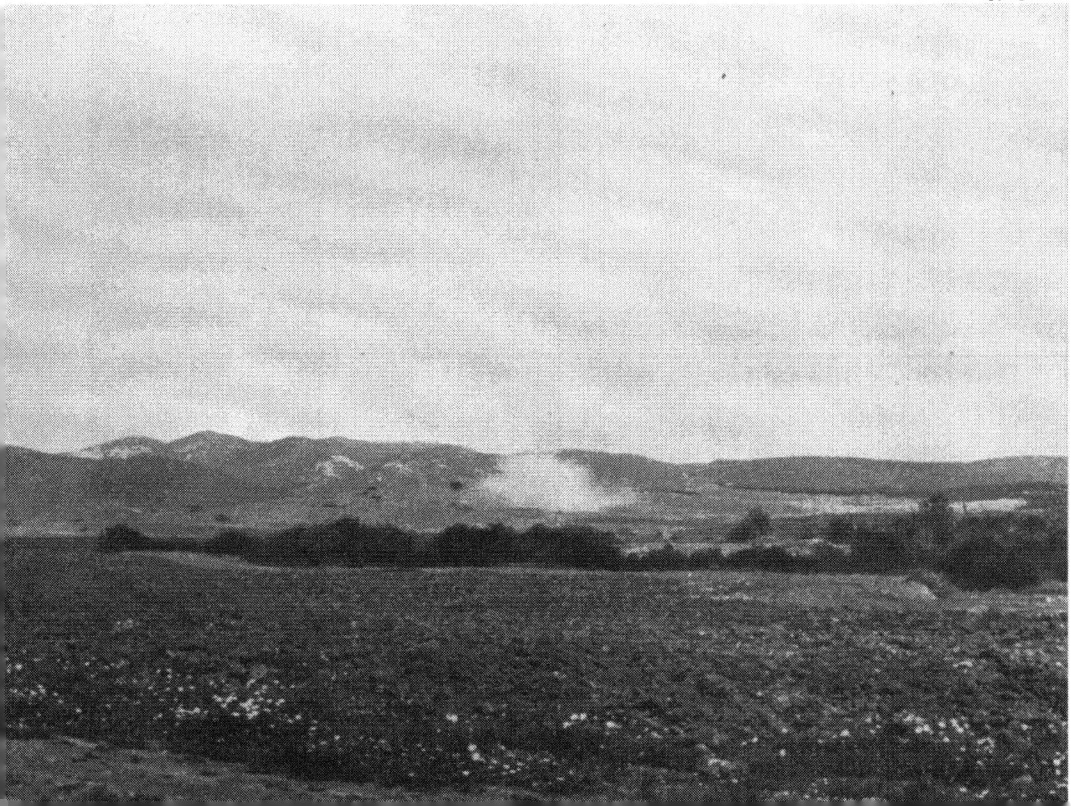

on the enemy side of the stream there was a group of large French 1943
farms which were explored almost nightly by patrols from both sides.
In Windmill Farm, or Y Farm, there was always trouble for those
who went in search of it. The Germans had been in the habit of
bringing down barrow-loads of mines and explosives with which to
booby-trap the buildings and block the approaches. They could sometimes be heard shouting or even singing as they worked, and on the
evidence of some of the songs the regiment was identified as Austrian
—a wild conclusion which was later shown to be correct. A patrol of
about fifteen Grenadiers set off one night to occupy Y Farm in the Mar. 27
hope of surprising the German mining party in the morning. It was
nearly light when they arrived, and, although the farm was found to
be deserted, the buildings were already heavily sown with booby-traps.
About thirty were touched off while our men were there, and one
Guardsman was killed and four wounded. The sound of the explo-
sions attracted German mortar fire, and as the patrol began to return
carrying the wounded men they were machine-gunned in the open.
They escaped without further casualties, but the worst was still to
come. The body of the dead man had been left in the farm, and a
carrier was sent forward in daylight to retrieve it. "An awful tragedy,"
wrote Colonel Bushman in his diary. "Having collected the body, the
carrier was just starting back when it received a direct hit from a
heavy mortar. This turned the carrier upside down and killed three of
the four occupants. Soon afterwards a party of fifteen to twenty
Germans was seen to come down to the farm, went up to the carrier,
and took something from it. Our artillery opened up, and claim to
have hit six of the enemy before they disappeared." This was not the
only loss suffered by the Battalion at Oued Zaaga, but it was by far the
heaviest in a single patrol. The pace then began to quicken: a feeling
of bitterness replaced the sense of mild adventure. Only two days later Mar. 29
they were relieved, and moved round by lorry to join the remainder
of the 24th Guards Brigade at Medjez el Bab.

Medjez, in contrast to the flower-spangled hills and water meadows *See Map p.* 318
by which it was surrounded, was as dismal a place as could be found
in all Tunisia. There was not a house which was untouched by shell
fire; the stench of corpses, buried only by loose heaps of rubble, fouled
the air, and mangy cats patrolled hungrily among fallen sheets of
corrugated iron. In these ruins No. 2 Company of the 5th Grenadiers
took up their station under Major C. W. Norman-Barnett. The remaining companies were distributed among the hillocks of Grenadier
Hill, which they occupied for the next three weeks. April 1-20

They found and remedied many deficiencies in the defences of the

1943 hill. They laid belts of mines across the gaps, wired in the most exposed positions, and deepened the trenches to suit a Guardsman's height. By day the men rested in dug-outs excavated from the reverse slopes; by night the majority moved into forward positions and slept but little. There was not much activity to disturb them, and such trouble as they met was mostly of their own seeking. At dusk two or three patrols would venture out over the same ground which had become so familiar to the 3rd Battalion. Normally they would return before dawn with the report that they had been to this place or that, and had found it free of enemy; at other times there would be a sudden encounter with a German patrol or a German outpost, shots and cries in the darkness, the scurry of crouching figures against a skyline, then silence and a slow return across the plough. In this way the Battalion lost two of their best officers: Lieut. B. E. Dunlop was killed on the 17th of April, and Lieut. J. C. Frederick was killed two days later.

The constant patrolling had a wider object than merely to hold the enemy at his proper distance. From the first week of their arrival at Medjez the Battalion had known that an Allied offensive was impending, and that their own Brigade had a part to play in it which would take them across the high ground which faced Grenadier Hill to the north-east. As the details of the plan were evolved they were able to familiarize themselves on these patrols with the actual routes which they were to follow, with the positions of the outer German trenches, and with the system of their minefields and defence. As they gained in experience and as D Day approached, the patrols grew more and more ambitious. They probed almost as far as the first objectives of the attack, and with the help of the sappers tested the whole area for mines and cleared tank lanes through our own minefields. There was a certain risk attached to these preparations. A single prisoner might arouse the suspicions of the enemy by some chance word. If the Germans discovered that a British attack was imminent, what was to prevent them from using the same gaps through the minefields for a thrust into the heart of our own lines?

This is exactly what occurred. The enemy became aware of our plans, not through the indiscretion of any prisoner but by air reconnaissance and by simple deduction. Medjez was not only a nodal point in Allied communications, the gateway at the foot of the Tunisian plain: it was also at the tip of a deep British salient. It was overlooked from the enemy-occupied hills to the north, and the road between Medjez and Oued Zaaga was impassable to Allied traffic. The 3rd Battalion had faced east and south: the 5th Battalion, from the same positions, faced north and north-east. When the 78th Division opened
April 7 their attack to regain the northern hills as far as the approaches to

Longstop, the Germans guessed accurately that this was merely a pre- **1943**
liminary to a general offensive: it was impossible to conceal from them the assembly of so large a force of tanks and guns round Medjez itself. The possibility of a German spoiling attack had never been overlooked. During the middle days of April there was therefore a double tension: the tension inherent in the approach of D Day, and the tension caused by the increasing likelihood of a German attack. When all the preparations were complete, within a single day of our zero hour, the enemy attack was launched.

The Germans called it, light-heartedly, Plan "Flederblüte" (Operation "Lilac Blossom"). Directed by von Arnim himself, it had as its object the cutting of the roads leading into Medjez from the south, followed by the isolation and destruction of all Allied forces lying east of the Medjerda River. With the German battle groups which operated farther south as part of the same plan we are not here concerned: they had no greater success than at Medjez itself. But the northern thrust of the attack was directed immediately south of Grenadier Hill. On that night the hill was fortunately held in greater strength than at any previous time. All four Grenadier companies were in position on the main knolls: a company from the Irish Guards, and later a company from the Scots Guards, were sent up to join them; and three companies of a battalion of the Duke of Wellington's Regiment had occupied an outlying ridge, known from its shape as Banana Ridge, which the Grenadiers had held during previous weeks with a single platoon. On the other hand, all the minefields had been lifted, nearly all the anti-tank guns had been taken out of their emplacements in preparation for the advance, and a group of field and medium artillery were actually in process of arriving at new positions under the lee of Banana Ridge.

Ninety minutes before the first shots were fired the Brigade were **April 20**
put on the alert by a message that a German attack was imminent. This warning (the "Wolf, wolf" of senior headquarters, which could never safely be ignored but so often resulted in no more than the loss of a night's sleep) gave them time to attend to their ammunition supply and to man the forward trenches. The enemy had been expected to strike to the north of Grenadier Hill directly at Medjez, but the first blow fell on the Duke of Wellington's on Banana Ridge. The Grenadiers heard a great deal of firing from that direction, but after a short while all communications with the ridge ceased, and the commanding officer of the Duke of Wellington's could only conclude that his companies had been overwhelmed. This fortunately was not the case. Yet the Germans had undoubtedly found a way through into the valley south of Grenadier Hill. They overran the guns, whose lorries could

1943 be seen blazing, and the 5th Battalion expected at any moment to see the first German troops riding up on to their own hills. It was then that they first heard the sound of the engines of German tanks. The latter did not, however, choose to risk themselves to the gullies of Grenadier Hill: they had a bolder plan in mind. They moved slowly up the floor of the main valley, supported by about two battalions of infantry, and in the early hours of the morning some half-dozen were already across the vital road which leads from Medjez to Goubellat. A few tanks penetrated even farther: one was knocked out in the drive leading to Brigade Headquarters; another reached the Medjerda bridge a quarter of a mile beyond before it too was destroyed. A second group engaged at point-blank range a battery of British field guns. But the main bulk of the German armour still lay back with the infantry in the valley, and it was this group which should at all costs be prevented from making further progress. Brigadier Colvin asked for the support of a squadron of Churchill tanks, and placed them on a rising ridge just west of the Goubellat road. At the same time, the Grenadier Pioneer Officer, Lieut. R. Freeman, hurriedly organized the laying of a belt of mines in the long grass ahead of the Churchills, and the anti-tank guns of the Grenadiers and Scots Guards were drawn into positions covering the same gap.

April 21 At dawn the situation was fairly well in hand. No enemy tanks were still at large west of the road, and a solid battery of Churchills, firing at a range which gave them an advantage over their lighter opponents, stood across the valley opening. The Grenadiers looked down upon this battle like spectators at a tournament. The tank duel was the issue on which depended the fate of the infantry of both sides. The Grenadiers, never themselves directly attacked, could contribute only their mortar and machine-gun fire to the slow process of destruction by the tanks. The mortars, under Lieut. B. M. Ogilvie, searched out the wadis which cut the valley floor: the machine guns, controlled by Lieut. J. M. Hargreaves, tore great gaps in the groups of German infantry when they fled across the open in search of better cover. The tide had turned by nine in the morning. Ten out of the twenty-five enemy tanks were abandoned: the remainder lurched back across the plain, and the infantry followed as best they could, some running from wadi to wadi, others mounted on armoured half-tracks. Not many escaped. The Grenadiers on one side, a battalion of the Loyals on the other, and—to the delight and surprise of all—the Duke of Wellington's on Banana Ridge raised their heads to shoot at the retreating enemy, while the tanks and artillery pursued them until the last survivors were out of sight and range. About two hundred German infantry were trapped in an angle of the valley and raised the white flag of

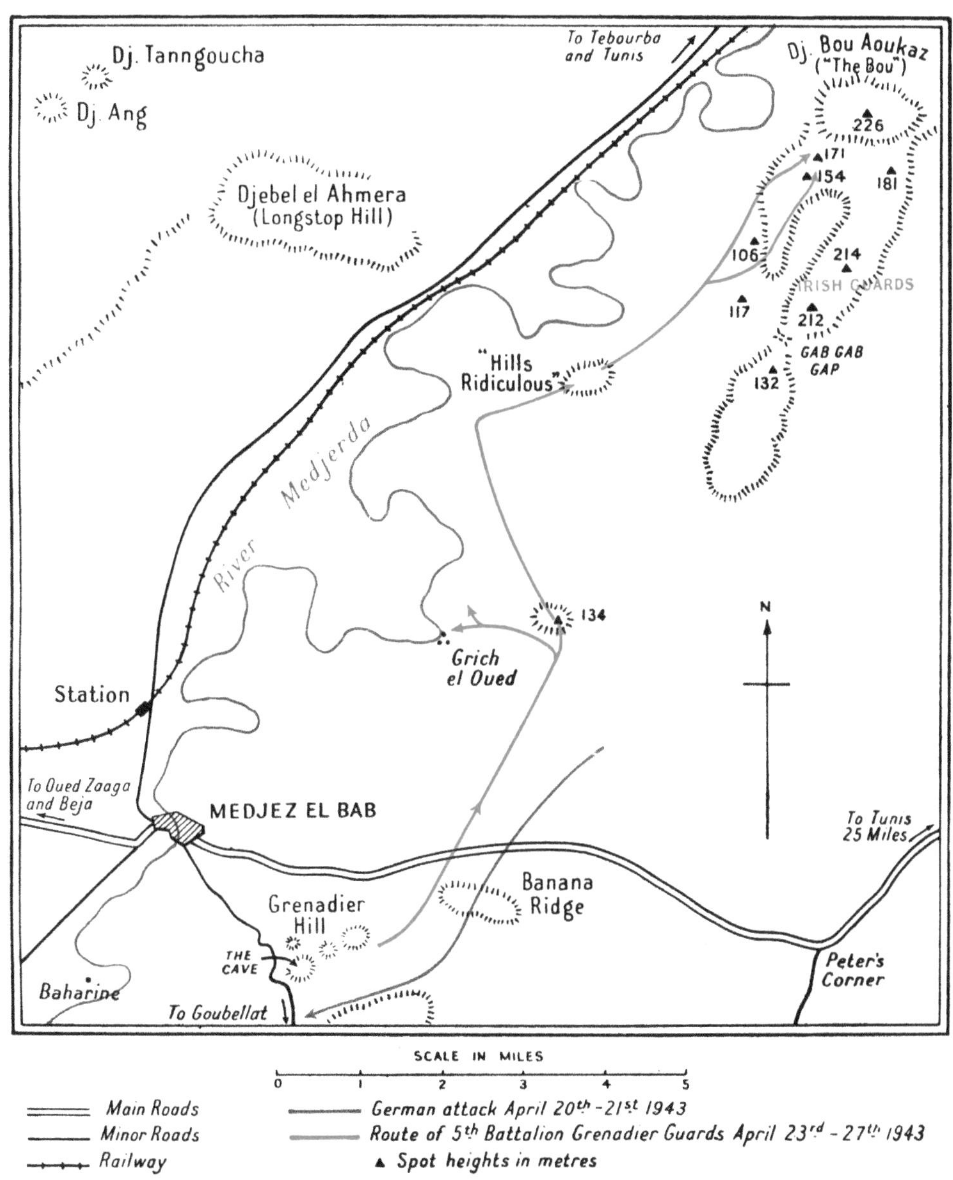

MEDJEZ EL BAB

surrender. The rest of the day was spent in marshalling the prisoners, recovering the guns, and completing the preparations for the British attack. The Germans had succeeded only in weakening themselves at a critical moment. On the British side casualties had not been heavy. Among the Grenadiers five other ranks had been killed and twelve wounded, mostly by the heavy shell fire with which the Germans attempted to cover their withdrawal. Of the officers, Lieuts. A. J. Courage and R. Freeman had both been wounded. **1943**

2

THE BATTLE OF THE BOU

Objectives and difficulties of the attack—The first two phases successfully completed—Daylight attack through cornfields results in heavy casualties —The Battalion capture all their objectives—Heavy German counter-attacks on all three battalions of the 24th Guards Brigade—German tanks threaten to cut our supply lines—Gallantry of the Irish Guards—Eight days' ordeal—The Bou captured by the Duke of Wellington's Regiment— Final results of the battle

The start of the British attack was postponed by twenty-four hours. Otherwise Operation "Lilac Blossom" had no effect upon their plans, and the success of the defence promised well for the success of the attack. There was one domestic matter which affected the Grenadiers. Their Commanding Officer, Lieut.-Colonel R. H. Bushman, had been obliged, just before "Lilac Blossom," to give up his command owing to a recurring attack of phlebitis. His place was taken by Lieut.-Colonel G. C. Gordon-Lennox, who remained in command of the Battalion for the next two years. At the same time, the Adjutant, Capt. T. A. Gore-Browne, was sent to a higher appointment at Brigade Headquarters, and was replaced by Capt. The Lord Stanley.

From the beginning the operations which culminated in the great Battle of the Bou were never intended to be decisive. In the previous December, it will be recalled, the 1st Guards Brigade were to have captured first Longstop and then the Bou, followed by an armoured break-through which might have carried the tanks into Tunis itself. Now, in April, the Tunisian campaign had developed to such a scale that six times the forces were needed to achieve only the first two phases of the December plan. The intention of the 78th Division was to capture Longstop; of the 1st Division to capture the Bou. Once they had achieved this the main attack by four other divisions would be launched farther south, up the axis of the main road leading from Peter's Corner to Tunis. The capture of the Bou would do three things

1943 to help this attack. It would clear the enemy off the higher ground from which they could overlook Peter's Corner; it would lead them to believe that the Allies intended to continue their main thrust up either side of the Medjerda, and so draw off their reserves; and it would create a deep salient on the flank of those German positions which were later to bear the full weight of the offensive.

Those two dark heights, Djebel el Ahmera and Djebel Bou Aoukaz, Longstop and the Bou, the most famous hills of the whole campaign, faced each other across the winding yellow stream of the Medjerda. Neither of them, during the past few months, had formed part of the German front line, for the enemy outposts on both sides of the river had been advanced several miles to the south-west; but both were within view of Grenadier Hill, and it was obvious to every soldier in the Medjerda plain that the key battles would be fought upon their crests. It was a disheartening prospect for the British battalions that they could not attack their main objectives directly, but would first have to fight a series of minor battles to clear the approaches: they would be weakened and wearied by these attacks, and instead of dissipating the enemy's strength at the same rate as their own they would merely be driving back his outposts to thicken the defences on the ultimate objective.

On the right bank of the Medjerda the Bou rose seven hundred feet from the northern end of a long ascending ridge. In the two-mile gap between the ridge and the river lay two isolated groups of lower hills. These had no distinctive names, but in the present account, following the fashion of the time, the southernmost group will be called Point 134, the northernmost Hills Ridiculous. Both, at the start of the operation, were in German hands: both were allotted to the Grenadiers as their first and second objectives. Simultaneously with their attack the other two battalions of the 24th Guards Brigade, the 1st Scots Guards and the 1st Irish Guards, were to capture the tail and centre of the main ridge leading to the Bou. The Brigade would then squarely face the final peak, and maintaining their momentum in two parallel columns, thrust with their remaining strength to gain the summit. The total distance which they were to cover from Grenadier Hill was about eight miles.

April 23 When all preparations were complete the Battalion filed off Grena-
1 a.m. dier Hill and assembled behind the western end of Banana Ridge in the form of a square. No. 2 Company (Major C. W. Norman-Barnett) were forward on the left, and No. 3 Company (Capt. J. G. F. Buxton) on the right: the other two companies and Battalion Headquarters were directly behind them. It was a wet and very dark night, and the fields of waist-high corn through which they passed were sodden with

rain and soon reduced their battledress to the consistency of damp cardboard. Keeping close together so that they would arrive simultaneously, and directing their course by compass, the men covered the larger part of the three miles of the approach march in complete silence. Only when they were within six hundred yards of Point 134 did the guns behind them begin to fire on the objective with high-explosive and smoke shells. The hills were not easily discernible through the dim light and drifting clouds of smoke, and it was the flashes of the enemy weapons and the Very lights rising from the trenches which gave the Grenadiers their direction during the final moments. It was a model assault. With scarcely a change in the formation of the Battalion or in the speed of their advance, they continued up the slight rise directly behind their creeping barrage. One officer had time to notice the pungent scent of rosemary and evergreen, for great stretches of these bushes had been torn by shell splinters and freshened by the rain. The first batch of prisoners surrendered readily enough to Lieut. P. E. C. Nugent and his platoon. In another quarter there was more trouble. After a pause of a few minutes Capt. Buxton led his company into a hand-to-hand assault with bayonets and grenades. He was killed by a bullet just short of the summit, and one of his subalterns, Lieut. R. J. Martin, was wounded two minutes later. The remainder carried all before them, and as it grew light Point 134 and the neighbouring hillocks were firmly in our hands. Over a hundred prisoners were taken, most of them Tunisian Frenchmen under German command (it was the only occasion during the war when Grenadiers found themselves in battle against the French), and among the booty was a field howitzer and an invaluable plan of enemy minefields between Grenadier Hill and the Bou. 1943

The Battalion spent the next four or five hours digging fresh trenches. When these had been excavated to safe depth, a company group was detached to mop up the system of hills and wadis round the village of Grich el Oued. The force, which was supported by seven Churchill tanks, was under the command of Capt. A. Heywood-Lonsdale. They struck due west from Point 134, hemming in the enemy against the river. The tanks fired from the two flanks upon the main centre of resistance, while the infantry moved up the centre, and the Battalion's mortars fired overhead, knocking out an anti-tank gun with their second round. Grich el Oued itself was found to be clear of the enemy, and from the surrounding hillocks a further score of prisoners were collected.

The Grenadiers were naturally much elated by their success. It was the first attack they had ever undertaken: they had breached the enemy's front line, and they had taken many prisoners and much

1943 material. They awaited confidently the orders for the advance to Hills Ridiculous, which now depended only upon the success of the Irish and Scots Guards on the right flank, where German resistance was proving more stubborn than the Grenadiers had yet encountered, and April 24 was not finally overcome until the next afternoon.

As soon as the first Brigade objectives were secured, they bounded April 25 forward to the second. The Grenadiers were unfortunate in their first attempt, for at the last moment the whole attack was postponed, after the Battalion had set off on their cross-country march. The Signals Officer, Lieut. A. R. Taylor, received the message at the rear headquarters and managed to pass it on by wireless to the Commanding Officer. Knowing that the cancellation of the attack at so late a stage would greatly astound and worry them, Taylor set off in a carrier to confirm the message by word of mouth. He did not know where exactly he would find them in that great stretch of mine-strewn country, and he had passed beyond them and reached the river bank before he heard their approach from the south. There was only one thing to be done. Dawn was not far off, and the Battalion had already covered several miles. The companies were formed up in threes, as though they were on a peace-time march, and, turning about, retraced their tracks through the corn, and arrived back on Point 134 before the enemy were even aware that they had left it.

April 26 Twenty hours later, at 1 a.m., they started out a second time towards Hills Ridiculous. The route they followed on both occasions was not direct: it was dog-legged, avoiding the minefields and higher and rougher ground which spread like a scab over part of the plain. They marched by compass, under the guidance of the Intelligence Officer, Lieut. G. W. Chaplin, and were brought up squarely facing the objective at the correct time and place. While they waited for the barrage the companies closed inwards into a tighter group, so that in the extreme darkness of the night they would not mistake each other for the enemy. The British guns, firing at right angles to their line of advance, dropped a few shells among the leading platoons, and they were obliged to accept a few casualties rather than waste the effect of their supporting fire by hanging back. They found the hills deserted. There were signs of recent occupation, the usual litter which the troops of an army will always leave behind them, but not a single rifle shot was fired, not a single prisoner taken. This marked the successful completion of the second phase. Amongst the few casualties was Lieut. B. M. Ogilvie, the Mortar Officer, who was wounded when his carrier blew up on a mine.

Between Hills Ridiculous and the Bou, which now loomed up closer and unavoidable, there was an expanse of cornfields, running

Photo: Dr. Epps

Grenadier Regimental Aid Post in Tunisia.

A Slit Trench in Tunisia.

The machine gun and water container are captured German equipment.

Crown Copyright

up to within a hundred yards of the long ridge which stretched away 1943
southwards from the Bou like the tail of a comet. This was the ground which the 5th Battalion would have to cover before they came within striking distance of the summit. They were to capture the head of the ridge, Points 154 and 171, while the Irish Guards, again advancing on their right, seized the equivalent heights, 212 and 214, on a parallel ridge farther east. To the Scots Guards was left the *coup de grâce*: they were to follow through the Grenadiers and assault the summit of the Bou (Point 226) from the side nearest to the river.

Since the capture of Point 134 there had been no direct contact with the enemy, although the quick and accurate reactions of the German artillery showed that the movements of the Brigade were being closely watched. They were shelled soon after their arrival at Hills Ridiculous, but the patrols which went forward to explore the ground ahead could find nothing worth reporting. Lieut. A. D. N. Clark, for example, patrolled several miles up the right bank of the Medjerda, investigated three deserted farmhouses, fell down the steep banks into the river, and returned wet and tired but without further adventure. The Divisional Commander, on receipt of this and other information, formed the opinion that the enemy were not holding the Bou in any great strength. They might attempt to hold off our attack by shell fire, but they had not the resources to offer more than token resistance. The advance must be resumed at once—that very night. Brigadier Colvin protested that he could not launch his Brigade at their most important objective without further preparation. In that case, he was told, the attack must take place in daylight the next day. This, reluctantly, he agreed to do, stipulating that they must start just before dusk, at 6.30 p.m., as there was so much open ground to cover. At noon on the appointed day zero hour was put forward by Divisional Headquarters to 4 o'clock that afternoon. This sudden last- April 27
minute change of orders affected the Battalion in several ways. It meant, first, that the time they had set aside for reconnaissance was so curtailed that it was possible to point out only to the company commanders their exact routes and objectives: the platoon commanders and men were told their tasks only as they moved forward to the start line. It also meant that the attack would be carried out in the heat of an African afternoon, and the men had not yet changed from their heavy battledress into the shorts and bush shirts of their tropical uniform; and it meant, finally, that at no stage of the attack would they have the advantage of surprise or the cover of darkness.

They had bombers and a heavy weight of artillery to assist them, but no tanks. The shells and bombs, though liberally scattered over the Bou itself and its approaches, failed to make much impression upon

1943 the German troops, who found shelter among the narrow, winding crannies of the hill. The Guardsmen emerged in deployed formation from behind Hills Ridiculous, and struck across the fields, each company diverging slightly from the others as they approached the ridge. Over the first mile they were little harassed, but the enemy were only waiting until they came within easy range of their mortars and machine guns, and then they opened up on the columns of Guardsmen below them. There was little that could be done in retaliation. The enemy weapons were well hidden and had splendid observation; our own men could not shoot back between the cornstalks: they could not pause nor take cover, for there was none at hand. On all sides men were falling, and the stretcher-bearers, stumbling against the dead and wounded, could only pause for a swift examination and mark the spot by sticking a rifle by its bayonet into the ground so that the butt showed above the corn. As the survivors cleared the edge of the cultivated fields they found themselves at the foot of the ridge: had the attack been made in darkness they would, with good fortune, have reached this point unscathed.

Operating as isolated platoons or even sections, and almost unaware of the fate of the others, they scaled the ridge and attacked the outcrops of rock on which they had fixed their eyes during the long advance across the plain.

Briefly, this was the fate of each company:

No. 1 Company lost two officers—Lieut. C. T. Keyser, who was wounded before they reached the ridge, and Lieut. G. G. H. Marriott, who was wounded on the summit of Point 117. The company commander, Capt. A. Heywood-Lonsdale, became separated from his platoons, and, being a small-sized man, could not spot their movements above the tall stands of corn. He struggled on alone—"it was like wading through the sea," he said—and came out into the open in time to receive the surrender of thirty Germans who were fleeing from Point 117. The bulk of the company was now led by Lieut. P. le R. Shephard, and it was this officer who performed one of the outstanding deeds of the day. With only a handful of men left to support him, he destroyed two German machine guns and captured ten mortars with their crews, before he himself was killed. Seventeen men only remained in No. 1 Company when Point 117 was finally cleared, and these linked up successfully with their comrades ahead.

No. 2 Company (Major C. W. Norman-Barnett), who took the lead on the left flank, pressed on in spite of terrible casualties to attack the farthest objective, Point 171. Their final effort was led by Lieut. D. B. Fergusson, who with twelve men captured sixty Germans and two light guns in the gully between Points 154 and 171, and then climbed

to the top of 171, where they remained alone all through the night. 1943
Lieut. A. D. N. Clark, a subaltern in this company, was among the wounded.

No. 3 Company met trouble early on. Their commander, Capt. S. J. L. Egerton, had been wounded as he was returning from the Battalion conference before the advance began, and Lieut. P. E. C. Nugent was killed when German machine guns opened fire from a group of Arab huts in the plain. The twenty Guardsmen who remained unharmed were led by C.S.M. C. Fielding on to Point 154, where they gave some support to Fergusson and his twelve Guardsmen on the far side of the gully.

Finally, No. 4 Company (Major M. G. D. Clive) also fought their way up to Point 154, having lost two of their three officers: Lieut. H. H. Carter was killed and Lieut. R. D. Rogers was wounded.

The 5th Grenadiers remained in possession of every point which they had set out to capture, but at a cost far in excess of what had been estimated. On the other spur the Irish Guards had also been successful, after overcoming even fiercer opposition, and it was now the turn of the Scots Guards on the left flank to pass through the Grenadiers and capture the Bou. Two of their companies actually gained the summit but could not link up with the remainder of the Battalion in time to secure a sufficiently strong foothold. They were withdrawn, and made a second attempt the next day, approaching by way of Point 181. This attempt was defeated by German snipers firing on the exposed slopes of the ridge, and the Scots Guards came back into reserve positions on Point 106, behind the Grenadiers.

All three battalions occupied these same positions during the next eight days. They were days of much hardship, imposing upon the men a strain which in its cumulative effect was more severe than that of the succession of attacks which they had just completed. It was not now merely a matter of waiting in open trenches as they had waited for three weeks on Grenadier Hill. The ridges were under constant and heavy fire, and barely a day passed when the Germans did not attempt to recapture what they had lost. Far from offering only token resistance to the initial attack, they had fought back most stubbornly, and now seemed prepared to throw in regiment after regiment, tank after tank, to crush the deep British salient. The left flank of the 24th Guards Brigade was secured by the Medjerda River, and later by the capture of Longstop by the 78th Division, but their right flank was completely exposed, and, though several other units of the 1st Division were sent up to plug the gaps, the long lines of communication stretching back to Grenadier Hill were open to attack at almost any point. The Germans saw their advantage. There was no need for them

1943 to attack the Grenadiers or the Irish Guards frontally: they had only to pass a strong force of tanks and infantry round their rear, slice across the narrow corridor of their communications, and so isolate the entire Brigade, hemmed in between the Bou and the river banks.

April 28 With this object the Germans began on the second day to attack through a slit in the eastern ridge known as the Gab Gab Gap. The Irish Guards had been obliged to leave it undefended in favour of concentrating the battalion on the defence of Points 212 and 214: the nearest British troops to the south were at least two miles away. About fifteen German tanks therefore had little difficulty in penetrating the Gap and rolling on to Point 117, a hillock about half-way between the Irish Guards and the Grenadiers, and well in rear of both battalions. The Scots Guards were lying on the reverse side of Point 117 itself. The Brigade were faced with complete encirclement. Unfortunately, the anti-tank guns of both the Irish and Scots Guards had not yet been able to find a way over the difficult country, and those of the Grenadiers were just out of range. The only remaining method of clearing Point 117 was by the concentrated fire of heavy guns, and this proved effective. The German tanks withdrew through Gab Gab, but only after they had become all too well aware of the weaknesses of our defence. They repeated the same tactics on the next day. On this occasion thirteen more tanks occupied Point 117, and their support-
April 29 ing infantry attempted to widen the gap by attacking the southern companies of the Irish Guards, knowing that tanks alone could never completely disrupt communications, and that infantry must have a firm base from which to operate. The defence of Point 212 therefore became an even higher priority than the neutralization of Point 117: the former was the cornerstone essential to both sides. While it remained in British hands the German corridor would never be wide enough to allow more than an armoured force to operate west of Gab Gab; if it fell, the consequences might be disastrous to the Brigade. It did not fall.

The Irish Guards bore the brunt of the fighting on the right flank, but the enemy's occupation of Point 117 was just as great a menace to both the other battalions of the Brigade. It left them only a very tenuous supply line up the right bank of the river, and the pressure of the fighting at the north end of the ridge often made it necessary for carrier loads of ammunition to run the gauntlet of tank fire in broad daylight. The food was brought up to the men after dark. It was cooked as close to the line as was reasonably safe, carried forward in a jolting jeep, held up, sometimes for hours, by shell fire, and finally man-handled in containers five hundred feet on to the top of the ridge: the stew was always cold when it arrived, but always very welcome.

The British artillery was responsible for the destruction of the **1943** majority of the German tanks, but the Grenadiers claimed at least one for their anti-tank platoon. A 6-pounder was hauled up to the lip of a crest, and with its third shot set a Mark IV tank on fire. As they were reloading, a salvo of mortar bombs exploded in the middle of the crew, wrecking the anti-tank gun and killing two Guardsmen. The Germans then opened fire on the Grenadier supply vehicles which had sheltered behind Hills Ridiculous. A lorry-load of ammunition was soon set ablaze, and the burning pieces of material, flung in all directions, spread the fire to the other vehicles. Under the direction of Capt. T. S. Hohler the drivers mounted their burning cabs and drove off to a more sheltered place, where all but seven of the trucks were salvaged for further use. This incident well illustrates the unusual situation which had arisen: the actual front line was firmly sealed; the communications on which it depended were dangerously porous. It was a mailed fist at the end of a withered arm.

The gallantry of the Irish Guards saved the entire Brigade. Their defence of Points 212 and 214 never faltered. Their strength was reduced by casualties to a dangerously low level—at one time there were no more than eighty men left north of Gab Gab—and their supplies, particularly of ammunition, were running very short at the moment when they needed maximum support. Partly to reinforce their garrison, and partly to secure their supply line, a body of some sixty Grenadiers from Nos. 1 and 3 Companies were led by Capt. Heywood-Lonsdale to join them. Their risky passage across the inter- **April 30** vening valley was accomplished in daylight with the loss of only four men, thanks to a thick smoke screen laid by the artillery, and they arrived on the eastern ridge just after the Irish Guards had repelled yet another attack in hand-to-hand fighting. Capt. Heywood-Lonsdale records that the first man they met was an Irish corporal dressed in an Old Etonian scarf. He took them up to his company, who were still in high spirits in spite of their four days' ordeal, and "there was great rejoicing." Two Grenadiers were killed during the three hours they remained with the Irish Guards. The latter were then relieved by a battalion of another brigade, and Capt. Heywood-Lonsdale was free to withdraw his little force back to the comparative security of Point 154. Once again they were covered by a thick blanket of smoke.

"Comparative security" must be taken to imply only that the Grenadiers were not normally subjected to actual ground attack. It does not imply that they were left in peace. The Germans overlooked their positions not only at close range from the Bou itself but also from the higher ground across the river, and it was difficult to hide so large a body of men in crannies where they would not be spotted

1943 from one or other of the enemy's observation posts. They dug their trenches as far down as the bed-rock, in places as deep as five feet, in others, particularly on the narrow crest, no more than a few inches, and they were obliged to seek extra protection by building up breastworks of stone round the lip of each trench. Every platoon position became a target for the German guns and mortars. The intense shelling continued sometimes for eight hours on end, and casualties
May 1 occurred at an average rate of twelve a day. Major M. G. D. Clive
was killed outright on Point 154, and Lieut. F. Crawford Boult, who
May 3 had come forward only two days before, lost his life at the same place.

On the day of the final German attack through Gab Gab three enemy tanks, including a Tiger, suddenly crushed their way through the corn between the river and the western slopes of the Bou, immediately in front of Point 171, and began shelling No. 2 Company at point-blank range. Major C. W. Norman-Barnett, peppered in many places by shrapnel and small stones, was fortunate to escape with his life. The threat was once again turned aside by artillery concentrations. "The tanks began scuttling around," wrote Colonel Gordon-Lennox, "like beetles in the corn," and finally drew away. Their comrades at the Gab Gab Gap suffered more heavily. By this time mine belts had been laid across the Gap, and a battery of 17-pounder anti-tank guns, a new and formidable addition to the British armoury, had taken up positions covering the approaches to Point 117. They destroyed ten of the German tanks that morning: one 17-pounder and a Tiger, firing at each other simultaneously, were simultaneously knocked out.

The German attacks were never again renewed. The day was fast approaching when the decisive Allied blow was to be delivered at Peter's Corner, and the 3rd Brigade of the 1st Division were ordered to complete the capture of the Bou before the main attack began. A battalion of the Duke of Wellington's, the same which had held Banana Ridge, assembled behind the Grenadiers in preparation for the assault. To their commanding officer we are indebted for this graphic description of the conditions he found on the ridge:

> "Our cautious activity at the observation post had been duly noticed, and the Germans, resenting our presence and probably guessing its import, proceeded to knock hell out of the Grenadiers' positions. I thus got my first realization of what that devoted battalion had put up with for ten days, and were still to put up with until we had cleared the Bou. The Germans knew exactly where the positions were, and the hail of mortar and gun fire descended upon Point 171 and the feature behind it. The whole position was systematically bombarded. My notebook, which I left on top of my trench, was punctured; my pencil shattered. I had a little leisure to watch the activities of the Grenadiers, and my

> already great admiration for that regiment and for the whole of the 1943 Brigade of Guards began to grow—it was to increase as long as I stayed with them on that unforgettable position. It will be appreciated that in those circumstances troops can do one of two things. They can lurk in the comparative safety of their slit trenches all day and become 'trench-bound' but suffer few casualties; or they can take every opportunity to leap out of their trenches when there is a lull, with the inevitable result that a few are caught by the opening burst of the next bombardment. I don't say which is better: the *moral* advantage of the latter is obvious, and it was that course which the Grenadiers adopted. They took every opportunity to hit back. They manned their mortars and fired at the German mortars which were out of their range; they sent out patrols; they encouraged their men to leave their trenches and perform their normal duties. In all cases it was the officers who were to the fore. It was the officer who left his trench first. It was the officer who went down the hill under fire and fetched the rations for his platoon. It was the officer who picked up the wounded and called the stretcher-bearers."

Later in this same account the commanding officer of the Duke of Wellington's describes the opening of his battalion's attack on the Bou:

> "The line of our advance skirted the fatal 171 wadi where I had set May 5 up my headquarters. Leaving 171 on their right and the Medjerda River on their left, the men pressed on towards the Bou. Then with a sudden and appalling crash down came the German defensive fire. The Duke's had good cause to thank themselves for concealing their presence. The Germans, blinded by the smoke of the barrage, obviously thought that the Grenadiers were staging an attack, and for the hundredth time the position of that decimated battalion was systematically shelled. It was, in its true sense, an awful sight. The noise was bewildering, the smoke was now eddying about in thick clouds, but in between its whirls could be seen the pathetically thin lines of Yorkshiremen pushing steadily on."

The attack was successful. Lieut. P. R. Freyberg had shown a squadron of Churchills the way up to the top of Point 181, and the combined thrust of infantry and tanks was sufficient to drive the enemy from the summit of the Bou. The 5th Grenadiers withdrew to May 6 rest among the litter of burned-out tanks round the Gab Gab Gap and later marched across country to a group of farmhouses north of the Tunis road. They took no further part in the Tunisian campaign, which had a bare week to run.

The total number of casualties suffered by the 5th Grenadiers since leaving Grenadier Hill amounted to six officers and fifty-four other ranks killed; eight officers and two hundred and eight other ranks wounded; and seventeen other ranks missing. Only three of the six-

1943 teen officers in the rifle companies who were engaged from the start remained unharmed on the morning of the 6th of May. The Battalion had achieved a great deal. In their long approach march, their three great bounds and their two battles, they had driven the enemy from position after position. It should not be forgotten that the Battalion were very tired and their ranks more than decimated by casualties when they first set foot upon Point 171. It was a rare event for a battalion to carry out three successive attacks with little pause between: rarer still for a battalion, after such employment, to be obliged to remain without relief for over a week. They endured every danger and discomfort of modern war—except bad weather. The shelling was so intense that it became legendary even in battalions outside their own. Writing more than a year afterwards of a battle in Central Italy, an officer commented: "The enemy's fire rose to a crescendo which could only be compared to that endured by the 5th Battalion on the Tunisian Bou." On that occasion it lasted for only a few hours. On the Bou the German guns were never silent for ten days on end.

It was only later realized what a tremendous contribution the 24th Guards Brigade had made to the Tunisian victory. Measured in terms of miles, they had made no very startling advance: they had captured no place whose name was known to the outside world, and they had not even taken their final objective, Djebel Bou Aoukaz. That was one aspect, the depressing aspect, of the battle. On the other hand, they had more than fulfilled their ultimate intention in drawing away from the vital sector a part of the German forces which was greatly in excess of their own strength. They had made so deep a penetration of one of the most sensitive parts of the line that the enemy thought it necessary to concentrate all the tanks of the 10th Panzer Division and the larger part of an infantry division in an unsuccessful attempt to regain what they had lost. In doing so they threw away the bulk of their remaining tanks and switched infantry reinforcements to a part of the front which was never more than a dead end. Thus the effect of the Battle of the Bou was twofold. It was a deception plan on the largest scale; and it gained for the Allies command over a wide stretch of enemy territory at a time when the loss of every mile reduced the Germans to a state of congestion and despair.

CHAPTER IV

THE END OF THE TUNISIAN CAMPAIGN

3RD AND 6TH BATTALIONS

1

THE LAST WEEK: 6TH TO 13TH MAY, 1943

Dispositions for the final offensive—A quick break-through—Simultaneous capture of Tunis and Bizerta—6th Armoured Division force the gap of Hammam Lif—The 3rd Battalion clear the town—Capture of the Bey of Tunis—The Cap Bon Peninsula sealed off against a German retreat—The 6th Battalion reach the southern coastline at Hammamet—The 3rd Battalion continue to Bou Ficha, where the remaining German divisions are trapped between the two British Armies—Capitulation of the Afrika Korps—Victory Parade in Tunis

THE north-eastern corner of Tunisia was sealed off by ten German and five Italian divisions, deployed in an unbroken loop from Mateur in the north to Enfidaville in the east. This pocket, this bridgehead, which had on the map the appearance of the type of situation which develops a week or so after the start of an invasion, rather than a week before its close, was geographically very small. From the top of a high hill such as Djebel Zaghouan it was possible to see its entire area. Allied aircraft which streamed overhead day after day to bomb Tunis and Bizerta could still be seen from the front line at the moment when they released their bombs. German reinforcements, landing at these bases by sea or air, would have only a single night's march before they occupied the foremost trenches. Strategically the issue was of immense importance. While this corner of Tunisia remained the last Axis foothold in Africa, the Sicilian Narrows were denied to Allied shipping, and the approaches to Italy and Southern Europe were guarded. At one time some of the Allied divisions now assembled round its perimeter had been fighting as far apart as Abyssinia and Morocco, and all their efforts over the past three years were now to culminate in these seven days of May. They were preparing to launch their final offensive. **1943 May.**

The Allies were disposed in four main groups. On the left flank, nearest to the north coast, were the American II Corps of four divi- *See Map p.* 344

1943 sions: the objective of their attack was Bizerta. In the left centre, between Medjez and Bou Arada, were the British V and IX Corps, consisting of seven divisions, whose objective was Tunis. In the right centre were the French XIX Corps of three divisions, who were attacking towards Pont du Fahs and Djebel Zaghouan. And on the extreme right flank, in the high mountains just north of Enfidaville, lay the Eighth Army, who were only to feign attack in order to hold the attention of the flower of the German Afrika Korps opposing them. Thus the whole front, on the morning of the 6th of May, burst into sudden flame, but only at two points were the attacks intended to be decisive: the attack by the Americans in the north, and the attack by the British IX Corps between Peter's Corner and the Bou. It is with the latter that we are more concerned.

In great secrecy the 7th Armoured Division, the 4th Indian Division and the 201st Guards Brigade had been brought round from the Eighth to the First Army, and assembled in the cornfields between Goubellat and Medjez el Bab. A large group of dummy tanks in the fields near Bou Arada had the intended effect of switching German armoured reserves to a point farther south, where they were out of reach of the later battlefield. The striking force of the IX Corps was composed of four divisions—two infantry divisions, the 4th British and the 4th Indian, and two armoured divisions, the 6th and the 7th. The infantry divisions were to punch the first hole through the German defences on a front of only three thousand yards north of Peter's Corner, and both armoured divisions were then to pass through the gap, in the now classic manner of the *Blitzkrieg*, and strike as hard and as fast as they could up the main road towards Tunis. Owing to the abnormal narrowness of the gap, both flanks would be exposed to the risk of German counter-attack, but from the outset this risk was not allowed to check the momentum of the armoured thrust. The capture of the Bou during the night of the 5th/6th of May had done much to lessen the danger on the left; but on the right, astride Peter's Corner itself, lay the whole of the Hermann Goering Division, one of the most formidable in the German Army. When they were bypassed by the assault and stranded in rear of our advancing divisions they would have three courses open to them. They could remain where they were, forming a bastion of defence but risking complete encirclement; they could leave their trenches and strike boldly northwards across the narrow corridor of our communications; or they could make their way back through the hills to reinforce the inner defences of Tunis. If they chose the first course, part of the Allied infantry would be diverted to attack them from the rear; if the second, they would be attacked frontally by the 78th Division, who were kept in reserve for

this very purpose; if the third, they would have no effect upon the **1943**
course of the operations until later. On the movements of the Hermann Goering Division depended much of the success and anxiety of the first and crucial day.

Both the 1st and 201st Guards Brigades were under the command **May 6**
of the 6th Armoured Division: it was the only occasion during all the Mediterranean campaigns when two Guards Brigades found themselves in such close association. They took no part in the initial attacks, but some of their officers and men climbed a hill overlooking
Peter's Corner to watch the opening of the barrage. The muzzle flashes **3 a.m.**
lit up the gun pits behind them with a dancing yellow light, and the shells, tearing overhead at the rate of five or six hundred a minute, burst a few seconds later on the opposite side of the valley like the flowering of a field of ruby tulips. When dawn came they could see through their field-glasses the infantry swarming over the hills and the Churchill tanks lurching up behind them. The attack had been very successful; the German infantry had run, throwing away their rifles; and the British armoured divisions were set in motion as early as 8 o'clock that morning. It was not an easy matter for the vast convoys to make their way forward. The main road could not be used until the Hermann Goering Division had been disposed of, and the vehicles were confined to two narrow tracks, from which the surface dust, already six inches deep, was whirled aloft by the strong breeze and churning tank tracks. A map-board would soon become too thickly coated to be legible, and every sun-tanned face became pallid white. The congestion of traffic was appalling. The bulk of both Grenadier Battalions took ten hours to cover as many miles, and when darkness came it was almost impossible to find the correct route among the maze of tracks and the litter of the morning's battlefield. The sappers, to make matters worse, exhausted their supplies of paint for the signboards. The 3rd and 6th Battalions became inextricably confused amongst themselves and with other regiments of the Division, and the last companies did not reach the main road south-west of Massicault until just before dawn. "Tunis 33 kms." read the first milestone they came to. Although the tiresome journey had taken the edge off their first enthusiasm, they had come through almost unscathed. A chance shell had killed a Guardsman in the 3rd Battalion and wounded Lieut. P. Maclean. In the 6th there had been no casualties.

Two contingencies had been allowed for in the original plan. If the opposition was stubborn the 201st Guards Brigade were to hold a corridor stretching south-west across the strip of plain between the main road and the hills, and the 1st Guards Brigade were to advance beyond them and occupy the high ground in rear of the Hermann

1943 Goering Division: this plan was known by the code word "Bread." If, on the other hand, German resistance seemed to melt away after the first assault, the whole Division would press on to Tunis without pause: to this alternative was given the code name "Butter." "Bread" had seemed to be the more probable of the two, and the 3rd Battalion had prepared themselves for another Djebel Mansour. To their great delight, "Butter" was echoed from wireless set to wireless set in the
May 7 early morning of the second day. The two Brigades were by this time in position side by side, south of the road just short of Massicault. While the tanks and armoured cars raced towards Tunis almost without opposition, the lorried infantry took to the fields, and with carriers and small patrols searched out the wadis and lower slopes of the hills to ensure that the right flank was not menaced. They soon discovered the answer to the question which had been in all their minds. The Hermann Goering Division were already in retreat. They were straggling back through the hills, having abandoned most of their heavy equipment without a fight, and, being either dispirited or unaware how far the Allied advance had penetrated, some of them came down too soon from the upper ridges and were taken prisoner by the patrols of both Guards Brigades.

Meanwhile, the van of the 6th Armoured Division was already in the outskirts of Tunis, and the Derbyshire Yeomanry, the reconnaissance regiment, reached the centre of the city at 4 o'clock that same afternoon, thirty-seven hours after the opening of the offensive. It was an amazing achievement. It had been obvious that the overwhelming weight of the assault, backed by a superiority in every arm, particularly in tanks, artillery and aircraft, could not fail to penetrate the crust of the enemy line; but, as one Grenadier put it, "we feared that there was pastry all the way through this pudding," and the German reserves might once again bring the whole attack to a halt. Those reserves did not materialize. Some of them had been drawn off by the Battle of the Bou: others were never given clear orders, and found themselves rudely pushed aside while they were making up their minds. The elaborate perimeter defences of Tunis were never manned. The anti-aircraft guns from the German airports were rushed to the city's outskirts, and their crews ordered to shoot at tanks—a role for which the guns were well enough adapted, but the crews quite untrained—and a score of 88-mms. fell intact into our hands. The Germans were astounded. The Derbyshire Yeomanry found German officers calmly sipping gin in the main hotel at Tunis. A captured major of the Hermann Goering Division refused angrily to believe the news until he was taken into the wireless car at the 1st Guards Brigade Headquarters, and was forced to listen to messages broadcast from

the centre of the city. When the B.B.C. news was switched on at 6 p.m. 1943
he then heard that Bizerta had fallen to the Americans almost at the same hour as Tunis had fallen to the British.

The Guardsmen had little immediate share in these triumphs, for they had been marching and driving all day some miles behind the tanks. It is true that Colonel Heber-Percy, from a hill-top ten miles to the south-east of Tunis, sent back the message: "I can see the lily-white walls of that blasted city"; but he was one of the few in the 3rd Battalion who did so. They were encamped at the foot of the hills south of the road, picketing the tracks by which the Hermann Goering stragglers were expected to return, and collected during the night a batch of surly prisoners. The 6th Battalion were given a more interesting task. Temporarily detached from the 6th Armoured Division and placed in the 4th Infantry Division, they occupied the hills immediately west of Tunis, and looked down upon its roof-tops. It had been feared that some determined German commander might seize these hills and threaten our communications—for the front was still very loose and enemy detachments were straying disconsolately between the lines—but nothing of the sort occurred. The 201st Guards Brigade rejoined the 6th Armoured Division two days later without incident.

The 1st Guards Brigade, following the remainder of the Division, cut across the network of roads which fanned out southwards from Tunis. The Grenadiers lay on the right of the Brigade, farthest from the sea, and for some time were happily occupied in searching for dumps of enemy equipment. They found a hospital in full operation and ordered the Italian doctors to continue with their very necessary work. They found a German workshop, stocked with tools and spare parts, and still staffed with civilian engineers from the Fiat works in Milan. They also found an Italian field post office, complete with typewriters and one thousand two hundred pounds in the strong box. They collected, almost in passing, four hundred Italian prisoners, for any man who chose had only to enter a house or peer into the recesses of a gully to be overwhelmed with anxious offers of surrender. One young Italian soldier, who was found to be an expert with the accordion, was attached to the officers' mess staff and relayed music to the outlying companies over the wireless. It was easy to forget, in the delight of these novel experiences, that the campaign was not yet over. The Battalion's most important tasks still lay ahead of them.

The simultaneous capture of Tunis and Bizerta had split the enemy's forces into two halves. The northern half was mopped up by the Americans. The southern half was larger and better organized, for it contained not only the refugee garrisons from the Tunis area but

1943 in addition the only enemy divisions which remained unshaken by the events of the past three days—the divisions which faced the Eighth
May 8 Army between Bou Ficha and Enfidaville. The enemy's foothold was now reduced to a perimeter which included Hammam Lif, Creteville, Djebel Zaghouan and Bou Ficha. They had little hope of holding out indefinitely in this narrow pocket: it contained no ports, no airfields and few supply dumps, but it might be possible for them to prolong the campaign by at least a few weeks if they were able to withdraw their southern forces into the fastness of the Cap Bon Peninsula: they might even save some of their best troops by defending its narrow, mountainous base long enough to organize their evacuation by sea and air. The issue of the campaign therefore depended on breaching the new defence line before the Germans had time to reorganize. The 6th Armoured Division were ordered to make this breach, and they chose to make it on the extreme left flank, at the town of Hammam Lif.

Hammam Lif was a small French bathing resort and the summer residence of the Bey of Tunis. It occupied the entire width of a corridor of low ground between the sea and the extinct volcano of Djebel Bou Kournine. The streets were laid out in a rectangular, grid-iron pattern, with the longer axis running parallel to the coast: the northern villas fronted the actual beaches; the southern and poorer houses were crushed against the foot of the precipitous cliffs. The Bey's palace stood on one side of the central square. The town formed

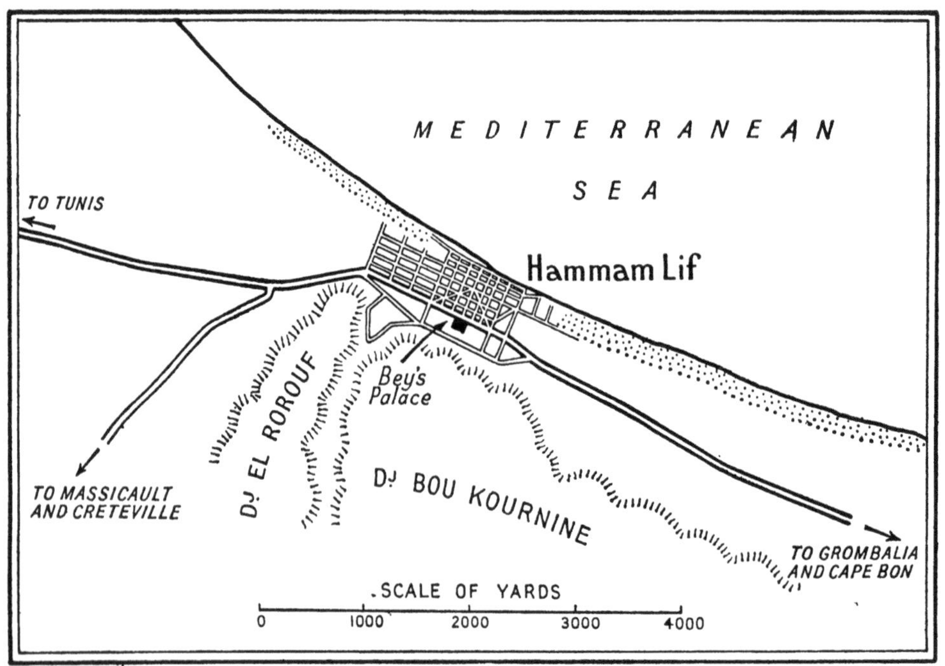

a complete block: there was no way into the plain of Grombalia 1943
except through its streets, and unless a passage could be forced, and forced quickly, the momentum of the whole offensive, the astonishing success of the past three days, would be thrown away.

Although the enemy were thoroughly disorganized, their local commanders were still sufficiently alert to appreciate the great tactical importance of Hammam Lif. They collected a strong force of infantry from the thousands of stragglers who had escaped south-east from Tunis, posted some of them, amounting to about two battalions, on the peaks of Djebel Bou Kournine, and the remainder at the western end of the town itself. The backbone of the defence was formed by a score of anti-tank guns, hastily sited in the gardens of the houses and actually inside any large buildings whose walls they had time to breach. They declared, in spite of these preparations, that Hammam Lif was an "open city," a meaningless phrase which was merely designed to calm the civilian population and cause the British to hesitate before they attacked.

There was no hesitation. Outside the town the 6th Armoured Division assembled its striking force, while the artillery poured a steady stream of shells over the shoulders of Kournine into the open streets. The Coldstream and Welsh Guards were brought up in their lorries to the western foot of the mountain, and after a very hasty reconnaissance, the Welsh Guards began to scale the steep slopes, watched by a thousand pairs of eyes from the plain below. Their tiny figures could be seen groping for a foothold between the brushwood and the rocks, and when they had reached a point just below the crest, to the flashes of German machine guns was added the livid explosion of grenades. They took the hill, at the cost of about sixty casualties, remained upon it all that night, and were joined by the Coldstream Guards during the hours of darkness. The two battalions were now able to look down upon the roof-tops of Hammam Lif, and saw the figures of German soldiers scurrying like rats between the houses, desperately revetting their makeshift defences, and bundling the civilians back into their cellars.

The 3rd Grenadiers had not themselves witnessed the capture of Djebel Kournine. They had lain that afternoon and night on the right flank of the Division in almost total ignorance of events upon the coast. They knew well enough the great importance of breaking the German line, and the Commanding Officer had been given a free hand by the Divisional Commander. "Push on as fast as you can," General Keightley had said, "and try to get the Creteville Pass"—the alternative approach into the Grombalian Plain farther to the south. With this object, Colonel Heber-Percy had been in conference with unit

1943 commanders of the 1st Armoured Division, which had appeared unexpectedly on his right, and the Battalion were planning a combined advance with the tanks early the next morning. The plan came to nothing, not only because the Creteville Pass was held more strongly than had been supposed but because the Grenadiers were suddenly sent for to assist in the capture of Hammam Lif.

May 9 The Battalion arrived outside the town to find that the capture of Kournine had not been sufficient to dislodge the Germans. The latter had managed to conceal their anti-tank guns in positions where few were visible from the heights above, since the roof-tops and outlying spurs of the hill hid many of the street corners from view. Every British general in Tunisia, it seemed, from the Army Commander downwards, had arrived to make a personal inspection of this vital point, and General Keightley was told that no matter if he reached the far side with only a score of tanks left in his Division, the Hammam Lif gap must be forced that day.

The Grenadiers were ordered to clear the town before dusk. Their plan was to advance under cover of a smoke screen from the sea shore towards the centre of the town, sealing off the northern street blocks by shooting down the railway line with their mortars and Vickers machine guns, and protecting their flanks with a troop of tanks on either side. It was while the company commanders were on the crest of Djebel Kournine, settling the details for this hazardous attack, that they saw below them a scene without parallel in the history of armoured warfare, an operation which seized the imagination of the world. The leading tanks of the Lothians and Border Horse, which had been probing cautiously round the western spurs of the mountain and exchanging shots with the German gunners on the outskirts, suddenly took matters into their own hands, and raced across the open ground in a long line, heading directly for the town. Several tanks were destroyed before they gained the first houses, but others behind them shot down the anti-tank gunners before they could reload. One squadron fought their way through the central streets; another jolted along the railway sleepers, their turrets revolving from side to side, and their guns firing without pause at every house which might contain a German. The defences were finally turned by the two troops on the left flank, which could be seen making their way along the sea shore and through the actual surf breaking on the beaches. The sand was just firm enough to bear the great weight of the tanks, and the shoreline appeared to have been the one avenue of approach which had been overlooked in the German scheme of defence. Barely half an hour after they had started the tanks emerged behind the town with its garrison at a hopeless disadvantage. A few days later the commander of a German panzer division remarked in captivity: "I was amazed at the break-through of the 6th Armoured Division through the defile of Hammam Lif. I did not think that it was possible." 1943

It was uncertain at that moment how many German troops remained in the town and whether they were prepared to continue their resistance once the British tanks were behind them. It was therefore very important that the town should be cleared immediately, if the Lothians were not to find themselves cut off from the remainder of the Division. The 3rd Grenadiers, who had started to march towards the outskirts when they received news of the break-through, were ordered to search the town methodically. Having started to do so, house by house and block by block, taking every precaution against snipers and surprise, they soon found that there were few Germans unwilling to surrender without further argument, and the enthusiasm of the civilian population made orderly progress almost impossible.

> "It was a most extraordinary scene," wrote a Grenadier officer. "As the French and the Arabs emerged from their cellars, the Sherman tanks were still thundering through the streets. There were dead Germans lying beside their guns, a blanket or a greatcoat hurriedly thrown over their faces; there were hundreds of prisoners being marched away; there were the pathetic funeral processions of the Arabs who had been killed by our bombardment. The civilians went mad with relief. They brought out wine and pastries and pressed them on the Guardsmen; they tore down the roses from around their doors and tried to drape them on the guns and tie them to the handlebars of the motor-cycles; the girls lavished their caresses on the men while they were reloading their Bren guns for the continuation of the battle; and I was dragged off to a lovely villa and plied with questions about some subaltern in Giraud's army whose whereabouts I was surely bound to know."

At this stage of the liberation a message was received from the Armoured Brigade which ran: "Bey of Tunis in Hammam Lif. Bodyguard made prisoner of war. Palace damaged by shell fire." Colonel Heber-Percy sent off his Intelligence Officer, Lieut. J. H. Lambert, to seize the person of the Bey, whose attitude during the campaign had never found much favour with the Allies. Lambert took as his guides two members of the bodyguard, whom he placed on the bonnet of his jeep, and edged his way through the throng of excited Tunisians before the palace doors. Upstairs, in the throne-room, he found the entire Tunisian Cabinet assembled among a litter of broken glass and smashed gilt chairs, awaiting the British envoys with some apprehension, and overwhelming them with offers of alliance as soon as they appeared. They produced a German document which declared that the Bey could live in Hammam Lif, "which would be regarded as

1943 neutral." Lambert demanded to see the Bey himself, and the Bey came out shortly afterwards from an inner room. Through his interpreter he inquired graciously after the health of Their Majesties The King and Queen, and offered to invest the British Divisional Commander with a high Tunisian order. It was declined with equal courtesy. General Keightley himself then entered the palace. He was received in the outer courtyard by two guards of honour: one from the Bey's own bodyguard, temporarily released from captivity for the occasion, and splendid in their uniforms of scarlet, black and gold; the other was provided by No. 4 Company of the 3rd Grenadiers under Capt. T. Bagshawe, whose appearance after their exertions of the past four days was hardly equal to the brilliance with which they presented arms. General Keightley did not remain long in the palace, excusing himself with the plea that he had a battle to fight, and the Bey was removed to Army Headquarters. "As he emerged from the palace with his escort of British soldiers," wrote an eye-witness, "a Tunisian colonel gripped me by the arm, his face deadly white, and muttered: 'Mon Dieu, mon Dieu: l'Empereur!' " Lieut. Lambert borrowed the Crown Prince's car and drove off to rejoin the Battalion, which had now passed on some miles beyond Hammam Lif.

Nos. 1 and 2 Companies were sent in search of German and Italian stragglers far up into the hills west of Grombalia, and spent a cold and almost fruitless night, hidden in the mist and out of reach even by wireless. Battalion Headquarters occupied a small farmhouse in the valley, after the Adjutant, Capt. J. D. Buchanan, had led a small party to clear it of a dozen German soldiers. They were all taken prisoner without resisting, among them a German officer wearing the Iron Cross, who was found lying face downwards feigning death. It was becoming too easy, almost ludicrous. The Derbyshire Yeomanry that night wirelessed back the message: "Found nineteen German officers dining off champagne. Champagne rather dry. Dinner good. Germans sampling bully beef." On another occasion, records Brigadier Gascoigne, a group of a hundred and twenty Germans emerged from a wood two hundred yards away from the place where he and General Keightley had set up their joint headquarters, and surrendered without showing fight or shame. From all parts of the Grombalian Plain,
May on this day and the next, the prisoners began to stream back in their
10-11 tens of thousands. On the 10th of May the 1st Guards Brigade alone marshalled five thousand into their cages and the 201st Guards Brigade, who had now rejoined the 6th Armoured Division, were responsible for almost as many more. In spite of this, some of the men found time for their first bathe of the year on the sands near Hammam Lif, the first bathe which most of them had ever enjoyed in the Medi-

terranean Sea. Across that incomparable bay they saw the cape of 1943
Carthage, they saw the gleaming white houses and minarets of Tunis, and they watched British and American destroyers nosing their way into its shattered harbour, while on the other side, over the Cap Bon Peninsula, the fighter aircraft soared and swooped like falcons in the sun.

The thirty-five miles between Hammam Lif and Hammamet were covered in two days, and the German divisions south of Bou Ficha were sealed off from any way of retreat into the peninsula. An officer of the 3rd Battalion left this picture of the great advance:

> "You must imagine a fertile valley, with the corn standing about three feet high and speckled with poppies. The sun shines brilliantly, turning the little farms into islands of dazzling white, and the sea into a vast bowl of wine. The background is therefore agricultural and Mediterranean. On to this you must impose, in the forward areas, one or two columns of smoke rising from vehicles which the Germans have destroyed in their retreat, a column of prisoners dressed in the drab uniform of the Afrika Korps, and the odd 88-mm. anti-tank gun, camouflaged with sheaves of corn, and the crew lying dead around it. Our armoured cars edge slowly forward. At every small ridge they halt, and the commander scans the country ahead through his binoculars. Behind them the great Sherman tanks, regularly spaced out in diamond patterns, move heavily through the corn. They avoid the roads and surround each farm with the greatest precautions. There is no shooting. The rate of progress is about a mile an hour. Behind them come the infantry in lorries, and then the country begins to wear a far more military look. The supply trains, the ambulances, the repair shops, the tank transporters, and the huge bridging lorries all begin to flood into the plain, and there is a mass of vehicles where only a few hours before the armoured cars broke fresh ground."

In the main, it was the tanks and armoured cars which led the Division during every available hour of daylight. Both Guards Brigades were held back clear of the roads, ready at a moment's notice to send off a platoon or a company for a specific task—to marshal another column of prisoners, to patrol the by-roads, or to search a group of hills which the tanks could not penetrate. The carriers of the 6th Battalion, for example, brought in five hundred German prisoners from a single sweep. At night time the infantry were normally moved up to the limit of the day's advance, and either remained close to the tanks to protect their harbours and allow the crews to sleep, or patrolled forward as far as they could on foot. There was always the danger that the Germans might still attempt to make their way back to the peninsula, and the bulk of both Brigades were strung out side by side along a wide stretch of the road, facing west, in order to block all possible routes across the plain. This cordon never

1943 trapped more than a few stragglers. There was no sign of a German withdrawal from in front of the Eighth Army. For the first time the strange rumour began to circulate that the Germans had no plan; that they had lost their heads; and that no alternative remained to their vast Army than total surrender.

The 6th Battalion saw their last Tunisian action on the 11th of May, in the hills just north of Hammamet. During the previous night they had been filling in craters to make the roads passable to the tanks, and then pressed on at dawn to sweep the high ground overlooking the coast road. The 2nd Scots Guards were the first to enter Hammamet itself, and the 6th Grenadiers sent a scout platoon to assist in the clearing of the town. They found an elaborate system of coastal defences—the Germans had clearly been expecting Allied landings at this point—as well as large supply dumps, a hospital full of German wounded, and a chain of smart hotels. Every lance-corporal was soon driving a captured Fiat or Mercedes car. There was no resistance from the mass of German and Italian soldiers wandering about the town. Many of them were men from the rear areas who had never envisaged such a situation, men from the field ambulances and post offices and tank repair sheds and bakeries. The Cap Bon Peninsula was crammed with such people, and the 4th Infantry Division had no difficulty in driving round by the two coastal roads to its northernmost point in the course of a single morning. There were a few half-hearted attempts at evacuation. At one point the armoured cars fired at a little fleet of rowing-boats, loaded down with German soldiers, and forced them to return to the shore. At another place, a platoon of Germans cut down some telegraph poles on which they sat astride and began to paddle hopefully towards Pantellaria. None of these attempts had any chance of eluding the destroyers which patrolled thickly round the whole coastline, or the aircraft flying low over the beaches.

May 12 The 1st Guards Brigade, who so often before had had the good fortune to be present on historic occasions, continued southwards from Hammamet in the wake of the tanks. They were heading directly for Bou Ficha, striking into the rear of the three remaining German divisions, and were held up only by the destruction of a few bridges and by some minefields sown hastily across their path. By midday they were shelling the same targets as the guns of the Eighth Army, and in the early afternoon it was possible to see, beyond the German-occupied hills, the yellow lorries which had set out eight months before from El Alamein. An Eighth Army officer described later to the Grenadiers how they had followed the progress of the 6th Armoured Division with tense excitement; and how, on that last day, they had raised their heads as much as they dared above the parapets and

Photo Dr. Epp

Grenadier motor-cyclist escorts column of German prisoners, driving their own lorries, after the final surrender in Tunisia.

Grenadier Intelligence Officer (Lieut. J. H. Lambert) interrogates German prisoners.

scanned the horizon for the first sign of their approach. First they 1943
heard the sound of gunfire from the north, and a little later saw the small puffs of dust raised by the tank tracks: finally, the reality—the sight of the Shermans bowling across the plain; and then they knew that the campaign was over.

It was not quite over. Von Arnim, the German Commander-in-Chief, was captured that morning in a village near Creteville, but as he had no means of communicating his orders to his divisional commanders, they were left to make up their own minds. The division holding the part of the front nearest to the coast was the 90th Light Division, the same which had so bitterly opposed the 6th Battalion at the Battle of the Horseshoe. Its commander, a general named Graf von Sponek, now ordered his men to destroy all their equipment except the bare minimum of personal possessions: all the remaining ammunition, all the weapons, almost all the vehicles except water-carts, all maps, wireless sets, binoculars and even watches, were smashed or burned. Having done this, von Sponek was prepared to surrender unconditionally. He himself received a British intelligence officer at his headquarters in a mountain gorge, and all along the crest of the ridge his men raised white flags and began to gather by their companies and battalions for the march into captivity. It was 4 p.m. in the afternoon of the 12th of May.

In this last hour of the Tunisian campaign the 3rd Grenadiers and 2nd Coldstream were ordered forward to complete the triumph. The Grenadiers drove up from Bou Ficha in their lorries and, preceded by a screen of carriers, continued across the open plain, past the halted tanks, and as far up into the hills as the broken ground would allow the vehicles to travel. Little more was required of our men than to assist formally at the great act of surrender. The Germans were already organized under their own officers and non-commissioned officers, and their discipline was remarkable. There was hardly a scowl, a surly gesture, or a slouching man. They appeared strangely undismayed by their defeat, having perhaps so strong a sense of the dramatic that a capitulation on this scale was almost as splendid a performance as a great victory. The German commanders were given permission to make a last address to their men. One of them broadcast a message to each of his companies, and ended by smashing his own wireless set; another declared that there was no disgrace in surrendering to the Grenadier Guards, "the finest troops in the British Army." To Colonel Heber-Percy, von Sponek remarked that his position at Bou Ficha had been impregnable—from the south; and to another officer he said that he could not have wished to fight against a nobler enemy. In this spirit the 90th Light Division filed off the hill-

1943 side, and marched under British escort to the cages at Bou Ficha, singing as they went the song which had already become the favourite in both Armies—"Lilli Marlene."

In a letter written on the next day a Grenadier thus described the last hours of this unforgettable afternoon:

> "I went down off the hill and drove a little way along the road, to where a bridge over a deep wadi had been blown up. I stood on one side of the chasm, and the advanced units of the Eighth Army on the other. The sappers worked vigorously to clear the minefields on either side, and a great metal bridge was laid in a few moments, resting on the crumpled tarmac. I remember noticing, as I waited, that by the buttress were two dead Italians and, of all things, a chicken (we ate it for dinner that night). When the bridge was completed I walked across and went up to the first officer I saw. 'Hullo,' I said, not knowing quite what to say. 'Hullo,' he said; and then, noticing the mailed-fist sign on my sleeves: 'You come from the 6th Armoured Division, I suppose?' I said I did. 'How do they feed you in the First Army?' Of such things do Englishmen talk on great occasions. . . . I started back as dusk was falling. The tanks remained in the positions where they had come to rest, and the crews, unshaven and very tired, had tumbled out, and each had lit a fire on which to cook the evening meal. Before tonight, of course, fires had been unheard of. This, then, was the final scene. The plain dotted with points of light, each reflecting dimly the shape of a Sherman tank; the tramp of feet as the Germans marched away to imprisonment; the sea shining in the moonlight; and the hills resounding with explosions as the Germans who were still at liberty fired their remaining ammunition dumps."

May 13 The 3rd Battalion went back the next day to an area between Hammamet and Nabeul, and the 6th Battalion came down to Bou Ficha. Both camps were very close to the sea, and the weather was already warm enough for the men to bathe and to lie out on the sands the whole day through. There was very little else for them to do. The prisoners of war had passed out of their hands into vast camps near Tunis, one of which was in the charge of the 5th Battalion. There were dumps of enemy material to sift, and occasionally a platoon would be sent out on receipt of civilian information that a party of Germans was hiding in the hills. Otherwise the Guardsmen enjoyed their rest, and
May 14 were taken in small parties to visit Tunis. One hundred and ninety-one officers of the three Guards Brigades in Tunisia assembled at a victory dinner at Nabeul.

May 19 The campaign was formally concluded by a parade of all arms and nations through the centre of Tunis. The 3rd, 5th and 6th Battalions each provided detachments for the march past, and the 3rd Battalion, in addition, mounted the British guard of honour under the

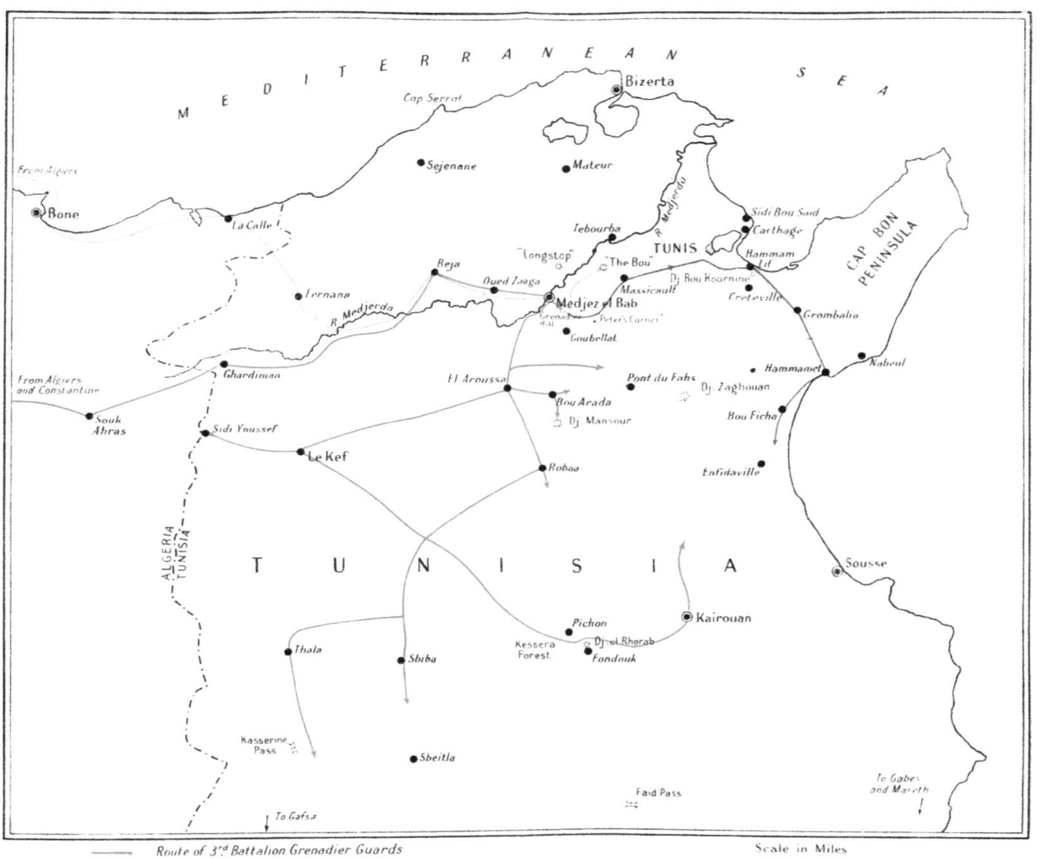

NORTHERN TUNISIA

Face page 344

command of Major A. C. Huntington, M.V.O. It was a Grenadier (Major G. E. Pike, until lately Brigade Major of the 1st Guards Brigade) who organized the whole parade, and another Grenadier (Major G. F. Turner, M.B.E., D.C.M.), of First Army Headquarters, who entertained many of the officers and men at Carthage the night before. On the morning of the parade the temperature rose to 92 degrees in the shade, and a number of men in the guard of honour who were suffering from dysentery collapsed through the heat. "Nobody noticed its gradual declension," wrote Capt. J. D. Buchanan, "with the exception of R.S.M. Hagell, who used all his cunning to remove each sick man in turn without any spectator becoming aware of it." The spectators included Generals Alexander and Anderson, and the salute was taken by General Eisenhower. In the march past the Guardsmen shared with the Moroccan Goums the loudest acclamations of the day. They then dispersed to their various stations throughout North Africa, and began to prepare for the next campaign—the invasion of Southern Europe. 1943

2

THE AFRICAN INTERLUDE

The aftermath of victory—Life in Tunisia—The French and the Arabs—The Grenadiers wait in Africa during the Sicilian campaign—Movements of the three Battalions before crossing to Italy

The conquest of North Africa had a profound effect upon Allied strategy, and upon the morale not only of the armies which had achieved it, but of soldiers and civilians in every country of the world. The official German attitude was to make light of their defeat: to say that this result was only to be expected when the Allies had concentrated all their efforts on this single object, while the Axis Powers had regarded the campaign merely as a side-show, and had succeeded in delaying the conclusion for three years with a very small expenditure of effort. Far from magnifying the Tunisian debacle to the proportions of a national disaster (the manner in which they had treated their reverse at Stalingrad a short time before), the German commentators admitted to only a small part of their true losses, and poured scorn upon the jubilation of the Allies. In Tunisia itself optimism among the British and American troops ran to the other extreme. They saw their armies reinforced, exhilarated by victory, and the initiative resting entirely in their hands; they saw the whole northern littoral of Africa at their disposal, with its chain of first-class ports and airfields; and, seeing, too, the long and thinly defended coastline of Southern

1943 Europe facing them across a narrow strip of sea, and the whole summer before them, they began, not unnaturally, to speculate. Sicily, Italy, Greece, Sardinia, even the southern coast of France, became in turn the favourite selection of the ill-informed. Each division began to jockey for a place among the assault troops. There was no resting on their laurels. The question universally, eagerly, asked was this: "When and where do we go from here?"

All three Guards Brigades in Africa, the 1st, the 24th and the 201st, had a long time to wait, and none of the Grenadier Battalions found themselves in action again until the 6th landed at Salerno in September. The other two had an even longer respite. None of the Guards Brigades took part in the invasion of Sicily, none in the subsequent landings in the toe of Italy. There was a sufficient striking force for both these operations without calling on some of the most triumphant divisions in the First and Eighth Armies. They settled down uneasily at scattered points on the coast and in the hinterland of North Africa, expecting on any day to receive their marching orders, speculating on their chances, grasping eagerly at any information concerning the new type of fighting across the Sicilian Narrows, and sick at heart that they were not there themselves. Unwillingly they relaxed.

There was all too much relaxation during those summer months of 1943. The heat was often crushing: on one day the temperature at Tunis rose to 120 degrees in the shade, the day on which a Guardsman in the 5th Battalion wrote home to say that he had tried to fry an egg on the scorching pavements, an experiment which ended only in failure and a yellow stain. Another remarked that it was so hot that he "tried to take his skin off," for clothes were soon discarded except for a pair of khaki shorts; and an officer wrote that "the men have turned into bronzed Apollos, and when one shouts for an orderly a semi-divine figure appears to whom one is ashamed to entrust one's trivial commission." The Sirocco, blowing directly from the Sahara, blooded the midday sun with flying sand, and smeared every paper with a film of grey; at night the temperature seldom dropped below 90 degrees. Fortunately, all three Battalions, during the worst of the heat, were bivouacked close to the sea, the 3rd and 6th Battalions, indeed, among the very sand-dunes, and the men spent a great part of their day in the water. The flies and mosquitoes, and the scorpions among the stones, added to their discomfort, and very occasionally there would be a sharp shower of rain, against which precautions had seldom been taken. To give the men a relief from camp life, each Battalion organized rest centres in the more agreeable parts of Tunisia—at Sidi Bou Said, overlooking the site of Carthage, and at Hammam Lif—where they would go in parties for three or four days at a time.

Tunis itself was never very popular with the Guardsmen: it was hot 1943
and dull, and the native quarter, the Kasba, was dirty and out of bounds. Expeditions were organized to places farther afield. Some leave parties penetrated deep into the Sahara Desert, where they would be welcomed with lavish entertainment among the outposts of the Foreign Legion; others went to Morocco, Malta, Gibraltar, and even to Southern Spain, while truck-loads of Grenadiers motored along the desert road to Cairo, where the 6th Battalion still felt more at home than in Tunis or Algiers.

They had little contact with the native French or Arabs. Of the French the majority were aloof without being hostile, but some would invite the men into their homes or take them boar hunting in the mountains. The Arabs remained greatly influenced by Axis propaganda. The Germans had paid them well in a spurious currency, and their aircraft continued to drop leaflets on the villages, together with sham pound and dollar notes overprinted with slogans such as these: "The day has come to fight against the Anglo-Americans and the Jews. You must kill them, cause sabotage, refuse to work for them. They have come to steal your rights. Beware of their lies. Bring up your children to hate them." The effect of this propaganda was seen in surly looks, and the unceasing theft of military property. They would creep into the camps by night, eluding the most watchful sentries, and lift rifles and whole kitbags from the sides of sleeping men, even, in some cases, the blankets off their bodies. The French gendarmerie would co-operate in periodic round-ups of the native villages: the haystacks would be pulled to pieces, and the earthen floors within their huts dug up in search of loot, but it was seldom that anything was recovered. As the amount of stolen arms and ammunition began to grow, it was feared that the Arabs were plotting something more sinister than systematic pillage, but so long as the Allied troops remained there in strength nothing very serious occurred. There was, on the other hand, a large section of the Arab population which was quite prepared to co-operate. They saw in the occupation troops a crowd of exploitable tourists. They had eggs and vegetables to sell, and especially fruit (figs, apricots, greengages, melons, dates, mulberries, lemons and oranges), which were not only consumed in vast quantities by the Guardsmen but sent home in ship-loads to their families in England. Typical of these friendly Arabs was the 3rd Battalion's "lemonade man," a Wog,* says the War Diary, of doubtful breeding. "He made

*"Wog" was the generic term for an Arab, current throughout the African armies. If he was a sheikh he was a "Head Wog": his village was "a woggery." Of the many origins suggested for this strange word, the least improbable is that the native labourers employed at the Alexandria docks wore armbands bearing the initials "W.O.G.S." (Workers On Government Service).

1943 thirty thousand francs out of the Battalion during the first week, but then was foolish enough to ask the doctor to attend to his daughter-in-law, who was down with typhus. The doctor immediately forbade a typhus-carrier to inhabit the Battalion area. The lemonade man was back the next day, however, with an enormous melon, which he tactfully presented to the Commanding Officer, and informed us at the same time that the person in question was only a distant cousin, and was dead, anyway."

For other entertainment the Battalions relied on the official E.N.S.A. concert parties and improvisations from among their own ranks. The Tunisian music-halls were reopened under British or American management, and films were sometimes shown by mobile cinema vans to audiences seated in the open air among the sand-dunes. But the evenings were rare when there was any organized entertainment, and after nightfall time was apt to hang heavily on a man's hands. A letter from home was one of his main excitements, and the writing of a letter in return one of his main occupations. With the introduction of air-mail letter-cards he could receive a reply from England in about a fortnight.

This was the background of the Guardsman's life during these summer months. At first his main military duties, in whichever Battalion he found himself, were concerned with prisoners of war. The greater part of the two hundred and fifty thousand prisoners captured at the close of the campaign were sent to England or across the Atlantic, but many thousands remained temporarily in the vast cages round Tunis, into which they had been shepherded direct from the battlefields. They gave little trouble to their guards. There were a few of the arrogant type who refused, even now, to face the facts: the man, for instance, who told an officer: "You may have captured Tunis but you will never retake Alexandria or Cairo," insisting that the Turks had declared war on the Allies, and had already advanced through Syria and Palestine to the Delta. The great majority were content to sun-bathe in thick, brown lines behind the wire, listening to the music of their own bands, or playing endless games of football. The Germans were allowed to administer their own camps and hospitals, and certain German officers and lorry drivers were given passes to go about their business in Tunis itself. The sight of enemy uniforms in the streets was at first so common that few concerned themselves with their presence. A story is told that a week after the last shot had been fired a determined German drove his own lorry from near Enfidaville to Nabeul, jammed in a slow-moving convoy with scores of British vehicles; he loaded his lorry with ammunition from a British dump, and returned unchallenged to carry on the war in the mountains.

More authentic is the story that hundreds of Italian prisoners lined 1943 the streets to cheer the Tunis victory parade before they were hustled back, protesting, behind barbed wire.

The 5th Battalion were made responsible for the cage outside the city at El Bardo, which was so large that the guard duties absorbed two complete companies. The Germans were kept separate from the Italians, who were in the majority, but the orderly running of the camp was hampered by the tendency of the French police to use it as a convenient lock-up for civilian offenders. Furthermore, crowds of Italian women, natives of Tunis, would arrive outside the camp gates with wine and bread for their friends and relations inside, and could be turned away only by a display of force. The camp commandant, Major C. G. Ford, was nevertheless able to marshal a parade of eight hundred presentable prisoners for the inspection by His Majesty The King when he visited Tunis on the 16th of June.

A great many of the prisoners who passed through El Bardo were shipped overseas from Bone, where the 6th Battalion were stationed. This Battalion, too, were employing some two hundred and fifty men a day on guards and escorts, and in addition they provided ship guards and train guards, as long as the westward flow of prisoners continued.

The 3rd Battalion at Sousse were occupied in a manner which needs fuller explanation. Soon after the 12th of May the 1st Guards Brigade were detached from the 6th Armoured Division and placed temporarily under the command of the 1st British Division—"for a special operation." This was the invasion of the Italian island of Pantellaria. The seaborne assault on the island was preceded by an air bombardment of an intensity which had never been seen before in warfare: it was an experiment, a rehearsal and a necessary preliminary to the bigger invasion of Sicily. The airmen believed that they could force the surrender of the Italian garrison by the weight of their bombardment alone, and their boast was justified. As the leading brigade of June 11 the 1st Division were landing at the shattered quayside, the Italian commander of Pantellaria signalled to Malta: "Beg surrender through lack of water"—an excuse which had not been foreseen at Sousse, but it was true that the Italian communications had been so disrupted that their men had had scarcely anything to eat or drink for the past three days. The 3rd Grenadiers, who had been prepared to follow up the leading brigades, were not now required even to set sail from Sousse, and their part in the operation was confined to guarding the prisoners who were brought back from the island. A few weeks later they assisted in the preparations for the invasion of Sicily, by staffing and organizing one of the transit camps through which the July assault divisions passed on their way to the docks. Many thousands of

1943 British and American troops were treated by the Grenadiers to their last cups of tea before embarkation, but scarcely one of them, hosts or guests, knew the destination for which they were bound.

As the flow and disposal of prisoners became more manageable, the Battalions had men and time enough to resume their tactical training. All of them were brought up to full strength, including reserves, by the arrival of a large draft of Grenadiers under Major W. E. P.
June 29 Miller. They staged at the reinforcement camp at Philippeville, which was commanded by Colonel R. B. R. Colvin, and here the three Commanding Officers converged to pick the officers and men for their Battalions. To Major Miller "it felt like an auction market, with all of us waiting to be bid for." In addition, the Battalions were now able to recover the majority of their men who had been wounded in the African campaigns, and with the flow of reinforcements from all these sources they were able to reorganize the Battalions from top to bottom, and in spite of continual casualties from dysentery and malaria to fit them for a new type of warfare. For it was at this time that the War Office decided to change the composition of the normal infantry battalions. All the heavy-weapon platoons (the carriers, the 3-inch mortars and the anti-tank guns) were detached from Headquarter Company and grouped together in a Support Company, leaving the Headquarters purely administrative. In the case of the 6th Battalion, the innovation was further complicated by the fact that they were transformed from a lorried-infantry battalion to an infantry battalion of the normal type. Fortunately there was still time for them to be exercised in their new role.

Owing to the extreme heat in the middle of the day, "Reveille" was sounded at 5 or 5.30 a.m. and training confined to the morning and evening, leaving the men free in the afternoon to sleep or bathe. The training at first took the form of small tactical exercises and shooting with rifles and Bren guns among the sand-dunes, but later whole brigades would manœuvre in the mountainous country of the Lower Atlas or the Cap Bon Peninsula. There were frequent visits to the old battlefields, the Bou, Mareth and Djebel Mansour, where the battle would be fought over once again, for the benefit of the newcomers, and as a reminder to the veterans of their past triumphs and mistakes.* A wider insight into the organization of war was obtained by those officers and men who visited airports and naval installations in the neighbourhood of their camps. The Guardsmen were able to make

*The bodies of the Grenadiers who were killed in action were collected into special cemeteries, and their graves marked with crosses. Those of the 3rd and 5th Battalions were laid to rest at Baharine, on the banks of the Medjerda, south-west of Medjez el Bab. The main cemetery of the 6th Battalion was at Mareth, at the foot of the Horseshoe.

several excursions into the Mediterranean on British warships, and a 1943
few flew on operational flights with the R.A.F. or the American Air Force over Sicily and Italy.

It remains to describe the stages by which each Battalion moved from place to place in North Africa before embarking for the campaign on the Italian mainland. We have already seen that immediately after the Tunis victory parade, the 3rd Battalion were at Sousse, the 5th at El Bardo in the environs of Tunis, and the 6th at Bone. None of them remained in these places more than a few months.

At the end of July, the 6th Battalion joined the 3rd at Sousse, and a fortnight later received sudden orders to move to Tripoli in Libya. The Battalion completed this journey partly by sea and partly by the overland route, and arrived to find that they were in the 56th Division, which formed part of the great Allied armada which was to land at Salerno. They were encamped two miles south of Tripoli, and spent three weeks practising embarkation and disembarkation from the infantry assault craft, a role hitherto unfamiliar to the 6th Battalion, although both the other Battalions had spent many months training in Scotland for combined operations which they never carried out. To harden the men they were made to march long distances round the fertile oases of Tripoli; they water-proofed their vehicles; and in great secrecy they planned. On the 2nd of September they went aboard their landing craft for the last time, and sailed for Italy.

The 5th Battalion also twice changed their quarters. After handing
over the El Bardo camp they marched with the remainder of the 24th Aug. 17
Guards Brigade (now under the command of Brigadier A. S. P. Murray, himself a Grenadier), down the hot and dusty road to Hammamet, a total distance of forty-five miles, which they covered in three days at the height of summer. The change was welcome. Their new camp was set close to the sea-shore among the olives and eucalyptus trees, from which the men strung up their mosquito nets, sleeping in the open in shallow holes scooped from the sand. For three months more they lived here, by turns bored and exhilarated, according to the weather, the latest rumour, or the job immediately in hand. This period was brought to an end in the last week of November by orders
to move to Bizerta, and from here they too sailed for Italy, not as Dec. 4
part of any invasion force but to land peacefully at Taranto.

Finally, the 3rd Battalion. They had nine months to wait before crossing the Mediterranean, and a second Christmas to spend in North Africa. After leaving Sousse the Battalion were at first spread
out over a wide stretch of Algeria, with companies detached on Aug. 11
prisoner-of-war duties as far apart as Philippeville and Souk Ahras. The remaining units of the 1st Guards Brigade (which was now com-

1943 manded by Brigadier P. G. S. Gregson-Ellis, also a Grenadier) were
separated by as much as a hundred and fifty miles, with the 3rd Welsh
Guards at Constantine, the 2nd Coldstream Guards at Bone, and
Brigade Headquarters at La Calle. The gradual flow of First Army
units to the Italian theatre had reduced the North African garrison
to a minimum, and the services of the few divisions left behind were
in great demand. Later the Brigade and the battalions began to close
Sept. 6 up. The 3rd Grenadiers were concentrated at Guelma, where they
occupied a French agricultural college (by far the most comfortable
billet they had found since leaving England), and moved finally to
Oct. 27 Constantine, to join the Welsh and Coldstream Guards. Here the
Battalion lived in Nissen huts and tents set among the pine woods a
mile to the east of the town. The energy they showed under Colonel
Heber-Percy in constructing a first-class camp, with gravel paths, canteens, and hard standings for their vehicles was well repaid when the
camp was deluged by the winter rains. Their association with the
other brigades of the 6th Armoured Division became even more intimate than before, not only as a result of the field exercises they carried
out in co-operation with the tanks and artillery, but in a more personal, social sense. The 3rd Battalion became closely linked with one
armoured regiment in particular, the 16th/5th Lancers, with whom
they shared their Christmas festivities at Constantine. The friendships
born in those days between the companies and the squadrons proved
invaluable to the ease of their later co-operation on the battlefields of
Italy.

Unit by unit, brigade by brigade, the 6th Armoured Division began
to melt away to Italy. The arrival of every despatch rider, every ring-
ing of the telephone, might bring to the 1st Guards Brigade their own
orders to cross the Mediterranean. When the orders finally came they
1944 were left with less than a week to pack up the accumulated baggage
Feb. 4 of nine months. They sailed from Philippeville to Naples with little
idea of what the future held in store.

PART TWO

THE ITALIAN CAMPAIGN

1943—1945

CHAPTER V

SALERNO AND MONTE CAMINO

6TH BATTALION

1

SALERNO

Strategy behind the Salerno landings—Allied order of battle—The invasion fleet sails from Africa—Italian armistice coincides with D Day—Allied optimism and German counter-measures—The landings are at first successful, but later checked at Battipaglia—201st Guards Brigade in a perilous situation—Withdrawal of the Brigade to a narrower perimeter—Vigorous German attempts to drive the Allies back to the sea—Link up with the Eighth Army—Combined advance towards Naples—Grenadiers in heavy mountain fighting

THE same three Battalions of the Grenadier Guards which had fought in North Africa—the 6th, the 5th and the 3rd—crossed in that order and at long intervals to the northern shore of the Mediterranean to take part in different phases of the Italian campaign. Only one of them, the 3rd Battalion, remained in Italy until the end of the war in Europe. The 6th Battalion were so weakened by casualties that they were withdrawn from active operations even before the Allied advance had reached the level of Rome, and the 5th Battalion had almost gained the northern limit of the Apennines before they too were withdrawn. Yet the Grenadiers took a very full part in the Italian campaign. Each Battalion, within a month or two of landing, became closely associated with one of its three great names: the 3rd Battalion with Cassino; the 5th with Anzio; and the 6th with Salerno. It is with the last-named that the first part of this chapter is concerned.

On the fourth anniversary of Great Britain's entry into the war the Eighth Army, under General Montgomery, landed at Reggio in the toe of Italy. They crossed the Straits of Messina to find the Italian shore almost undefended, and their advance up the Calabrian peninsula developed quickly, delayed by little more than the destruction of bridges. This was the shortest, the most obvious, line of attack. But it was not the main attack, which followed six days later with the landing of the Fifth Army, under the American General Mark Clark, on 1943 Sept. 3 Sept. 9

1943 the beaches between Salerno and Paestum. Its object was twofold: first to cut off the retreat of the German divisions confronting General Montgomery; and, secondly, to seize the port of Naples and convert it into the main base for the combined advance towards Rome. Salerno was chosen as the point of invasion not only because its beaches were more suitable for the landing of a large force than any part of the coastline farther north, but because it lay just within range of aircraft operating from Sicily, and even the Hurricanes, fitted with special tanks, had only sufficient fuel to remain over the battle zone for a quarter of an hour. The fate of the whole enterprise seemed to depend upon securing a foothold deep enough and quickly enough to enable the Fifth Army to survive the ten days which were expected to elapse between their landing and their junction with the Eighth Army advancing from the south. For this purpose they needed an air-field within the limits of the beach-head to give them close fighter support; they needed to secure the ring of hills which closed in the Plain of Salerno on its eastern side, in order to deny the enemy observation over the beaches and the shipping in the bay; they needed, finally, to dominate the main coastal road, which ran through Paestum and Battipaglia to Salerno and Naples, and so cut one of the main channels of supply to the southern German divisions, and force them to retreat, if they could, along the tortuous roads of Central Italy. The opposition on the actual beaches was not expected to be heavy, as the coastal defences were known to be manned by wavering Italians; but it was also known that the German 16th Panzer Division lay at Eboli, with a battle group at Battipaglia, and the counter-attacks of these troops would certainly lead to critical fighting during the first few days.

See Map p. 366 Let us examine in more detail the Fifth Army's plan of invasion. There were two Corps in the Army: the VI American Corps of three divisions, and the British X Corps, which consisted of the 46th and 56th Infantry Divisions and the 7th Armoured Division. The Americans, landing on a one-divisional front, were allotted the southern sector of the Salerno beaches from the River Sele to Paestum. The British divisions landed on the northern sector between the Sele and Salerno itself. Within the British sector the further sub-allotment of sectors was as follows, reading from south to north:

56th Division

Right: 167th Brigade, between the Sele and the Tusciano.

Left: 169th Brigade, between the Tusciano and the Asa.

In reserve: 201st Guards Brigade.

46th Division 1943

Between the Asa and Salerno.

7th Armoured Division

In reserve to the whole Corps.

The object of the entire force, as we have seen, was to capture the Plain of Salerno and the ridge of high hills which shielded it from the east and north. But within their respective sectors each division had a more immediate object, to be achieved, if possible, within the first twenty-four hours. That of the 56th Division was to capture the airfield of Montecorvino, and the town of Battipaglia. Without the first there could be little fighter cover; without the second the Allies could scarcely hope to prevent the 16th Panzer Division from moving along the main lateral road and attacking the beaches at almost any point they chose. The 167th and 169th Brigades were to lead the assault on the beaches, and advance inland as far as they could, while the 201st Guards Brigade landed behind them a few hours later, prepared to carry out any task which the situation demanded. It seemed that an attack on the airfield and Battipaglia would be their most likely role.

All this was explained in detail to the troops as they sailed northwards from Tripoli across the Mediterranean. The convoy was not at **Sept. 2-8** first a large one, for the invasion force was embarking at widely scattered ports, but during the voyage the different units of the fleet joined forces to cover the sea with shipping from horizon to horizon. The Grenadiers were sailing in three L.C.Is.,* and their vehicles were carried in L.C.Ts.† The former were most unsuitable for a voyage lasting as long as a week: below decks there was no sleeping accommodation other than hard, upright benches, and whenever the sea grew rough the whole craft from end to end was drenched in flying spray. Except for a single day, the weather fortunately remained fair, and though there was great anxiety about the manœuvring of so large a mass of ships in such dangerous waters, there were no enemy attacks upon them until they were within sight of Salerno itself. They sailed round the north-west angle of Sicily, and anchored off Termini, to **Sept. 7** await the arrival of other units, and give the men a rest from their cramped quarters and the continual motion of the sea. That night, apparently still unobserved by the enemy, the armada headed directly for the coast of Italy.

They sighted land before they expected it. "We saw quite plainly **Sept. 8** the Italian coast on one side," wrote a Grenadier, "and on the other,

*Landing craft, infantry.

†Landing craft, tanks.

1943 just visible on the horizon, the outlines of hundreds of ships of every size." Looking ahead at about 4 p.m., many of them observed the silhouette of a high island, lying detached from the end of a long peninsula. It was the Isle of Capri. They were astounded, appalled, that they should have arrived within sight of the beaches nearly twelve hours before zero hour. An hour later, as the convoy began to slow down, a further incident seemed to confirm the growing rumour that, unknown to them, the plan had been changed at the last moment. A launch picked its way between the assault ships, and an officer with a megaphone shouted up to each in turn that the Italian Government had signed an armistice with the Allies. There was immense jubilation on board. "I collected the half-bottle of sherry which I had been saving to give me courage on the following morning," wrote the Grenadier Carrier Officer, Capt. G. C. Maxwell, "took it to the bridge, and with the skipper and first lieutenant celebrated the downfall of Italy, and drank to an unopposed landing." The news was confirmed by the B.B.C. at 6 p.m. Nobody, not even Brigadier Gascoigne nor the Commander of the 56th Division, had had any prior knowledge of the Italian surrender.* Some thought that the convoy would now sail directly into Naples harbour. Their optimism was dampened only when a few German aircraft came over to bomb the ships, and the convoy wheeled eastwards as originally planned. When darkness fell they began to glide slowly towards the beaches.

The Germans had, in fact, received definite information at midday on the 8th of September of the approach of the Allied invasion fleet, but they were uncertain whether the landing was to be attempted at Salerno, Castellamare or Vietri. At Salerno they had held an exercise on the previous afternoon to practise the repulse of just such an invasion as took place thirty-six hours later, but the Italian armistice came upon them with equal surprise. An officer of the 16th Panzer Division wrote this description of the measures they took to save the situation on shore:

> "A sergeant from the heavy machine-gun section came running up to me in great excitement. 'Sir, a message has just arrived. I have been ordered to take over the Italian position. Would you, as an officer, undertake this mission?' I made my arrangements: one half of the section was to give me cover and open fire if I signalled with a white tracer. I went with the other half of the section, and in no time at all had disarmed the personnel of the Italian heavy machine-gun nest. I

---

*"My own opinion," wrote Brigadier Gascoigne afterwards, "is that the announcement was made in sufficient time to enable the Germans to remove the Italians from the local defences, with the result that we had far stiffer opposition to cope with right from the beginning than would have been the case if the announcement had been postponed for twenty-four hours."

1943

told them that their country had capitulated and that after being disarmed they could make their way home. It happened just as I expected. They threw their weapons away, and showed their joy that the war was now over for them, and they could go home. Much more difficult were the negotiations with the artillery position. . . . The Italian commander did not seem at all keen to comply with my order, and I was forced to give him a short-term ultimatum—to hand over or to be fired on by my men. When the officer realized that it was a case of 'either—or,' he came to a decision, and handed over his battery. . . . The whole thing did not take more than about forty-five minutes."

Sept. 9

At 1 a.m. the entire invasion fleet lay at anchor about nine miles off the coast, and at 2.15 a.m. the assaulting waves set off from their parent ships in a calm sea and under a bright moon. The Grenadiers did their best to snatch a few hours' sleep. In the direction of Salerno they saw one or two fires blaze up as the Germans set alight to the main warehouses and blew up the mole, but from the beaches there came little sound of shooting. The first wireless messages from the shore told them that the landing had been achieved without great difficulty, and a screen of infantry had already been thrown out to a depth of two or three thousand yards inland. On the American sector there had been slightly more opposition, and one brigade had so far failed to gain a foothold ashore. But the situation, on the whole, seemed very favourable when the 201st Guards Brigade were ordered at dawn to move in through the smoke screen to the beaches. No. 3 Company of the Grenadiers were the first unit of the Brigade to land —it was the first time that any body of Grenadiers had set foot on the mainland of Europe since the evacuation from Dunkirk—and they had a dry landing, stepping straight from their L.C.Is. on to a soft strip of shelving sand. The L.C.Ts. off-loaded their vehicles shortly afterwards at a point slightly farther north, and the whole great mass of men and lorries converged on the agreed assembly area in a field half a mile inland. At this stage the German artillery became more active. The larger ships anchored in the bay attracted most of their fire, but they soon also ranged accurately on the beaches. While the vehicles were churning their way with some difficulty through the sand two portees received direct hits: two Guardsmen were killed, and Lieut. T. A. Thwaites, the Battalion Machine Gun Officer, was wounded. These were the Grenadiers' first casualties of the campaign.

7.15 a.m.

It is now necessary to examine more closely the nature of the country over which the crucial fighting of the next week took place. The beaches, every yard of which was used for the landing of some part of the vast invasion forces, were suspended in a great arc some fifteen miles long, between Salerno and Paestum. On the morning of the 9th of September the mountains to the north and east were veiled

1943 in mist, but on subsequent days they were often seen rising sharp and clear to a height of five thousand feet, and gave the enemy an uninterrupted view of the entire beach-head. The plain at the foot of the mountains was quite flat as far as the main coastal road, beyond which the ground began to swell violently into the lower foothills. Almost the entire area of the plain was under intensive cultivation and was speckled with farms. The wheat had just been cut, but the tobacco plants and vines still stood eight feet high in the fields. The ground was intersected by a network of dykes and ditches, some filled with water and some concreted, and the rivers meandered across the plain in wide, flat beds, forming in places marshes and deep pools. The military import of these natural features was threefold. In the first place, it was not easy for infantry to see their way ahead nor to move silently and in deployed formation through the high, thick crops. In the second place, the ditches made it impossible for lorries and carriers, and difficult for tanks, to move across the open country: they were confined to the few roads and narrow tracks, where one breakdown or one unlucky shell-burst would block the progress of the remainder of the column behind. And, in the third place, the supreme importance of seizing the mountain crests became even more evident than the study of maps and air photographs had suggested many weeks before.

Once the Grenadiers had re-formed in the assembly area they were ordered to continue the advance between the encircling arms of the leading brigades, and deepen the bridgehead as quickly as possible in the direction of Battipaglia. They had already discovered that their advance would not be unopposed, for Major C. Earle, O.B.E., on leading No. 3 Company to the eastern limit of the assembly area, found himself under mortar fire, and a carrier which patrolled up the road was destroyed within a few hundred yards, two of its crew being killed. No. 3 Company took the lead in the first advance. In order to give them the support of his 3-inch mortars, Lieut. M. D. Ridpath climbed a tower to observe the country ahead; he was seen by a German tank, and was killed by a direct hit, which also wounded Capt. E. B. M. Vaughan. No. 3 Company soon met trouble, and delayed their second attempt until after nightfall. This time they had fair success as far as a network of lanes north of Verdesca, where the leading platoon were caught by a sudden volley of bullets and hand grenades. Several men were killed, among them Capt. I. A. Moncrieff-Brown, who was leading one of the forward sections, and several
Sept. 10 others wounded. The advance was again halted, and a third advance by this same company at dawn became involved with a group of German tanks and infantry in half-tracks, and in spite of an excellent

outflanking move by Lieut. G. R. Stokes-Roberts they could make no **1943** further progress. In this attack Lieut. R. M. Drake was killed outright at the head of his platoon.

The number of casualties began to mount, and the feeling of tremendous optimism with which the Battalion had landed began to wane. The 16th Panzer Division were now fighting back strongly, and taking skilful advantage of the close country to absorb the shock of the first British attack before it had even reached the main road. But it was evidently not their intention to fight out the battle on the lower ground. Almost at the same time as Major Earle launched his third attack, the Germans began to withdraw, and Nos. 1 and 2 Companies, passing on his right flank between No. 3 Company and the Tusciano stream, were able to advance unopposed as far as the road just west of Battipaglia. Major G. E. W. Potter, M.C., commanding No. 2 Company, drove over the bridge into the town itself, and there found a small party of Royal Fusiliers from the 167th Brigade in uncertain possession of its southern half. While Major Potter was there a force of about two hundred German infantry attacked from the north and recaptured the town, and were prevented from pouring over the bridge only by a squadron of Scots Greys, who moved their tanks forward to cover its western end. Major Potter made his way back across the Tusciano at a point farther south, and rejoined his company.

On the left flank of the Grenadiers the 3rd Coldstream Guards had occupied the aerodrome at Montecorvino—it was unusable by the R.A.F. because it lay for many days in the very front line—and the 2nd Scots Guards launched the first of their attacks on a large tobacco factory, lying just south of the main road. The factory was not captured until a week later. *See Map p.* **362** Its thick concrete walls were proof against the light shells of the British field artillery, and the Germans had garrisoned it with a battalion of infantry and several tanks firing outwards from inside the buildings. Here the Scots Guards were involved in heavier and more costly fighting than the Grenadiers had yet undergone, but the latter found themselves on the right flank in a position of great danger and discomfort. They held a salient, "a finger pointing at Battipaglia," bounded by the main road on the north side, by the Tusciano on the east, and by the railway on the south. Both of their flanks were wide open: on the far bank of the Tusciano the Royal Fusiliers had withdrawn about a mile south of Battipaglia, exposing the Grenadiers to attacks across the dry stream-bed and over the railway bridge; while on the left flank there was a gap of one thousand two hundred yards between the Grenadiers and the Scots Guards, which the Germans were not slow to discover. Immediately ahead, a spur of the central mountains ran down to Castelluccio, where the

1943 Germans set up an observation post which overlooked every recess of the Battalion's position, and survived all the concentrations of land and naval gunfire. The Brigadier sent up two companies of the Coldstream to assist the Grenadiers, and Colonel Kingsmill placed them along the line of the road, so that his own companies could pay more attention to the threat from their rear; they were fighting, during these days, almost back to back.

Sept. 11 Before launching their first full-scale attack to drive the Fifth Army back to the beaches, the Germans began to probe the front line to discover the points of greatest weakness. Two attacks along the railway embankment were beaten off, and a necklace of mines which the pioneer platoon strung across the British side of the Battipaglia bridge destroyed a German tank which attempted to cross. The barrier formed by the bed of the Tusciano was a sufficient barrier on this side. The real danger was from the north and west. The cultivation between the road and the railway was so thick that the only way to stop German infiltration by night would have been to block every yard by men standing shoulder to shoulder, "by actual bodies on the ground." For this, even with the Coldstream reinforcements, there were not sufficient troops, and, although each platoon was a closely knit entity, there remained small gaps between the platoons, larger gaps between the companies, and, as we have seen, wide open spaces between the battalions. The Germans operated with small battle groups of twenty or thirty men and perhaps a couple of tanks, who would penetrate these gaps and join up in rear of our foremost positions, always on the move, and always striking, suddenly, from a new direction. On the night of the 11th of September a serious situation arose. After a heavy artillery concentration a typical German battle group attacked across the road and forced the temporary withdrawal of part of the Coldstream companies and of No. 2 Company of the Grenadiers. Nos. 1, 3 and 4 Companies and a squadron of the Scots Greys remained firm, but it seemed at one moment, before it was realized that the enemy were not after all in very great strength, that the whole Battalion were in danger of being overrun. At Battalion Headquarters all the documents and marked maps were destroyed as a precaution against capture, and the regimental aid post hung out their Red Cross flag to protect the wounded. There was a great deal of random firing in the darkness, both from in front and from across the river on the right. The Commanding Officer, Colonel Kingsmill, collected what men he could from his Headquarters, formed them up behind the railway embankment, and led them forward to regain the line of the main road. The enemy had vanished. It had been little more than a raid, a *Kraftprobe,* a test of strength; and before dawn the position

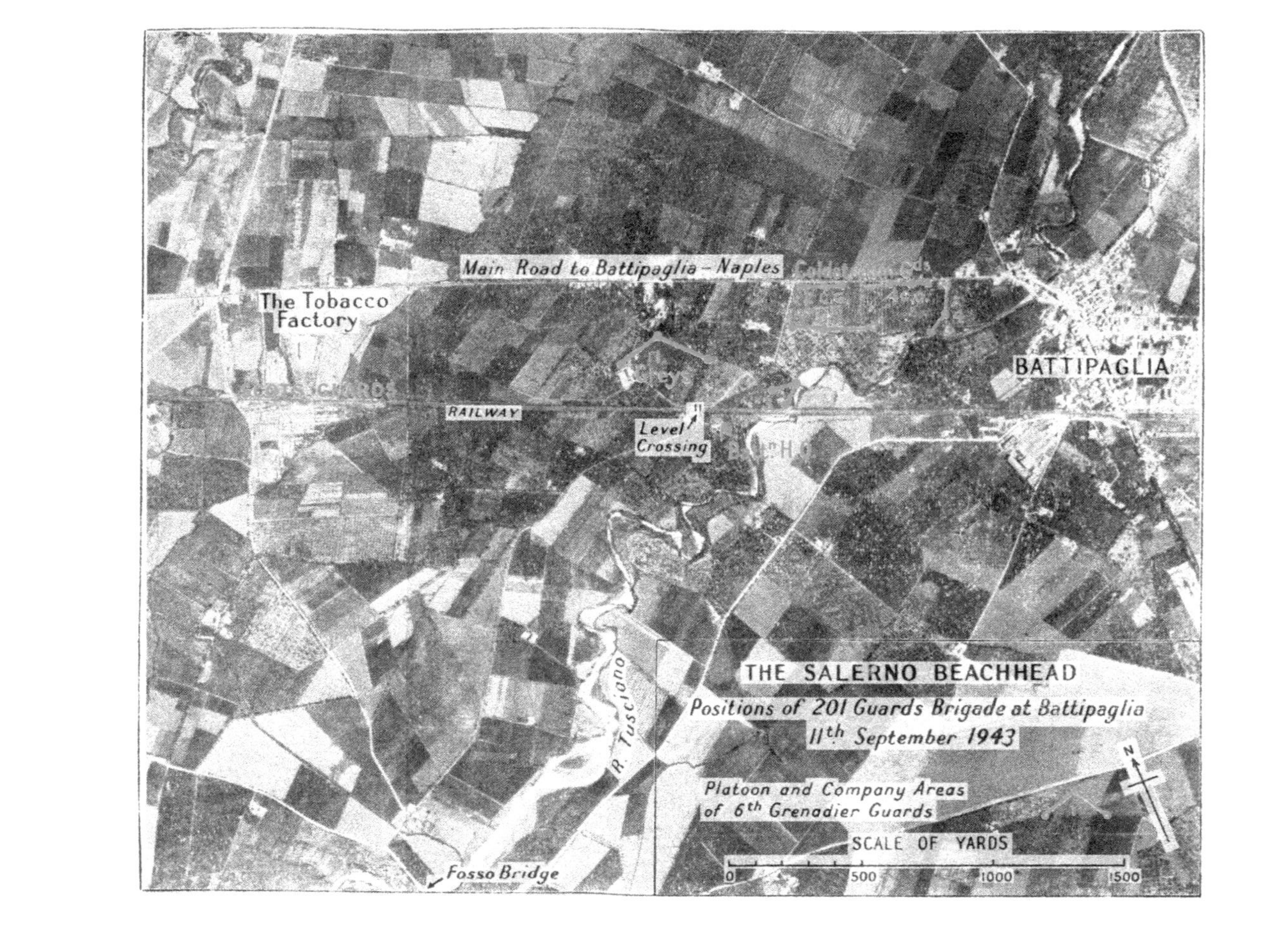

Main Road to Battipaglia – Naples
The Tobacco Factory
BATTIPAGLIA
RAILWAY
Level Crossing
R. Tusciano
Fosso Bridge
THE SALERNO BEACHHEAD
Positions of 201 Guards Brigade at Battipaglia
11th September 1943
Platoon and Company Areas of 6th Grenadier Guards
SCALE OF YARDS
0
500
1000
1500
N

was completely re-established. Among the casualties of the night the 1943 Battalion lost two more officers: Capts. J. V. Hermon and Hon. F. C. Wigram were both killed outright by mortar bombs.

The perilous situation of the Brigade could not be maintained indefinitely. They were still holding the most advanced position in the whole of the Fifth Army, and there was no likelihood that they would be able to deepen the bridgehead until the troops on either flank had moved up to the same level, and so loosened the German grip on the tobacco factory and Battipaglia. To remain in the salient could serve no useful purpose and merely exposed them to unnecessary risks. Sept. 12 Brigadier Gascoigne therefore decided to withdraw the Grenadiers and Coldstream to new positions about a mile in rear, where they would be in closer contact with the troops on their right and left, and their own sector of the line would be shorter, more compact, and allow the 6th Grenadiers to be placed in positions of close reserve to both the other battalions. A withdrawal from close contact with an enemy who is continually on the alert is one of the most risky operations of war, and in this case it was complicated by the chance that there was only one level-crossing over the railway line, and one bad and boggy track available for the tanks of the Scots Greys, four heavy anti-tank guns, and some eighty vehicles of the Coldstream and Grenadiers, as well as all the infantry. If one vehicle was hit or ditched, the remainder would be isolated behind it. Having carefully weighed up the risks, the Brigadier further decided that the withdrawal of the vehicles must take place at dusk, in order to give the drivers a better chance of clearing the bottleneck without accident; the infantry would not follow them until after nightfall. To their surprise, this large-scale withdrawal was successfully carried out within full view of the enemy without attracting more than a few random shells. There was not a single casualty. By 8.40 p.m. the last company of infantry had also withdrawn, and Capt. G. C. Maxwell, who had waited behind for twenty-five minutes with a protective screen of carriers, heard not a single movement ahead. The only remarkable incident which occurred was the destruction of the Battipaglia bridge by the Germans at the same time as the last companies withdrew. Why they should have cut their lateral road in this manner is still not explained. They were not at this stage also planning a withdrawal—indeed, they soon occupied the ground which the Guardsmen had evacuated—and the only other crossing of the Tusciano was by the Fosso bridge, which remained securely within the new British perimeter.

The withdrawal of the Grenadiers marked the temporary end of offensive operations by the X Corps. To some the withdrawal had given new spirit, a new sense of security: others viewed with keen

1943 disappointment the melancholy fact that after five days' heavy fighting, involving the loss of so many officers and men, the invasion forces were still no more than five thousand yards from the beaches on which they had landed. They knew, too, that they must await enemy attacks in ever-increasing strength as the German divisions from the south joined forces with those already at Salerno. The area in which the Allies could still manœuvre was already reduced far below the margin of safety. On the left flank the 46th Division were clinging with difficulty to the narrow shelf which they had captured during the first few hours, and Salerno itself was still in enemy hands. On the Paestum sector the Americans had achieved no greater success. At one point German attacks penetrated to within less than a mile of the beaches, and amphibious dukws and even jeeps took up hull-down positions among the dunes only a few yards from the water's edge. All their hopes rested on the advance of the Eighth Army from the south. General Alexander, when he visited the 201st Guards Brigade on the 15th of September, said that there could be no question of evacuating the Fifth Army, and that they had only to hold firm to their perimeter for a few days more, "when General Montgomery will make himself felt on this battlefield."

His optimism was fully justified by events, but the days of waiting were full of anxiety. The Grenadiers, who were nominally in reserve to their own Brigade just north of Verdesca, were informed that they were the only mobile reserve in the entire X Corps, and they must be ready to move at a moment's notice to any part of the British sector. From this unpalatable role they were saved only by the landing of the
Sept. 13-17 7th Armoured Division. The Battalion remained for five days in rear of the Coldstream Guards, never directly attacked themselves, but suffering acutely from the strain of continual shellfire, which arched over their heads in both directions, from the German guns in the hills and from the British warships cruising in the bay. Colonel Kingsmill, on one occasion, was slightly wounded in the arm by a piece of flying
Sept. 13 shrapnel. On the 13th the Coldstream were heavily attacked by the 26th Panzer Division, which had now arrived from the south, and beat them off only after expending fifty-four thousand rounds of small-arms ammunition, while the British gunners fired for ninety minutes without pause. Prisoners taken in this attack said that its intention had been to break through to the very beaches, and fifty tanks had been waiting to pass through if the German infantry had been able to force a breach. Such was the scale of the attacks, and such the extreme peril of the Allies.*

*The Brigade Major of the 201st Guards Brigade, Major L. R. C. Stucley, who was sick with diphtheria when the Brigade landed at Salerno, was evacuated from the beaches after trying desperately to carry on with his work, and died in North Africa on the 16th of September.

Three days later the 26th Panzer Division made a second attempt 1943
in broad daylight: this also failed, and it marked the close of their Sept. 16
attacks. The first reports of a German withdrawal were unfounded. Lieut. The Master of Saltoun, M.C., led a patrol to Battipaglia and found it still occupied, and they escaped with great difficulty: one Guardsman was killed, and the Master, becoming separated from his patrol, found his way back to our own lines only two nights later. On
the 18th the link between the Eighth and Fifth Armies was firmly Sept. 18
forged at Paestum, and the sound of German demolitions on the line of the main road indicated that the enemy were at last retreating to the hills. The whole Allied force followed cautiously but quickly. The Guards Brigade found the tobacco factory and Battipaglia a mass of rubble, but free of German troops; and No. 4 Company of the Grenadiers were sent with the 44th Reconnaissance Regiment up the road to Olevano in the lower foothills. Their vehicles were held up by a demolished bridge, but they crossed on foot during the night and held a covering position while the sappers bridged the gap behind them. The remainder of the Battalion awaited further orders just north of Battipaglia.

The combined forces of the Fifth and Eighth Armies were now able to wheel north-west towards Naples, and though there was but a single road passing between precipitous hills, they broke through to Pompeii without great difficulty. The 201st Guards Brigade had no share in these Vesuvian triumphs, for they were diverted along the secondary
road which ran due north from Salerno to San Severino. The Grena- Sept. 19
diers took over from the Sherwood Foresters an awkward sector of the line lying astride the valley floor just south of Ponte Fratte. Further progress was blocked by a German strong-point in the cemetery, and the short stretch of road between there and Salerno was under enemy observation and enemy fire. The Adjutant of the 6th Battalion, Capt.
P. C. W. Alington, was wounded by a salvo which landed close beside Sept. 23
him on the road, and though his wounds did not at first appear to be serious, he died the next day.

The Germans withdrew of their own accord, but the Brigade had Sept. 24
followed only a short distance when they found the defile barred once again farther north. They took to the hills on the left of the road. It was the Grenadiers' first experience of mountain fighting, and they found conditions which were often repeated during the next few months but were seldom more disagreeable. They were ordered to attack Point 270, a steep hill covered with brushwood, up which it was possible for a company to move only in single file along rough tracks. The Italian civilians had told them that there were no Germans on the summit, a fact which their own observations through field-

1943 glasses had tended to confirm; but it was false. Heavily laden as they were (for the ideal equipment for mountain fighting had yet to be evolved), the Guardsmen of the two leading companies reached the crest to find the Germans about to withdraw, and after an exchange of grenades our men remained in possession of the hill while the enemy retired to a higher ridge beyond. This success had been achieved at no great cost, but only then was it fully realized that the problems of administration in this type of warfare were as great as, or even greater than, the problems of tactics. Battalion Headquarters, in a tunnel close to the road, was three hours' journey on foot from Point 270. How were the wounded to be evacuated over this great distance? How were food, water and ammunition to be taken forward to the companies? Furthermore, it was extremely difficult to find the way in darkness among this mass of hills; and because the wireless sets were out of range the exact situation from hour to hour was never known, and no artillery fire could be called in support of the widely scattered companies. Major Sir Hugh Cholmeley, who was acting for the Commanding Officer, went forward with the reserve companies, and after reviewing the situation on the spot took the decision that Point 270 was untenable. He ordered the Battalion to withdraw to the slopes of Monte Taborra, a thousand yards farther south, leaving No. 4 Company, who had captured a farm on the left flank, in a position from which they were able to assist the Coldstream on the next day. To reinforce the Grenadier porters, a squad of Basutos shouldered some of the more vital loads and began the slow ascent into the hills. With the rain and the darkness and the shell fire, many of these supplies did not reach their destination, but that at least the wounded might receive attention the Medical Officer, Capt. Chestnut, took the regimental aid post to a point just below Monte Taborra, and worked without ceasing to relieve their sufferings. Gdsm. Butterworth, one of his stretcher-bearers, went twice down the forward slopes of Taborra to collect casualties under heavy fire, and his example was followed by many others. Among the officers, Lieut. P. J. O. Meyrick was killed during No. 2 Company's attack on Point 270, and Lieuts. D. A. L. Lawrence and J. R. A. Brocklebank were wounded.

For two days the Battalion remained at Taborra while the Coldstream passed ahead of them and at great cost attacked Point 270, which had been reoccupied by the enemy. On the 26th patrols re-
Sept. 27 ported that the Germans had withdrawn out of sight, and the Brigade could at long last be relieved. The Grenadiers came back to a block of requisitioned flats in Salerno, which their Quartermaster, Lieut. B. H. Pratt, had prepared for their reception. The Battalion were able to wash the clothes they had not taken off for three weeks, and enjoy the few luxuries which Italy had to offer.

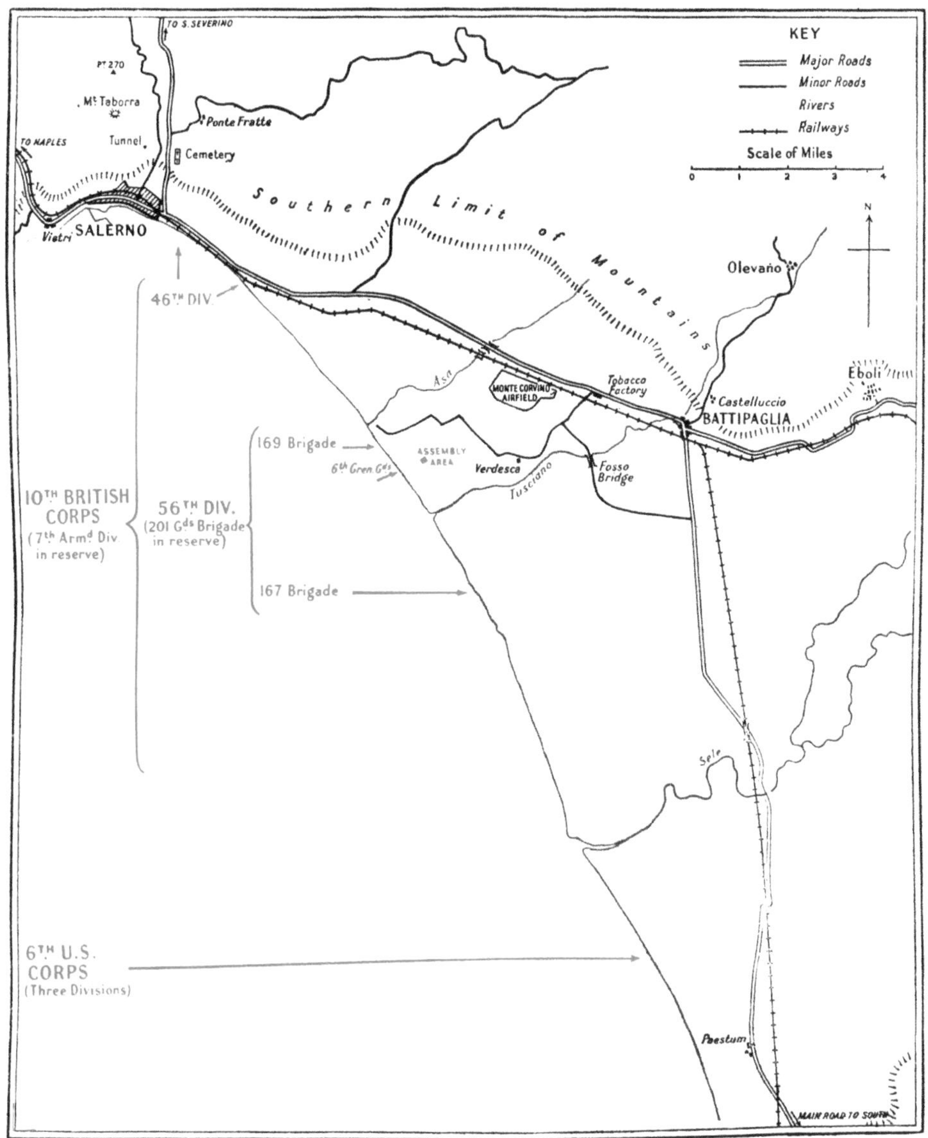

THE LANDING AT SALERNO

Face page 366

2

CAPUA AND THE APPROACH TO MONTE CAMINO

The 6th Battalion ordered to force a crossing of the Volturno at Capua—Last-minute change of plan—Nature of the fighting north of Capua—Capture of Hill 860—The preliminaries to Monte Camino

For the 6th Battalion the respite from the battle lasted ten days **1943** while the Allied armies captured Naples and overran the broad plain to the north until they were halted on the line of the Volturno River. The Grenadiers had time to visit, as tourists and not as conquerors, the historic sites of the Neapolitan littoral; Pompeii, which was a disappointment to most of them, so closely did it resemble the recent scenes of devastation which they themselves had helped to cause; and Naples, a shambles of ruined dockyards, ridden with typhus and overflowing with a pitiful population of frightened, excited urchins. Only the Sorrento Peninsula remained almost untouched by war: places such as Amalfi, Ravello and the Isle of Capri were transformed during succeeding months into holiday camps and rest centres for the convalescent wounded of all the Allied forces.

After waiting for a few days in the orchards near San Severino, the Grenadiers were moved up to the town of Capua, on the Volturno. **Oct. 7** *See Map p.* **442** Only Nos. 1 and 2 Companies were stationed in Capua itself, the remainder of the Battalion lying farther south. The town is built inside a deep loop of the river, which surrounds it on all but one side, and the Grenadiers, from their spy-holes in the houses on the southern bank, looked across the two arms of the stream to see the German sentries at fifteen-yard intervals watching closely for the first signs of an Allied crossing. There was little activity. A B.B.C. commentator described Capua as "the hottest place on earth," but it was very far from that. The men were billeted in cellars, where they were safe from desultory shell fire, and could even move about the central streets without risk of being observed from the far bank. They suffered no casualties. Their chief concern was to control the excitable population. Many of the young Italians, feeling that they must contribute in some way to the liberation of their own city, were all too eager to make the most of their brief occupation of the front line, and began to shoot wildly across the river with any type of weapon on which they could lay their hands. This practice was stopped by Major Marsham ("Il maggiore commandante"), who soon achieved such prestige in Capua that not only military but the most intimate domestic affairs

1943 were brought to him for advice, accompanied by gifts of cold chicken, tongue and Italian champagne. While it lasted the occupation of Capua was by no means unenjoyable.

It was, however, overshadowed by the prospect of an extremely dangerous operation. The 201st Guards Brigade were ordered to force a crossing of the Volturno at Capua itself. Both the bridges had been totally destroyed, and the only method of gaining a lodgement on the far bank was to cross in assault boats under the very eyes of the enemy. Always a costly form of attack, it was rendered in this case physically very difficult by the high banks on both sides. It would first be necessary to carry the heavy boats through the rubble-blocked streets of the town; to lower them down a twenty-five-foot vertical wall to the water's edge, embark the troops, cross the swift-flowing river, and scale twelve-foot mud-banks on the far side. Though all this movement would be carried out in darkness, and as far as possible in silence, there was little chance that the enemy, only two hundred yards away, would not soon become aware of that danger, and flood the stretch of river with flares and fire. Nevertheless, the plan remained
Oct. 11 unchanged. The Grenadiers were withdrawn from Capua to Caserta, and there, in the gardens of the old Royal Palace, they practised carrying their boats up and down the steep banks, and ferrying them across the ornamental ponds. At the last moment, twenty-four hours before zero hour, news reached the Battalion that the higher commanders had thought again of the appalling risks involved, and the Capua plan was cancelled. The Volturno was to be crossed by other troops at more favourable points to the east and west of the town, and all that was required of the Grenadiers was to send a small force to simulate an attack at Capua itself. For this task No. 4 Company were sent back
Oct. 12 to the river bank, where, without loss to themselves, they fired mortar smoke bombs across the stream and heard on their right and left the barrages and fusillades of the genuine assaults.

On the left flank the assault failed; but the Americans on the right captured a bridgehead which was deep enough to dislodge the entire German line. The whole of the 201st Guards Brigade marched over
Oct. 15 the pontoon bridges on the American sector, and took over an angle of the new salient. The Germans made no attempt to counter-attack. They had plans for a winter line much farther to the north, and they were prepared to withdraw to it under pressure, remaining long enough and stubbornly enough in each intervening position to force the Allies to deploy their strength, and to tire themselves out before they reached the main line of resistance. It was in this type of warfare that the 6th Grenadiers were involved until the time came for them to leave Italy. There was no hope of a clean break-through, no sudden

thrusts, no opportunity in this mass of hills and worsening weather to 1943 use the tanks to fullest advantage. The line was drawn tight across the breadth of Italy from mountain-top to mountain-top; every lane, almost every mountain-path, was a supply route; every house in a zone five miles on either side of the front line was a billet or a headquarters, and the civilian population cowered as best they could in the cellars or the caves. Slowly the Allies made progress, the Eighth Army leaping river after river on the Adriatic coast, the Fifth Army clawing their way from mountain to mountain on the west. To the outer world the Italian operations were disappointing. Occasionally a spot-light would be thrown on a single name—Ortona, the Sangro, Cassino, Camino—but for those lesser hills or rivers or villages which required a battalion, a brigade or a division for their capture there was no publicity. It was an endless repetition of the same type of incident, the same degree of hardship, the same small gains, which made little impression on the daily sketch maps in the newspapers of the world.

The 201st Guards Brigade took their place with countless others of many nations, each pursuing different but parallel channels up the length of Italy. From the bed of the Volturno just east of Capua rises a long chain of hills leading northwards in ascending ridges towards Cassino. This was the ladder which the Guardsmen scaled rung by rung during the next weeks. Their first few actions were not difficult. After a hard climb through trees and boulders, or having crossed by night a bare patch of open moorland, they would arrive on a numbered but nameless summit to find only the litter which the Germans had left behind; if the defenders were still there, they were either asleep or prepared to surrender. Three heights were thus gained, with ten prisoners of war and no casualties. The attack on the last hill of Oct. 17 this particular series, Point 860, was preceded by all the elaborate arrangements of a full-scale brigade assault. The Grenadiers were split by the watershed between two parallel valleys, unconnected by any roads, and it was a full day's journey to reach Battalion Headquarters from the farther side. The problem of supply over these great distances was solved only by employing as porters the entire Coldstream battalion, three hundred Basutos, fifty Italians and forty mules—and even then some of the Grenadier platoons were left without water for twenty-four hours.* The attack itself was a greater success than they had dared to hope. The day before two excellent patrols, led by Lieuts. T. W. Huntington and J. R. A. Brocklebank, Oct. 22

*The equipment carried by each Guardsman on this occasion was as follows: rifle, Bren gun or tommy-gun, steel helmet, pick or shovel, small pack (mess-tin, spare socks, emergency rations), water-bottle, and a hundred rounds of ammuniton for each rifle. Greatcoats and blankets were brought up later by the porters. No washing or shaving kit was carried, as there was no water on the hill-top.

1943 had found the enemy well established on the approaches to Point 860. There was, in fact, an entire German battalion on the summit. The Battalion were saved unnecessary casualties by two devices: first, by a very heavy artillery barrage which swamped the defences and concealed the direction of the attack; and, secondly, by avoiding the few pathways and attacking up the steepest part of the mountain. At first light the advance began. The Guardsmen hauled themselves up from tree to tree, expecting at any moment to come upon the German outposts. Instead, they found the enemy stunned by the barrage. Without waiting to fight, the Germans fled down the far slope, some of them still in their underclothes, pursued by bullets from one of their own machine guns which Lieut. J. R. S. Wace had found abandoned on the summit. At 7.15 a.m., at least two hours before they had expected it, the Battalion and Brigade Headquarters in the valley below heard floating back to them the bugle call of No. 2 Company (Major G. E. W. Potter, M.C.)—the signal of complete success. They had captured one of the most dominating hills in this part of Italy.

One of the main secrets of mountain fighting had already been learned on Monte Taborra, that the best defence against counter-attack is to strike farther ahead once the main objective has been captured. This rule was followed with great success after the capture of Point 860. The other Grenadier companies leap-frogged ahead, and were in turn passed by the Scots Guards, who exploited the initial success to an area which they could now overrun without great difficulty, instead of waiting a few days to launch a separate attack. The Brigade were well aloft on a high, flat ridge—"like a golf course," was one officer's description—and, being in little danger themselves, they could afford to wait until the other divisions on their right and left had advanced to equivalent positions. At first they were short of food, although the Coldstream porters did their utmost to carry up the heavy boxes of compo rations, and arrived with their loads, almost asleep on their feet. They were always short of water, and could not wash. At nights they were very cold, and found it difficult to sleep cramped into the bottom of a slit trench. But the days were usually sunny, and they could watch at their leisure the Americans battling below them, our light bombers attacking the hill-top villages ahead, and Naples behind them grappling with a German air raid. After six days they
Oct. 28 moved down into the valley, and some of the men were able to sleep under a roof for the first time in a month.

Such were the preliminaries of the two great Battles of Monte Camino. The 6th Battalion entered upon this fresh engagement with two months of almost uninterrupted fighting behind them. They were hardened, experienced, but very tired. They had already lost many of their best officers and non-commissioned officers, and others were sick with jaundice, malaria, dysentery or desert sores. Yet they were not dispirited, and, though they well realized that a success such as they had achieved at Point 860 depended upon a degree of good fortune as well as a degree of good management, their confidence had grown. They had just that superiority in equipment, morale and numbers which an attacking force requires in order to overcome an enemy in positions of static defence. The whole Guards Brigade needed, and indeed expected, a period of rest far removed from the battlefields; but when the order came for another effort, they accepted it without question. 1943

3

THE BATTLES OF MONTE CAMINO

Importance and topography of Monte Camino—Night advance up Bareback Ridge—The highest point remains in enemy hands—Four days of very great hardship—Two Grenadier companies cut off—Situation temporarily restored—The Battalion withdrawn and Monte Camino later abandoned to the enemy—Rest period at Caserta—Second attempt to capture Monte Camino—201st Guards Brigade in reserve—The Queen's capture the mountain—Exploitation of this success by the Grenadiers towards Rocca d'Evandro—Significance of the two battles

The name of Monte Camino became known to the troops at the end of October, mentioned casually at first as "another hill," something large but vague, darkening the map, but lying beyond the skyline. During the next week, as the line edged up to the Garigliano River, Camino swung clearly into view, and assumed from its forbidding size, and the fact that it happened to be the next obvious barrier, a prominence which increased day by day. It has now taken its place with Salerno, Anzio and Cassino as one of the great sites of the Italian campaign. "Murder Mountain," it was later called: and the French Moroccan troops, casting round for some symbolic site where they might erect a memorial to their British Allies, chose, very properly, Monte Camino. Close to its summit, set among the rocks where the Grenadiers made their historic stand, there rests a marble slab, inscribed with these words:

AUX COMBATTANTS BRITANNIQUES
TOMBES GLORIEUSEMENT AU MONTE CAMINO
NOVEMBRE—DECEMBRE 1943
LES GOUMS MAROCAINS

1943 At first sight Camino seemed to differ little from the mass of grey hills by which it was surrounded, and at a later date the Allied convoys on their way to Rome would circle its eastern slopes without so much as a glance at its snow-clad summit. It is little more than three hundred and thirty feet higher than Point 860, but what distinguishes it from its neighbours is not so much its height as its mass. It fills completely, with its outlying spurs and gullies, the seven-mile gap between the Naples road and the Garigliano. As such, it became a bastion in the German defence system. It is still not certain whether Kesselring had intended Camino to form part of his winter line, or whether it was to be merely a final testing ground before he withdrew to Cassino. What is certain is that the Allies hugely under-estimated the strength in which it would be held. A single brigade, the 201st Guards Brigade, was given the task of forcing this barrier; and of that Brigade a single battalion, the 6th Grenadiers, was all that could be spared for the assault on the summit of Camino itself. In the end, a month later, it required the deployment of an entire Corps to complete the task which the three battalions had come within measure of accomplishing unaided.

Nov. 5 To the officers making their first reconnaissance from a point four miles to the south Camino stood out against the sky as a long, wavering ridge terminated by a pyramidical hill. The plain at their feet was filled with orchards and vineyards, little farms and villages, and beyond them rose a steep, sharp spur leading directly to the western end of Camino. It was the obvious approach, indeed the only approach, for the southern face of the massif was almost precipitous. *See inset Map p.442* They christened it (though not in such polite terms) "Bareback Ridge." At the top of Bareback Ridge, where it began to level out into the main crest, was Point 727. On the crest itself there were three places of importance: at its western end, Point 615; in the centre, immediately beyond 727, the twin humps forming Point 819; and on the extreme right, the pyramidical summit of the whole mountain, which became known as Monastery Hill, from a small chapel on the very peak. With four companies it was impossible to capture each one of these prominent points, and Colonel Kingsmill decided to concentrate on three of them, Points 727, 615 and 819. Once these were in our hands it was intended to strike with the other battalions over the western shoulder down to the Garigliano Valley, so cutting the German supply route to Monastery Hill and forcing their withdrawal from the entire position. The Coldstream were to clear the immediate approaches to Bareback Ridge, allowing the Grenadiers a clean start for their sterner task. The Scots Guards were kept in reserve for the second phase.

The first misfortune which befell the 6th Battalion was the loss of 1943
their Commanding Officer just before the battle started. Colonel Kingsmill was returning with the orders to his own headquarters, when his jeep overturned down a steep slope, and though uninjured he was so badly shaken that he was persuaded to hand over the command of the Battalion to his Second-in-Command, Major Sir Hugh Cholmeley, D.S.O.

The Grenadiers watched the beginning of the Coldstream attack Nov. 6
from a group of shattered villages close behind. They could clearly see the movement of the Coldstream platoons, the tracer bullets flying to and fro, the arching smoke bombs and burst of shells. But they could also see, as dusk passed into night, that the Coldstream were not likely to complete their task up to schedule, and rather than waste valuable hours of darkness Major Sir Hugh Cholmeley decided to launch his own Battalion without further delay. Just before midnight the Grenadiers began their long climb up Bareback Ridge. In front there was a battle patrol led by Lieut. W. J. Hackett-Pain, followed by the four rifle companies strung out in a long column. The hillside was lit up by huge brushwood fires, ignited either accidentally by smoke shells or intentionally by the Germans, and the Battalion were obliged to hug the sheltered side of the ridge in order to avoid the fire of the machine guns which the Coldstream had not yet eliminated. They did not lose many casualties during this ascent. It was more a test of physical endurance. Their rate of progress was no more than five hundred yards in an hour, as the slope was a glacis of huge boulders, and the men's feet were continually catching in the crevices or slipping backwards on the loose shale. The artillery barrage which was to have helped them to gain their final objective still seemed very remote, and they knew that its effect was being largely wasted. It was already
within half an hour of first light when the leading company reached Nov. 7
Point 727, having been driven almost to desperation by false crest after false crest; the men behind them, already very exhausted, knew that they would have to face the final assault in broad daylight.

There was a four-hundred-yard stretch of bare ground lying in front of Point 819. No other method was possible than to form up on its southern edge and summon up all their reserves of strength for a dash across the open. No. 2 Company (Capt. R. M. C. Howard, D.S.O.) carried this out with great success, while No. 3 Company (Major E. T. Cook) took advantage of a belt of trees to attack from another direction. The Germans continued to fire until the last moment, and then fled, pursued down the far slope by our men until they were recalled by Capt. Howard to consolidate on the summit. Among the officers, Lieut. B. Henshaw was shot through the chest early on, and Lieut.

1943 H. P. G. Cholmondeley, who had shown outstanding courage at this critical moment, was also killed.

In spite of their gains, the position was already one which gave rise to great uneasiness. The enemy had not withdrawn far, and seemed determined to regain what they had lost. Point 727 was held firmly enough by Nos. 1 and 4 Companies, but Point 819 was a far larger feature than it had appeared from a distance, and it was as much as Nos. 2 and 3 Companies could do to hold their own without undertaking further action. Point 615 was not yet captured, and there were no troops to spare for it; while Monastery Hill, which had never been one of the objectives, dominated the entire position from close quarters. The German counter-attacks did not begin immediately, but from their positions of superior observation they began to rake systematically with mortar and machine-gun fire every hillock which they had surrendered earlier that morning. Capt. Howard, for instance, recalls that, having laid down his equipment and walked a few yards away, he turned round to see it spattered with bullets from Monastery Hill; while Capt. Whatman found himself crouching against the front wall of his stone sangar while bullets ricocheted off the back wall. Even on Point 727 it would take an hour to crawl the four hundred yards between No. 1 Company and Battalion Headquarters. This was not all. The Germans soon discovered the gap—the "Saucer"—which existed between the two halves of the Battalion, and crept round with battle patrols in darkness or under cover of mist to attack isolated platoons from every direction, and interrupt the porterage of supplies.

Nov. 8 The headquarters of No. 3 Company and a complete platoon of No. 2 Company were overrun, and although on the second night Lieut. C. V. I. Snell managed to make his way through with food and ammunition, the two forward companies were virtually cut off for three days, and fed off their emergency rations and those taken from the bodies of the dead. The seriously wounded were obliged to remain on the hill-top, where twelve of them died of exposure, while the walking wounded had the choice of staying in these abominable conditions or running the gauntlet of German patrols in the Saucer. Most trying of all was the weather. There was a bitter tearing wind from the east which at times grew to such violence that movement was possible only on all-fours; few had more than gas-capes to protect them from the cold, and those who took their boots off could not replace them in the morning, for their feet had swollen to twice the normal size. To this were added hail and rain storms almost without pause, and the few trees which might have given the men some protection were torn to

Nov. 9 ribbons by shells and bullets. On the third day, as though every resource of man and Nature was combining to complete their utter distress, there was a small earthquake.

The scene farther back has been well described by a British war correspondent: * 1943

"An earthen track zigzagged up the sheer face of the mountain to the Monastery. There were no trees, only coarse grass, and so the enemy on top had a perfect field of fire. Rainwater was cascading down the track at such a pace that it unseated boulders and loose rocks, and these went careering to the bottom. There were two processions on the track, one going up and the other coming down, and the whole of this moving human frieze was under shell fire. You could see it all from the bottom if you arched your neck. The upward travellers were mostly Italian mule teams carrying blankets and boxes of ammunition. Then there were single soldiers, each one with a heavy box of rations on his back, and they were bent double by the incline. As they lifted themselves upwards step by step their faces were only a few inches from the mud. . . .

"The stretcher-bearers were on the downward journey, eight men to a stretcher. They carried the stretchers on their shoulders and they slithered rather than walked. Often they dislodged a boulder, and the whole party wobbled uneasily. For the most part the patients, their blood mixing with the pools of water on the canvas stretchers, would be held at an angle just short of over-balancing.

"Every minute or two a shell came down. They hit first on one side of the track, then the other, then in the angles of the sharp bends. Whenever a shell hit the track itself a gap would open up in the procession. At first this gap was filled with smoke. Then as the smoke cleared you would see the fallen men scattered about on the steep grass and the mules stampeding."

By the fourth day the situation on Point 819 was growing desperate. **Nov. 10** A company of Scots Guards under Capt. Rathbone (who was killed soon after his arrival) had fought their way through on the previous evening to join Nos. 2 and 3 Companies of the Grenadiers, but these three companies in all did not amount to more than a hundred men, and the Saucer was still closed behind them. In No. 2 Company Capt. R. M. C. Howard, D.S.O., had been three times wounded, in the arm and through both legs, but remained with his men to inspire them with fresh confidence; Lieut. J. R. S. Wace was badly wounded in the arm; and the third officer, Lieut. J. R. A. Brocklebank, was killed when he sat up to fire at a German patrol twenty yards away. In No. 3 Company Major E. T. Cook had died of his wounds on the hill-top. Capt. J. D. Whatman, M.C., assumed command of the whole force, and it was largely due to this officer that the Grenadiers were still able to hold the enemy at bay. In the rear companies Lieuts. O. M. Sainsbury and B. A. F. Hervey-Bathurst were both wounded.

The Germans now began to counter-attack in earnest. The isolated companies reported on the wireless that "the enemy are closing in all

*"Eclipse," by Alan Moorehead. Quoted by permission of the author.

1943 round and we think the end seems near," for they were so low in ammunition and the Germans were so close that a single determined rush, regardless of casualties, might at any moment have overwhelmed the little group of slit trenches and sangars. "Many slit trenches," wrote an eye-witness, "were manned by dead, propped up with their steel helmets and weapons." They were saved not only by their own vigilance and endurance (yet who could have blamed them if after all these days their spirit had weakened?) but by the support of the artillery and mortars behind them. The shells were screaming overhead to burst less than a hundred yards away, and sometimes one or two would fall short among our own men. A German officer stood up to shout, in English, that further resistance was useless: he was answered by a fusillade of fire, and this incident marked the end of the German attacks on the final, hardest day of all.

That night the Grenadiers were withdrawn from Point 819, and the Coldstream Guards relieved their other companies on Point 727. There were two outstanding difficulties to be solved before this withdrawal could take place. The first was to warn the outlying companies of the plan without at the same time betraying it to the enemy. Major Cholmeley was unwilling to risk passing so vital a message over the wireless, and he entrusted it to Capt. D. A. S. Adair to carry verbally to Capt. Whatman. Capt. Adair was successful in crossing the Saucer, and, having delivered his message, he started back from Point 819 with a few Guardsmen, carrying between them Capt. Howard, who was the most seriously wounded of all those who survived. They had not gone many yards when they were intercepted by a German patrol and forced to return to 819. Capt. Adair set off to deal with the patrol before making another attempt to evacuate Capt. Howard, and was never seen alive again. For a long time hope was not abandoned that he had been taken prisoner; but his body was found, and unmistakably identified, when the battlefield was searched again more than a year later. He was the son of Major-General Adair, Commander of the Guards Armoured Division.

The second difficulty was to secure and hold open a corridor for the withdrawal of the isolated companies. Although two companies of the Scots Guards were now established on the eastern flank of Camino, they were not in touch with Point 819, for the enemy lay between them. Lieut. Hackett-Pain attempted to clear the Saucer with a patrol from the rear, but could not guarantee that the opening was secure. It was therefore decided that a battalion of the Oxford and Bucks should clear a passage between the Grenadiers and the Scots Guards. At nightfall this attack was successful, and the three companies filed back down the mountain track to the village of Mieli at its foot.

Four hundred and eighty-three Grenadiers had gone up to Camino, 1943
and only two hundred and sixty-three returned. Of the survivors, some
could scarcely move from frost-bite, and others arrived back at Mieli
in a state of such exhaustion that even the prospect of rum, blankets
and a hot meal after all those days of cold and rain and near-starvation
could not rouse them to stir another yard. They slept in the caves and Nov. 12
shells of houses, indifferent to the heavy gunfire around them.

Two days later Camino was abandoned to the enemy. The reasons
for this bitter decision were the strain on the supply system and the
shortage of fresh troops to launch an attack on Monastery Hill,
without which Point 819 was a profitless death-trap. As Brigadier
Gascoigne was discussing the plan for withdrawal an artillery concentration came down on the Grenadiers' Headquarters, wounding him
in the lung and both arms. Lieut.-Colonel Kingsmill, who had returned
that morning, temporarily took over command of the Brigade, and
left Major Sir Hugh Cholmeley once more commanding the Battalion.
It was an inauspicious start to a manœuvre which many viewed with
greater misgivings than the original ascent of the mountain. If the
enemy had obtained information of this withdrawal they could have
sealed the paths by shell fire and simultaneously attacked. They did
neither. On a dark and stormy night the long columns of the Brigade Nov. 14
filed past the Grenadier check point in silence and without casualties,
and for two days afterwards the enemy continued to bombard the
empty trenches. This was poor consolation for the men who had fruit-
lessly endured such great hardship, who had left behind them on that
hill-top the bodies of so many friends. They had come so near to
success: disappointment and weariness were the only outcome, and
the knowledge that they had done their best was their only reward.

They drove back to Caserta, to those same barracks where they had Nov. 16
lodged before the crossing of the Volturno. The Americans made
them very welcome (Caserta was now the Allied Force Headquarters
for the whole of Italy), and after the Battalion were well rested they
refreshed themselves with entertainment locally and in the rest camps Nov. 24
of the Sorrento Peninsula. On the 24th of November, having paraded
before General Mark Clark, they returned to the front-line zone and
prepared to make a second attempt to capture Monte Camino.

This time the 201st Guards Brigade were not alone. The immediate
objective was unchanged—to capture Camino and clear the left bank
of the Garigliano—but to accomplish it two British divisions were
deployed in the direct attack, and an American division operated up
the road on their right flank. Camino itself lay entirely within the
British sector, and its nodal points, Monastery Hill and Point 819,

1943 were to be captured by the Queen's Brigade of the 56th Division. The 201st Guards Brigade were held back for exploitation over the left shoulder of the mountain in the direction of Rocca d'Evandro. This meant, in effect, that, although the hardest fighting was left to fresher troops, the Guardsmen were obliged to await the success of the Queen's Regiment before their own operation could start; and in order to take immediate advantage of the capture of Camino they must lie very close behind the fighting zone. Accordingly, they were moved
Dec. 4 up to the base of Point 727, and while the Queen's fought among those familiar rocky knolls, the Guardsmen waited for two days in conditions which were scarcely less unpleasant than those they had experienced three weeks before. The rain was no less drenching, no less unyielding; the cold and the wind as wearying as they had ever been; and, though the companies were shielded by a high cliff from most of the mortar fire (crouching against its foot like sheep in a storm), the German shells struck the cliff-top and toppled boulders on to their place of shelter. They lost several casualties before they had fired a shot themselves. Hardest hit of all was their Brigade Headquarters. Lieut. A. I. Inchbald, the Grenadier Liaison Officer, was wounded and died two days later in a field hospital; and on the same day Brigadier R. B. R. Colvin, D.S.O., who had taken over command only a week previously, narrowly escaped with his life and was evacuated by the medical services. Colonel Kingsmill assumed temporary command of the Brigade, and Major Sir Hugh Cholmeley once again took his place as Commanding Officer of the 6th Grenadiers.

Dec. 6 At their third attempt the 2nd/5th Queen's, to their undying fame, captured Monastery Hill. The Coldstream had already moved up to occupy Point 615. Thus the Camino triangle was at last secured, and the Grenadiers were ordered to take up the pursuit without delay. They advanced in two stages. The first was made by night to a position below that of the Coldstream. Though the first two companies managed to cross the open ground while it was still dark, the tail of the Battalion column, struggling as they were with thirty-five-pound loads and a gale which bit with brutal force into their faces, found themselves in the gathering light exposed on Bareback Ridge to the last shots which the German snipers were able to fire from Monastery Hill. To avoid the wind as much as the bullets, they took to crawling on hands and knees between the rocks, and the whole Battalion assembled behind Point 615 without casualties, but with only a few hours in hand before they were launched towards Rocca.

They had two preliminary objectives, the heads of two spurs which ran down towards the river. The first, the Acquapendola Spur or Point 550, was allotted to No. 3 Company (Major C. Earle); the second,

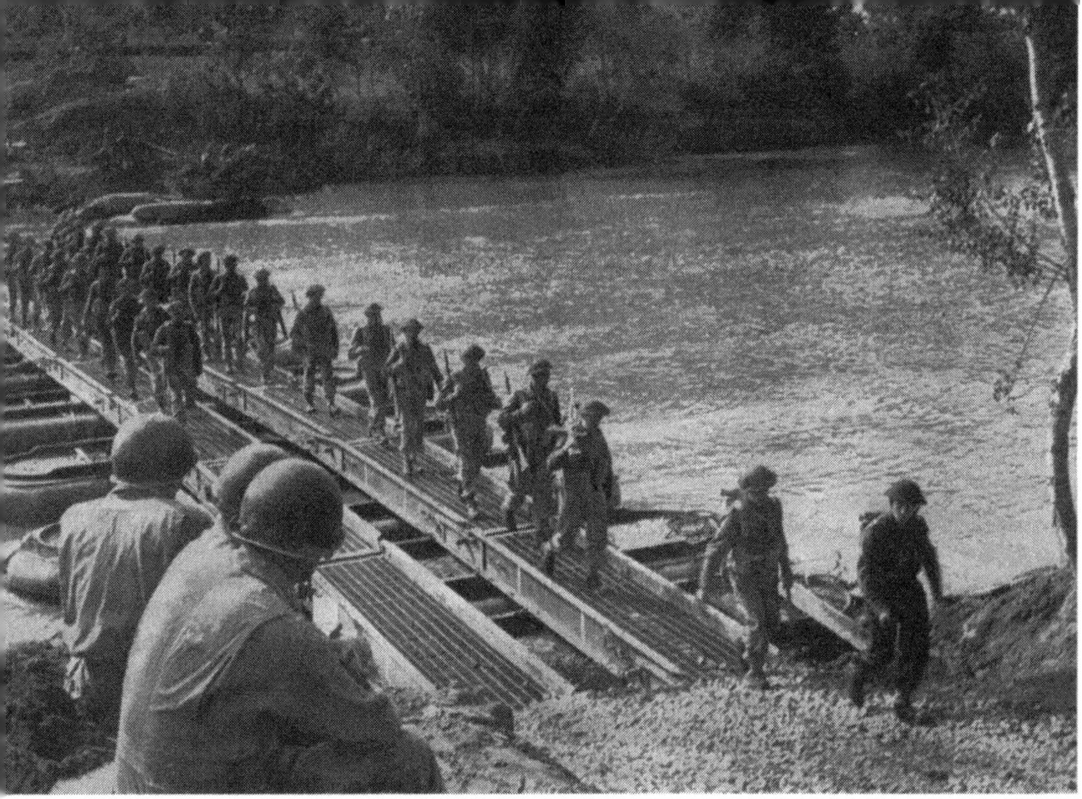

Crown Copyright

Troops of 201st Guards Brigade cross the River Volturno, watched by American Engineers.

Preparing for the assault on Monte Camino. Monastery Hill is the pyramidical peak in the centre background.

Crown Copyright

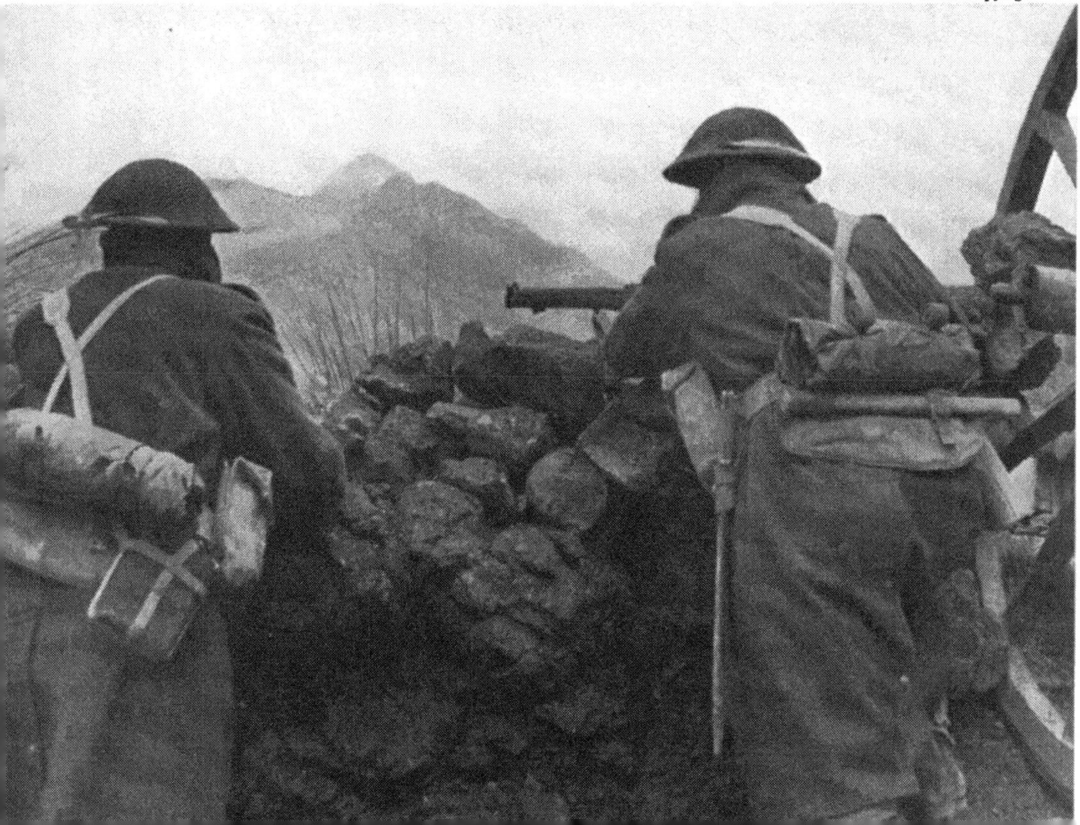

Point 470, to No. 4 Company (Major H. C. Hanbury, M.C.). They 1943 advanced in daylight. It was slow going between the rocks and the thick coppice, and the light-hearted reminiscence of Major Sir Hugh Cholmeley that "I failed to shoot a wood-cock with my revolver that got up at my feet" reflects more the spirit of the Battalion than the atmosphere of that painful advance. It has been thus described by Major P. C. Britten, the commander of No. 1 Company:

> "Somewhere on our flank a sniper was firing with great effect. Then we were spotted, and were chased off the hills by some most unpleasant shells. One landed so close that it bruised my arm with the force of the explosion. John Glyn, who was acting as Adjutant, was wounded. We had the plan and the artillery programme, and there was nothing to do but wait an hour until zero. I gave out the orders and tried to put what cheer I could into my words. At midday the barrage came down, and the party was on. Over the hill we went and down across the slope. Our own shells screamed overhead. . . . We were now miles from anywhere, and not even a path to go back by. Ahead I could see companies getting near their objectives. Could it really be that there were no Germans on our hill? It was terribly tiring, and intensely exciting. The Germans were not long in opening up, and were deadly accurate. However, by this time we were down in the cracks in the rocks, or had built up stone sangars."

There had in fact been no short-range opposition, and Points 550 and 470 were both occupied before dark. In addition to Capt. Glyn, Capt. The Lord Ardee was wounded in the hand and Lieut. P. Addison in the leg. It took eight men twelve hours to carry the latter officer down to the nearest point which even a jeep ambulance could reach.

After the capture of Monastery Hill the Germans still clung tenaciously to the remoter offshots of Monte Camino, among them Rocca d'Evandro itself, and the centre and tail of both the spurs of which the Grenadiers now occupied the upper ends. Between Point 470 and Rocca lay a deep valley which the village overlooked from the top of a hundred-foot cliff, and any advance in this direction, in spite of urgent encouragement from the Divisional staff, who had not seen the physical difficulties, was clearly impossible before the cliff and spurs had been cleared of enemy. The first move was made by Lieut. T. W. Huntington with a patrol of three men. They located a machine-gun post just south of No. 3 Company's position, and, having killed one of the crew, they called on the others to surrender. In reply Lieut. Huntington was shot dead, and his body was later recovered at great risk by Sergt. F. Fletcher. Two further patrols, one from No. 3 Company under Lieut. P. Parr and the other from No. 1 Company under Lieut. G. R. Stokes-Roberts, went down into the valley by night and confirmed what the Battalion had already suspected, that the route to

1943 Rocca from the south was almost impassable to infantry and blocked by a close network of German machine guns.

Dec. 8 The situation remained unchanged for two days. Neither of the forward companies could make any progress down the series of terraces below them. No. 3 Company tried a second time, and failed; and the commander of No. 4 Company, Major Hanbury, was wounded. But meanwhile, on either flank of the Grenadiers, Allied advances were beginning to have their effect. On their left, nearest the Garigliano, the Scots Guards had come up almost level with them; and on their right the Americans were pressing up the main valley east of Camino, and the remainder of the 56th Division were fighting their way along the ridge leading north-west from Point 819 towards Rocca.

Dec. 9 The 9th of December, more than a month after the Camino operations had started, saw the end of the story. Major Earle led No. 3 Company down the Acquapendola Spur, overcoming one after another three German machine-gun nests lying at the bottom of the twenty-foot terraces, and Lieut. Parr stalked and knocked out a fourth. The Germans evacuated the whole position that night. Two Grenadier patrols entered Rocca almost simultaneously from different sides, and found it abandoned. They occupied Rocca Castle, whose thick walls were impregnable against German shell fire, and in spite of the ruins around them and the stench of decaying bodies they could relax in comparative comfort and security.

Two letters were found in Rocca d'Evandro, left behind by some German soldiers in a mood of bitterness or sentiment. The first read: "When the Russians occupy Europe, and the Americans England, what happens to you then?" And the second: "Much loves from a German soldier. When is the war lost for yourselves? Good-bye, Tommy."

Good-bye, Tommy. So they, too, felt that a great episode had just closed. The two Battles of Monte Camino were soon to be overshadowed by more tremendous events. Cassino was more dramatic, Anzio more adventurous. But Camino remains in the minds of those who fought among its rocks as a memory which will never be blurred. One of them will tell you of the wind, and the pools of water streaked with blood; another of the unbearable tension of those nights on Point 819 when they knew not in which direction to hold their rifles in readiness, for the enemy were all around them; while to a third the name "Camino" will recall how he toiled up the goat track night after night with wet loads of food and ammunition, and the shells tore into the hillside at his feet. It is not true to say that the first Battle of Camino was typical of the fighting in the Apennines, for it combined all the worst elements of all battles: extreme danger, intolerable weather, a

position inferior to the enemy's, long duration, and, at first, failure 1943
To the Grenadiers Camino seemed so tragic because there was so little to show for all that they had suffered, even after the second battle had at last been rewarded by success. No town was captured as a result, no river crossed, no clean break made in the German line. The enemy were forced back no more than a mile or two to another mountain, and these mountains stretched endlessly up the length of Italy. How, they felt, would it ever end? A clear answer to that question can now be given. The Germans were defeated by the attrition of countless battles, of which Camino remains a striking example; by their losses in dead and prisoners; by the exhaustion of those who survived and the wastage of their war material; by their growing despondency in continual defeat, matched by the increasing confidence of the Allied troops. In such a cause, no soldier's life is thrown away in vain.

4

THE GARIGLIANO

The Brigade in position on the Gulf of Gaeta on the extreme left of the Allied line—The Battle of Trimonsuoli—Winter deadlock

The 6th Battalion's story is almost finished. They had three months more of service in the field, and one more major battle, before they were withdrawn from Italy a year after they had first engaged the enemy in the Battle of the Horseshoe. These final months, December, 1943, to February, 1944, were spent in static positions near the mouth of the River Garigliano, on the extreme left of the Allied line overlooking the Gulf of Gaeta. When the Battalion first took over this new Dec. 17
sector there was no Allied bridgehead north of the river, and German patrols were still active on the southern bank, penetrating as far into the plain as Brigade Headquarters, cutting telephone wires, waylaying despatch riders, and harassing by every possible device the Allied preparations for crossing the Garigliano. Yet compared to the battlefield they had just left it was a quiet sector. The weather had temporarily improved, and though the seaside meadows were waterlogged and overlooked by the German-occupied hills to the north, the Battalion were grateful for the cover of a few shattered farmhouses
and the regular delivery of their supplies. They spent Christmas in the Dec. 25
line, borrowed a church from a Catholic priest (who was much disturbed by the reaction of his congregation to its use for a Protestant service), and in the afternoon started to play a game of football until it was spotted by the Germans and broken up by shell fire. Having

1944 taken part, in a subsidiary role, in a feint attack across the river, the Battalion were withdrawn for their first period of relief in the opening **Jan. 4** days of the New Year. They rested near Aversa.

They did not return to the front for nearly three weeks. By this time a shallow bridgehead had been gained on the north bank of the Garig- **Jan. 20** *See Map* p. 416 liano, but so shallow was it that the river crossing was under constant observation, and the bridge was kept permanently blanketed by a smoke screen. The front line was scarcely four hundred yards north of the river, half-way up the first foot-hills which led to the massive cliffs of the Aurunci Mountains, and the Grenadiers at Trimonsuoli led a troglodyte existence in slit trenches dug between the olive trees and rocky outcrops. The shell and mortar fire was unceasing. In five days seven other ranks had been killed and forty-three wounded; while among the officers Lieut. G. R. Stokes-Roberts, who had survived so many more critical situations, was killed by a mortar bomb, and two company commanders, Capt. M. W. Lowry-Corry (No. 2 Company) and Major P. C. Britten (No. 1 Company), and one other officer, Lieut. A. J. Savill, had all been wounded.

Rather than remain in a position of such inferiority, the Brigade attacked (it was their last battle) in order to gain the crest of the lower ridge. The Coldstream were operating on the left flank, and the Grenadiers on their right were ordered to capture two low hills, separated by an orange grove, eight hundred yards ahead of their present line. According to the plan, the hills were to have been captured in the evening, allowing them time to spend the night in consolidation, and be prepared to resist a counter-attack at dawn. It worked out very differently. **Jan. 29** No sooner had the right-hand company (Major H. C. Hanbury, M.C.) moved forward from their trenches than they were caught in a crippling barrage, and only twelve men arrived at the foot of the objective itself. On the left No. 3 Company (Major E. Penn, M.C.) had better fortune at the start, but on approaching their hill they heard the clicking of German rifle bolts, and the platoon commanders had time only to shout "Down!" before the first volleys crashed over their heads. Both companies were now held up and much weakened: it was already extremely dark, and the two reserve companies were not only beyond striking distance but had never seen the ground in daylight. Nevertheless, Colonel Kingsmill decided that both reserve companies must be employed if the hills were to be captured before daylight, and they began to feel their way forward in the darkness, guided by wireless messages from behind and the sound of firing from in front. After many hours of searching, No. 2 Company (Capt. M. W. Grazebrook, M.C.) linked up with No. 4 Company (Major Hanbury) just as dawn was breaking, and found that they had

ten minutes in which to form up for the attack. An artillery barrage **1944**
came down at exactly the right place and time, and the two companies
surged up the hill together as soon as the shell fire had ceased. It was
a very successful attack, in which Lieuts. V. E. Naylor-Leyland and
R. O. H. Crewdson took leading parts. They cleared the hill in hand-
to-hand fighting, taking thirty-seven prisoners. Meanwhile, on the **Jan. 30**
other flank, Nos. 1 and 3 Companies had also joined forces, and by
much the same methods, led by Lieuts. H. W. Freeman-Attwood and
the Master of Saltoun, they captured the other hill. The total number
of prisoners was seventy-eight, and twelve German machine guns were
taken in addition. On our own side thirty-five Grenadiers were killed
and one hundred and thirteen wounded. Among them were Lieut.
O. M. Sainsbury, who was killed, and Major Hanbury, Capt. Grazebrook and Lieut. Crewdson, who were all wounded, the last-named
for the second time that day. The Germans did not fail to launch their
usual counter-attack during the afternoon. It was beaten off by a
combination of artillery fire and close shooting by the Grenadiers.
When the gun barrels grew too hot for further firing a fighting patrol
was led to the end of the farther ridge by Lieut. R. P. Parr, and there
he, too, after successfully beating back the Germans, was killed. "We
managed to keep them off," wrote Capt. Grazebrook with masterly
understatement, "as it is very boring to have to take a thing like that
twice."

After another short period of rest the Grenadiers returned to **Feb. 5**
relieve the Scots Guards on the left of their original positions, and
remained for another ten days within the Garigliano bridgehead, in
positions of great discomfort. The rain had now begun to fall in
earnest. The advance was halted by the weather, the strength of the
natural physical barriers ahead, the weariness of our own troops, and
the determination of the Germans. The Anzio experiment had failed:
Cassino had already withstood two heavy attacks. On the lower
reaches of the Garigliano there was even less prospect of advancing,
and the 1st Guards Brigade, who had now arrived in Italy, were
engaged five miles farther north in clinging to our small lodgement in
the Aurunci Mountains. The 6th Grenadiers spent many cold and
weary days overlooking Gaeta Bay, watching the cruisers shelling the
enemy coastline, laying wire and mines, and patrolling in and out of
olive groves in No Man's Land. In this way they lost their last casualties of the war. Lieut. J. E. Renton was badly wounded, and Lieut. **Feb. 9**
The Master of Saltoun was trapped in a minefield while on patrol.*

*The fate of the Master of Saltoun has never been discovered, and he is the only Grenadier officer who remains (1948) posted as "Missing." Italian civilians said that they had seen him being carried away wounded back to the German post, but thereafter news of him ceased.

1944 Feb. 18- Mar. 5 Their final three weeks in the line were marked by no very unusual incident. The Battalion Headquarters was in the village of Minturno, and the companies fanned out over the rocky hillocks in front of it. A few doors and shutters were blown off by shell fire, but these crumbling Italian villages were stronger than they looked, and the tenfold retaliation by the British gunners discouraged the Germans from wasting what little ammunition they had. A Grenadier officer has well expressed the atmosphere of Minturno in these lines:

. . . Time to start,
And with five anxious men behind me I will creep
Full of cold fear down the old muddy track
Past the burned tank outside the town, through the wet
Vineyard where our forward sentries stay, wondering if we'll come back.

. . . . . .

A peak-capped figure rises, falls:
Hell wakes the night.
A wounded German calls.
Now forward! End the fight
And back!
Back to a dim light in Minturno;
A candle flickering on a cellar floor,
Glazed eyes, tired faces, sleeping shapes, signallers making tea,
A weary Major, murmuring over maps and message forms, and we,
Pushing aside the muddy blanket cov'ring the door
Are now at home again, out of the night's inferno.

5

THE DISBANDMENT OF THE 6TH BATTALION

Mar. 7 After their final relief by an American battalion the 6th Grenadiers returned to good billets at Piano di Sorrento, ten miles south of Naples. Their arrival coincided with the return of the 5th Battalion from Anzio, and the two Battalions spent the next few days in each other's welcome company, refreshing themselves with the many attractions of the Bay of Naples, and dodging as best they could the cloud of lava dust which spread over the camps from the erupting crater of Vesuvius.

They also had a more serious purpose. It had long been realized **1944**
that the supply of reinforcements to the Grenadier Regiment was not sufficient to maintain six battalions in the field, and now that the invasion of North-West Europe was not far off it was decided to remove one battalion from active operations. The 6th were the youngest in years, though not in experience. Their veterans were to return to England, and the remainder reinforced the 5th Battalion and provided
a pool of reserves. Accordingly, seventeen officers and nearly four **Mar. 13**
hundred other ranks were transferred from the 6th to the 5th Battalion, a further two hundred went to the I.R.T.D.* (which was commanded by a Grenadier, Lieut.-Colonel G. C. Harcourt-Vernon, D.S.O., O.B.E., M.C.), and not more than eight officers and a hundred other ranks remained for the homeward journey.

Thus it was at Sorrento that the historical 6th Battalion were properly dissolved, and though their name lingered on for nine months more in a variety of functions, they never again went into battle.

The nucleus, still under the command of Lieut.-Colonel Kingsmill, **April 11-22**
sailed from Naples to England. They were welcomed at Windsor by their Colonel, Her Royal Highness Princess Elizabeth, and at the beginning of May the veterans of Mareth and Camino mounted the King's Guard at Buckingham Palace. The Battalion, still little more than a skeleton of their proper strength, were then sent up to Wilton Camp at Hawick in Scotland. Here they were transformed into a cadre battalion (though they still retained their name), and under the command of Lieut.-Colonel R. H. Bushman they began to train as Guardsmen a large number of men who had been serving with the Royal Air
Force and the Royal Air Force Regiment. This duty fully occupied **June-Dec.**
the summer and autumn months, and by November the intake was considered sufficiently trained to embark for service overseas. Some of the Grenadier officers went with them, but the majority were dispersed among the other battalions of the Regiment, and the few men who remained joined the Training Battalion. On the 4th of December,
1944, the Adjutant, Captain R. C. Rowan, declared the 6th Battalion **Dec. 4**
formally disbanded.

*Infantry Reinforcement Training Depot.

CHAPTER VI

THE ANZIO BEACH-HEAD

5TH BATTALION

1

THE LANDING

The Battalion cross from Africa to Italy—Strategy behind the landings at Anzio—Allied order of battle—The expedition sails in great secrecy from the Bay of Naples—Landings on 22nd January, 1944, almost unopposed—Irritating delays before the advance inland begins

1943 THERE are some phases of a campaign which are no more than a chain of small incidents, dully repetitive, and startling only in their cumulative results: there are other phases which are complete in themselves, lengths snipped off, as it were, from the ribbon of history, which strike the imagination not because so much was achieved but because so much was aimed at. When a great deal is at stake, and failure or success depends upon a few men, war is raised from the level of mere operations to the level of drama. Such, for the 5th Battalion Grenadier Guards, was Anzio.

They saw the beginning but not the close of that campaign. They landed in the beach-head on the first day close behind the assault troops, remained there for six weeks, and were then withdrawn to Naples with the remainder of the 24th Guards Brigade because they were too weakened by casualties to sustain another battle. To narrow down still further the period of their main exertion, it should be realized that during those six weeks the Grenadiers were actively engaged for little more than a fortnight—from the 25th of January to the 10th of February: in that time the Battalion lost twenty-nine officers out of their normal establishment of thirty-five, and five hundred and seventy-seven other ranks out of the eight hundred which compose a battalion's complement at any given time. These figures give some indication of the violence of the opening stages of the Anzio campaign. What they do not show is the amazing ebb and flow in the fortunes of both the Germans and the Allies: "On one day," wrote a Grenadier, "we would be in high spirits and boast that we would be the first to enter Rome; on the next we would be speculating on the 1943 chances of a successful re-embarkation from the beaches." It is this fluctuation which gives the Anzio story its peculiar fascination.

It is first necessary to describe briefly the stages by which the 24th Guards Brigade became involved in the Anzio operations. They had sailed with the 1st Division from Bizerta to Taranto in Southern Italy **Dec. 4** at the end of 1943. They moved up the heel of Italy in slow stages to Canosa, a scruffy, off-white town in Apulia, more than a hundred miles behind the Eighth Army's front, and were encamped nine hundred feet above sea-level between the main snow-capped ridges of the **Dec. 8-31** Central Apennines and the sea. There was, as usual, a succession of rumours about their future destination, and one definite order: for a period of four days on either side of Christmas the Division made active preparations to relieve the 8th Indian Division in a sector of the line on the Adriatic coast. This order was cancelled for a reason which was then known only to the Brigade Commander (Brigadier A. S. P. Murray, Grenadier Guards), and on the first day of the New Year the **1944** advance parties moved westwards across the whole width of the Italian peninsula to the neighbourhood of Salerno. They were fol- **Jan. 3** lowed by the entire Brigade two days later. The Grenadiers were billeted in a series of macaroni factories and private villas round Gragnano, a small town wedged into the mountains of the Sorrento Peninsula, about three miles from the sea and overlooking the Bay of Naples.

The reason for this move was that the Division had been earmarked for the Allied landings at Anzio (Operation "Shingle"). It was explained in detail to the Commanding Officer and company commanders on the 11th of January, and to the men on the day of embarkation. The objects and plan of this new enterprise were as follows: *See Map p.* **442**

The advance of both the Eighth and Fifth Armies had been brought to a halt, the former on the line of the Sangro River, the latter on the Garigliano. Cassino had become the keystone and the symbol of the desperate German resistance from sea to sea. One or two isolated mountain-peaks could perhaps still be captured by the deployment of an entire division, but beyond them were other peaks no less formidable, and while the Germans used this respite to prepare reserve lines far in rear of the present front, our own men were already very tired, and some dispirited. A new method of attack was required to regain mobility. Tanks were of little use in the mountains, the infantry were too closely matched by their opponents to be capable of far-reaching successes, and the effect of our artillery and Air Force was steadily diminishing as the Germans constructed stronger and stronger lines

1944 of defence. There remained the sea. Here our naval superiority was unchallenged, and the long double coastline of Italy presented the Germans with a problem of defence which was a constant anxiety to them. They had not the forces to defend every beach: they depended upon a few divisions held centrally in reserve north and south of Rome. They did not expect to defeat any fresh Allied invasion on the waterline: they hoped merely to contain it within a safe perimeter until they had mobilized their strength to throw the Allies back into the sea.

The strategic conception behind the Anzio operations was formulated at a conference held at Tunis on Christmas Day, 1943, at which were present Mr. Churchill and the principal Commanders-in-Chief of the Mediterranean theatre. In his official report, Field-Marshal Sir Henry Maitland Wilson gives this account of the conference: "After General Eisenhower had described the general military situation, Mr. Churchill said that it would be folly to allow the campaign in Italy to drag on and to face the supreme operations against Europe in the spring with the task in Italy half finished. The case for the drive on Rome was not merely the capture of the city, important politically as that might be, but the annihilation of the enemy's army and the securing of a line to give sufficient depth for the protection of the Naples—Foggia area to admit the full development of its port and airfield facilities. Such strategy would speed up the Italian campaign and so facilitate the launching of an attack in early spring against Southern France by releasing personnel and equipment of all branches of the three Services, and would give us additional ports from which to launch the attack over shorter sea routes."*

The neighbourhood of Anzio and Nettuno was chosen by General Alexander for the same reasons as had governed the choice of Salerno four months before. The long, sandy beaches were suitable for the simultaneous landing of a large force; in Anzio there was a port capable of being developed for the necessary amount of supply traffic, and it was within range of aircraft operating from the Naples airfields. Once the force was firmly established ashore it would be within striking distance of Rome, and by a direct advance of twelve miles would be able to cut the main coastal road and railway through the Pontine Marshes on which the Germans depended for the supply of their divisions lying between Cassino and the sea. Assuming that the initial landings were successful, the Germans were expected to react in one of two ways. Either they would panic, evacuate Rome, and

*From the "Report by the Supreme Allied Commander, Mediterranean, to the Combined Chiefs of Staff on Italian Campaign, 8th January, 1944, to 10th May, 1944" (H.M. Stationery Office, 1946).

attempt to withdraw their Cassino—Garigliano forces before their 1944 escape route was finally closed; or they would take the bolder course of withdrawing part of their southern army to assist their reserve divisions in containing the Anzio invasion. To make their task more difficult if they chose this second alternative, it was arranged that the Fifth Army would deliver another assault at Cassino to coincide with the landings at Anzio; and to prevent German reinforcements hurrying down from the north the Allied air forces attacked the marshalling yards at Florence, Pisa, Arezzo and Terni. In either case, the testing time would come within the first few days, for whatever they did, the Germans would have to act quickly. For the Allies the main problem was to decide whether to take every advantage of surprise and send out weak striking columns as soon as they had landed, in order to give an impression of greater strength than they in fact possessed, or whether to establish themselves firmly in a narrow perimeter around Anzio and Nettuno, and wait until a sufficient force had been put ashore to give the subsequent break-out towards Rome every chance of success. This second plan was the one adopted by General J. P. Lucas, the elderly American commander of the entire expedition.

He had at his disposal from the start the VI United States Corps, consisting of three divisions, the 3rd U.S. Division, the 1st U.S. Armoured Division and the 1st British Division, in addition to a force of British Commandos and American Rangers. The 1st British Division (Major-General W. R. C. Penney), with which we shall be chiefly concerned, consisted of the 2nd and 3rd Infantry Brigades and the 24th Guards Brigade. The last-named, unchanged since Africa, had three battalions: the 5th Grenadier Guards (Lieut.-Colonel G. C. Gordon-Lennox, D.S.O.), the 1st Scots Guards and the 1st Irish Guards. On D Day, Saturday, the 22nd of January, 1944, the Rangers *See Map p. 394* and Commandos were to land at Anzio and Nettuno and secure the port, while the two infantry divisions landed north and south of them on the open beaches—the 3rd U.S. Division in the bay south-east of Nettuno and the 2nd Brigade, with the Scots Guards under command, about six miles north of Anzio. The remainder of the 24th Guards Brigade were not to land until a firm beach-head had been secured, and the American armoured division were to follow behind the infantry.

The 5th Grenadiers embarked on four L.C.Is. at Castellamare di **Jan. 20** Stabia, having marched to the docks past the Lieutenant-Colonel of the Regiment, Colonel J. A. Prescott, headed by the Band of the Irish Guards. Lines of ordered ships stretched across the Bay of Naples, glittering in the sun, while Vesuvius, meditating on its eruption a few weeks later, looked down upon them crowned by a plume of drifting

1944 smoke. They remained in the bay all that night, cramped on the narrow benches below decks, and heard, most of them for the first time, the plan and detailed orders for the adventure on which they were embarked. The convoy of two hundred and forty-three ships of all types, preceded by a screen of destroyers, sailed out to sea past
Jan. 21 Capri at 11 o'clock the next morning. They sailed south all that afternoon, to deceive any enemy aircraft or agents watching from the shore; turned west after dark, and finally due north. They had seventy miles to cover before arriving at the rendezvous off Anzio. At dawn
Jan. 22 the Grenadiers lay three miles off their appointed beach. The sky, which was cloudless, was filled by British and American fighters waiting for air opposition which never came, and on shore the Grenadiers could pick out through their field-glasses the indolent movements of the leading British troops. There had been no opposition to their landing. There were a few casualties from beach mines, an 88-mm. gun was firing aimlessly at the beaches from some distance inland, but of troops manning the coastal defences there had been no more than a weak German company and a few Italian gunners spread over the entire width of the invasion shore. The Scots Guards had captured a few prisoners from a German regiment, who claimed that they were there by accident: they had been sent to shoot cattle for food.

The Grenadiers also saw from the decks of their L.C.Is. the features of the ground which they had already studied so carefully on maps and air photographs. They recognized the long, low line of dunes, the scrub and coppice of the immediate hinterland, the neat, white farmhouses of Fascist agriculture, and, a dozen miles beyond, the cultivated slopes of the Laziali Hills, backed by the higher ridges of the Apennines. Rome lay in a hollow, fifteen miles to the north. At 9 a.m. the Grenadiers were called ashore, ferried by dukws from a sand-bar where the bigger craft ran aground, and marched peacefully down the road to a concentration area a few miles north of Anzio. How very different from Salerno! They halted to await orders and developments. To their surprise, the men were allowed to settle down on the wet, sandy soil amongst the scrub, in defensive positions, it is true, but in no danger except from a few random shells which caused the first casualties of the campaign: five Grenadiers were wounded on the beaches. Of ground counter-attack there was no sign. Brigadier Murray was able to drive in his jeep to Anzio, meeting on his way a few bewildered Germans, who fled at his approach, and found the port securely in the possession of the Rangers. The officers of the Brigade had so little to do that they whiled away the time by playing bridge and were able to sleep that night in their pyjamas.

This was all very pleasant, but there was scarcely a man of that

force who did not ask, and who does not still ask, why the situation **1944**
was not immediately exploited. There was something uncanny about the silence, and yet no patrols went forward to find out what was happening beyond the three-mile perimeter which had been secured. Some were reminded of the Suvla Bay landings in 1915, when an opportunity was thrown away for want of a flexible plan. They asked why the American armoured division, or such elements of it as were already ashore, could not be sent out in battle patrols to add to the enemy's confusion, if they did nothing else. It was no longer any secret that the Allies had landed in force at Anzio, and behind the German lines, as we now know, the news had produced a momentary panic. The base establishments and some of the headquarters in Rome were hurriedly evacuated to the north, and preparations were made to withdraw from the Cassino front. There can be little doubt that had the Allies struck boldly on the first or second day they would have gained much of the ground which was won later only in bitter fighting. It might, on the other hand, have exposed them to great risks if the Germans had recovered in time and taken advantage of their wide dispersal to counter-attack down to the very beaches. General Lucas was faced by a tremendous decision: to risk all in the hope of gaining all, or to adhere to the consolidation plan and make sure of his tight perimeter until he built up his strength to strike. The second plan was the one he chose. By midnight on the 22nd, thirty-six thousand and thirty-four men and three thousand and sixty-nine vehicles had been put ashore.

All Saturday and all Sunday the 24th Guards Brigade waited in **Jan. 22-23**
their reserve area close to the beaches, and the other brigades of the 1st Division penetrated no more than three miles inland, meeting one or two small groups of Germans, but not even the skeleton of an
organized line of resistance. On Monday the Brigade were told to send **Jan. 24**
an "armoured reconnaissance" patrol through the perimeter to discover where they would first meet serious trouble, and on the results of this patrol was to depend a more ambitious advance planned for the next day. The patrol was to be sent out by the 5th Grenadiers.

2

THE FACTORY AT CARROCETO

Description of the beach-head area—First Grenadier patrol to Carroceto —The Battalion's advance the next day meets stiffer opposition—Capture of Carroceto and the Factory—German counter-attacks held off with heavy casualties to both sides—A tragic incident—Irish and Scots Guards advance towards Campoleone—The whole of the 1st Division threatened with encirclement—Withdrawal to a shorter line

1944 Before describing their first venture it is necessary to give some account of the country over which they moved, and where the bulk of the fighting developed during the next few weeks. The area in which the Anzio beach-head was contained was for the most part flat and thinly cultivated, penetrated by few roads, and lying just outside the limit of the Pontine Marshes, which Mussolini had so intensively developed before the war. From the air it has today the appearance of a blackened prairie, intersected by a network of water-courses branching inland like the veins of a dying leaf. On the whole, it seems un-Italian, inhospitable, a poor approach to Rome: the woods are low and thin, the farms derelict and scattered, as if only exiles from the rich country to the north and south-east could be found to scratch a living from its soil.* The Appian Way marks the northern boundary of this prairie, separating it from the splendid villas and vegetation of the Colli Laziali or Alban Hills. From the point of view of military operations, three geographical factors are of importance. First, the Laziali gave the Germans observation over the entire area of the beach-head: on clear days it was possible to see the surf breaking on the shore, and almost every movement in the open country between; only the woodlands, the villages, the branching gullies and the few folds in the ground gave any concealment. The German gunners could mark the fall of every shell, and every Allied gun which fired betrayed its position by a stab of naked flame. Secondly, in the British sector the system of wadis (the African term survived among the armies in Italy) and the sodden ground between them made it very difficult for tanks to move off the roads, and the advance of infantry was slow and risky. Thirdly, there was only one road which ran northwards

*Anzio and Nettuno themselves are rich bathing resorts, quite different in character from their immediate hinterland. This contrast seems already to have existed in the days of Imperial Rome, cf. Horace, Odes I, xxxv:

O Diva, gratum quae regis Antium . . .
Te pauper ambit sollicita prece.
(O goddess, thou that rulest pleasant Anzio,
Thee the poor peasant entreats with anxious prayer.)

from Anzio towards the Laziali Hills, piercing like a skewer the entire **1944**
depth of the beach-head. With this road we shall be much concerned. It was straight and tarmacked, running through low scrub and pine woods for the first six miles out of Anzio, then emerging into open, grassy country which began to swell and roll with greater boldness as it rose into the southern foot-hills. At two points the road was crossed by bridges, both of which became key-points in the Anzio fighting. The first bridge, which carried a lateral road a mile beyond the northern edge of the woodland, was known as "The Flyover." The second, two and a half miles farther on, had carried an embanked railway which had long been disused, and whose surface was now nothing more than a cinder track. This became known as "The Embankment." Parallel to the road, and only a few yards to the west of it, ran a light railway which pierced the Flyover and the Embankment by two other bridges, lying side by side with the road bridges.

The Grenadier patrol which had been briefed on the previous evening was given a task which normally would have been carried out by tanks and not by the handful of carriers and anti-tank guns which
were all that they were allowed to employ. They set off at dawn, under **Jan. 24**
the command of Lieut. J. M. Hargreaves, in high spirits, without knowing what they would meet beyond the Flyover, at that time the farthest limit of the beach-head, but in a mood of exploration, determined, if it were possible, to continue to the gates of Rome itself. They *See Plan*
reached the Embankment without incident, passed through into the *p.* **410**
village of Carroceto on the far side, and were immediately fired upon from a large group of buildings a few hundred yards beyond. These buildings formed a Fascist agricultural settlement known as Aprilia, but as the name was not yet marked on any map it was christened by the Grenadiers "The Factory," and the name clung to it throughout the Anzio campaign. The enemy's fire was not heavy, and the carriers were able to race backwards and forwards between the houses of Carroceto, pausing to observe at intervals where the Germans were situated and to return their fire. Lieut. Hargreaves threw a grenade into the entrance to a dug-out, and much to his surprise six Germans immediately tumbled out and surrendered. They were the Battalion's first prisoners. Soon afterwards the opposition began to thicken. Two or three self-propelled guns waddled out from among the Factory buildings, and a company of German infantry were seen to approach from the east, threatening to cut the road south of the Embankment, while Carroceto itself was bombarded with increasing violence. The patrol had done their task. They had pin-pointed the first German road block, and, being unable to make any further progress, they withdrew with their prisoners to the Flyover.

1944 On receipt of this information the Divisional Commander ordered the Guards Brigade to advance in strength the next day, clean up the area of Carroceto, and continue to the junction of roads and railways at Campoleone, which would then become the base for the break-out of the main tank forces. The 5th Grenadiers were to lead the Brigade column. As there was only one road, and the country on either side was impassable to vehicles, the Brigade were forced to advance in a long, slender column, with a striking force at its head and a reserve of all arms following a long way behind. There were only sufficient lorries to carry two Grenadier companies; the remainder of the Battalion and the Brigade were set to march the eight miles from Anzio to the Embankment. Owing to the different speeds of the two halves of the column, there was bound to be some delay before the full strength of the Brigade could be deployed. The mobile column of over ninety vehicles, with the carriers once again in the lead, followed by two
Jan. 25 troops of tanks, began to wind through Anzio at 5 a.m., and once clear of the town hurtled northwards at great speed between woods and fields white with the early morning frost. The reconnaissance of the previous day led them to approach the Embankment with great caution. The road was found to be mined where it passed under the Embankment, and Lieut. Hon. V. S. de R. Canning's platoon deployed all along the top of the railway bed, looking out over Carroceto and the Factory. As Lieut. Hargreaves ran to join them he was killed outright by one of the first shots fired that day. His Commanding Officer wrote of him: "He was one of the most competent and reliable young officers that I ever knew."

The enemy were at once seen to be in greater strength than the day before, and by this time they were wide awake to their danger. They now occupied not only the Factory but the houses of Carroceto village and some farm buildings south of the Embankment and in rear of Lieut. Canning's platoon; one account states that twenty-five German machine guns were directed on to the small strip of the Embankment which we already held. Today's effort was no mere reconnaissance but a determined attempt to enlarge the beach-head, and as a first step it was clearly necessary to capture Carroceto and the Factory. No. 1 Company (Capt. T. A. Gore-Browne) were ordered to attack across the Embankment and seize the village. Lieut. Canning himself was already wounded in the head, and he had lost all his section commanders except one, so that the main burden of the assault fell on Lieut. A. E. P. Needham's platoon, while the others gave him whatever overhead support they could, and one or two tanks cautiously penetrated the bottleneck of the bridge to shoot into every house they could see on the far side. Lieut. Needham's platoon were faced by the

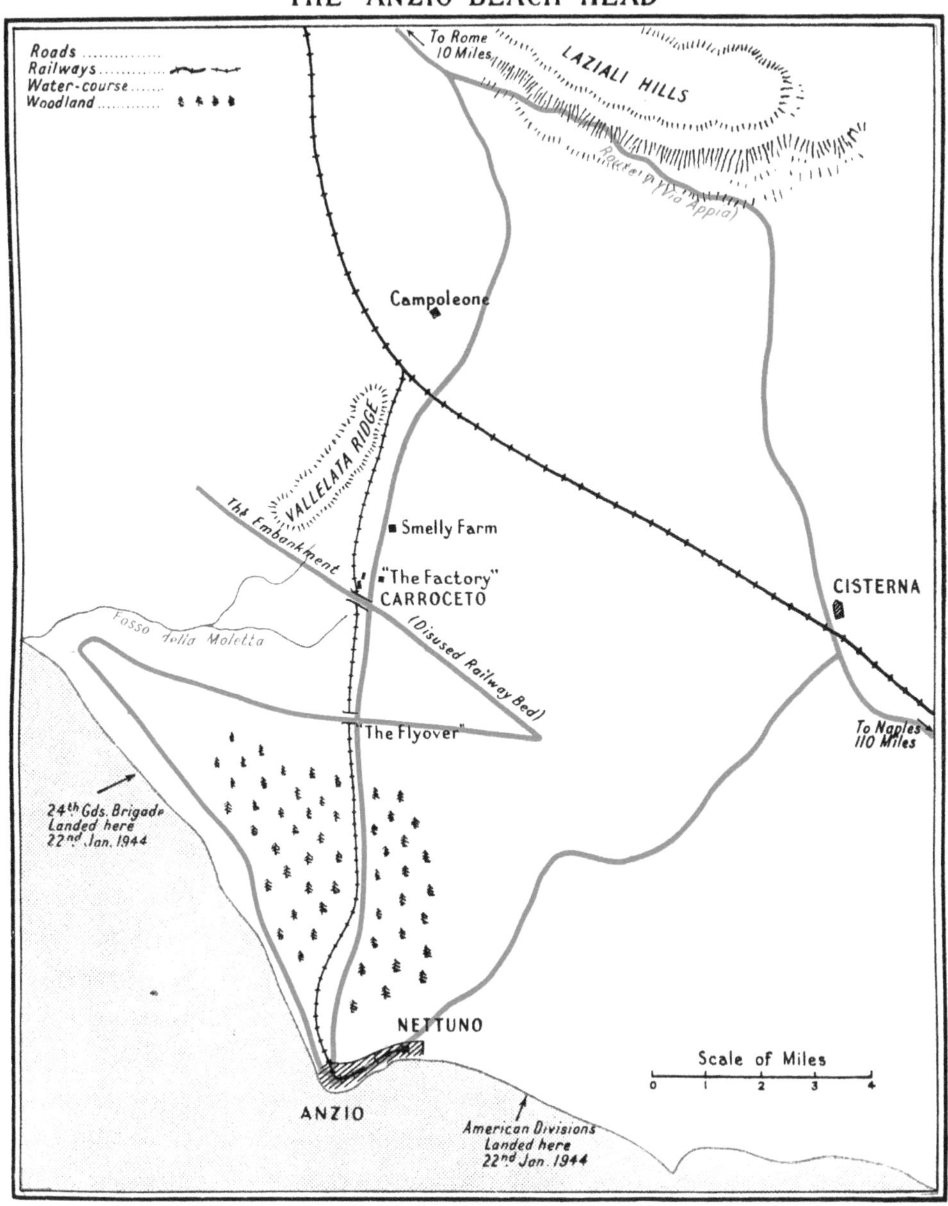

Face page 394

unpleasant necessity of slipping down the enemy side of the Embankment and climbing a wire fence at the bottom before they could dash across the open to seek the doubtful security of Carroceto. They did not suffer many casualties, and still had sufficient strength in hand to clear the buildings one by one. The first few houses and the station were found unoccupied, and when they finally came upon a group of Germans they found them barricaded behind closed shutters and a crowd of terrified Italian civilians cowering in the cellars. This and all the remaining houses were cleared most successfully, and as the surviving Germans made off to the north a German outpost emerged from a culvert in the Embankment under the very feet of the Commanding Officer and surrendered without further argument. Carroceto was in our hands. With how much less cost could it have been captured two days before! 1944

No. 1 Company continued to advance later in the day to occupy without opposition two houses on either side of the kilometre stone M.25, but in doing so they lost their commander, Capt. T. A. Gore-Browne. A shell from one of his own supporting tanks struck a telegraph pole close by, wounding him and several others. Lieut. Needham, who had been lightly grazed in the hand, took over command, and, apart from several alarms, this company remained untroubled for the next twenty-four hours while the main battle raged for the possession of the Factory. To this we must now turn our attention.

During the engagement at Carroceto No. 3 Company had remained with their vehicles some distance down the road, and the marching column had closed up behind them. The road was already under shell fire, and among the early casualties was the Second-in-Command, Major E. J. B. Nelson, M.C., who was wounded in the back by an air-burst. While the men moved farther up to take cover, their officers assembled on the Embankment to plan the attack on the Factory. The plan was simple, the distances involved were short, and the whole objective lay clearly before them. No. 2 Company (Major J. E. Anthony) attacked the east side of the Factory, and No. 4 Company (Major W. E. P. Miller) the west side, advancing simultaneously to clear the massive modern buildings on either side of a central avenue. They started at 2.15 p.m., the sun at their backs and full in the faces of the enemy (a chance which saved the Grenadiers many casualties), and as they crossed the open ground they were covered by a barrage of high-explosive and smoke shells. Although they could not see each other for the smoke, the two companies reached the southern buildings simultaneously and began to work their way through a maze of corridors and courtyards, ferreting out the Germans from the cellars and upper storeys, battering down the doors and scrambling up the stair-

1944 cases, which were already half-choked by rubble. Aprilia was a much larger place than had at first appeared. The buildings, which were two and three storeys high, included a cinema, a school, a garage, a large block of flats, and a church, covering in all about ten acres, and providing innumerable positions from which the Germans continued to snipe for about half an hour. Even when the two leading platoon commanders, Lieuts. A. D. N. Clark and H. R. F. Luttrell, had gained the northern limits of the Factory, there were still many enemy who remained concealed behind them. The first to appear was a party of thirty, who came forward under a white flag from a tower at the north-east corner of the Factory and surrendered to Major Miller; and shortly afterwards, when No. 3 Company came up to search the buildings more thoroughly, Lieut. A. J. Gurney came upon another thirty Germans waiting in a single room. The total number of prisoners, including those taken at Carroceto, amounted to more than a hundred. Their great success had cost the Grenadiers many valuable men. The most severe loss was Major J. E. Anthony, who was killed while leading his company across the open ground. Major Miller was also slightly wounded.

Once the Factory had been finally cleared of enemy, No. 3 Company (Capt. T. S. Hohler, M.C.) was moved to the rising ground on the right flank, while Nos. 2 and 4 Companies remained in possession of the main blocks. With No. 1 Company at M.25, all four companies of the Battalion were now in the front line, leaving them with both flanks open and no local reserves; the Irish Guards moved into Carroceto, and the Scots Guards were not far behind.

It had been a fine day's work, but the Battalion were already weakened by casualties and knew well that they would not be allowed to remain long in undisputed possession of so important a place. Although patrols were sent forward with regularity to search the buildings and ditches ahead, the enemy managed with great skill to creep back unobserved during the night to within two hundred yards
Jan. 26 of the Factory, and to occupy the huts outside its north-eastern corner. Shortly after dawn they opened fire from these new positions with belt after belt of machine-gun bullets, and five self-propelled guns came up to pump shells into the Factory from point-blank range. No infantry assault was actually delivered, and in a moment of panic the Germans abandoned those guns which had not already been destroyed by the Battalion's anti-tank platoon, which accounted for three, or by artillery fire, leaving them to be blown up on the next night. Their infantry were also mopped up in large numbers, seven of them emerging into captivity from a cellar within the Factory itself.

The situation at the huts was more serious. Lying on slightly higher

Air Ministry

The Anzio Beach-head.

The Factory at Carroceto (right centre), looking north-east towards the Laziali Hills.

[*Compare with plan facing page* 410]

ground, and presenting the enemy with a screen behind which they could form up for attack, they were the key to the defence of the whole Factory area. When it was seen that the Germans were in occupation of the huts and actually driving away civilians who had taken refuge there, Colonel Gordon-Lennox ordered No. 3 Company to capture them by an immediate attack. This was carried out successfully by Lieut. D. M. A. Wedderburn's platoon, who found and overcame an enemy force of about twenty-five men. Lieut. Wedderburn was not left in peace for long. At 10.30 a.m. two German tanks advanced directly on the huts, and began cruising about between the wooden walls. As he had no form of anti-tank defence and his platoon was reduced to eight men, Lieut. Wedderburn withdrew, leaving the huts for the second time that morning in German hands. There was no choice but to attack again, and there were no other troops available than No. 3 Company, who by this time were extremely weak, their headquarters having received a direct hit from a shell while the wounded from the first skirmish were being treated inside. Capt. Hohler returned with his new orders, to find that a Guardsman who had been blinded some time previously in the huts had had his leg blown off while lying on a stretcher; another had lost both legs; and several others, including the Company Sergeant-Major, were also wounded. In these conditions it was remarkable how quickly the attack was organized. They crossed the open ground in front of the huts, losing five men killed on the way, and though the tanks withdrew as they approached they turned farther up the road to send a stream of tracer bullets flying through the flimsy walls. Hohler's forearm was shattered, and he found himself left with only one wounded Guardsman out of his entire headquarters. Lieut. Wedderburn, who had so far survived unhurt, took up a position with a single Piat mortar to guard against the expected return of the tanks. 1944

> "The company commander," records the War Diary, "feeling faint, went into a hut and sat down beside some sacks, to be joined by a Guardsman from No. 13 Platoon whose Bren gun had jammed. Suddenly Wedderburn's voice was heard shouting 'Fire! Fire! Fire!' but no explosion followed. (The Piat bomb had not gone more than a few yards.) A few seconds later the turret of a tank appeared a few feet away with its guns trained on the hut. Almost at the same time there was a gurgling noise, and the company commander saw the Bren gunner being led away with a Schmeisser jammed into his ribs, having been caught unaware with his gun in pieces. Capt. Hohler rather carefully laid down, put his steel helmet over his face, turned up his toes, and lay as one dead. The wounded Guardsman was then led off as well, but the ruse worked, and Capt. Hohler was not disturbed by any Germans."

He himself managed to make his way back after some time, but

1944 Lieut. Wedderburn and the bulk of his platoon were captured, and the huts were once again abandoned to the enemy.

In this battle two out of the three platoons of No. 3 Company had been reduced to the size of weak sections, while the third, under Lieut. A. J. Gurney, had been attacked by the tanks in a small farmhouse two hundred yards to the south-east of the huts. They had avoided severe casualties by lying on the floor of the upper storey, only to find that the outside staircase had been blown away, and they escaped with difficulty after nightfall by a rope of sheets. Lieut. Gurney himself was slightly wounded. The position was greatly improved by laying a belt of mines round the open right flank, and in the early afternoon a platoon of No. 2 Company supported by a group of American tanks recaptured the huts, and remained there in undisputed possession.

The Factory had become the crucial point in the whole British sector of the line. Lying not only at the tip of its deepest salient but astride the main north-south road, the Grenadiers had borne the greatest weight of the fighting in the past two days. One of their company commanders had been killed, the other three were all wounded; and soon after dawn on the second day their Commanding Officer, Lieut.-Colonel Gordon-Lennox, was hit in the ankle as he was making a reconnaissance of the ground in front of the Factory; and, though he continued to command the Battalion from a stretcher for the next twenty-four hours, he was evacuated on the next day, handing over the command to Major W. E. P. Miller. Among the rank and file of the Battalion the casualties already amounted to about a hundred and thirty, and many of those who were not actually wounded were much shaken by the fatigue and tension of forty-eight hours' continual fighting, and by a bombardment which exceeded even the legendary intensity of the shell fire on the Tunisian Bou. They had captured and held the Factory and Carroceto, and it was now the turn of other battalions to deepen the beach-head in the direction of Campoleone.

Jan. 27 The American Rangers moved up to give the Grenadiers some welcome protection on their right flank, taking about a hundred prisoners from the area of the huts; and the 1st American Armoured Division, making their first appearance on the battlefield, broadened the salient on the left wherever they were able to work their tanks forward among the branching wadis. In the centre the 1st Scots Guards relieved the pressure on the Factory by advancing as far as the buildings which became known as Smelly Farm. It was, of course, still the intention of the Allied Higher Command to carry out their original plan: to fight through to the Appian Way and capture the Alban Hills. Although there were now sixty-eight thousand eight hundred and eighty-six men, five hundred and eight guns and two hundred and thirty-seven tanks ashore at Anzio, it was clearly no easy matter. Five German divisions had already been identified on this front, and of these two came not from the local reserve or from the Cassino front but from Northern Italy and France, and more might follow.* Surprise and the overwhelming superiority of the first few days were no longer on our side: our only advantage was that no battalions of the 1st Division, with the exception of the 5th Grenadiers, had yet been very heavily engaged. By a process of rapidly leap-frogging one battalion past another it was hoped to throw the Germans off their balance and so recover the conditions of open warfare in which the tanks could be used to their fullest effect. **1944**

The Scots Guards were at Smelly Farm, the Irish Guards in Carroceto, and the Grenadiers, after being relieved in the Factory by a battalion of Sherwood Foresters, were ordered to move up on the left of the Scots Guards in preparation for a big effort on the next day. To settle the details of this plan, Major Miller ordered his company commanders to meet him at Smelly Farm. It was then that the incident occurred which was the greatest single disaster to befall the Grenadiers during the Anzio campaign. **Jan. 28**

The Order Group, consisting of Major C. G. Ford, Capt. R. Freeman and Lieuts. Chaplin, Luttrell, Taylor, Clark, Harding and Gurney, together with three other ranks, left the Embankment in three jeeps to join Major Miller in Smelly Farm. None of them had ever before visited the Scots Guards in their new position, and the turning to Smelly Farm off the main road was more insignificant than appeared from the map. The little convoy of jeeps swept past it unaware, and continued up the road for about three-quarters of a mile until they were halted by a demolished culvert just where the road passed through a small cutting. Realizing then for the first time that they must have come too far, they ordered the drivers to turn the jeeps around, and while they were doing so, grenades and Schmeisser bullets came flying into the group of officers and men. They had driven into the middle of a German outpost. It was impossible to fight back from a position of such disadvantage, unthinkable to surrender, and their only course was to take to their heels and run back down the road. For several hundred yards they were in the direct line of fire. The first to be killed was Lieut. G. R. H. Harding; the next was Major C. G. Ford, who was shot through the back of the head; and the third was Lieut. H. R. F. Luttrell. Lieut. A. J. Gurney was wounded and

*German intentions were greatly clarified by the capture of a German order of the day, signed by Hitler. It read: "The Gustav Line [Cassino front] must be held at all costs for the sake of the political consequences which would follow a completely successful defence. The Fuehrer expects the most bitter struggle for every yard."

1944 taken prisoner, and of the Guardsmen one was killed and both the others wounded and captured. The four remaining officers escaped with their lives only owing to the folly of the German machine gunner, who fired behind instead of in front of them, and to a pall of smoke which blew across the road from a burning jeep. They returned on foot to Smelly Farm to receive their orders. Major Miller felt bound to ask for a postponement of the plan, not so much because of the shortage of officers (though of the thirteen officers in the rifle companies who had landed six days before only four were now left) but because of the difficulty of assembling a new Order Group in time to point out their objectives in the failing light. His view was supported by the Brigade and Divisional Commanders, and the Battalion were withdrawn that night to a reserve area round the Flyover. Not only was the loss of the four officers at this moment and in so wasteful a manner a tragic conclusion to the brilliant four days' fighting in the Factory, but they feared that the Germans would find on the bodies the maps and written orders which would give away the Division's immediate intentions. However, the enemy were too slow-witted to appreciate their good fortune. When the site of the ambush was overrun on the next day the jeeps and bodies were found undisturbed, the maps and papers intact.

Jan. 30 The Irish Guards took over the positions which the Grenadiers were to have occupied on the left of the Scots Guards, and these two battalions fought hard to gain another thousand yards on either side of the road. They captured a hundred and sixty prisoners, and opened the way for the 3rd Brigade to advance as far as the main Naples—Rome railway, which runs through Campoleone. This was the deepest extension of the beach-head made by the Allies until the break-out in May (for the Americans, too, had been held up in their attacks on Cisterna). Once the 1st British Division had been halted, the Germans, turning to the offensive, created a critical situation which did not ease until six weeks later. The eyes of the world were upon Anzio. The annihilation of the beach-head became a political issue of the first importance to the Germans. Inspired by Hitler's direct order, they were determined to convince the Allies that a seaborne invasion, in any part of Europe, could result only in complete disaster.

The main weight of the first German attack fell on the flank of the Irish and Scots Guards; but the Grenadiers had been moved back to the Embankment before the battle and were not left undisturbed. The Embankment was the base of the five-mile salient which now stretched northwards to Campoleone. There was great depth to the position of the 1st Division but very little width. All three battalions of the 3rd Brigade were clustered in a tight knot just short of the railway line, the Irish Guards and a battalion of the Gordons lay immediately behind them on either side of the road; the Scots Guards were on the Vallelata Ridge; and the 2nd Brigade stretched eastwards from the Factory. The whole of the salient so formed was open to attack at any point on both flanks. While this threat existed it was scarcely possible to renew the northward thrust, and it soon became apparent that the British would have great difficulty even in holding what they had already gained. The Grenadiers slightly broadened the base by sending No. 2 Company (Capt. R. J. Martin) a mile north-east along the Embankment, where they dug and wired their isolated position among a litter of American corpses and equipment abandoned some days before. It was this company which, on the night of the first German attack, became directly involved in the battle; the others could do little more than wait under intense shell fire, and hope that the enemy thrust would not penetrate as far as Carroceto. It did not: but the two forward platoons of No. 2 Company were driven back just before midnight, and the situation was saved only by salvoes of mortar bombs and shells which laid a screen across the threatened point. Both Capt. Freeman and Lieut. Q. H. M. Gage were wounded. In the early hours of the next morning a platoon of No. 4 Company, led forward by Lieut. Hon. J. R. B. Norton, M.C., assisted No. 2 Company to re-occupy their old positions.

1944

Feb. 1

Feb. 4

This had been no more than a subsidiary thrust. Far more dangerous was the enemy force which managed for the space of some hours to force their way between the Irish and the Scots Guards, isolate the Gordons, and cut the road by small-arms fire in rear of the entire 3rd Brigade salient. "The situation," wrote Brigadier Murray, "was now very serious. I told the Divisional Commander that I expected an attack on Carroceto which, if successful, might involve the encirclement of the best part of the Division." Fortunately a brigade of the 56th Division, which had landed at Anzio that very morning, moved straight into the battle and were able to recover the Gordons' position on the right of the road. The Irish Guards, by remaining firm when at one moment they were surrounded on all but one side, held open the 3rd Brigade's escape route. Even after the battle had died down and columns of prisoners began to shuffle down the road to Carroceto, it was obvious that little was to be gained and much to be risked by holding out in so exposed a position. The Division could advance no farther. That night the 3rd Brigade were withdrawn and the whole line shortened. The Irish Guards came back into reserve after a night of appalling hardship, the Scots Guards drew in their outposts to Carroceto station and the tail-end of the Vallelata Ridge, and the Grenadiers adjusted their positions on the Embankment to face north-west. The

1944 Brigade were ready to meet the second German offensive, which came three days later.

3

THE GULLY

Dispositions of the Battalion before the German attack of 7th February—Two Grenadier companies cut off and eliminated—The enemy sweep on towards Battalion Headquarters in the Gully—Tactical importance of the Gully—Major Sidney's exploit for which he is later awarded the Victoria Cross—German attacks held off at point-blank range—Attacks renewed the next night—A short withdrawal to a new line—The Commanding Officer, Colonel Huntington, is killed—Battalion relieved

For the 24th Guards Brigade the fighting in the beach-head reached its climax on the 7th and 8th of February, and the 5th Grenadiers found themselves once more in a position so crucial that it is no exaggeration to suggest that the fate of the whole Corps depended upon their efforts. The story of these two days is one of the high-lights in the record of the Regiment during this war. To grasp its full significance it is necessary to study the accompanying plan and air photograph in all their detail, and to understand clearly how the Grenadier companies were disposed before the attack, what support they had on either flank, and what were the German intentions.

See Plan p. 410

Feb. 6 Up to the eve of the second German offensive almost nightly re-adjustments were made in the line, for it was a difficult problem to find the correct balance between compactness and the necessity to block every possible avenue of approach. The Battalion faced both north and west, with one flank resting on the Embankment and the other on a water-course. At first No. 4 Company had been placed in an outpost position along the Embankment about two miles north-west of Carroceto, but later the line was shortened, in the manner shown on the plan, to form a parallelogram with one company at each corner. The companies were by no means closely interlocked, either one with the other or with the battalions on either flank. There was at least five hundred yards of undefended ground, for instance, between Nos. 1 and 2 Companies: No. 2 Company never had a very clear idea where the nearest platoon of the Scots Guards were to be found, and No. 3 Company were separated by half a mile from the North Staffordshires on their left. In particular, No. 1 Company (Lieut. P. R. Freyberg), in the outer angle of the parallelogram, felt most uneasy, being too far even from their nearest neighbours to expect much assistance against an enemy night attack, and exposed to

assault from every direction. The Battalion, moreover, were very tired. 1944
It is true that they had received reinforcements both from their rear echelon at Gragnano and from a draft of officers and men who arrived fresh from England—with them had come the new Commanding Feb. 3
Officer, Lieut.-Colonel A. C. Huntington, M.V.O., direct from the 3rd Battalion in North Africa—but there had been no time for the new men to become acclimatized to such intensive fighting as they were now called upon to face. Nor is it surprising that some of the veterans of the Factory battles were showing signs of strain. A renewal of the German attacks was expected at any moment. Their rest was disturbed by constant false alarms, uninterrupted shell fire, the need to improve their scattered defences, and the rain and the cold. "We all had a blanket apiece," wrote Lieut. Freyberg, "but that is not much protection when even the puddles freeze."

During the morning this message was received from Brigade Head- Feb. 7
quarters: "Prisoner says that attack scheduled for last night in neighbourhood of railway bed had been put off for twenty-four hours. Could give no reason." As a normal precaution, patrols were sent out at nightfall to discover whether the Germans were forming up for attack. The patrol from No. 1 Company, led by Lieut. M. J. Hussey, went westwards along the Embankment, and were startled to observe in the bright moonlight three long columns of Germans, about a battalion in strength, moving resolutely in the direction of No. 3 Company. Lieut. Hussey hurried back with this report, but as there was no sign of an artillery barrage the danger was not considered to be immediate. Shortly afterwards the Germans attacked, following an advance in almost complete silence. It was later discovered from a captured operation order that the enemy were seeking to repeat the tactics which they had used with such success at Campoleone, by striking simultaneously at several points on the left flank. If they could cut the road behind the leading battalions they would isolate the whole Carroceto salient and tear a gap in the most sensitive part of the beachhead perimeter through which they could later pour their tanks. The infantry attack was delivered by three main columns: one from the north-west aimed at Carroceto itself; a second striking directly along the Embankment towards the bridges; and a third whose object was to cut the road farther south. The Grenadiers thus found themselves suddenly transfixed by all three prongs of the attack.

During the middle hours of the night all companies, as well as both flanking battalions, were engaged in heavy fighting, and it was not easy for Colonel Huntington to form a clear idea of the situation, since wireless messages from the forward companies were few, and later ceased completely. His own headquarters was in great peril, and not

1944 a single officer or man of the two outer companies escaped to inform him of the position ahead. Only now (1947) is it possible to piece together the events of that night from the accounts of repatriated prisoners of war.

The first company to be attacked, at about 9.30 p.m., was No. 3 Company (Capt. N. D. M. Johnstone, M.B.E.), who were thinly spread out along the western edge of the parallelogram, based on a deep wadi which ran the whole length of the position. The platoons were necessarily very widely distributed in order to guard the many ramifications of the wadi. The first they knew of the attack was the sound of firing from the area of the right forward company of the North Staffordshires, and shortly afterwards they realized that the Germans had found the gap on their left flank and were already digging in behind them on the Buonriposo Ridge. At the same time, two of the three platoon commanders, Lieuts. R. S. Longman and D. D. Boulton, reported German columns moving directly upon them from the north-west. No. 3 Company were therefore virtually surrounded. Lieut. Boulton's platoon replied to the attack with great spirit, and Lieut. Boulton himself was killed as he manned a machine gun; Lieut. Longman's platoon was overrun by another German column; and a third fell on Capt. Johnstone as he advanced with two sections of the remaining platoon to restore the situation. The company were now not only surrounded but swamped by a greatly superior force. With nine other survivors, Capt. Johnstone managed to link up with No. 1 Company on his right, and gave them some assistance on their left flank.

By this time No. 1 Company (Capt. T. A. Gore-Browne, who had barely recovered from his previous wound) were also heavily engaged. Their battle centred round a small group of farm buildings on a spur overlooking the Embankment which had been occupied by Lieut. Freyberg's platoon. The Germans approached from an unexpected direction ("I was suddenly aware," wrote Lieut. Freyberg, "that a lot of Germans had suddenly materialized, as it seemed, out of the air"), and for the next half an hour they fought among the haystacks of the farmyard, each side doubtful whether they were firing at friend or foe, at one moment finding themselves prisoners of war, at the next turning the tables on their captors. For a short time the Germans gained possession of the farm, but lost it again to a combined counter-attack by the platoons of Lieuts. Freyberg and Hussey. At this stage Capt. Gore-Browne was wounded for the first time; he preferred to take his chance where he was rather than wander over territory which was probably already occupied by the enemy. What did they know of the situation around them? They had held firm to all their own platoon positions, but there was a strong German force immediately in front 1944 who were unlikely to remain inactive after their first repulse; they could hear the Scots Guards firing heavily on their right; from Capt. Johnstone they learned that a wide breach had been torn open between the Grenadiers and the North Staffordshires, and there was evidence of this not only from the machine-gun fire on the Buonriposo Ridge but from wireless reports that the tide of the German attack had already penetrated as far as Battalion Headquarters, more than a mile in rear. There seemed to be only one avenue of escape left to them —the Embankment. If they remained where they were, they could probably hold out until the morning, but in daylight the ring would be completely closed and the company would be dominated from the high ground on two sides. If, on the other hand, they withdrew before the Embankment was cut, they could join forces with No. 2 Company and hold a tighter perimeter defending the vital road bridge and in closer touch with the Scots Guards. In default of instructions from Battalion Headquarters, with whom all communication had ceased, this was the decision taken by Capt. Gore-Browne (now wounded for the second time) in consultation with Capt. Johnstone. The combined Nos. 1 and 3 Companies, amounting to little more than fifty survivors, began to withdraw at about 3 a.m. directly along the Embankment, not knowing whether the Germans were already across it, nor indeed whether No. 2 Company were still in the same positions as before. The first to leave was a jeep towing an anti-tank gun. It was ambushed by a German block across the Embankment not three hundred yards east of the company's original position, and the head of the following column of marching men was prevented by heavy fire from making further progress. This was the end. They were completely surrounded, and the Germans on the Buonriposo Ridge began calling on them to surrender, closing in from every side. The company split up into groups, each under the guidance of an officer or non-commissioned officer, and began to make their way independently across the open ground as best they could, dodging from gully to gully, but found the whole area alive with German soldiers. They were all taken prisoner, some that night, some at dawn the next morning; and many of them, in seeking to avoid capture, were wounded before they gave themselves up. The officers were Capts. T. A. Gore-Browne and N. D. M. Johnstone and Lieut. M. J. Hussey (all wounded and taken prisoner), and Lieuts. P. R. Freyberg, M.C.,* and R. S. Longman (both taken prisoner).

*Lieut. Freyberg escaped a few days later and made his way to the Papal residence at Castel Gondolfo, which was neutral territory. From here he was smuggled, hidden in a delivery van, into the Vatican City, where he remained until the liberation of Rome on the 4th of June. He then rejoined the Battalion for the advance up Italy.

1944 Meanwhile, the remainder of the Battalion was also coming under attack. After three companies and the headquarters of the North Staffordshires had been overrun or surrounded, the southern German column, led with great determination, swept round to attack No. 4 Company of the Grenadiers (Major W. E. P. Miller) from the left flank and rear. No. 4 Company had been considered as the reserve company, and none of the other three was in a position to give them any aid: nor could the Scots or Irish Guards spare a single man, for they too were fully engaged, the former at Carroceto and the latter in plugging the gap left by the North Staffordshires. To avoid the loss of No. 4 Company in addition to Nos. 1 and 3, Major Miller was instructed to withdraw his platoons to new positions just west of the gully which sheltered Battalion Headquarters. This they did, but were so closely pursued that both forward platoons were soon afterwards overwhelmed before they had had time to dig in. The platoon commanders, Lieuts. A. J. Courage* and E. D. Collie, were both captured, the latter having emptied his revolver and rifle into a group of Germans before he found himself encircled by bayonets.

This left the Grenadiers at the climax of the battle with, first, No. 2 Company (Capt. R. J. Martin), who were now under strong attack on the Embankment, and had withdrawn their forward platoon to better positions from where they could enfilade the mass of Germans; secondly, with a company of American parachutists, who had been hurriedly brought up on the right of Battalion Headquarters; and, thirdly, with the few men of Headquarter Company and Battalion Headquarters in the Gully, who now occupied the centre of the picture. From a parallelogram the shape of the Battalion's position had shrunk into a short, thin line, and nothing remained between them and the road. As so much depended upon the defence of the Gully, it is worth reproducing the fuller description of it written by the Battalion Intelligence Officer, Lieut. G. W. Chaplin, M.C.:

> "A track leading south-south-west from the Embankment dipped into the Gully, the walls of which rose higher as the track went farther in. The stretch which concerned Battalion Headquarters was shaped like a question-mark. As one entered, the right-hand walls stood as high as twenty-five feet, composed of some sort of crumbling sandstone. At the north-east edge of the loop of the question-mark the walls grew lower until there was a broad earth ramp leading from the floor of the gully to a crossing place over a deep ditch about fifty yards to the west. At the bottom of the stalk of the question-mark there was just room for a truck containing a wireless set, and two tents in line, one used for a telephone exchange and orderly room, and the other for the Commanding Officer and the Adjutant."

---

*Lieut. Courage was killed, while trying to escape, a few days later.

Two points should be added: the walls of the Gully were honeycombed by small caves in which a few Italian civilians cowered during the whole course of the battle; and, secondly, the southern end of the Gully lay wide open, the nearest companies of the Irish Guards being well out of reach. 1944

Once No. 4 Company had been overrun, the Germans swarmed over the top of the Buonriposo Ridge to threaten the Gully from above. Several German machine guns appeared on the spur in front, firing directly down on Battalion Headquarters, and the Guardsmen who had been stationed on a low mound on the floor of the Gully "were immediately drilled off it." Nevertheless, the defenders of the Headquarters and the Americans on the right were able to return a steady stream of fire, and the Pioneer Officer, Lieut. C. C. P. Hodson, set up a 3-inch mortar which he fired at the minimum range of a hundred and fifty yards. In the bright moonlight they saw the Germans charge down towards them, "shouting to each other," says one account, "in an almost hysterical manner." They were brought up short by an obstacle which they had not expected—the Ditch. It was V-shaped, with steep, slippery sides, and a stream running along the bottom; most important of all, it was choked almost to the brim by an impenetrable mass of brambles. For some time the Germans ran uncertainly up and down the far side, losing heavily in casualties to the concentrated fire of the Grenadiers and Americans, but then they found the crossing place mentioned in Lieut. Chaplin's description. It was no more than a rough track hewn through the brambles by some Italian peasant long ago, but once they were through it they were immediately opposite the shelving entrance to the Gully, and unless halted in time they would be in a position to roll up the whole Headquarters from the south.

At the risk of repetition, it must be emphasized that the Gully was the last defended line west of the road, and if the enemy had broken through at this point they would have cut off not only the remnants of the Grenadiers but the American parachutists, the Scots Guards in Carroceto, and the London Irish Rifles in the Factory, as well as opening a passage to the tanks, which had been heard moving up in readiness behind the German infantry. There was never a more critical moment. The fate of the whole beach-head was about to be fought out in the narrow strip of ground between the Ditch and the Gully.

It so happened that the crucial part of the Gully opposite the Ditch crossing was held by Major W. P. Sidney,* the commander of Support Company, with a handful of men. He advanced alone to the edge of

*Now Lord de L'Isle and Dudley, V.C.

1944 the Ditch, stood upright in the face of intense fire, and held off the Germans with his tommy-gun. The gun jammed. Major Sidney withdrew to the edge of the ramp leading down into the Gully, and, though one or two Germans had now succeeded in crossing the Ditch, he prevented an inruption into the floor of the Gully by flinging grenades at any who showed themselves. The grenades were handed up to him by two Guardsmen who were priming them as fast as they could. In their eagerness, one grenade was detonated prematurely, killing one of the Guardsmen and wounding Major Sidney in the legs and forehead. He remained for some minutes more at his post, blocking single-handed the gap on which the enemy now relied to complete their triumph. Then he was again wounded in the face by a German stick grenade. By this time the first German onslaught was spent, and others of his own men coming up to his assistance prevented further penetration. For this exploit Major Sidney was awarded the Victoria Cross, the second to be won by a Grenadier in this war.

There were still one or two Germans on the side of the Ditch nearer the Gully, and until they had been driven off the danger remained as great as ever. Lieuts. G. W. Chaplin, M.C., and W. S. Dugdale, M.C., and a few men scrambled up the northern end on to the ledge between the Gully and the Ditch, and began to work their way southwards, disposing of any Germans they found on the ledge or in the Ditch itself, where many of them were trapped, finding it almost impossible to free themselves from the brambles or to scale the slippery sides. At the farther end the Grenadiers found themselves suddenly confronted by four Germans. Their own weapons being out of order, they jumped the thirty feet down into the Gully and survived unhurt.

Feb. 8 It was now 3.30 a.m. and the full moon stood high in the sky. After their first repulse the Germans attacked the Gully a second time. The desperate position of the Grenadiers is reflected in this message sent by the Adjutant, Capt. The Lord Stanley, M.C., who for the past few hours had been broadcasting a running commentary from his tent on the Gully floor: "Nothing heard of No. 1 Company for forty-five minutes. Nos. 3 and 4 Companies believed overrun. Ourselves surrounded, and there is a German on the ridge above me throwing grenades." This second attack was repulsed by small-arms fire at close range, and by the skill of the artillery officer, Major Greig, who directed the fire of his guns by minute corrections nearer and nearer the very lips of the Gully. As the light strengthened, the German attacks died down. Looking around them at dawn, the Grenadiers saw the ground in front of them littered with German corpses; and over on their right the men of No. 2 Company moving unconcernedly about the Embankment. The latter had passed a difficult night repelling the central German column; being cut off from their own headquarters, they had drawn food and ammunition from the Scots Guards on their right. The North Staffordshires had been completely overrun, and the Irish Guards had taken their place. Of the Germans immediately facing the Grenadiers there was little sign. Whenever a head appeared on the Buonriposo Ridge a British or American rifle would open fire at once, but during the hours of daylight there was no renewal of the attack. The Battalion Headquarters prepared to face a second night as grim as the first. 1944

The total force in the Gully and its extension to the north now amounted to no more than twenty-nine Grenadiers, of whom four were wounded, and about forty-five Americans. Leaving the latter to line the track between the end of the Gully and the Embankment, widely spread out to give the impression of strength where there was only weakness, Colonel Huntington divided his own men into three groups. Lieut. J. A. Lyttleton and D./Sergt. Armstrong and six men were placed in the southern loop; Lieuts. W. S. Dugdale and Hodson and seven Guardsmen held the northern entrance with the only workable Bren gun; and Lieut. Chaplin with two Guardsmen and six Americans was placed on the ledge above, lying out on the open slope from where they could directly command the Ditch. By the time everyone was in position it had already been raining hard for an hour. It was impossible to keep dry or warm, and the rain turned to sleet. As expected, the Germans renewed their attacks, and, having failed once, returned for a last effort to break through. "There followed," says the War Diary, "the now-familiar advance to the Ditch and the sight of more miserable Germans walking up and down trying to find their way across. Those venturesome souls who did entrust themselves to the bed of the Ditch made almost as much noise splashing as they did shouting. . . . The enemy who were unwise enough to come within grenade range were dealt with, and the stretch of the Ditch nearest to the defenders on the ledge was used as the killing-ground. The 36 grenade once again proved itself the most valuable of all weapons for night fighting."

In this manner they held their own through the first part of the night. By this time the rain had reduced the Gully to its normal function as a water-course, and the tent from which Capt. The Lord Stanley was still relaying his wireless messages was a foot deep in water. Partly because it was impossible to fight from a stream-bed, and partly because of their great exhaustion and the weakness of the line, Colonel Huntington obtained Brigadier Murray's permission to withdraw from the Gully to the area of the road bridge during the early hours of the morning. It was an extremely risky manœuvre. All the

1944 men and three of their vehicles (the others were abandoned) left the
Feb. 9 Gully by its southern exit at 3.30 a.m., crossed the muddy fields to the road, and then turned north to the Embankment. From a hundred yards away the Germans could not have failed to observe their movement, but they did not fire, thinking perhaps that they had at last attained their object.

In this opinion they were quite mistaken, for the line was not broken: it was re-formed on the road, facing west, and was now more closely knit than before. Battalion Headquarters returned to their old position in a culvert under the Embankment just east of the road, and after breakfast—their first hot meal for forty-eight hours—a party of reinforcements under Lieut. Norton came up to the support of No. 2 Company, who had not moved from their original area. Before the latest arrivals had time to move into their positions No. 2 Company were once again attacked and were forced to draw back another hundred yards before the Germans were again halted by artillery and machine-gun fire. It was during this attack that the Commanding Officer, Lieut.-Colonel A. C. Huntington, was killed. He was standing outside the Headquarters culvert directing the fire of an American tank when a German machine gun, firing down the length of the Embankment, shot him through the chest: he died instantly. Major E. J. B. Nelson, M.C., barely recovered from his own wound, took over command of the Battalion. He was the fourth officer to take command since they had landed at Anzio less than three weeks before.

That night the survivors of the Gully battle, having been seventy-two hours without sleep, were relieved by a scratch force of four Grenadier platoons, and were sent back for rest beyond the Flyover. Even with a hundred reinforcements, the Grenadiers were still too weak to defend more than the immediate area of the road and railway bridges under the Embankment, which it was vital to keep open at all costs so long as the Scots Guards were still at Carroceto. The enemy attacked twice during the night, and both Capts. A. T. A. Holland and J. A. Orme were wounded. The Germans were repelled to such good effect that a stretcher-bearer appeared with a white flag at 2 a.m.,
Feb. 10 asking for a truce to bury their dead. This was refused, because the Scots Guards were then facing the crisis of their battle two hundred yards away: their Adjutant reported that the station building was being shot down by a tank over the heads of their battalion headquarters. Brigadier Murray told the Divisional Commander that he thought it unlikely that the Brigade could hold on for another night. Two very strong attacks had resulted in the loss of two Scots Guards companies and one Irish Guards company, and eventually the Scots Guards were forced to abandon Carroceto, and joined the Grenadiers.

ANZIO BEACH-HEAD :- The Embankment and Factory Area

Positions of our own troops on February 7th 1944 marked in Red
Companies of 5th Battalion Grenadier Guards shown thus .... (3)

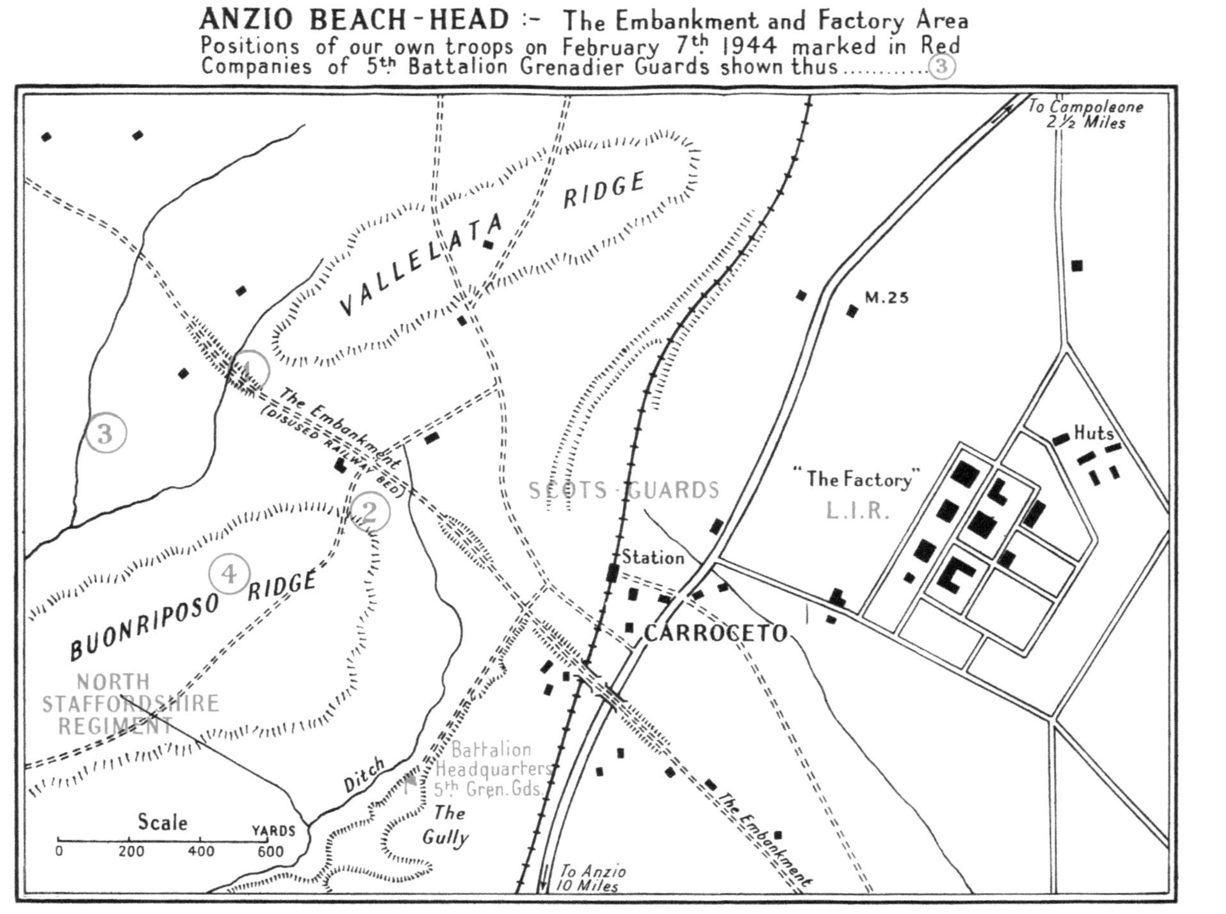

Air Ministry

The Anzio Beach-head.

Carroceto Station (top right) and The Ditch and Gully (centre)

Major W. P. Sidney receives the Victoria Cross from General Alexander.

Crown Copyright

The Factory also fell into German hands, and the beach-head was contracted to the line of the Embankment. "Now we were back where we started," is the tragic record of the War Diary, "having inflicted and suffered tremendous losses, and the future was obscure." 1944

The Grenadiers were relieved by the Duke of Wellington's after nightfall, and returned into reserve between the Flyover and the beaches. "The troops turned over the railway line into the dim area of trees and scrub which comprised 'B' Echelon. Everything that was possible in the way of comforts was prepared. A vast, hot meal was doled out and taken in mess-tins to the little bivouacs dotted round the area. The only thing left was to sleep, and that with a clear conscience, without the prospect of a midnight alarm. A chapter, which had opened on the 21st of January, was closed. The Battalion were out of the line." They were told on the next day by the Commander-in-Chief, General Alexander, that they "had made history and tradition worthy of the finest in all the military history of the Brigade of Guards." As a special mark of distinction the name of the 5th Battalion Grenadier Guards was the first of all British battalions fighting at Anzio to be released by the censors to the outside world.

4

THE LAST PHASE

Desperate German attempts to eliminate the beach-head—No evacuation was possible or contemplated—Grenadiers in skirmishes among the wadis —The Brigade withdrawn to Naples—Their total casualties at Anzio

The Battalion's "B" Echelon, where they spent the next week, was **Feb. 11-16** a rest area only in name, for the whole beach-head up to the very docks at Anzio was within range of the German heavy guns, and enemy aircraft would come streaking over to machine-gun the road or drop a pattern of butterfly bombs. There was no relaxation in the German offensive. The Embankment was captured on the 12th of February, and soon afterwards the Germans started to attack down the east side of the road with a whole division of infantry and sixty to seventy tanks, penetrating at one moment to within a hundred yards

1944 of the Flyover. The contracting outline of the Anzio beach-head was now a familiar feature in the newspapers of the world. In the House of Commons Mr. Winston Churchill quoted a message from General Alexander affirming that there would be no evacuation. The German infantry, on the other hand, were told that the Allies were already re-embarking, and that in a few days, after a final effort, they would return to Berlin and lead their prisoners in triumph through the streets. The leaflets which they dropped bore the clumsy legend: "Tommy, you are going to Neptune, not Nettuno. You will all be sunk when you re-embark." Very different was their present experience. The 15th Panzer Grenadier Regiment, for example, formed up one thousand three hundred strong for their attack on the Flyover on the 18th, were twice thrown back, and the next morning, now reduced to a weary four hundred, advanced a third time shoulder to shoulder, only to be slaughtered by our shells and bullets. Thirty-two thousand rounds were fired that morning by a single company of British machine gunners, and for every German shell twenty were sent over in return, while wave after wave of Mitchell and Liberator bombers reduced Carroceto and Campoleone to the pitiful state in which they still remain; eight hundred and thirteen bombers dropped nine hundred and seventy-two tons of bombs during this action alone. It was no unusual sight to see twenty German tanks burning in the plain, and ammunition was so plentiful that the whole Corps artillery would be used to demolish a single house.

The situation was serious enough, but there was never any thought of evacuation. Politically it would have been a great blow to Allied prestige, and tactically it would have been an impossibility, so large was the force and so close to the beaches were the enemy. The beach-head would be held if necessary by the very orderlies at a divisional headquarters, and all the men of the supply companies, of the R.E.M.E. and the R.A.S.C., dug their trenches in a final Corps reserve line. The attacks across the open country between the Embankment and the Flyover could probably be halted indefinitely by shell fire and tanks, but more disturbing was the threat to the north-west angle of the beach-head, where a German parachute division were becoming increasingly bold and skilful in their use of the complex system of winding gullies. "Patrols would move forward from their company areas and vanish without trace," says the 1st Division's History of Anzio, "while on other occasions our own troops would leave the cover of their wadis to assault one held by the enemy, and on return find Germans in occupation of their own positions. So, in the mud and pouring rain, among the deep, overgrown wadis to the west of the main road, this grim game of hide-and-seek was played out." "Be

careful," was a more tense warning at the time, "these parachutists 1944
have a habit of eating a platoon for breakfast every morning."

To this area the 24th Guards Brigade moved after a week's rest. Feb. 17
They were commanded, after the departure of Brigadier Murray, first by Brigadier M. D. Erskine, D.S.O., and later, on his arrival from the United Kingdom, by Brigadier A. F. L. Clive, D.S.O., M.C. They were not in the front line, which lay along the Fosso della Moletta, but in reserve a mile south-west of the Flyover, with the immediate task of blocking any German patrols which infiltrated through the thick country towards the British gun lines. It was impossible to construct satisfactory defensive positions when every field of fire was limited by trees and brushwood, and every trench would fill with water as soon as it was dug. As a start, a belt of wire was put down round the entire Battalion position, and the track leading to their headquarters was made passable by loads of fascines and rubble brought from the bombed houses in Anzio. Every night the Quartermaster, Lieut. H. N. Lucas, M.B.E., brought up his convoy of supplies, often at considerable risk, for the beach-head was now so narrowed that the Germans could keep almost every yard of that perilous road under continual fire. It was fortunate that so many of their shells failed to explode.
On one occasion, when the Germans had pin-pointed the small patch Feb. 23
of wood which contained both the Grenadier and Brigade Headquarters, and deluged it with shells, ninety per cent. of them were duds. On another occasion, wrote Capt. Chaplin, "while two or three stretcher-bearers were standing round near the regimental aid post eating their evening meal, an 88-mm. shell whistled in, bounded off two trees, and landed between two men talking together; it spun slowly round and round at their feet, steaming as it did so on the wet ground. They were not in the least perturbed." One of the few casualties in the period between the Gully battle and the time the Battalion left the beach-head was Lieut. J. A. Lyttleton, who died of his wounds in hospital. Apart from Lieut. J. H. G. Shephard, who had been wounded when the Battalion first moved up into this position, there were no other officer casualties.

The Brigade had long been promised a relief, for they were no longer in any condition to re-enter a full-scale battle. Among the Grenadiers the casualties had been appalling: nine officers had been killed, twelve wounded and eight taken prisoner of war (of whom four were wounded before capture); fifty-two other ranks had been killed, two hundred and twenty-two wounded and three hundred and three were missing. In spite of reinforcements, they had been obliged to reduce the number of their rifle companies from four to two. On the 8th of March they embarked at Anzio docks, under fire up to the very

1944 Mar. 9 moment the ships drew away from the harbour. On the next morning they docked at Naples, and drove to billets at Sorrento. The silence, after the continual hammering of the guns at Anzio, seemed most strange.

CHAPTER VII

THE CENTRAL APENNINES FEBRUARY—MAY, 1944

3RD AND 5TH BATTALIONS

1

THE GARIGLIANO BRIDGEHEAD

Arrival of 3rd Battalion from Algeria—Their first positions on the Garigliano—Nature of winter fighting in mountains—Monte Cerasola —Concentration of 6th Armoured Division in Italy

DURING the whole eventful period between the landings at Salerno **1944**
and the landings at Anzio the 3rd Battalion of the Regiment had remained in North Africa, where little more than the normal newspaper accounts of the fighting in Italy had reached them. It was nine months since the Battalion had been in action, and there were now many new men among them who had never yet seen a German except in captivity, or themselves fired a gun with intent to kill. They therefore crossed the Mediterranean to Naples with almost the same degree **Feb. 4**
of wonder and expectation with which, more than a year before, they had landed at Algiers. What would Italy be like? The people? The billets? The wine? Was it true that the Germans were deserting in hundreds, and that all the fighting in the mountains was no more than a shield to cover a sudden withdrawal to the Alps? And what of the future of the 1st Guards Brigade, now divorced from their familiar 6th Armoured Division, arriving solitary in this strange country, with no foreknowledge of their destination beyond Naples, or of the part which Caserta thought them fit to play?

The *Ville d'Oran*, carrying the bulk of the Brigade, slid alongside the shattered quays of Naples harbour in the middle of the morning, **Feb. 5**
and from the rails the men looked down upon the familiar symbols of British staff work—British lorries, mobile canteens, military police, the flutter of official papers upon a millboard. As the box-cars of the Italian railway carried them northwards to Capua they saw that the countryside was also gripped and scarred by war. They saw lines of

1944 parked tanks beneath the olive trees, ropes of dusty telephone cables festooned across the roads, English military notices scrawled without apology upon the white and pitted stucco of a half-demolished house. As the darkness deepened (for the rail journey of twenty miles lasted for seven hours) they saw the northern sky lit up by flashes, and mountain ridges jump suddenly into relief. At first they thought that it was summer lightning, but later they also heard, or rather felt, the roar and trembling of the guns. Leaving their train at Capua, they were taken in lorries to a village called Cascano, and in the morning climbed to a *See Map p. 416* ridge near by, from which they looked across the valley of the Garigliano, and were told that somewhere in those snow-covered mountains beyond lay the German winter line.

The 3rd Battalion had arrived in Italy at about the time when the Allied effort was sinking to its lowest ebb, through the exhaustion of the troops, the bad weather, and the physical obstacles of mountain and river. The Garigliano had indeed been crossed, but at a price which left the 46th Division too weak to climb more than half-way up the mountain mass which rose abruptly from the northern river bank. Their bridgehead was little more than two miles deep. The enemy were still numerically as strong as the Allies, and were confident in the knowledge that such a very local penetration of their winter line could have no strategic consequences in country where there were few communications better than mule tracks, and that behind them lay one defensive position after another, to which they could withdraw if the Allies renewed their attacks. Yet the British had not abandoned their efforts to break through, and when the 1st Guards Brigade, fresh from Africa, suddenly arrived at Cascano it is not surprising that the tired veterans of the 46th Division should have looked to the newcomers to bear the brunt of the next attempt. Indeed, the Brigade Commander (Brigadier J. C. Haydon, D.S.O.), who had flown out from England to meet his battalion commanders for the first time on the previous day, found that his Brigade were expected to go immediately into action and strike deep into the hills in order to loosen the German hold on Castleforte. Into the details of this operation it is unnecessary to enter, for it was postponed and then abandoned soon **Feb. 7** after the preliminary phases had begun. But the Brigade, two days after landing in Italy, were already waiting in the heart of the Garigliano bridgehead when the final order for the cancellation of the plan came through, and once they were there it was too late to return them for a period of acclimatization behind the lines: the situation was too serious: the men on the spot must remain there to resist increasing German pressure.

It so happened that the first position held by the 3rd Grenadiers on

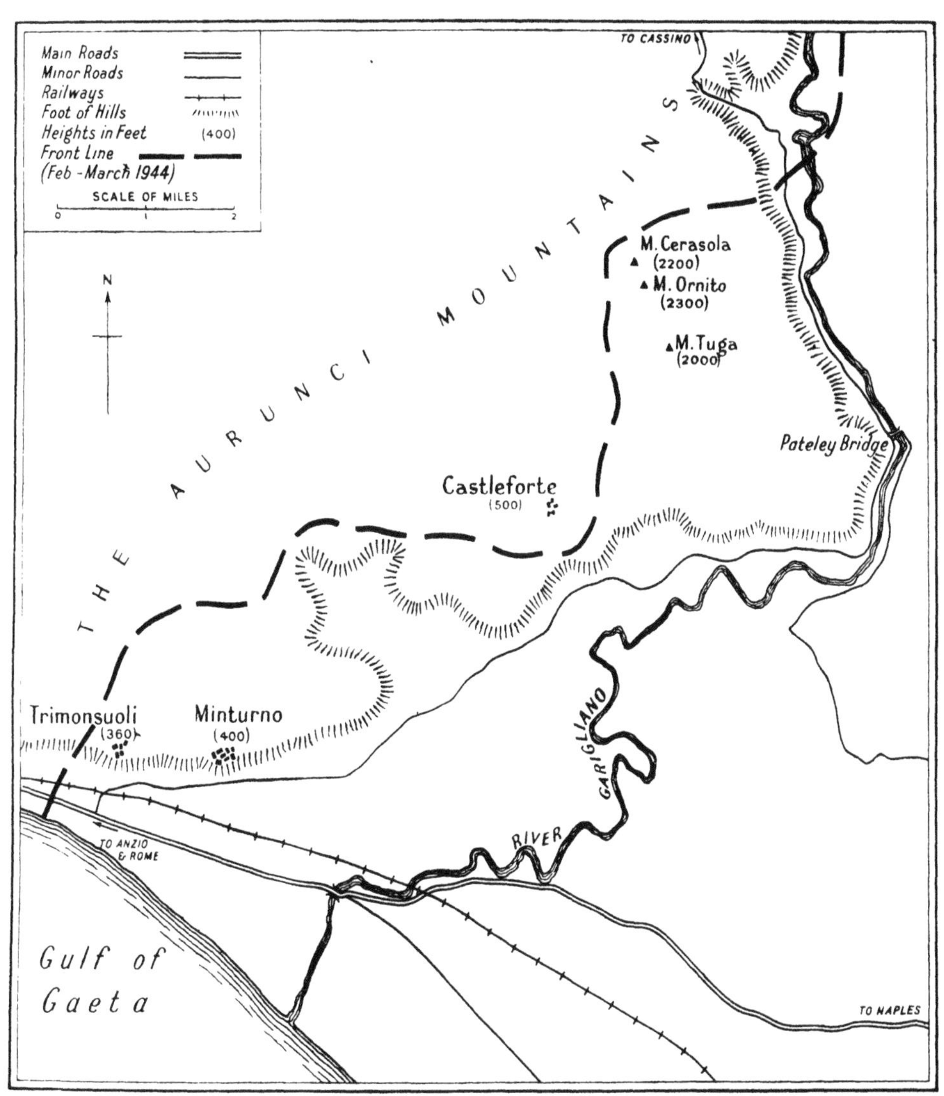

THE GARIGLIANO LINE, WINTER, 1943-1944

the Garigliano was one of less danger and importance than those 1944 allotted to the 2nd Coldstream and 3rd Welsh Guards. Of the four hundred casualties suffered by the Brigade in their first fortnight in Italy, the Grenadiers' share was but thirty-eight. They did, however, endure to the full the physical hardships of that mountain fighting, and a description of this aspect, rather than a catalogue of small patrols, will best illuminate the nature of the campaign in Italy in the winter of 1944.

Imagine, then, a tossing mass of hills of about the same height and same degree of ruggedness as the mountains of the English Lake District. Their steep slopes were covered by chutes of small, grey stones, between which you would sometimes find a timid Alpine plant, but more often a rusting splinter of a high-explosive shell. There was no road nearer than that which ran beside the river, and though it was less than three miles to the front-line trenches from the nearest point which could be approached on wheels, the steep climb would take a fully laden man as much as three and a half hours. If he were wounded near the summit the stretcher-bearers could not bring him down to an ambulance in less than five hours, sometimes eight, and many men died upon the jolting stretchers before reaching the end of the journey. The tracks followed the easiest gradients, circling slowly round the natural contours of the hills, and, though their foundations had been well laid by generations of Italian peasants, and widened and revetted by British engineers, a four-inch covering of liquid mud would overlie the solid stone after every shower of rain. The traffic of men and mules could not be interrupted to allow the tracks to dry, and every fresh print of foot or hoof only increased the labour of the ascent for those following behind. Day and night the stores of food and water and ammunition were carried up into those remote mountains, for the first part of the journey by strings of mules and then doggedly man-handled beyond the point where increasing shell fire made the tracks impassable to every animal but man. Apart from a few rough sheep-pens, which were reserved for the medical aid posts and perishable stores, there were no ready-made shelters on the upper levels of the hills, and the men would rig up their small bivouacs or sling two ground-sheets between the rocks, and there, despite the wet and cold, they accustomed themselves to snatch a few hours' sleep. The British soldier soon adapts himself, physically and mentally, to the most intolerable conditions. Very few of them developed even an ordinary cold, though they lay soaked to the skin for hours on end; and as the days passed, a hint of domesticity began to creep into their makeshift arrangements. "My bivvy," it became: "My rock"; and to the main dumps and landmarks on the upward routes were given names which

1944 contrasted strangely with those printed on the Italian maps: "Harrogate," "Cheshire," "Pateley Bridge," and "Skipton Dump."

In these miserable surroundings—"Kein Menschenleben," as one of the German prisoners remarked—the 1st Guards Brigade held off almost daily attacks against the centre of the Garigliano bridgehead. The Grenadiers, in their positions on Monte Tuga overlooking Castleforte, suffered more from shell fire than from direct attack. There was the occasion when a hundred and forty-two shells fell on No. 1 Company in the course of a single night without causing any casualties; and on another day a shell landed at Battalion Headquarters, six feet away from the sleeping head of the Commanding Officer, Colonel Heber-Percy, and left him unharmed. But the Battalion also had a more aggressive role to play. They constantly patrolled the dead ground ahead of them—from one of these patrols Lieut. R. C. Murdoch brought back three most valuable prisoners—and when the Coldstream appealed for support in resisting the sixth and final attack on Monte Ornito Capt. P. Maclean led No. 2 Company back into the hills, and defended one of the foremost Coldstream positions against a most violent assault. In this battle Sergt. A. Treeby won the first Distinguished Conduct Medal to be awarded to the 3rd Battalion in
Feb. 20 Italy. It was a tragic conclusion to their efforts when Capt. Maclean was killed by a stray shell long after the main danger had passed.

After a short period out of the line the Grenadiers returned across
Mar. 5-13 the Garigliano to hold one of the key-points in the bridgehead, Monte Cerasola. The companies were very closely grouped round the inside rim of a natural bowl, with the Germans in equivalent position on the outer side of the rim. An air photograph of the position, taken early one morning after a fall of snow, showed clearly how close the rival defence systems approached to one another: the tracks made by the porters of both sides could be seen branching from the thick stems of the main supply routes to innumerable small, black points; a strip of clear snow separated the two lines: on the photograph it was less than a millimetre wide; on the ground it was about twenty yards. What did it mean? It meant that the men of No. 3 Company (Capt. J. H. Lambert), who occupied the most forward sangars, would sit all day huddled in greatcoats, their eyes fixed on the ridge in front, their Bren guns resting ready on the sill of the sangar. From time to time a shower of grenades came sailing over from the far side, against which they erected a shield of wire-netting, mounted like a semi-circular windscreen upon the top of the sangar wall. On only one occasion did a party of Germans show themselves on the ridge, probably newcomers who were unaware that the British were no more than a few yards down the far slope. They were immediately shot down, and their

bodies lay for days on the very summit, almost within touching 1944 distance of both sides but unapproachable by either. From Brigade Headquarters came the suggestion that one of these corpses should be pulled down and examined for documents, as it was uncertain which German battalion opposed us on this sector of the line. A long pole fitted with a hook, a sort of gaff, was made by the sappers, and Colonel Heber-Percy himself pulled in the corpse, catching the hook in its Mar. 8 rotten clothing. The documents found on the body told us all that we wished to know, and a day later the identification was confirmed by the desertion of two Poles, drafted by force into the German Army, who said that the morale on their side of the ridge was sinking very low indeed. As for the Grenadiers, they took their own hardships very philosophically. "What I really hate," wrote a Guardsman, "is that every morning we have bits of cold bacon on the same tin plate as a mess of apricot jam. The jam gets into the bacon, and the bacon gets into the jam."

The Battalion returned for a rest to the village of Calvisi, some Mar. 20 twenty miles north of Capua, where the local population were obliged to share each other's homes in order to make room for the Grenadiers, and to accustom themselves to totally unwonted standards of sanitation and cleanliness, looking on with growing wonder while their houses were forcibly disinfected and whitewashed. Once they were suitably accommodated, the Guardsmen were allowed to go on day expeditions to Naples, where there were two main attractions: the opera, for which they developed an increasing taste, and the eruption of Vesuvius, by which whole villages were ploughed away, and the sun eclipsed by a vast cauliflower of smoke and dust.

The main object of their return to Calvisi had been the reincorporation of the 1st Guards Brigade into the 6th Armoured Division, whose other units had now arrived in Italy from North Africa. At the same time the Brigade were transferred from the Fifth to the Eighth Army, and it was at first intended that the Division should remain out of the line until the opening of the offensive on the 11th of May. This expectation was disappointed when the Army Commander, General Sir Mar. 25 Oliver Leese, visited the Battalion and informed them that the shortage of troops was such that the Brigade would be temporarily placed under the command of the New Zealand Division (Lieutenant-General Freyberg) and hold a sector of the line on the River Gari south of Cassino. At a later date they would be moved into Cassino itself.

Of the preliminary period on the Gari not much need be said. It Mar. 29-April 6 was a quiet, defensive sector, set back a few hundred yards from the river bank among copses and small farms. Colonel Heber-Percy re-

1944 duced the operational strength of his Battalion to the minimum, taking only two hundred and fifty men with him into the line. They lost some casualties from shell fire; they patrolled down to the river regularly and thoroughly. But in the main their activity fell into two categories: the control of the civilian population, who still wandered negligently through the battle zone; and the study, the careful, anxious study, by consultation and direct observation, of the problems peculiar to Cassino itself. They moved into that famous town on the night
April 7 of the 7th of April.

2

CASSINO

Tactical and psychological importance of Cassino—Appearance of the town after heavy bombardment—Life in the 3rd Battalion among the ruins—The porters—Headquarters in the crypt—Character of the enemy parachutists—Strategy of General Alexander's offensive of 11th May, 1944 —The Grenadiers wait below ground in Cassino while the battle rages in the Liri Valley—Cassino abandoned by the Germans

Cassino had already become the focus of the world's interest in the Italian campaign. There was the moral controversy over the bombing of the Benedictine Abbey; there was the military problem raised by the repeated failures to capture the town, failures in which Americans, Indians, New Zealanders and British had all suffered terrible casualties; and there was the human interest in the strange troglodyte existence lived by the German and Allied garrisons who faced each other across a few yards of rubble in the centre of the town. The Fifth and Eighth Armies shared the opinion of the world. When the 1st Guards Brigade heard that they were to occupy Cassino they received the news with an apprehension which events showed to have been scarcely justified; for there were few men who would not agree, after several days' trial, that conditions in Cassino were in fact far preferable to those that they had recently experienced in the Aurunci Hills.

In the first place, they were not called upon to attack nor to resist attack, nor even to patrol. After the failure of the last Allied assault on the 15th of March, General Alexander had decided that Cassino should be outflanked and not directly seized, and that the troops in the town itself would have no other task than to remain there until the converging pincers of the two great flank attacks had closed behind the German garrison, or at least forced upon them a precipitate withdrawal. For Cassino, though it lay across Route Six, one of the two

Cassino from an Observation Post on Monte Trocchio. *Crown Copyright*

The Monastery is obscured by the explosion of falling bombs. At its foot is the town of Cassino, and behind the snow-capped peak of Monte Cairo.

The Crypt in Cassino.

Combined Headquarters of the 3rd Grenadiers and 2nd Coldstream Guards. *Crown Copyright*

main roads from Naples to Rome, was not in itself of supreme tactical 1944 importance: it blocked no bottleneck, and dominated none of the disputed ground. The German defence system, which had been See Plan p. 426 evolved long before the war at Italo-German staff exercises, hinged not on the town but upon Monastery Hill behind it, and on the River Gari, which sliced across the plain southwards from Cassino. From the former the Germans had an uninterrupted view over the whole area, and wherever a man moved within two miles of the town he felt upon his back a hundred pairs of unseen but all-seeing eyes; and on the west bank of the Gari they had constructed a string of earth fortifications which had so far defied all attempts to cross the river.

It was with the town itself that the Grenadiers were most immediately concerned. In peace time it had been a place of great prosperity, a market for the rich surrounding countryside, and a resort of the pilgrim-tourists who for many centuries had come to visit the Abbey where Saint Benedict had founded his order. Under the Fascist regime the town had been enlarged, and the main buildings reconstructed in a sturdier, more palatial, style, worthy of the town's traditions. For this reason many of the buildings had survived to a remarkable extent the heaviest pounding by bomb and shell which any place had received in the history of warfare. This is no exaggeration. As the air photographs show, there was scarcely a square yard in the centre of the town which was not pitted by a bomb crater, there was not a single roof left intact, and many of the smaller houses had not only been destroyed but completely obliterated, the rubble from their walls spread over a wide, amorphous area or sunk beneath the mud. The streets, even the main road to Rome, were barely distinguishable from the foundations of the buildings on either side; and where once they had opened out into piazzas and ornamental gardens, now there was nothing but an interlocking chain of craters, deep cauldrons of black water. Yet Cassino in its ruins did not have the appearance of shabbiness: it shone; it glistened in the sunlight; its wounds were veiled by a film of powdered stone and marble, and from between the fallen blocks of stone began to spring a carpet of grass and flowers.

From Monte Trocchio, which was the observation post that accommodated a daily crowd of visitors and gunners, Cassino appeared quite deserted. A haze of smoke drifted slowly over the ruins, and from time to time a heavy British shell would raise a spurt of stone and dust from the Monastery walls. The most powerful field-glasses could not detect a single human movement. Yet there were one thousand five hundred men hidden among the houses, half of them men of the German 1st Parachute Division, and half men of the 1st Guards Brigade; there were no civilians. The troops lived in the

1944 shored-up cellars of the houses, and where there were no cellars they constructed rough shelters on the ground floors, partly from the rubble of the upper storeys and partly from sandbags and timber frameworks. Let us examine more closely one such platoon position, a house known by the code name "Mary," which was occupied in turn by Lieuts. D. I. Rollo, M.C., J. W. Harkness and R. Neville, all of the 3rd Grenadiers. Twenty men lived without moving from this house for about ten days at a stretch. "Mary" had no cellar, but she was fortunate in possessing a ceiling over which a mountain of debris had piled up, rendering her water-tight and proof against all but the heaviest German shells. Somewhere beneath the rubble was the corpse of a British soldier killed during the earlier fighting, and the stench of decay became so intolerable that some of the men plugged their nostrils with mosquito cream. In the day time only one sentry was necessary to watch with a periscope the approaches to the house from every direction; at night there were four sentries, one to each corner. For the men not on duty there was very little to do. They read, they wrote letters, they made themselves endless cups of tea, and in that stuffy atmosphere they slept far longer hours than were strictly necessary. Although they were cramped and bored, they were at least warmer and drier and safer than they had been on Monte Cerasola. On the other hand, there was a great sense of isolation, for, though the next platoon were less than fifty yards away, they could no more see their comrades than they could see the Germans a hundred and fifty yards in front. There were only two ways in which they kept in touch with the outside world. The first was by the telephone and wireless, by which every position was linked with every other. And the second was by the nightly arrival of the porters with their supplies for the next twenty-four hours. These porters were as important to the Battalion as the sentries who manned their forward posts, and the part they played was no less dangerous. There was little danger once you were buried inside the town: the danger lay in entering and leaving it.

The porters were selected from among those men who do not normally go into action with the Battalion—the cooks and cobblers, the storemen and the Quartermaster's staff. One of them, for instance, was the Battalion's oldest soldier, Gdsm. Miles, who had served in the Regiment for twenty-four out of his forty-two years. The porters were divided into two teams under an officer (either Lieut. R. H. Firth or Lieut. V. B. Cubitt), and each team would porter for four nights in succession, and then rest for four nights. In addition to food, water and ammunition they would carry in special items such as periscopes, letters, newspapers, petrol for cooking, wire-netting, new pairs of boots, timber for revetments, and quicklime for the destruction of un-

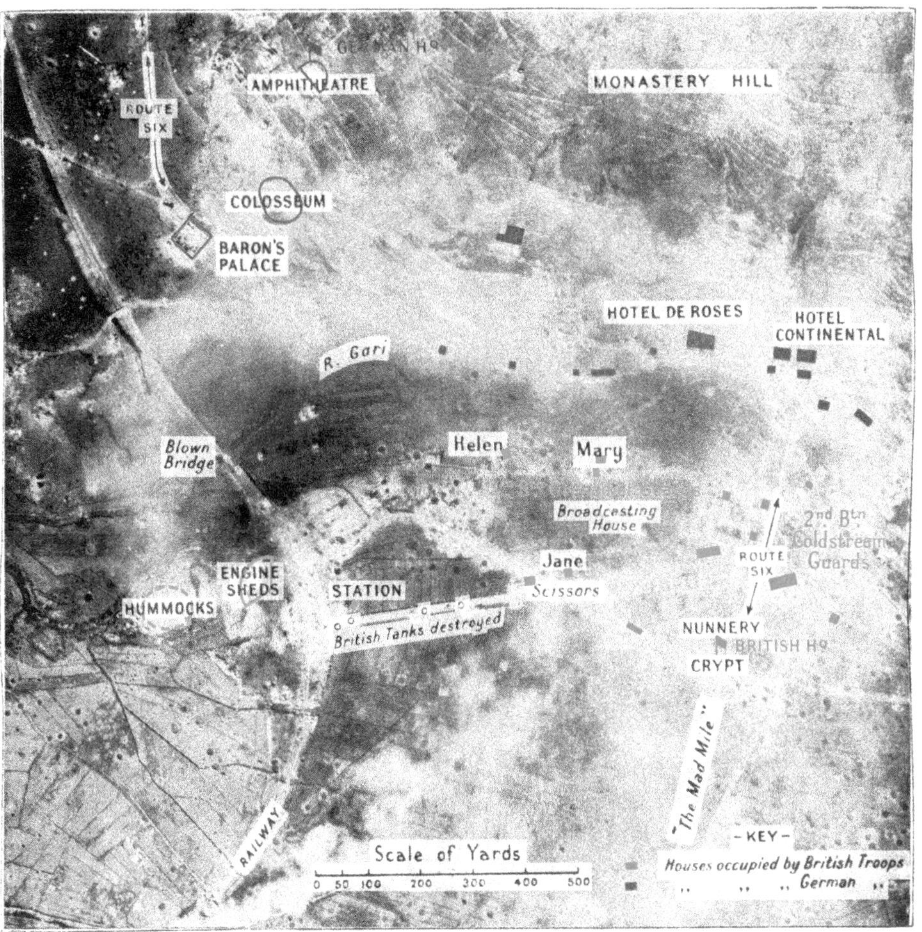

MONASTERY HILL
AMPHITHEATRE
ROUTE SIX
COLOSSEUM
BARON'S PALACE
HOTEL DE ROSES
HOTEL CONTINENTAL
R. Gari
Blown Bridge
Helen
Mary
Broadcasting House
2nd Btn Coldstream Guards
Jane
Scissors
ROUTE SIX
ENGINE SHEDS
STATION
HUMMOCKS
British Tanks destroyed
NUNNERY
BRITISH HQ
CRYPT
"The Mad Mile"
RAILWAY
Scale of Yards
0 50 100 200 300 400 500
- KEY -
Houses occupied by British Troops
" " " German "

CASSINO

buried bodies. All these stores were packed into rucksacks, and at 1944
dusk the porters began to pick their way in single file up that torn stretch of Route Six which was later christened "The Mad Mile of Cassino." Once it had been a fine highway, but now it was rougher than a cart track, quite impassable to any vehicle, for the surface had been pounded to pieces by shells, and in places where a heavy bomb had fallen it gaped wide open. They came to know well the incongruous civilian landmarks scattered along its length: the tottering newspaper kiosk, the ruins of a petrol filling station, a café recognizable only by its signboard hanging by one corner from a slab of wall. Other landmarks recalled more recent events—the series of broken Bailey bridges uselessly spanning a stretch of water, tanks turned lop-sided into a ditch, the body of an American nurse—nobody knew how she had come to be there—pinned beneath the shattered girders of a bridge. The water had overflowed the banks of the Rapido to flood the country on either side, leaving only the road high and dry, like a dyke in Holland. The Germans knew that Route Six was the only possible approach to the centre of the town, and nightly spattered its whole length with mortar bombs and raked it with machine-gun bullets. Burdened as they were—six gallons of water was a typical one-man load—the porters could not run from one covered position to another like an infantryman advancing under fire: they could merely listen with a practised ear for the flight of a falling mortar bomb, or watch the strike of bullets in the dust, and so quicken or slow down their step over the most dangerous section of the route, each man following the stumbling figure ahead of him.

> "When you arrive at Battalion Headquarters," wrote a Grenadier, "you always feel the contrast between the misery of your approach and the welcome that awaits you. Here you find the familiar faces which you have seen in a hundred such headquarters, the same hubble-bubble chatter, gossiping and demanding gossip with the self-assurance of soldiers who have been in the same sector for some time and know the habits of the enemy and the strength of their own position. So you get the gaiety and friendliness and alertness of a rather good club in a place which all of you at home must imagine to be quite appalling."

The headquarters to which he refers was shared between the Grenadiers and the Coldstream, and was located in the crypt of a church which lay beside Route Six at the eastern entrance to the town. The Welsh Guards, who held the northern sector, had their headquarters in the town jail, and it is a measure of the strange conditions in which they lived that the subterranean dungeons of an Italian prison should have been considered the best billets in the whole of Cassino. The crypt housed the commanding officers of the two battalions, their

1944 adjutants, medical, intelligence and signal officers, and about thirty men. There was no room for more, and all were carefully hand-picked to serve the headquarters of both battalions, usually in more than one capacity. The church overhead had been completely destroyed, and the entrance to the crypt was through a small hole tunnelled through the rubble. No natural light ever found its way in, and very little fresh air. They slept late, breakfasted at midday, and needed to rouse themselves into activity only during the first half of the night, when they received visitors from the outside world, and the Germans too began to show signs of life.

General Heidrich's 1st Parachute Division, the veterans of Crete and Sicily, had achieved immense esteem for their successful defence of Cassino. In the northern and more congested part of the town only the width of a ten-foot alley sometimes separated a house occupied by the Welsh Guards from a house occupied by the German parachutists, but in the southern sector, held by the Grenadiers, the ground was more open and the No Man's Land as wide as a hundred and fifty yards. From long observation both sides knew with fair accuracy which buildings were occupied by the other, and as patrolling was unnecessary (and also impossible because of the mines and the waterlogged ground), aggressive activity was limited to short-range and long-range shooting. The Germans would fire into Cassino with every weapon in their armoury from a rifle grenade to a monster railway gun, but the British answered only with the fire of medium weapons, their artillery and heavy machine guns and mortars, to avoid betraying by small-arms fire their posts within the town itself. "A most remarkable achievement," reads a contemporary account, "was the accuracy with which our 25-pounders were able to isolate an enemy-occupied building and pound it to pieces without touching our own troops fifty yards away." The effect of this shooting was seen in the daily processions of German stretcher-bearers moving through the streets under cover of a Red Cross flag.

Like night animals the Germans emerged from their warrens at dusk, and, thinking quite mistakenly that their movements were already veiled by the gathering darkness, they began to porter their supplies, take exercise upon the main road, or carry in huge baulks of timber to reinforce their cellars. It was therefore not difficult to pinpoint their main hide-outs, and the most notorious were given names by successive Allied battalions—names such as "the Hotel des Roses," "the Hotel Continental" and "the Baron's Palace." The carelessness of the Germans in their dusk activities was never modified by their experience of British retaliation. They would expose themselves to quite unnecessary danger, as a prisoner later admitted, in order to

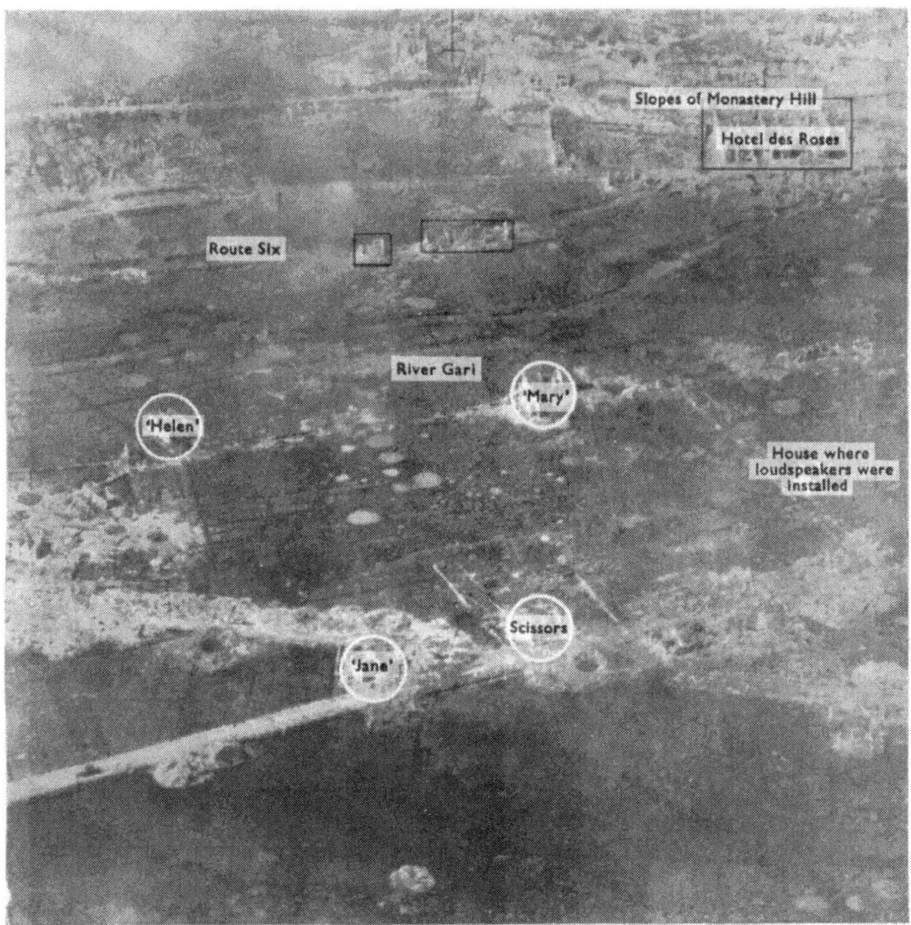

Air Ministry

Cassino: The centre of the Grenadier sector.

The buildings enclosed in circles were those occupied by the Grenadiers: those enclosed by squares were in German hands.

maintain their self-respect. A German, he said, who spent a fortnight 1944
in Cassino automatically qualified for the Iron Cross, and he wished to earn it by a display of courage. They were bored, these tough parachutists: they liked fighting, not waiting. From time to time they would try to enliven the proceedings. They would creep about with pole-charges; their signallers would chip in on British wave-lengths with such innocent remarks as "Comrades, what are you doing?"; and on the morning of Hitler's birthday, the 20th of April, the German part of the town was seen to be festooned with vast Nazi flags. Meanwhile, they knew well enough that a fresh Allied attack was imminent, and night after night the Grenadiers could hear the sound of hammering and blasting, of pile-driving and excavation; fresh trenches would spring up overnight almost within range of a hand grenade; the tank embedded in the Hotel des Roses would suddenly warm up its engines. It came as a relief to the Guards Brigade to hear that no direct assault upon the defences of Cassino was contemplated.

In the interval between the two periods of their occupation of April 23
Cassino the Battalion returned to Calvisi, and it was here that they learned that their Commanding Officer, Lieut.-Colonel A. G. W. Heber-Percy, D.S.O., had been promoted to command the 12th Infantry Brigade. It was now nearly two years since he had taken over command of the Battalion, eighteen months of which he had spent overseas, and during that time he had raised the Battalion to a pitch of excellence which earned from General Leese the tribute that "it is the best trained battalion in the British Army." It was Colonel Heber-Percy's tireless energy which had spurred on his men in battle and out of it; his constant inventiveness; his determination that nothing in a battalion's training need be dull if familiar problems are approached each time from a fresh point of view; his defiance of the merely conventional, his inquisitiveness, his physical courage, his gaiety: almost, one might say, his boyishness, for with his mature instinct for what was possible and what was not possible in war, he combined an unflagging delight in personal leadership and adventure. In capacity more than equal to the command of a brigade, as his later brilliant record showed, at heart he retained the qualities of an eager subaltern who welcomes danger as an opportunity for fresh achievement and as a closer bond between himself and his men. He was succeeded in command of the 3rd Battalion by Lieut.-Colonel J. A. April 25
Goschen.

The secret of the Allied offensive had been well kept. When they first held the Cassino sector, from the 7th to the 23rd of April, not even the commanding officers had known what plans were afoot, and May 4
when the Brigade returned to the town an elaborate cover-plan was

1944 devised to conceal the facts from all but the most senior officers. The full details were not published to the Guardsmen until a few hours before the start of the operation.

"From the East and West, from the North and South, blows are about to fall which will result in the final destruction of the Nazis and bring freedom once again to Europe, and hasten peace for us all. To us in Italy has been given the honour to strike the first blow." So ran General Alexander's order of the day. The object of this attack was not merely to capture Cassino and debouch into the Liri Valley; nor would the offensive stop short at the relief of the Anzio beach-head or the liberation of Rome. Its object, again in the words of the Commander-in-Chief, was no less than "to destroy the German armies in Italy." Since the beginning of the campaign the Fifth and Eighth Armies had been strung across the whole width of the peninsula, battering with limited forces against a number of separate points in the enemy line. This strategy was now reversed. With great secrecy the bulk of the Eighth Army divisions were transferred to assembly areas behind Cassino, the Fifth Army were concentrated on a narrow sector of the Lower Garigliano, and the Adriatic coast and the Central Apennines were left thinly held by a number of independent formations, of which the 24th Guards Brigade was one. The large force so amassed attacked on the fifteen-mile sector between Cassino and the sea. In so far as it affected Cassino itself, the plan included a simultaneous assault both north and south of the town. The Polish Corps *See Map p. 426* were to capture Monastery Hill, while the 4th British Division forced a crossing of the River Gari, and, sweeping north-west, linked up with the Poles on Route Six about three miles west of the town. Cassino would then be cut off, and if the German garrison had not already made their escape or still refused to surrender, the town would be cleared from the south by the 10th Brigade, supported on their right flank by the fire of the 1st Guards Brigade.

May 11 At 10.45 p.m. on the 11th of May there was a sudden pause in the spasmodic gun fire. All in the town were waiting below ground, and all those behind the lines stood watching at the farmhouse doors. At 11 p.m. exactly seven hundred Allied guns split the night with the greatest barrage fired in five years of war.

The Germans were certainly surprised by the time, the direction and the violence of the offensive, and their immediate reaction to the barrage was to send up scores of coloured Very lights all along the line, but particularly from Cassino itself, as if they expected the main blow to fall there. The Grenadiers encouraged this idea by firing into the town throughout the night, but when morning came the enemy had defined the areas of the first assault, and both sides settled down

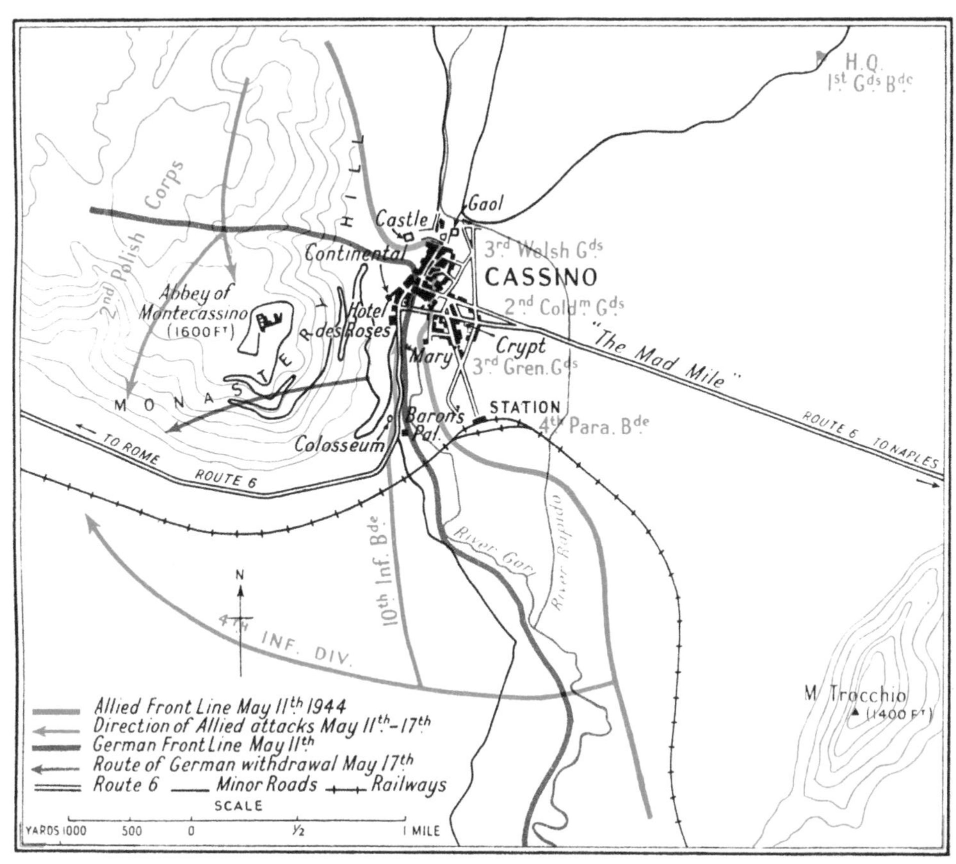

THE CASSINO OFFENSIVE, MAY, 1944

Face page 426

to wait in a mood of calm alertness. One German was seen that morning cleaning out his billet with a broom. The town was shrouded in smoke blown up from the Gari battlefield, and frequently nothing more could be seen from Monte Trocchio than the Monastery floating on a sea of mist. The reports which were received during the first few days were not very encouraging. The 4th Division had failed to bridge the Gari on schedule, and the Poles had been flung back almost to their starting line. Later the pincers gradually began to close, and the Guards Brigade watched with closer and closer attention the movements of the German parachutists in the town. "Are they still there?" "Are they going?" were questions asked by the higher headquarters several times a day, and even the men in the most advanced posts could never answer with certainty. How easy it would be, now that the moon was waning and the town was blanketed in smoke, for the enemy to slip silently away, leaving behind just sufficient men to simulate normal activity! When the small items of information were pieced together the conclusion was hazarded that on the evening of the 17th of May (when the 4th Division's carriers were already across Route Six, and the Poles were making good progress in their second assault on the Monastery), the enemy might have thinned out slightly, but he was still holding the town in force. This conclusion was soon shown to be correct. At 8.50 p.m. that night there was still a gap about a mile wide through which the Germans could escape, and the Divisional Commander decided that the time had come to make use of the broadcasting apparatus which had been erected in the middle of the town. Accordingly, all artillery fire in the area of the town was suspended, and in a place where there had always been a tendency to speak in whispers, the silence was broken by an enormous voice, repeating in German:

1944 May 12

May 17

> "If you wish to surrender, come out with your hands up. Come out while it is still light down Route Six leading east out of the town. If you surrender after dark we shall not know whether you are trying to break out or to surrender, and you will probably be shot. You have fought well. To fight on is senseless. Look over your shoulders. The Poles are at the gates of the Monastery. If you don't believe us, send out patrols. Cassino is lost to Germany."

A few shots were aimed at the loud-speakers, but not a single deserter came over.

At about midnight the gap was narrower but still open, and the Grenadiers suddenly saw the Germans rise from the ruins and swarm over the shoulder of Monastery Hill, moving in groups and by quick dashes from rock to rock. The whole slope was heavily bombarded, but undoubtedly the majority of the parachutists safely passed

1944 May 18 through the barrage, and then through the gap. At 8 a.m. the next morning the German wireless announced with some justification that Cassino had been successfully evacuated. Only a handful of men were left behind in the town, and they came forward with white flags when the broadcasting began again. At 10 a.m. the 10th Brigade advanced according to plan, meeting no opposition apart from one or two snipers' shots, and at 10.30 the Polish flag was seen flying from the Monastery. The first direct contact between the 10th Brigade and the 1st Guards Brigade was made by Brigadier Heber-Percy, who waded through the water-logged ground from the Hotel des Roses to the building occupied by Major Jameson. Then the Press arrived, followed by the gunners, the sappers, the tank crews, and all the others who had contributed to the defence and capture of the town. The Army Commander, General Leese, was given tea in the crypt, and in the late afternoon the Grenadiers, as they had so often promised themselves, marched out of Cassino in daylight.

3

THE 5TH BATTALION ON THE RIVER SANGRO

Reorganization after Anzio—Mountain positions at San Pietro—Move to Vastogirardi—"The Nelson Column"—The 24th Guards Brigade join the 6th South African Armoured Division

Mar. 9-28 After their return from Anzio the 5th Battalion enjoyed three weeks' rest in the neighbourhood of Sorrento, revisiting the many small places which they had discovered before embarking for the beach-head, among them Ravello, Positano, Ischia and Pompeii, but not, to their regret, the Isle of Capri, which was out of bounds to all but American troops. The little villages of the peninsula in which they lived were built high above the Bay of Naples in ascending layers of brown roofs and stepped streets paved with lava blocks, while beyond the huddle of houses the hillsides were striped by terraces and orange groves, and the black outlines of distant promontories fell sharply into the sea. They were very happy. The 5th Battalion, and the 24th Guards Brigade as a whole, were growing fresh limbs, imbibing new blood. In place of the two companies which the Grenadiers had lost at Anzio two more were formed from the younger men of the 6th Battalion, whose veterans were soon on their way home to England; and in place of the Irish Guards the 3rd Battalion of the Coldstream joined the 24th Guards Brigade.

By the end of March they were ready for fresh enterprises, but first **1944**
came a period of training at Montesarchio, for the original companies **Mar. 28-April 11**
of the 5th Battalion had never yet fought in high mountains, and high mountains formed the staple terrain of Central Italy. It was while they
were at Montesarchio that General Alexander visited the Battalion to **April 2**
present the ribbon of the Victoria Cross to Major Sidney in the presence of the latter's father-in-law, himself an old Grenadier, Field-Marshal The Viscount Gort, V.C.

Until the opening of the May offensive the 24th Guards Brigade
held in turn two wide sectors of the Central Apennines overlooking *See Map p.* **442**
the River Sangro. They were scattered over thirty miles of mountain during the same period that the 1st Guards Brigade held a six-hundred-yard frontage in Cassino. In the first position the 5th Grenadiers had two companies at Vastogirardi and two companies farther forward in the village of San Pietro. Vastogirardi was out of sight and out of all contact with the Germans, a hill-top village with cobbled stairways in place of streets, and a rectangular block of sturdy houses on the summit, forming the citadel, in which No. 3 Company were lodged. Their duties were, first, to send patrols ahead of the main line; secondly, to organize the Battalion supplies; and, thirdly, to restore order among the civilian population. This last task was undertaken by Major T. S. Hohler, M.C., who soon arranged not only a system of ration cards but a juridical scheme based on his own sound sense and an unofficial court at which he attempted to dispense justice among the more quarrelsome Italians.

At San Pietro Nos. 1 and 2 Companies found that the Germans had destroyed every building except the church and three small houses, in order to deny to the Allies the comfortable quarters which they themselves lacked on the far side of the Sangro Valley. The Grenadiers slept in tents, but the local population had refused to abandon the ruins of their homes. They lived in odd corners of the rubble, in makeshift shelters, and a Grenadier records with sorrow and admiration that he watched two Italian farmers digging through a glacis of fallen bricks and plaster to reach their field beneath, and finally extract a small basketful of seed potatoes. They hated the Germans, these peasants: quietly but deeply, they hated them; and to the British, who were now in possession of what remained of their villages, they gave all they could: some of them even gave their lives when acting as guides or scouts on our behalf. From a village within the German lines a message was received one day to ask whether we would mind shooting a little farther away, as the Germans had all gone, and there were so few houses left now. There were no other complaints.

Of the Germans the Battalion saw very little. From San Pietro they

1944 looked across the deep, wide valley of the Sangro to a vast apron of grassland speckled with grey rocks and farmhouses, and rising in wooded humps to a skyline of mountains six thousand feet high. Among the rocky pinnacles on the crest there were isolated German outposts, so far away that it was only on the eighth day that the Grenadiers' intelligence section announced with some surprise that they thought they had seen three Germans. The patrols which crossed the Sangro from our side did not have time to do more in the course of a single night than explore some of the farms and villages on the lower slopes. Of enemy patrols there was no sign.

A fortnight later the larger part of the Battalion moved a few miles
April 28 farther south to Castel San Vicenzo, leaving No. 2 Company at Vastogirardi under Major E. J. B. Nelson, M.C. The Grenadiers arrived at Castel San Vicenzo in a snowstorm to find that their company positions were sited most uncomfortably on the slopes of enormous empty hills, with two platoons on the very summit of the four-thousand-foot Monte Curvale. Here the shelling was more regular and more intense than at San Pietro, but again there was no enemy in sight, and attempts to find the Germans by night-long patrols were usually fruitless. Among those who went out on these exhausting expeditions were Lieuts. Freeman-Attwood, King-Smith and Williams, and the Commanding Officer, Lieut.-Colonel G. C. Gordon-Lennox, did his share of the patrolling.

It was, however, the force at Vastogirardi, nicknamed, after its commander, "The Nelson Column," whose activities during this static period of the 5th Battalion's story were the most adventurous. In the
May 6 first week of May they suffered a sad loss in the death on patrol of Lieut. V. S. de R. Canning, who trod on a mine and was killed out-
May 11 right with his Italian guide. Five days later No. 2 Company carried out a raid upon the German-held mountain-crest with the intention of creating an incident on this part of the Italian Front to coincide with the opening of the Cassino offensive, and so give the Germans cause to wonder whether this remote sector of the line was also coming under strong attack. In order to approach within striking distance of the six-thousand-foot crest, the company moved forward the night before to the far bank of the river, lay concealed there for the whole of the next day, and then continued up the track to the foot of the pinnacles where the Germans were thought to be lying. As they waited there, cold and lonely, they saw the gun-flashes spring up from the direction of Cassino, and felt the ground tremble beneath their bodies, but the distance was too great for them to hear the accompanying roar. For several minutes the sky, as one of them described it, "was bright like the dawn: then the moon came up and killed the flashes of the

guns." At a prearranged moment Lieut. T. A. Jones's platoon opened fire from two hundred yards away, the artillery brought down their concentrations on the same spot, and in the ensuing silence one German machine gun fired nervously in the direction of the patrol. Nothing more happened, for nothing more was intended. They returned stumbling down to the path to the river, and back to their ruined village of San Pietro. 1944

The Nelson Column rejoined the remainder of the Battalion, and in a few days they returned together to Solopaca. Here they learned that the 24th Guards Brigade were to join the 6th South African Armoured Division which had just arrived in Italy from Cairo and included many veterans of the two South African divisions which had fought under Wavell and Alexander in the Libyan campaigns. From the very start the relations between the Guardsmen and the South Africans were extremely cordial, and, as the next two chapters will show, the fortunate chance which united them at the outset of the advance up Italy resulted not only in many victories gained in common but in friendships which have never since been allowed to die. May 21

CHAPTER VIII

CASSINO TO FLORENCE

3RD AND 5TH BATTALIONS

1

THE SUMMER CAMPAIGN OF 1944

General account of fighting in Tuscany and Umbria—Devastation in the Liri Valley followed by rapid advance farther north—Attitude of Italian civilians to British troops—Contrast between British and German soldiers

1944 IT has not often been possible in previous chapters of this History to link the operations of the separate Battalions of the Grenadiers by more than a stretched and tenuous thread. With the exception of the final week of the Tunisian campaign, each Battalion had been engaged in battles which were tactically independent and geographically remote from one another, and whose only connection was the strategic plan of which the men knew very little at the time. From the start of the three-hundred-mile advance up the leg of Italy from Cassino to the valley of the Po, the fortunes of the 3rd and 5th Battalions were more closely interlocked and directed towards the same immediate ends. Though they marched under the command of different divisions and different corps, the two Battalions kept pace with each other, sometimes at the head, sometimes at the tail of their respective columns; sometimes swung farther apart by the grain of the hills and valleys, and sometimes diverted along different channels of the same sluggish stream; but rarely was there as much as twenty miles between them. The actions which they fought during those summer months varied greatly in their circumstances, but the whole atmosphere of the advance was common to them both. Before describing the detail of their operations it is therefore proposed to give a general account of this phase of the Italian campaign: to answer the question "What was it like?" before answering the question "What actually happened?" And in passing to the narrative of events, the operations of both Battalions will be interwoven, with the object of re-creating the impression, very strong at the time, of the simultaneous, interdependent piston-strokes of a multicylindered engine.

First, the country. The Grenadiers had had little chance to discover 1944
how warm and serene Italy can be. The weather hitherto had been foul, and on remote mountain slopes or in sodden, battered villages they had found little to excite their admiration. Only the Sorrento Peninsula had lived up to the picture-postcard idea of Italy which most of them had preconceived. But now, as they passed into undamaged Tuscany and undamaged Umbria, they found the real Italy at last: the Italy of wagon teams of white oxen lumbering along a lane with a load of grapes; of little towns upon a hill-top with roofs of russet-brown and a campanile lazily tolling out the hours; of cypresses, orange groves, and tall poplars on a river bank. They found, too, that the weather, once the spring had passed into summer, was warm and dry enough to make a night under the open sky no hardship but a delight, and any field by the wayside a pleasant resting place.

The change from a war-like to a peaceful landscape was not at first apparent, for the Liri Valley had been fought over with an intensity that left indelible scars. The Grenadiers did not take part in those first battles, but this description, written by an officer a short time afterwards, gives a good idea of what they found:

> "Never have I seen, not in Tunisia, not in England, not in France in 1940, a country which looked more like the conventional idea of a country at war. A village street is like a row of decayed teeth. In the remains of one house, a gun team have slung a tarpaulin over the roofless walls, and they are cooking their dinner with the sticks of furniture which remain: in the next, where only the cellar is still intact, a wretched peasant family looks up at you from the earthen floor, crouching on their haunches all day long, and refusing to leave: from any house which has a few rooms fairly water-tight there will come a glow of hurricane lamps, the buzz of telephones, and officers running to and fro. Having been obliged to shell this village, and then impose ourselves piecemeal on what remains of it, one feels almost ashamed of this constant traffic of heavy lorries which is steadily grinding the decent civilian life out of the place—this constant passage of khaki, which is probably all these people have known and will ever know of the English. And when the battle passes it may be exhilarating for us, but it will mean that every village we reach will be reduced to the same state."

It did not turn out as gloomily as he foresaw. Contrast with that picture of devastation another letter written a month later, when both Battalions were advancing up the Tiber Valley:

> "To a troop of tanks or a platoon of men in the vanguard the countryside looks quite deserted: hot, untouched, sunny, sleepy, and even welcoming. One of the odd things about this campaign is that its battles are fought in places just like the fields at home. We are sent to attack green hills with cows grazing on them, or villages where you

1944 can see the peasant women hanging out their washing. For a moment there is a crash of artillery which does little harm to anyone or anything, and then the tanks burst through the hedges into the fields, while the infantry dart about behind them. The material damage done by these girations is little more than a herd of cattle would do if they ran amok among the corn. And then suddenly you see that it is not the country but human beings who have really suffered. You meet the Guardsmen or their German prisoners returning along the leafy lanes with their faces grey and haggard, sometimes talking incoherently; and there among the poppies and the wheat you will come upon the body of a young soldier, his dead hands biting deep into the soil."

Perhaps the Italian civilians suffered more than any. The war which the armies had been making and following for years would suddenly burst upon them in the middle of an afternoon. The familiar names of their villages and little towns would for the space of a few hours be circled on the maps of rival commanders, mispronounced upon a score of wirelesses, lifted from obscurity into the *communiqués* which the world would read the next day. A sloping field, which to the farmer had merely been an awkward piece of ground to plough, would be reconnoitred by a German subaltern, occupied by a tired dozen of his men, shelled, attacked, and then captured, leaving behind strips of jagged metal, and two humps, perhaps, beneath a rough, wooden cross. The armies could have no respect for private property. They imposed themselves upon the country like a plague of locusts. No door was closed to them, and while they brought with them every resource necessary for life and battle, the peasants in their own homes had often so little that they would dig up the empty army ration tins for scraps of food. When they were wounded (being too inexperienced to judge the risk they ran from the feathery shuffle of a falling mortar bomb), they had no other recourse than to crawl to Allied aid posts for their charity and skill. Sometimes they would take to the mountain roads, walking with bundles on their heads through the dust, and look up with shy smiles at the troop carriers. "I once saw an old man," records a Grenadier, "being carried for miles by his two sons, seated in his kitchen chair." In spite of all their hardships, the Italians remained well disposed to their liberators, quite unaffected by the German propaganda posters which represented us as rapacious brutes, mostly black. They would come forward to meet the leading troops with a basket of cherries, a bottle of wine, or a clutch of eggs in a straw hat. For them our arrival meant the end of the war. An instance of this attitude stands out vividly in the mind of one Grenadier. His jeep happened to be the first to enter a hill-top village bypassed by the main advance. As he drove into the little piazza he was puzzled to see the children run screaming to their mothers' aprons. This had never happened before. And the explanation? The children thought that he was a German officer returning to reoccupy the village. After making himself known and taking a glass of wine with the priest and mayor, he came out to find his jeep festooned with country flowers and the children dancing round it. 1944

The qualities of the British soldier were perfectly adapted to his present task. His friendliness, his power of improvisation, his acceptance of every situation as he found it, his capacity to cast away all worry about his own personal future, which comes partly from confidence in his leaders and partly from sheer ignorance of what is going on. Indeed, the interest he showed in what was happening on the Russian front, and, after the 6th of June, in Normandy, was often more marked than his interest in the Italian campaign. At the beginning of the offensive he understood well enough what was the immediate object—the capture of Cassino—for he could see with his own eyes the shell-bursts and the clouds of dust which marked the farthest points reached by the converging pincers. But when the battle loosened, when the dam burst, and the flood of the Allied advance poured along a dozen separate channels, the soldier's horizon was apt to be confined by the mountains bordering his own particular valley. There were the high-lights—the relief of the Anzio bridgehead, the liberation of Rome, the crossing of the Tiber-Arno watershed, the breaching of the Gothic Line, and the first sight of the Po Valley and the Alps. But more often the men and junior officers were engaged in battles of which they did not know the full significance in relation to the strategic plan. For hours, and sometimes days, they would wait patiently in dusty fields while others broke fresh ground ahead of them. Ordered suddenly to put on their equipment and climb back into their lorries, they would be driven off to unknown destinations, lurching along hot by-roads all through the day or night, delayed at intervals by blown bridges long enough to brew a can of tea by the wayside; then on again, down the steep diversions which the bulldozers had carved out of the stream-banks, or rattling across the loose boards of a Bailey bridge. So they came once more to the van of their Division, past the tanks, within the range of gun fire, and then heard a shot or the rattle of a machine gun. Where were they? There was no time and no real need to explain the wider situation. Out came the maps, a small, isolated square of Italian soil; a hurried identification of features on map and ground. "The Germans are here and there, perhaps here too. The bridge is blown, the tanks held up. We must have this ridge by nightfall." Then the battalion, company and platoon plans, in increasing detail: "That hedge . . . will the 2-inch mortar reach? . . . Get them under cover of this farm . . . and

1944 No. 3 Platoon on your right . . . in half an hour from now." So the battle started; a few more fields, another village, abandoned by the Germans, entered by our own men, and so "captured." And this minor skirmish would make its mark upon the great operation maps of rear headquarters, and even affect the bulge of the broad, black line published the next day in the newspapers of the world. The exact position of the front line, the line joining the points reached by the leading tanks or sections of a hundred different columns, was always of great importance. Beyond it lay country which looked no different from the country already in our hands; but somewhere across that calm, unbroken stretch of fields lay a curtain dividing friend from foe, guns that would shoot to defend you from guns that would shoot to kill.

Brushing aside the curtain, let us examine the conditions under which the Germans fought and lived. The Italians who experienced, as we never could, the odd sensation of seeing one army suddenly replaced by another, would immediately be struck by the contrast between the two. Our men were confident, healthy, even rather languid; the Germans were tired, sick and nervous. It was not only that they suffered from the psychological effects of constant retreat and the hostility of the people which grew, as the summer advanced, into open partisan warfare. There was also the physical exhaustion imposed by lack of transport and Allied air superiority which prevented the use in daylight of the few German lorries which remained. They marched by night, and it was a relief to halt at dawn to defend the slope of some rocky hill, for then they could rest and they could hit back. Not many of them, even in the moments of greatest hopelessness, would take the final step of desertion, but their attitude when taken prisoner would often be one almost of gratitude to their captors, and the Guardsmen were puzzled by the contrast between their present exhaustion and even tearfulness and their brave performance on the recent battlefield. The Germans had been told by their officers that the British take no prisoners, or hand them over to the Russians for execution. Is it, then, surprising that they should have fought their hardest to evade capture, and then be overwhelmed by relief to find that they were treated no more harshly than one of our own soldiers under arrest? They never knew us as we knew them. They never saw a billet occupied by the British the night before as we saw theirs. They never handled the litter of personal equipment and letters as we handled theirs. The number of prisoners which they took was very small, of deserters none at all. All they knew was that our supplies, our equipment, our morale were apparently inexhaustible, our determination inflexible, our initiative unchallengeable. On their side the advantages were few. They could leave behind mines and booby-traps, and blow up the bridges. They were withdrawing back on their own supply 1944 dumps at the same time as the Allies were putting a greater and greater distance between their front line and their bases. But little more. They did not know what they were heading for: we knew, without a shadow of doubt.

2

CASSINO TO ROME

Development of the offensive—The 3rd Battalion and the Battle of Monte Grande—Capture of Arce—Capture of Rome by the Americans—The 5th Battalion reach the Tiber

Our object was the destruction of the German armies in Italy. Our method, to make the maximum use of our three great advantages—our mobility; our ability to concentrate our strength at a single point while the Germans were obliged to disperse theirs over the whole width of the front; and our possession in the Anzio bridgehead of a large striking force poised upon the flank and rear of the German lines of communication. A quick and easy success at Cassino was not what General Alexander either expected or desired. He wished to draw in the German reserves to the battle in the Liri Valley, weaken their field force, cripple their communications by air bombardment, and then, when they were utterly confused, launch his own reserves simultaneously from Anzio and Cassino. An eventual break-through was never in doubt; what was more uncertain was whether Kesselring would be able to withdraw his shattered forces in time and in sufficient strength to form a new line farther north. As so often before and after in the Second German War, the world was electrified by the announcement of a great new offensive, only to be disappointed by the smallness of the gains in the first few days. The Liri Valley was a new Alamein, a Sedan, a Vitebsk, a Caen. And then, quite suddenly, the break-through; full retreat and full pursuit. But while the world once more applauded, the generals worried. It was going *too* quickly. The Germans were not hemmed in and fighting: they were escaping. With every score of miles overrun without a fight, the chance that the German Army could be annihilated grew more remote. It was not another Tunis, for the leg of Italy is a long one, and broadened out at the hip into the Fortress of Central Europe. Once the first opportunity to encircle the Germans had passed, the Fifth and Eighth Armies had

1944 no final destination to which they could point and say: "Once there, it will be the end."

Neither the 3rd nor the 5th Battalion of the Grenadiers was involved in the fighting in the Liri Valley, for both formed part of that mobile reserve which waited to exploit the issue of the battle. After the fall of Cassino the 3rd rejoined the 6th Armoured Division, and the 5th took their place for the first time in the 6th South African Armoured Division. *See Map p. 442* Not long afterwards both Battalions moved up behind the tanks, and jolted over the rough cart tracks which temporarily served as supply routes, into the less-damaged country south of the Melfa River. The 5th Battalion's first task was to hold secure a group of hills May 27-30 at Castrocielo, overlooking Route Six, but they met no enemy there, and the Tactical Headquarters of the Eighth Army settled in beside them. They were cramped and uncomfortable, but in no danger. The 3rd Battalion, on the other hand, were soon involved in a battle which was fiercer than any other in which they were engaged throughout the campaign: the Battle of Monte Grande and Monte Piccolo.

These two hills lay on the south side of Route Six at a point where *See Plan p. 440* the road and railway together pass through a narrow defile, approaching the small town of Arce. It was here, the first natural barrier lying astride the Liri Valley, that the Germans left a rearguard from the 1st Parachute Division to gain a breathing space for the bulk of their armies which were draining off the hills and by-roads for their long march to the north. There had been reports that part of the Canadian Division had occupied Monte Grande, but owing to some misunderstanding or over-optimism the Canadians had come down from the hill-top, allowing the Germans to creep back and build the rough emplacements by which the 6th Armoured Division were faced the May 26 next day. Crossing the Melfa River by a ford, the 3rd Grenadiers, mounted on the tanks of the 16th/5th Lancers, were carried for some miles up Route Six before discovering the trouble that lay ahead. They occupied the village of Coldragone without a fight. At this moment a few German motor-cyclists ventured down the road to meet the fire of the Lancers, and the Grenadiers dismounted from the tanks to continue the advance on foot into the mouth of the Piccolo-Providero Pass. While No. 4 Company (Capt. A. K. C. Nation) were forming up on the road for this advance they were suddenly deluged by a storm of shells which killed five men and wounded seventeen others. Any attempt made by the tanks to move off the road along the dusty tracks was blocked by increasing shell fire, directed, as they then realized, by the Germans on top of the two hills ahead. The Grenadiers were halted, and a company of the 3rd Welsh Guards passed beyond them during the night to occupy the lower slopes of

Monte Providero. Grande and Piccolo were still strongly held by the Germans. It would require an attack by the whole of the 1st Guards Brigade to capture them. 1944

Little did the Grenadiers realize that the entire Eighth Army waited on the result of this attack. It was the first check since the break-through, and if a delay were imposed at Arce the momentum of the pursuit would be slowed down. Nor did they realize by what stubborn opposition they were faced. From the start, the importance and the difficulties of their task were therefore under-estimated through lack of accurate information, and it cannot be denied that the Battalion as a whole lacked that fierce determination which carried them through to success in previous and later battles. They felt lost: they could not see the objectives clearly through the thick foliage of the lower ground: there was no time to explain to every man exactly what was required of him: and during the preparatory phase of planning and giving orders they were exposed to heavy shell fire which prevented them from resting, and from assessing with calm and clarity the task by which they were confronted. In all this lay the seeds of their ill-success.

Monte Grande was separated from Monte Piccolo by a deep cleft. Each was a bare, rocky hill about six hundred feet high, curling round in a crescent to form a natural breastwork defending the town of Arce. Brigadier Haydon ordered the 2nd Coldstream to capture Piccolo and the 3rd Grenadiers to capture Grande, by a simultaneous night advance. The Grenadier plan, as formulated by Lieut.-Colonel J. A. Goschen, was as follows: Nos. 1 and 3 Companies were ordered to advance side by side to the peak of Grande, while No. 2 Company, moving in a wider sweep round the left flank, cleared a string of houses at its foot and then captured the centre of the ridge. No. 4 Company were kept in reserve.

Shortly before 3 a.m. the Grenadiers, following the tail of the Coldstream, began to move forward up the dark and twisting lanes to the foot of the hill. The first to meet trouble were No. 2 Company (Major M. E. M. Sandys), who were approaching the houses, closely bunched on a narrow track, when a salvo of German shells fell among them, and they suffered at least twenty casualties before coming within sight of a single German. Lieut. A. M. Denny rallied the survivors, but they were now too few to carry out their original task. They were halted and reorganized at the foot of the hill. Unaware of the consequent insecurity of their left flank, Nos. 1 and 3 Companies had already advanced up the hill to the main summit, stumbling over the steep terraces and passing at one point through the fire of their own guns, which was falling short of the enemy's line. Until the last May 28

1944 moment they were not shot at by the Germans, but just as they were breasting the final ridge a machine gun opened fire from behind them, lower down the hill. Lieut. M. A. R. R. Cooper led his platoon towards it, but was himself almost immediately wounded. The remainder continued up the slope. At about 5.30 a.m., just as dawn was breaking, No. 1 Company swept over the highest knoll and continued down the far slope, to discover that the Germans had withdrawn a few yards, but had by no means given up the position for lost. They shot upwards at the advancing Grenadiers, and among the casualties was Major A. G. Way, M.C., the commander of No. 1 Company, who was severely wounded in the stomach. The company were reorganized on the summit by Lieut. D. I. Rollo, M.C., and side by side with No. 3 Company (Major J. G. C. Jameson) they began hastily to build stone sangars for protection against the expected German counter-attack.

It came half an hour after the capture of the hill, at a time when the men had been obliged to lay down their arms to carry stones for the construction of the sangars. One platoon of No. 3 Company were forced to withdraw, and the two companies now lined a low wall which ringed the summit, while the Germans occupied a pimple of rock slightly above them, and began to shoot down with terrible short-range accuracy at any Guardsman who raised his rifle or machine gun to reply. For a time the Germans were kept at bay. The British artillery fired as close as they dared, with great risk to the Grenadiers but with great effect upon the enemy, and among the men on the hill-top there were several who performed outstanding acts of gallantry. Gdsm. Eaton, M.M., of No. 3 Company, alone accounted for eighteen Germans; and Gdsm. Atkinson, M.M., of No. 1 Company, advanced into the open upon another group, firing his Bren gun from the hip, and shot down a German officer and four men. Had it not been for two setbacks it is probable that the Battalion would have been able to hold their own, just as the Coldstream Guards, who had captured Monte Piccolo, remained upon it until the end of the battle. The first setback was the shortage of ammunition; the second was the fact that No. 2 Company had stopped short of their objective, and the farther end of the Grande ridge (marked "A" on the plan) was never captured. Steps were taken by Colonel Goschen to remedy both situations. He ordered Lieut. R. H. Firth to take two carrier-loads of ammunition to Nos. 1 and 3 Companies; and he ordered No. 4 Company (Capt. A. K. C. Nation) to advance along the crest to capture Point "A." Both, through no fault of their own, arrived too late. Lieut. Firth was delayed by a direct hit upon one of his carriers within a hundred yards of Battalion Headquarters, and had begun to organize the man-handling of the ammunition boxes up the hill when he found that the

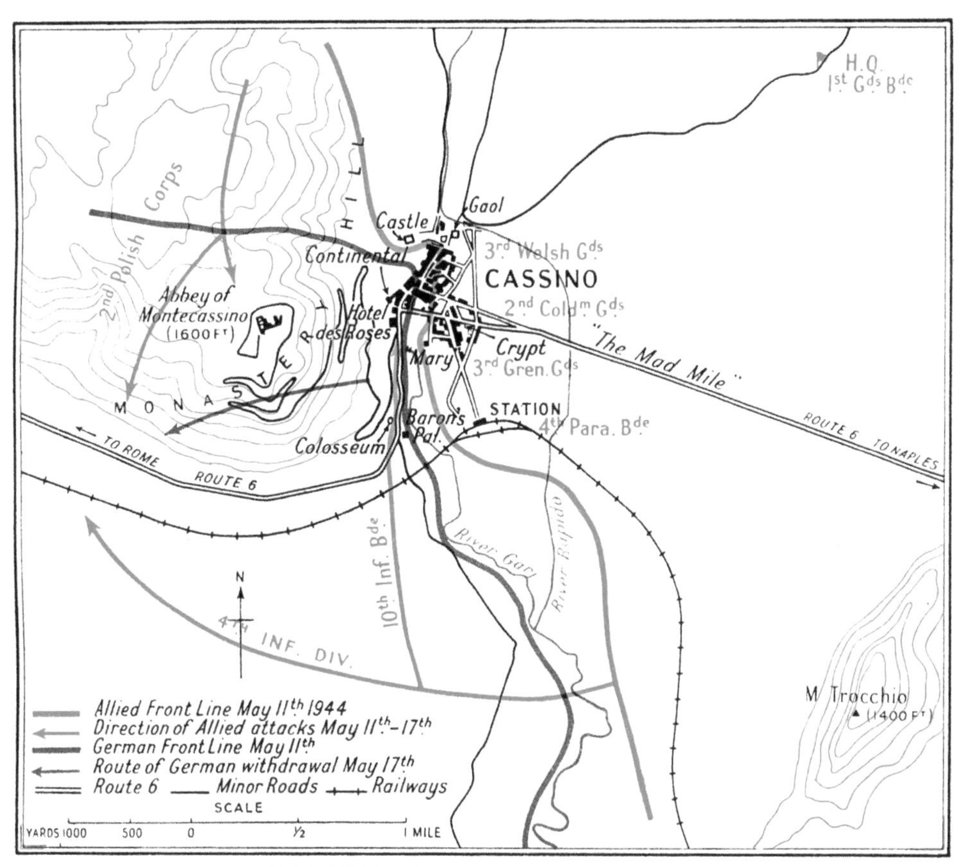

THE CASSINO OFFENSIVE, MAY, 1944

Face page 426

withdrawal had already begun. And Capt. Nation was leading his 1944
company up the terraces when he too saw that the forward companies were beginning to come back. This withdrawal had been ordered at 7 a.m. by Colonel Goschen for two reasons. He realized that even if Lieut. Firth arrived in time the ammunition which he was carrying would not be sufficient to beat back another counter-attack; and, more important, a wide outflanking movement by the Germans, originating from Point "A," was already threatening to cut off the Grenadiers from the Coldstream. Small groups of enemy were beginning to penetrate the cleft between Grande and Piccolo, and on the left flank German machine guns were seen to be firing from the near slopes of the hill. Apart from this, the companies were much weakened. Among the officers in No. 1 Company Major Way and Lieut. Cooper were wounded; and in No. 3 Company Lieuts. J. W. Harkness and R. C. Murdoch. A fifth casualty was the Battalion Intelligence Officer, Lieut. T. H. Faber.

The Grenadiers withdrew in broad daylight down the slopes of Monte Grande, protected from the pursuing Germans by the tanks of the 16th/5th Lancers firing low over their heads. C.S.M. Waters was outstanding for his coolness and courage in organizing that difficult retreat. They re-formed in the plain protecting the left flank of Monte Piccolo, and neither were attacked nor renewed their own attack during the remainder of that day. After nightfall the Germans, having delayed the Allied advance by forty-eight hours, abandoned both hills under the threat of the 8th Indian Division's attack on Rocca d'Arce. A patrol led by Sergt. Roberts of the 3rd Grenadiers found the summit of Monte Grande free of all enemy except for some thirty German corpses, and the next morning the British tanks entered May 29
Arce unopposed. The battle had cost the 1st Guards Brigade two hundred and eighty-three casualties in all; of the Grenadiers, sixteen men were killed and fifty-five wounded.

Not for many days and for many miles did the Eighth Army again encounter such strenuous opposition. The strong flank attack by the Anglo-American Corps from the Anzio beach-head had forced the southern group of German divisions to abandon all attempts to hold the Allies south of Rome, and only by a systematic destruction of the bridges did they delay our advance. The 3rd and 5th Battalions joined the slow convoys moving towards Rome, following the tanks of their respective divisions at such a distance that the wireless messages from the front were scarcely audible and the exact position of the spearheads uncertain. The two Guards Brigades moved on in fits and starts as road space became available, crawling through the night along

1944 roads which traversed almost undamaged country, where only a group of German prisoners, a ditched tank or a blown-up lorry showed that a half-hour's skirmish had been enough to unlock the gateway to another valley or another small town. One evening, when both Bat-
June 4 talions were near Fiuggio, a message flew from wireless set to wireless set: "Our big cousins have entered the great city"—a poor, excited and needless veiling of the news that the Americans had liberated Rome. Two days later, this announcement was overshadowed even in
June 6 the Eighth Army by General Eisenhower's first *communiqué* on the landings in Normandy.

There were many occasions when both Battalions were warned that they would be needed for local operations, but only the 5th were actually called forward, and then their plan, hurriedly conceived in a mood of great excitement, led to nothing but disappointment. They had been ordered to capture the Tiber bridge at Castel Giubbileo. They were to have priority, so they thought, over all roads leading to their objective, and No. 1 Company were mounted in a fleet of jeeps supported by a squadron of South African tanks. This flying column, whose mission was one which the world should have heard of with
June 5 astonishment and delight, was halted before they had gone many miles by the troops of three nationalities who had preceded them. Major Sidney, V.C., was held at pistol-point by an American military policeman, who threatened to shoot him if he dared to advance any farther to clutter up the roads. They arrived at the bridge many hours later to find that it had already been blown up and that a French regiment was sitting peacefully on the near bank. Their only consolations were the desertion of twelve Germans who swam the Tiber, and the discovery of an abandoned train full of German equipment, to which they helped themselves liberally.

There was great congestion on the Roman Campagna. The 24th Guards Brigade on the Tiber banks and the 1st Guards Brigade bivouacked near the ancient site of Palestrina were but two of a hundred formations, British, French, American, Canadian, South African and Polish, which had come to rest before the gates of Rome. They had set out by many different roads, but all—their own eyes ranging over that vast encampment showed them that the proverb was indeed true—all had led to Rome. Like Shelley in 1819, they saw before them "arches after arches in unending lines stretching across the uninhabited wilderness, the blue defined line of the mountains seen between them; masses of nameless ruins standing like rocks out of the plain; and the plain itself, with its billowy and unequal surface, announced the neighbourhood of Rome." Above a low horizon, from a dark, formless mass of houses, as it might be from a wood, rose clean and clear the dome of St. Peter's.

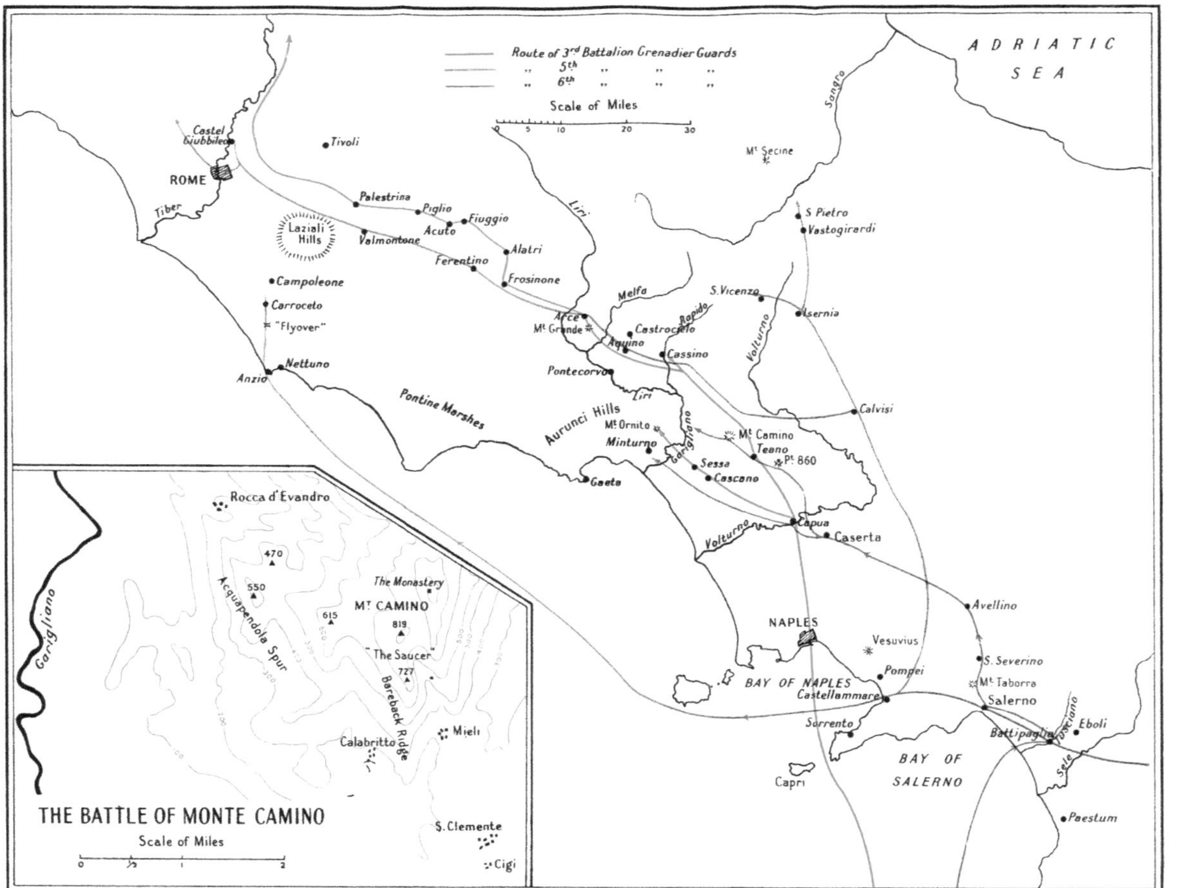

CENTRAL ITALY

Face page 442

3

THE 5TH BATTALION: BAGNOREGIO AND THE RIVER ASTRONE

Advance through Rome and Viterbo towards Orvieto—Checked at the precipitous village of Bagnoregio—A two-day battle culminating in the capture of the village—Advance checked again at the River Astrone—After some fighting the Battalion cross the river

After the fall of Rome the two Battalions were more widely separ- **1944**
ated by intervening hills, and each was involved in a series of small
battles which kept the front loose and porous, allowing the Germans
no time to recover their breath or their cohesion. Yet by the middle of
June the dream of encircling the entire German Army had faded:
they had escaped the trap. Now the prime object was to pursue them
closely with a score of branching columns, following the valley bot-
toms where their retreat had been rapid, climbing the hills on either
side when they turned to bar the valleys. While the fighting was still
fairly open, each Battalion was engaged in two actions which were
serious enough to be classed as battles—the 5th Battalion at Bagnoregio and the Astrone River; the 3rd Battalion on the approaches to
Perugia and Arezzo.

Leaving the Tiber banks at dusk, the 5th Battalion drove through **June 7**
Rome three days after its capture, crossing the river by one of the
many bridges in the city's centre which the Germans had not destroyed. It was a disappointing way in which to visit Rome for the first
time. Though the night was brightly moonlit, the eight-mile column
of tanks and lorries crawled painfully through dim streets which might
have been the streets of any European capital, and they passed no
recognizable monuments to stamp their memories with an unforgettable impression. Apart from a few old women and lounging American soldiers, there was no stir in the streets, and the air was filled with
shouted orders and the grinding of tracks and gears. After resting for *See Map*
a while on the outskirts of Rome, the Brigade passed on to Civita *p.* **524** **June 8**
Castellana in the wake of the South African tanks, and from there
continued to Viterbo. On the next day the Grenadiers entered the **June 11**
forefront of the battle for the first time since leaving the hills above
the Sangro River.

The immediate objective was Orvieto, twenty miles north of
Viterbo, a distance which had been covered almost daily by the South
African Division since the fall of Rome. On this day the Germans felt
strong enough to impose a local check north of the Viterbo Plain,

1944 where the country is sliced up by gorges and escarpments and the Bolsena Lake narrows down the width of the front by half a dozen miles. Of the two roads which led from Viterbo to Orvieto, the main, westerly, road through Montefiascone was taken by a French division, and the secondary road, three miles to the east, by the 6th South African Armoured Division. In the normal manner, an advance guard of tanks went ahead as soon as it was light, reporting by wireless their arrival at successive identifiable points—railway crossings, groups of houses, junctions with by-roads, all of which had previously been given code names for easy reference on the map (thus "Jack O.K.," "Five hundred yards short of James," was the type of short message which flowed back constantly on the air). A short way behind the tanks came No. 2 Company (Capt. J. A. Orme), carried in six jeeps and trailers; and behind them Nos. 1 and 4 Companies dropped off small parties to explore a little way down the side-roads and make certain that there was no threat to the open flanks. So they continued through the morning, moving more slowly than usual, for a thick mist and drizzle limited visibility to less than fifty yards, and the tanks were blind and cautious.

Not much occurred until they reached the deep ravine south of the village of Bagnoregio. Then suddenly the leading tank was fired upon from across the demolished bridge, and a spurt of bullets whipped across the road. Thereupon Nos. 2 and 4 Companies of the Grenadiers left their vehicles and advanced through the woods at the side of the road, pushing their way through damp undergrowth and past empty trenches littered with the rubbish of a German camp. They came down to the stream-bed on either side of the bridge, and crossed over to the far bank, still hidden by the mist but well aware that the Germans were entrenched somewhere among the steep terraces above them. On the right of the road No. 4 Company (Major C. B. Frederick) found an intact wooden foot-bridge, but immediately lost a few prisoners to a German post on the far side. On the left of the road No. 2 Company at first had better fortune, for some of them, led by Lieut. G. W. Lamb, were able to clamber unobserved up the first few terraces and drop down upon a group of ten German parachutists, who surrendered; later they also freed the prisoners taken from No. 4 Company. While the mist still hung low over the ravine it was scarcely possible to advance any farther without risk of mistaking friend for enemy, or penetrating the German screen in one place only to find that they themselves were cut off. In the middle of the afternoon the mist lifted, and the two platoons of No. 2 Company (those commanded by Lieuts. Lamb and Jones) were exposed in a most dangerous position on the far side of the stream, with the Germans immediately above them. By crouching against the foot of the terraces **1944** they avoided heavy casualties, but they could do nothing. At dusk Colonel Gordon-Lennox withdrew the whole company to the near bank. In the course of the day seven men were killed and thirty-three wounded, among the latter Capt. J. A. Orme, the acting commander of No. 2 Company.

The lifting of the mist had also shown them for the first time by what a formidable obstacle they were confronted. The village of Bagnoregio was an Acropolis, filling the narrow width of a high, rocky spur, the walls of the nearest houses lying flush with the sides of an almost precipitous cliff; each window overlooking the deep and tangled ravine seemed to contain a machine gun, each tumbled cluster of rocks a German sniper. There was no chance of forcing such a barrier without very heavy casualties. Brigadier Clive therefore decided to concentrate his attack on the ridge west of the village, where the approaches were easier for tanks and infantry, and the Brigade's left flank would be given some protection by the simultaneous French attack on Monterado. Twice the tanks of the Pretoria Regiment **June 12** attempted to force a passage over the narrower part of the ravine, and twice they returned in the gathering darkness without making great progress. The Battalion meanwhile remained on the left of the road south of the stream under such heavy fire that on this second day of the battle fifteen more men were killed and twenty-five wounded. There was one incident in particular which caused them great distress. A carrier patrol led by Lieut. T. A. Thwaites and the Mortar Officer, Lieut. M. G. R. Kingsford, had gone forward at the same time as the tanks and were caught in the close-range fire of a German platoon. Lieut. Thwaites was killed immediately by a mine, and Lieut. Kingsford received wounds from which he later died. Sergt. Howe took charge of the survivors, and, thinking mistakenly that it was his duty to seize the ridge ahead, made two efforts to reach it. When darkness fell he sent back the wounded on the two remaining carriers and himself returned first through the German and then through the French lines. That night the Germans unexpectedly withdrew, and the attack arranged for the next morning became, in the changed circumstances, a careful but bloodless advance. The tanks at last found a way across **June 13** the stream, the 3rd Coldstream followed, and finally the Grenadiers approached Bagnoregio from the west at the same time as a South African battalion entered from the other end. They met in the centre of the village. The Italian population were hiding in caves. A few shots rang out from the north, but the Battalion were now safe among the houses, and while the tanks and lorries rumbled through all night they slept undisturbed.

1944 The pursuing forces leapt ahead of them at their previous rate, ten miles on an average in each day, a speed, wrote a Grenadier, "at which a very indolent tourist would in peace time have made his way from Rome to Florence," but remarkable in this mountainous country where every bridge was destroyed and an armoured division was attempting to push forward along a minor road which was little better
June 15-18 than a farm track. The Battalion spent three days on the banks of a crystal-clear stream outside Orvieto, moving round the poplars to find some shade from the midday heat, and huddling under anti-gas capes (which throughout the war were used as waterproofs) when a sudden storm drenched their makeshift camp. From Orvieto they slithered up
June 18-21 the greasy tracks to Citta di Pieve, finding tanks and trucks overturned at every corner, and came after ten days' comparative peace
June 24 once more within sound and range of gun fire at Sarteano. The enemy had just left the town, and in the middle of the main square stood a German Tiger tank, still steaming like a kettle from its internal fires. The Grenadiers climbed the Castle Hill and from the top they had a wide view over the tossing country of Umbria and Tuscany. To the east they could see Lake Trasimene, a silver dish crumpled at the edges, near which the 4th and 78th Divisions and the 3rd Battalion of their own Regiment in the 6th Armoured Division were halted among the mines and hills and marshes on which the Germans had based their temporary "Trasimene Line." But their attention was caught by a more unusual sight. Two miles ahead they saw through their field-glasses Germans digging trenches. The Trasimene Line evidently extended to their own front. As at Bagnoregio, here too it was based upon a deep valley, the valley of the River Astrone, and if no tanks could cross it, yet another infantry battle would be necessary in order to force a way through.

When the 5th Battalion drove out from Sarteano they were heavily shelled on the road, and, abandoning their lorries, the companies took to the scrub-covered hills on the left overlooking the Astrone
June 24-27 Valley. For three days they remained there while the 1st Scots Guards attacked on their left flank, and the Grenadiers themselves sent several patrols each night down to the river to find a place where the tanks could cross. The Astrone left the Battalion with particularly disagreeable memories. There was first the heat and then the cold; there was the constant and accurate shell fire which caused the majority of the sixty casualties they suffered in these three days, among them Major Frederick and Lieut. C. C. P. Hodson, who were both wounded; there were those vile patrols down to the river, when the men would stumble all night among the brushwood and branching water-courses, never certain when they had reached the river itself,

and fearful for German patrols and even the few German tanks 1944
which were thought to be lying on the near side. On one of these
patrols Lieut. M. N. Conville was wounded, and the party which
found him two mornings later was fired upon and Lieut. Conville, as
he lay on the stretcher, received four more bullet wounds, from which
he happily recovered. And there was finally the incident of the Royal
Engineers. A platoon from No. 4 Company had been detached to June 25
protect a section of sappers while they mended a hole in the road.
Through some oversight, the whole party approached the site still
mounted in their trucks, and discovered only when it was too late that
the Germans were already in position. The trucks were riddled with
bullets and the greater part of the platoon was lost.

The Grenadiers were not by this time in a very optimistic mood.
However, by the enemy's sudden withdrawal they were spared the
full-scale attack which had been planned. Two deserters gave themselves up to the Battalion's Chaplain, Rev. D. J. Browning, with the June 27
welcome information that their friends had abandoned the opposite
ridge. The news seemed at first to be false, for when No. 3 Company (Capt. Whatman, M.C.) marched down the road towards the bridge they were fired upon near the river-bed, and two or three tanks and carriers were knocked out behind them by a long-range gun. While the whole plan for a Brigade night attack was revived, No. 3 Company waded through the shallow water to the far bank and immediately found themselves in the middle of a thick minefield. One of their officers, Lieut. C. V. I. Snell, was killed by a mine under the north arch of the bridge. At dusk the company determined to investigate further. Lieut. C. I. M. Williams went forward up the far slope with two or three men, found the ridge clear of all enemy, and called up the remainder of his company to occupy the crest. They were joined later in the night by two other companies, guided by Lieut. H. W. Freeman-Attwood, and the advance to Montepulciano was continued by the Scots and Coldstream Guards at first light. The 24th Guards Brigade had by this time come a hundred and twenty miles from Rome, and two hundred and twenty from Cassino.

4

THE 3RD BATTALION: PERUGIA AND AREZZO

Advance up the east bank of the Tiber—The 3rd Battalion engaged in several minor actions—The bulk of the German Army escapes to the north and holds a delaying line between Perugia and Lake Trasimene—Grenadier battle for Perugia—Lieut. Lascelles wounded and captured—Entry into Perugia by the Grenadiers—Fighting beyond the city—Move to approaches of Arezzo—The 1st Guards Brigade attack hills south-west of Arezzo—Capture of the town—Advance up the Arno Valley—Visit of His Majesty The King—The Grenadiers within sight of the Gothic Line

1944 The foregoing account of the advance of the 5th Battalion from the Tiber to the Astrone will have indicated how large was the number of men who were killed and wounded in small engagements of which the outside world heard little. Once the excitement of the pursuit had worn off, the 5th Battalion seldom had any other stimulus than their sense of duty and a confidence that their commanders would never order them into any action which was not strictly necessary or properly supported. On the other hand, the 3rd Battalion were fortunate in having another stimulus to success. Their two main battles during this period were closely linked with two names, Perugia and Arezzo, of which the world had certainly heard and the world would certainly talk. Fighting within view of the walls of these two great cities, they were offered a more immediate prize for their exertions than the 5th Battalion ever held within their grasp: and, though the 3rd Battalion too had their share of minor actions which seemed remote from the main strategic plan, their casualties, compared to their sister Battalion's, were fortunately light.

See Map p. **524** Circling round the outskirts of Rome, which they never entered, the 6th Armoured Division were directed up the left bank of the Tiber towards the two communication centres of Narni and Terni, through which the German divisions from the central part of the old front were in full retreat. If these towns could be captured ahead of the bulk of the German troops the Allied offensive would achieve almost all that General Alexander intended; but if the Germans managed to hold them long enough for their rearguards to fight clear, their crisis was over. Though huge areas of Italy would be abandoned to the Allies, the German armies would remain relatively intact, and be able to re-form a continuous line farther north. Hence that six-mile strip of plain between the Tiber's left bank and the Central Apennines became more important than any other part of the front. The enemy concentrated across its width two of their best and most coherent divisions, with orders not to fight stubbornly on a single line, which would expose them to the risks of another break-through, but to impose delays by demolitions and small rearguard actions, absorbing and checking the weight of the Allied advance in the manner of a hydraulic buffer. All the ingenuity of their engineers contributed to these tactics. Not only was every bridge and every small culvert blown up, but wherever the road ran for some distance over unbroken ground the tarmac would be torn up by patterns of small craters; branch-tracks and roads were systematically mined; trees bordering the road were felled across it; the very railway lines were cut at fifty-yard intervals by small charges of gun-cotton, and the sleepers split by a great steel hook mounted on the back of the last wagon to pass over them. The 6th Armoured Division followed as fast as they could repair the roads. The tanks moved ahead, keeping to the road where the surface was intact, and when they came to a block, shouldered their way through the hedges despite the risk of mines and overturning. Often it was impossible to find a way round. Often a team of bulldozers would work for three or four hours, shearing a channel down the banks of a stream, before the tanks could pass across it; or a screen of German guns on the far side would make a further advance too costly; or darkness would fall. It was on these occasions that the infantry were called forward to seize a bridgehead behind which the engineers could work in safety, or to extend by a night advance of a few miles the gains which the Armoured Brigade had made during the day. At every moment either the tanks or the infantry were advancing or attempting to advance, each assisting and depending on the efforts of the other. Never before or after did the Armoured Division work in such smooth and close co-operation. **1944**

Before reaching Perugia the 3rd Battalion (under the command of Lieut.-Colonel E. J. B. Nelson, D.S.O., M.C., since the end of May) were engaged in two small actions, each typical of this phase of the advance. The first was at Fara Sabina, a triangle of roads eighteen miles north of Rome. There had been some German resistance during the day, but a bridge south of the village was still intact, and at night **June 8** the Grenadiers advanced to capture it, moving through the cornfields between the Tiber and the road. As they drew near, the bridge was blown up ahead of them, but they managed to cross the stream, and entered the railway station to find that the enemy had flown. During the remainder of the night the sappers worked on a Bailey bridge, which was christened "Grenadier Bridge," one of the many which spanned the streams of Africa and Italy, and in the morning the tanks crossed over to resume the pursuit. The second action took place fifteen miles farther north, at a point where the hills closed down to

1944 the Tiber to form the narrow defile of Poggio Mirteto. Here the enemy's resistance was unusually stubborn, and the 2nd Coldstream Guards in particular suffered many casualties from shell fire. At first a daylight infantry attack was planned, but the Divisional Commander (Major-General V. Evelegh) later agreed that the attack could be made at night, provided that the Grenadiers captured a river cross-
June 10 ing on the far side of the defile by 1 a.m. The Battalion moved out at dusk into a barrage of German shell fire which exceeded anything they had experienced since Monte Grande. Led in person by Colonel Nelson, they branched off into the hills east of the defile, intending to come down upon the river crossing by a wide and indirect approach. To guide them for the first part of their five-mile advance they followed a line of pylons; after that it was a test of careful map reading. Colonel Nelson achieved what he had promised. He reached the river with a quarter of an hour in hand, and, though the bridge was again blown up as they approached, they found a ready-made ford, over which the tanks passed at dawn. In this action a dozen men were wounded, including Lieut. P. A. Buchanan.

In the six following days the Division advanced seventy-five miles. Either the tanks or the 61st Brigade, the other infantry brigade of the 6th Armoured Division, were in the lead throughout the period, and their advance was bloodless and almost enjoyable, the Eighth Army having by this time swum clear of the trail of destruction which their own guns or the enemy's had left farther south. The roads from Narni to Todi, and from Todi onwards to Perugia, were almost indestructible, being built along ridges and watersheds where the natural drainage had made the smallest culvert superfluous. Only at Narni was there
June 14 a lengthy hold-up. The main route crossed the River Nera just below the town, at a point where the river swirled through a deep gorge, and nothing but a high-level Bailey bridge of unusual length could carry the tanks across. The sappers, working all day and night, completed it in twenty-four hours, and the Grenadiers had time to close up with the rest of the Division at Narni. Looking down the length of the great valley towards Spoleto and Assisi, they saw upon that gently swelling counterpane of fields and little woods no sign of war, no sign that until the previous day it had been the channel by which a large part of the German Army had escaped.

For the Germans *had* escaped. Narni was found to be deserted; as also were Terni and Rieti. When the tanks moved across the Nera they were able to drive as light-heartedly as char-à-bancs to Todi, and still there was no sign of the Germans. The cheering civilians of Todi had
June 17 had time to placard their city with proclamations welcoming the Allies; they pointed excitedly to the north, imitating with grotesque

gestures the despair and exhaustion of the last German troops they had seen, and shouted above the clatter of the passing convoys: "Perugia! Perugia!" **1944**

The 26th Armoured Brigade, who had been ordered to bypass Perugia and head for the north-east corner of Lake Trasimene, were almost within sight of the city when the first shots they had heard for many days rang out among the fields, and the more sombre note of artillery and anti-tank guns mingled with the brisk rattle of the machine guns. Perugia was defended. The Grenadiers had already been ordered forward in their lorries to assist the tanks of the 16th/5th Lancers. No. 2 Company captured one anti-tank gun intact, the 16th/5th two others, and then the Battalion swept up to the top of a terraced ridge known as Monte Corneo, from where at a distance of two miles they looked across to the high, grey walls, the towers and palaces, of Perugia. **June 18** *See Plan p.* **452**

> "I walked up to a villa on top of Monte Corneo," wrote a Grenadier, "where one of our forward companies had just moved in. There was a Comtessa there, terribly distressed for the fate of her furniture and especially for her parquet floors, over which gently clumped Guardsmen in hob-nailed boots. The Germans had just gone. They had left plates of half-eaten sausage on the kitchen table, and copies of the *Voelkischer Beobachter* littered the drawing-room floor. Just outside in the garden a salvo of German mortar bombs spattered earth and shrapnel all around us, but hurt nobody. Again one sensed this odd contrast between the peaceful serenity of the country scene (where everything is in leaf and flower, and there just ahead calmly lies this lovely city) and superimposed upon it the crumps and rattle and gear-changing of war."

There were three incidents that evening which brought them sharply back to reality. During the afternoon a small party set off from Battalion Headquarters in a carrier and a light tank to find a signal route to the top of Monte Corneo. Although they followed the tracks left by one of the Shermans, they had not gone far before the carrier blew up on a mine, wounding Lieut. Hon. H. L. T. Lumley-Savile and one Guardsman. A jeep ambulance was called for, and while the wounded were being placed upon it two motor-cyclists rode up the same track. Before they could be warned they touched off two more mines, which killed one man and wounded two others so severely that they subsequently died. Though he was also badly wounded, Capt. A. D. Angus, M.C., was the only one of the party who could still stand. Having driven back the jeep with its first load, he later returned for the remainder, as only he knew where the mines lay.

The other two incidents both occurred after nightfall. Lieut. H. Farebrother was badly wounded on patrol by a German grenade, and

1944 died later that night; and Lieut. The Viscount Lascelles, a nephew of the King, was wounded and taken prisoner when leading a second patrol. The circumstances of his capture, which was announced with triumph the next day by the German wireless, were strangely unfortunate. He had had no other intention than to go as far as the Fork (see plan), where No. 3 Company of the Battalion were in position, in order to discover whether the road as far as that point was passable for tanks. By a misunderstanding the guides whom No. 3 Company had put out to meet him were stationed on a different track from the one followed by his patrol, and Lieut. Lascelles continued up the road until he was met, not by the expected guides, but by a volley of German bullets. He himself was wounded in six places, and, though he took cover in a ditch, the Germans found him early the next morning, and an ambulance jeep reached the spot just too late. As they began to carry him back to their own lines a concentration of British artillery scattered his captors, and Lieut. Lascelles, together with two Guardsmen and an officer of the Royal Engineers, were once more at liberty in No Man's Land. They took refuge in the house marked "A." Before further help could reach them the enemy encircled the house in large numbers, and recaptured Lieut. Lascelles and his companions.

No. 3 Company (Capt. J. H. Lambert) were lying just short of the Fork, dug into the gardens of a group of houses, and No. 1 Company (Major T. S. Hohler, M.C.) lay close behind them. Neither could advance to the cross-roads owing to strong opposition, and both were
June 19 exposed on both their flanks. At first light the Germans began to attack No. 1 Company from the direction of the railway line, and, though they were held off and many casualties inflicted upon them, they occupied a house between Nos. 1 and 3 Companies from which they were evicted only when a tank battered it to pieces at point-blank range. The events of the day were more encouraging. The Coldstream Guards, the 61st Brigade and the tanks of the 17th/21st Lancers all made deep advances on the left flank, which not only protected the Grenadiers on this side but upset the entire German line. The cross-roads and the railway station now became the prime objectives for the Grenadiers and Coldstream respectively. Not a shot was fired either from or into the city itself. On the Grenadier sector No. 4 Company (Capt. A. K. C. Nation) managed to advance to within a few hundred yards of the cross-roads by bypassing the Fork on its right, but when No. 3 Company attempted to move up level with them they lost two of their supporting tanks, and many men of the leading platoon were wounded. These casualties were brought back under intense fire by Lieut. J. Penn, M.C., and by Sergt. Spiller, D.C.M., who extricated the wounded one by one at great risk to himself. But it was no longer

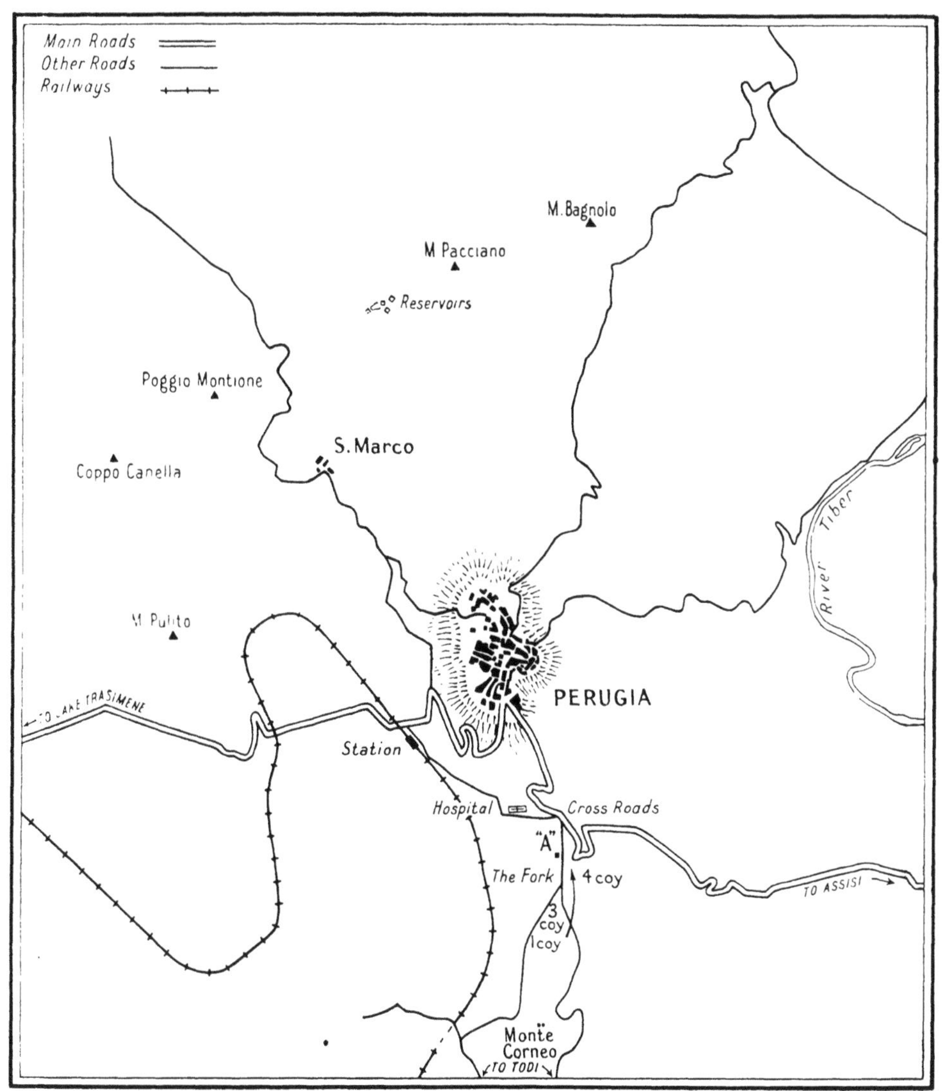
Main Roads
Other Roads
Railways
M.Bagnolo
M Pacciano
Reservoirs
Poggio Montione
S.Marco
Coppo Canella
M. Pulito
TO LAKE TRASIMENE
PERUGIA
River Tiber
Station
Hospital
Cross Roads
"A"
The Fork
4 coy
3 coy
1 coy
TO ASSISI
Monte Corneo
TO TODI

PERUGIA

a stalemate. The 61st Brigade were already across the Perugia—Trasimene road west of the railway loop when, at 4.30 a.m., the Coldstream reported that the station was in their hands. At dawn the Grenadiers' No. 4 Company occupied the cross-roads without a fight, No. 2 Company came up soon afterwards to join them, and No. 1 Company searched the hospital on the far side without any incident other than the complaint by a British medical officer that their presence in the hospital was an abuse of the Geneva Convention. He wished, he later added, to occupy it himself.

1944

June 20

But what of Perugia itself? Except for one crater in an outer street, the city was so far untouched. Did the Germans now intend to fight from its ramparts, or would they take the broader view that its value as a national monument was greater than its value as a very temporary tactical obstacle? Looking upwards from the cross-roads at about 8 a.m., the Grenadiers paused and wondered. While a gang of willing Italians heaved aside the trees which the Germans had felled across the road, others clamoured round Capt. J. F. Rowley (No. 2 Company) insisting that the Germans had left Perugia the night before, and that there was no reason why the British should not immediately enter the city. The events of the next half an hour were thus described by another Grenadier officer who joined Rowley at the cross-roads:

> "We looked at each other. Although Colonel Nelson had received and passed on clear orders to occupy Perugia, we wondered what to do. Your armoured cars should enter first. The sappers should go ahead in case the road was mined. The Italian might be leading us deliberately into an ambush. But we thought that these opportunities do not often occur, so we piled a small force into four jeeps and drove, the Italian guide sitting on the bonnet, up and up, round and round, into the centre of the town. In the main square there were few people as we drove in. They stopped to stare for a few seconds and then rushed towards us, cheering and flinging out their arms. All the doors and windows were suddenly flung open and a great crowd welled into the street, converging on our dusty little caravan. I had the impression of thousands of laughing faces, of people stretching out their hands to be shaken or even just to touch my grubby pair of shorts, people throwing carnations and roses and lilac, so that soon our jeep looked like a float in a fête des fleurs. Finally we came to a halt before the cathedral. They swarmed round us. I have never seen such looks of wonder and genuine happiness. They seemed unable to believe that the English would look like other men, and we for our part caught their spirit, laughed off their embraces, and sent back by wireless, a little self-consciously, the message that Perugia was indeed liberated. The Mayor was then produced at the end of a long lane, which was cleared for him by the carabinieri, and he made us a sort of official welcome. We discussed practical details. The Germans had blown up the water mains: we assured him that A.M.G.O.T.* would bring up water within

*Allied Military Government, Occupied Territories.

1944 the hour. Were there any German wounded left in the hospitals? He would take us round them himself. Would he assure us that the political prisoners would be released immediately? And would the carabinieri continue to police the streets and keep them clear for the passage of the tanks to the far side of the town? All this, he assured us, would be done."

These triumphs were confined to those few Grenadiers who had the good fortune to pass through the centre of the city. The majority of the 1st Guards Brigade circled round the outer roads and found their way barred by another screen of German infantry and guns drawn across the hills on either side of San Marco. The enemy had spared Perugia, and even after its occupation by the British their guns fired not more than an occasional round into the city. But the Germans were no longer on the run. Both north and south of Perugia their resistance was no mere display of strength by a makeshift rearguard. It was an organized line of defence, a link in the chain of the Trasimene Line, which stretched the whole width of the Italian peninsula. From now onwards they withdrew according to their own plan, steadily and indeed calmly, from one preselected position to another, until they halted on the Gothic Line in the Northern Apennines.

The 6th Armoured Division were thankful for the enforced delay. Their one hundred and fifty tanks were badly in need of the maintenance which they could now receive, drawn up in rigid rows in one of the main piazzas where the Perugians and the German prisoners gathered to stare at the mechanics as they worked. Inside the town normal civic life was revived while the German guns were still within easy range. The shops reopened; an opera, a theatre, and several cinemas resumed regular performances; and in the evening, after the daily siesta, the streets were filled with strolling groups of young Italians, for whom the British were now no longer liberators but rather self-assertive guests. Less than two miles to the north the British and the Germans sat facing each other. From the towers flanking the northern Etruscan gate of Perugia both scenes were immediately visible: the bustling civic life below and behind; the stealthy activity of the front line just ahead. Ten minutes in a jeep would take you from peace to war.

The 3rd Grenadiers were ordered, on the day after the fall of Perugia, to launch a local attack west of San Marco in order to deny the Germans observation of the immediate approaches to the town, and to open up the road to Trasimene. While their Commanding
June 21 Officer, Lieut.-Colonel Nelson, was on reconnaissance near San Marco he was wounded by a mortar bomb (it was the third wound he had received since coming overseas), and the command of the Battalion was temporarily taken over by Major P. H. Lort-Phillips.

The attack was successfully carried out without more than a single 1944
casualty. Starting just before dark under cover of a heavy barrage June 22
which stunned the Germans and cut their telephone wires, the Grenadiers captured in turn the hills of Monte Pulito, Coppo Canella and Poggio Montione, took five prisoners, and linked up at dawn with the 3rd Welsh Guards at San Marco.

Four days later the whole of the 1st Guards Brigade were involved in a more serious attack designed to free Perugia once and for all from the menace of direct German observation of the town, by capturing the hills of Monte Bagnolo (Grenadiers) and Monte Pacciano (Coldstream and Welsh Guards). The Grenadiers' battle centred round a
farmhouse on the hilltop where the Germans at first resisted strongly, June 26
but later in the night they withdrew and Lieut. M. H. Jenkins crawled ahead of his platoon to find nothing on the top but the stench of dead cows. Ten Germans gave themselves up to a patrol led by Lieut. Hedley-Dent. The Battalion's success was marred only by the death of Lieut. V. B. Cubitt, their Anti-Tank Officer, who was killed by a
German shell at Battalion Headquarters the next morning. June 27

At this time the information provided by Italian civilians (who passed easily between the lines and were even able to telephone on one occasion from a German headquarters to the British headquarters in Perugia University) gave ample warning of the enemy's general withdrawal. As soon as the news was confirmed deep patrols were sent out by all three battalions of the 1st Guards Brigade, which between them cleared forty-eight square miles of new territory in as
many hours. The Grenadier patrols were led by Lieuts. A. M. Denny June 29-30
and J. W. Harkness. The country on the west bank of the Tiber was steep and thickly wooded, the weather very hot, and the Guardsmen hampered by a great load of equipment. The experience, however satisfactory in its results, was therefore most unpleasant. Lieut. Denny's patrol found four Germans hiding in a house; but, though Lieut. Harkness advanced more than eight miles north of Monte Bagnolo almost to the banks of the Tiber, he made no contact with the
enemy. On the next day the whole Brigade was relieved by an Indian July 1
division, and the 6th Armoured Division were switched to the area between Lake Trasimene and Arezzo. The battle was once more becoming extremely mobile.

After spending four days in stubble fields south-west of Lake
Trasimene, the Brigade drove up its western shore to a new area near July 6
Cortona, where they began almost immediately to plan their attack on the hills overlooking Arezzo. The situation was an unusual one. On the left of the main road the country was flat and closely cultivated;

1944 immediately on its right a long chain of rugged hills stood about a thousand feet above the level of the plain, rising and falling in successive ridges and gullies until it dropped down to the l'Olmo Defile, through which passed the road and railway leading to Arezzo, two miles to the north-east. It was at once clear that the l'Olmo Gap must be forced before Arezzo could be captured and that the key to l'Olmo was the high ground overlooking it to the north and south. The tanks had already managed to probe up the road to within a mile of l'Olmo, but the Germans had deployed a complete division across the gap and were shelling its approaches with an accuracy that made any further advance by the tanks quite impossible. The 1st Guards Brigade were therefore ordered to strike up into the hills and clear the ridge from south to north. The final object was to capture the l'Olmo Gap and allow the tanks through to Arezzo; the initial object was to establish a firm base on the lower end of the ridge around the farm of Stoppiace, from where the Brigade could begin their main advance on more level terms with the enemy. This initial phase was the Grenadiers' contribution to the capture of Arezzo.

See Plan p. 458

Owing to various delays and changes in plan the Brigade had an unusually long time in which to prepare for the battle, and they made good use of it. At a series of conferences the exact routes were worked out, and the exact time and points fixed at which each of the three battalions would pass through the others to take up the pursuit, so that the impetus of the first successes would not be lost and the enemy, once thrown off his balance, would constantly be pressed back by the onslaught of fresh British troops. Brigadier Haydon, the commanding officers of his battalions and almost every company commander, examined the configuration of the ridge, not only on air photographs and by direct observation from ground-level but also from artillery spotting aircraft which flew them one by one in a wide circle over Arezzo and its approaches. Moreover, the Grenadiers sent No. 1 Company (Capt. D. I. Rollo, M.C.) to establish an advanced base at S. Andrea, and from here patrols went forward nightly towards l'Olmo and up the lower slopes of the hill towards Stoppiace, both to test the strength of the German position and to explore the routes by which the Battalion were to follow. One of these patrols was accompanied by Major
July 10 Lort-Phillips, who was still acting as Commanding Officer. On another Lieut. Hon. J. D. Berry suddenly heard a party of about twenty Germans coming down the l'Olmo road singing "Lilli Marlene" at the tops of their voices, and by holding the fire of his men until the last moment he killed fifteen of the enemy without loss to himself. At the moment of his triumphant return to S. Andrea, the headquarters of No. 1 Company was attacked by another German force of about the

same size, and for half an hour there was a confused skirmish among the houses and ammunition trucks. "Someone tried to throw a grenade out of an upper window," records the War Diary, "but it hit the window-frame and fell back into the room, whereupon he jumped out of the window, and held on to the sill with his fingers until the grenade had exploded, and then climbed safely back." The Grenadiers had six casualties in this affair, but the Germans were repelled. 1944

After dark on the evening of the main attack the Brigade, with the Grenadiers in the lead, motored up the sixteen miles from Cortona and then marched two miles to their starting point above S. Andrea. July 15
At 1.30 a.m. No. 3 Company (Major J. G. C. Jameson) advanced up the hill under cover of the fire of four field regiments, two medium regiments and two heavy batteries. Passing within a hundred yards of Stoppiace, they were fired upon from their right rear, but this they left to a New Zealand brigade who were simultaneously attacking Monte Lignano, and passed on through the darkness to the fringe of a wood which lay astride the crest. Among the trees they surprised a handful of bewildered Germans, and others who came up from Stoppiace to investigate were also captured without great difficulty. One German boldly shouted: "Put up your hands, you English swine!" to which Lieut. J. S. M. Pearson-Gregory replied: "Come here, that German!" and he meekly came. The most risky part of the operation had been accomplished with complete success and without a single casualty. No. 4 Company (Capt. P. R. de L. Giffard) found but one German left in Stoppiace itself; and the food upon the kitchen table was still warm. The Grenadiers had already driven a deep wedge between two German battalions, established themselves firmly astride the ridge, and now turned north along the track leading to l'Olmo. Major D. V. Bonsor, M.C. (No. 2 Company) passed his two platoons through No. 3 Company towards the Battalion's last objective, Point 575, and it was only then that the complicated plan began temporarily to go astray. On the right Sergt. F. Lovett, M.M., accounted for two machine-gun posts before he himself was badly wounded in the stomach; and on the left Lieut. P. Hedley-Dent lost his way in the thick undergrowth and came up eventually to Marzupino Farm to find it strongly held. His platoon captured the farmhouse and took several prisoners, but as he renewed his advance to Point 575 a sudden shower of German shells wounded eight of his eighteen men, and he was left too weak to continue. No. 2 Company assembled round Marzupino, and shortly after dawn the 2nd Coldstream passed through the Grenadiers to capture the central part of the ridge. In the gathering light the men of No. 3 Company were able to look down across the northern plain to Arezzo, and beyond it saw

1944 a gleaming loop of the River Arno. It was the first sight of the river which any part of the Allied armies had yet obtained.

This was the end of the 3rd Battalion's participation in the battle for Arezzo. They had lost no more than three men killed and ten wounded, and had captured thirty German prisoners. First the Coldstream and later the Welsh Guards fought their way to the northern end of the ridge. By nightfall German resistance had crumbled. The Welsh Guards occupied the villa of Paradiso overlooking the l'Olmo Gap, and at dawn the next morning one of their companies climbed
July 16 the opposite slope to the empty German trenches at M. Castellare. The tanks of the 16th/5th Lancers passed through the defile and entered Arezzo at 9.20 a.m. There was no excited crowd of civilians here as there had been at Perugia to acclaim their entry. The town had been severely damaged by the Allied air forces, and a population which was notorious for its Fascist sympathies had long since taken refuge in the surrounding hills. The German *communiqué* laconically announced that evening: "After a hard struggle the deserted ruins of Arezzo were abandoned to the enemy."

For the 1st Guards Brigade there followed a period of six weeks until the end of August, of which there is no need to give more than a short account, for, while the 5th Battalion were fighting desperate battles in the Chianti Hills, the 3rd, ten miles away to the east in the floor of the Arno Valley, were merely maintaining contact with a retreating enemy, and one day was apt to be very similar to the next. The advance by the 6th Armoured Division followed a valley which was called the Val d'Inferno, but until it became a battlefield seldom has a name been less appropriately bestowed. It is true that on the right flank rose the grey, pathless massif of the Prato Magno, and on the left the softer outlines of the Chianti Hills sometimes assumed, especially in the evenings, the proportions of a mountain range. But on the wide floor of the valley itself Italy was at her gentlest and most luxuriant. The Arno, lying between long rows of poplars and cypresses, was no formidable obstacle like the Tiber: at almost any point it was possible to drive a jeep across the pebbly bottom of the river, and the Bailey bridges, swung low across the water, were a luxury of which the Guardsmen only appreciated the real necessity after an infrequent shower of rain. On the left bank of the river there was a succession of small towns strung like bright beads along the road; but on the east bank, where the 1st Guards Brigade operated during the whole of this period, there was merely a multitude of tracks, little villages, farms, villas and castles. The countryside was thickly cultivated with corn, vines and fruit trees, all approaching the

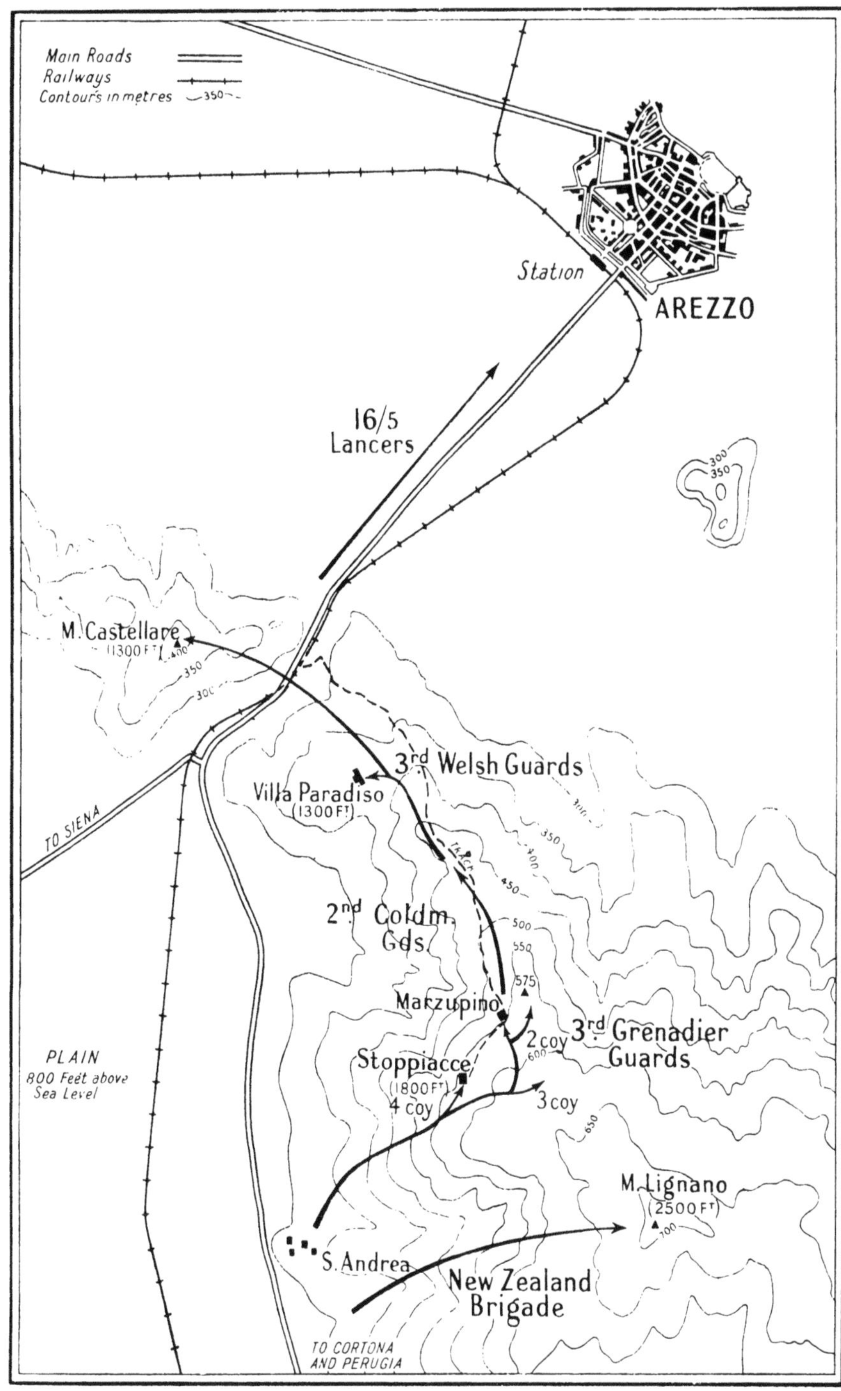
Main Roads
Railways
Contours in metres
Station
AREZZO
16/5
Lancers
M. Castellare
(1300 FT)
3rd Welsh Guards
Villa Paradiso
(1300 FT)
TO SIENA
2nd Coldm.
Gds.
Marzupino
575
3rd Grenadier
Guards
2 coy
Stoppiacce
(1800 FT)
4 coy
3 coy
PLAIN
800 Feet above
Sea Level
M. Lignano
(2500 FT)
S. Andrea
New Zealand
Brigade
TO CORTONA
AND PERUGIA

AREZZO

season of their harvest, and the Guardsmen would often find themselves lying close to a peach grove from which they could gather the warm fruit as liberally as apples from a Kentish orchard. A month of almost unbroken sunshine poured into this happy valley. 1944

The men were not fighting the whole time. At intervals each battalion in turn was withdrawn for a week's rest to the banks of the Upper Arno, with only the distant sound of gun fire to remind them of the war; and sometimes they sought their relaxation even farther afield, at Siena, on the shores of Lake Trasimene and in Rome.

According to the Adjutant, Capt. G. H. Micklem, the immediate enemy, the German 715th Division, were "a nice quiet type, who did not do much, and when they did do anything they did not do it very well." There had been no change in Kesselring's ultimate intention to withdraw to the safety of the Gothic Line, but his withdrawal was now keyed down to a slower rate in order to postpone the Allied attack on the Gothic Line until the more difficult autumn months. The Germans rarely counter-attacked, and were willing to withdraw under pressure; but if left alone they stayed where they were. On the 6th South African Division and the 4th Division fell the main burden of thrusting the enemy back through the Chianti Hills towards Florence, and little more was required of the 6th Armoured Division than to keep pace with the advance on the outer flank, and miss no opportunity to harass the German rearguard and threaten the security of their successive lines of defence. The Division soon evolved their own peculiar technique. From long experience of German habits they were able to guess with some accuracy the moment when the enemy were about to withdraw. Bridges behind the German front line would be blown up, their artillery would register the demolitions, and their outposts begin to thin out; civilians and prisoners would usually bring confirmation of what had already been surmised. But the only certain proof of a withdrawal was the actual inspection of empty German trenches by our patrols. On receipt of the civilian reports an infantry company moved up cautiously to occupy the next ridge, and as soon as possible made fresh contact, probing night after night to discover the limits of the new German line, to give the artillery their targets, and themselves warning of another withdrawal. The sappers repaired the bridges and cleared away the mines, and behind them the whole apparatus of the Armoured Division—the guns, the headquarters, the workshops, the medical centres, the supply lorries—were stepped up for the next phase of the advance. In this way, two, three and even as much as five miles were gained in twenty-four hours, followed by a pause of a week or more.

Before they were engaged in these new operations there were two

1944 incidents of domestic importance which affected the Grenadiers. On
July 26 the main road leading from Arezzo to Siena, while it was still under
German observation and within range of the German guns, four
hundred men of each Battalion were assembled to cheer His Majesty
The King and General Alexander as they drove slowly past in open
July 29 cars. And three days later the command of the 1st Guards Brigade
passed from Brigadier Haydon to Brigadier C. A. M. D. Scott, D.S.O.,
when the former left Italy for a new appointment in Washington. At
about the same time, the Grenadiers moved from Arezzo to the east
bank of the Arno opposite the town of Montevarchi.

At first the main duty of the Brigade was to guard the Division's
right flank against German infiltration into the valley from the Prato
Magno. Spread over fifteen miles of foothills, small picquets occupied
the scattered farms and villages, and sifted the mass of conflicting
civilian information. By night they patrolled between their isolated
posts and into the deep re-entrants of the mountain ahead. Their
greatest single success was the ambush which was laid by Lieut.
J. S. M. Pearson-Gregory and caused the Germans at least thirty
Aug. 1 casualties for the loss of only two Grenadiers. After a few days the
Brigade were switched to the main front between the Arno and the
Prato Magno at the moment when the Germans had decided to withdraw a full dozen miles to the north. During the next three nights the
Grenadiers, who were placed in the most advanced positions, followed
up from ridge to ridge—first a patrol, then a platoon, then a company
and finally the remainder of the Battalion, all carefully interconnected
by a wireless network. The advance was always exciting, often most
satisfactory, but it was rarely achieved without some casualties. On
the second day, for instance, the Battalion objective was an old castle
Aug. 2 perched above the Arno on a low ridge. As far as the foot of the castle
hill all had gone well: there had been no sign of the enemy except for
twelve prisoners captured by No. 2 Company in the initial stages, and
the mines had been avoided by keeping clear of the roads. Then
Lieut. R. D. D. Thomas took the first patrol up to the castle itself, and
on entering its only gateway he was shot dead from inside the courtyard. The small German garrison escaped, and Lieut. P. R. de L.
Giffard entered with his platoon. His first action was to climb the
tower to obtain a view of the country ahead. At the top he found the
ideal observation post, a small, stone room with a slit window, and,
hearing Colonel Nelson climbing the stairs behind him, he stepped
back from the window to tell him of his discovery. As he did so his
foot trod on a loose flagstone, and there was an immediate explosion.
The mine or booby-trap which the Germans had left beneath it shattered Giffard's foot, which was later amputated. A third casualty was

C.S.M. Waters, one of the finest men in the Battalion, who was killed by an S-mine. 1944

The next night the Battalion continued another two miles to San Mezzano, an enormous villa (starred by Baedeker on account of its lavish Oriental style), which dominated the country for miles around. Three prisoners were captured in the garden. In the villa's great, empty rooms, hung with crystal chandeliers, and faced with tiles and painted mirrors, the Battalion relaxed, and brewed their tea upon tessellated floors, while upstairs the gunners sat at half-open windows, and in unusual luxury and safety directed the bombardment of the German lines. The Welsh and Coldstream Guards passed ahead of the Grenadiers, and while the latter rested, the elaborate mechanism of the Armoured Division was wound up for another effort.

In this the Grenadiers were not unrepresented. Serving in the 3rd Battalion of the Welsh Guards was a Grenadier company, formed entirely from men of the old 6th Battalion, under the command of Major D. Willis. They had joined the Welsh Guards shortly after the Battle of Arezzo. A patrol from this company, led by Lieut. R. H. Aug. 7
Leeke, went forward to attack a German-occupied house standing on a spur a hundred yards from the Arno banks. At a distance of a few feet from the house Lieut. Leeke was so severely wounded that he died later that night. Three of his Guardsmen, who were left wounded on the ground, were treated by the Germans in the brutal manner which they normally reserved for Italian Partisans. Far from giving them medical attention they kicked them to prevent them sleeping, and poured out water in the dust before their eyes. These wretched men were rescued after two days of this torture by Capt. R. A. Paget-Cooke, M.B.E., a Grenadier officer serving at the 1st Guards Brigade Headquarters.

Twice more the Grenadiers moved into the front line before the Brigade reached the level of Florence, but on neither occasion were they severely tried. Colonel Nelson reduced the number of men to the minimum necessary to hold a thin line—for there was no danger of counter-attack—and to a greater and greater extent he relied upon civilians and Partisans to obtain the necessary information about enemy movements. An ex-officer of the Italian Army, Lieut. Aldo, did great service to the Battalion in directing these civilian patrols, and ended by offering the Grenadiers the free use of his flat in Florence, with its nineteen bedrooms and three bathrooms. And always at hand for the interrogation of prisoners or an enterprising patrol was the young Luxembourger, Réné Helling, who had worn the Grenadier uniform ever since the Battalion borrowed him from the Foreign Legion after the Battle of Djebel Mansour in Tunisia.

1944 Sept. 2 In the first week of September, after the Germans had evacuated Pontassieve, the Grenadiers moved to a new position east of that town, from where they were able to look across to the towering massif of Monte Falterona, one of the main bastions of the Gothic Line. Here finally before them, three hundred and fifteen miles from Cassino, lay the objective of the great offensive. Already on the Adriatic coast the Eighth Army were preparing the attack which carried them past Rimini into the valley of the Po.

5

THE 5TH BATTALION: THE ADVANCE TO FLORENCE

Rapid advance through the Central Apennines—A sharp attack beaten off at Campi—"Tramping to Florence along the Chianti Hills"—Capture and bitter defence of Grenadier Ridge—Fighting among the vineyards south of Florence—First sight of the city

If the 1st Guards Brigade were able to advance up the Arno Valley with light casualties and comparatively little effort, it was mainly due to the strong pressure exerted upon the enemy by the 4th Division and the 6th South African Armoured Division; in this pursuit the 24th Guards Brigade played a leading role. Though their routes lay little more than eight miles apart, the nature of the fighting in which the 5th and 3rd Battalions were engaged was extremely different, not only in its intensity but in the type of country over which they operated. The 3rd Battalion had been fighting close to good main roads linking major towns and running up the floors of wide valleys; the 5th were dependent on third-rate roads, dirt tracks, and even pathways which they hewed through the virgin bramble. Moreover, they had no consecutive valleys to follow: thrown among a tangle of high, remote hills, they cut across the twisting network of country lanes from ridge to ridge, making always for the highest ground on their line of advance. Sometimes they were shut in by steep gorges, sometimes they looked down from hill-tops which no other summit within their wide horizon seemed to challenge. For them there was no pleasant period of relaxation, no cities to liberate (Siena lay well to the west of their path, and Florence they were not the first to reach), and even during the days of most rapid pursuit the Guardsmen were too exhausted to remain exhilarated for long.

July 1 From the south of Montepulciano, one of the loveliest of small

Italian hill towns, the Grenadiers moved up behind the 3rd Coldstream to hold a network of small road junctions, and broke no new ground until civilians brought them the information that it was safe to proceed to Serre. This village had been extensively mined, but the villagers turned out in a body to help the sappers, and to offer their assistance as guides through the difficult country ahead. The Battalion pressed on during the same afternoon to Rapolano, and found that it too was clear of enemy troops. From the summit of the town they watched the bridges for miles ahead crumbling one by one as the Germans detonated their explosive charges. For the moment the inhabitants of Rapolano gave the Grenadiers an hysterically affectionate welcome. "The embarrassed Guardsmen," according to one account, "were showered with flowers, bombarded with unripe pears, and the hard red wine was almost forced down their throats." In the hills to the east were other villages, to which small patrols paid formal visits of liberation. Lieut. R. G. King-Smith and his platoon received all to themselves the plaudits of San Gimignanello. But at Poggio San Cecilia, Lieut. G. W. Lamb was surprised to see the village gates slammed in his face, the local Mayor having mistaken his platoon for returning Germans. When the mistake was discovered the gates were flung back, the wine flowed, and the villagers could not do too much in the way of welcome and apology. It had been a good day for the Battalion.

1944 **July 3**

The next day was even better. The tanks and infantry advanced twenty miles during the day from Rapolano to Campi. At intervals the column was held up by bridge demolitions, and four bulldozers in turn were blown up on mines as they scraped diversions across the stream-beds. On two occasions, however, the leading company hustled a German demolition party off a bridge before they could blow it up. Castelnuovo was entered at midday by the Intelligence Officer, Capt. G. W. Chaplin, M.C., mounted on his captured German motorcycle, and he was told that the Germans had left but a few hours before. Brigadier Clive therefore decided to press on beyond the Brigade's allotted objective for the day, although the road ahead ran dead straight for several miles and was overlooked from its farther end. In the evening Grenadier foot patrols reached a road junction a mile north of Campi. In the village they recaptured, after an interval of sixteen months, two Guardsmen of the 6th Battalion who had been taken prisoner on the Mareth Line.

July 4

After this quick advance the Battalion waited nearly a fortnight in the Campi Valley, having already outstripped both the French troops on their left and the 6th Armoured Division twenty miles away on their right. An equivalent advance on both flanks was indispensable

1944 before the 24th Guards Brigade could again take the lead. The Germans, too, saw no reason why they should abandon the broad hill of Monte Luco, which dominated the valley from the north. At first they behaved with great lack of caution. Only a few minutes after the Battalion's arrival an officer of the Hermann Goering Division sailed into the British lines on a motor-cycle, carrying with him a map marked with the local German troop positions; and that same night a patrol of eight walked into the middle of Lieut. Hon. J. R. B. Norton's platoon, and two German armoured cars dashed round the corner to run over the bodies of their own dead and wounded. But later the Hermann Goering Division adopted more thorough and aggressive methods. From their observation posts on Monte Luco they systematically bombarded each of the Grenadier positions in turn, and even on days when there was little other activity it was not unusual for the Battalion to lose as many as six men killed and fifteen others wounded from this cause alone. (Lieut. C. Oldfield was one of the casualties.) The more static the position became the more vigorously did both sides dispute the ground which lay between them. Patrols went out by day and night in each direction. On two occasions the Commanding Officer himself, Lieut.-Colonel G. C. Gordon-
July 6 Lennox, narrowly avoided capture. On another, a patrol led by Sergt. Simmonds, M.M., just anticipated a German patrol in the occupation of a large villa, which was found to contain valuable paintings evacuated with their grateful curator from the Siena Museum. During the
July 10 early hours of one morning a German patrol approached No. 3 Company, to meet a stiffer reception than they had expected; according to the account of a Grenadier officer, "when the first outburst of fury, shouting and grenade throwing was over, a blasé voice with an immaculate accent shouted from the direction of the German patrol: 'I say, steady on up there, you chaps!' It was the German lieutenant who was later killed when retrieving his helmet from the road."

As it turned out, this last patrol was a preliminary reconnaissance for a sharp attack which the Storm Battalion of the Hermann Goering
July 12 Division launched upon No. 3 Company two days later. In the early morning, as Lieut. C. I. M. Williams, M.C., was returning with four German prisoners seized during a patrol, a heavy barrage descended upon the company, shortly followed by a group of violent men armed with small rocket guns and a flame-thrower. The latter fortunately misfired, spilling a pitiable flame less than six feet long, and its bearer was killed by a Bren gun before he could repair it. The others found themselves in the middle of a Grenadier minefield, but, persisting bravely with the attack, managed temporarily to cut off the two forward platoons from their company headquarters. Lieut. R. G. King-

Smith was wounded by a grenade, and the company commander, Capt. J. D. Whatman, M.C., by a mortar bomb. Nevertheless, the two isolated platoons, now commanded by Sergt. W. Grandfield, M.M., held off the attackers, and by 7.30 a.m. the situation had been restored by the arrival of a reinforcement platoon under Lieut. M. R. G. Llewellyn. It was led in to the attack by Major W. J. L. Willson. Upon one of the German prisoners was found a diary in which he had had time to write a running commentary on the battle. The last entry read: "It is now 0700 hrs. Fighting still continues and we have many wounded. I have to carry wounded back under fire." The enemy, according to later reports, picked up twenty-six of their own dead: the Grenadier casualties were nine wounded. Lieut. Llewellyn was most unfortunately wounded later that day when a Grenadier section mistook him for a German and opened fire; the Engineer officer with him was killed. **1944**

The French troops on the left celebrated their national festival by a **July 14**
deep penetration of the German line, and two days later Arezzo was
captured by the 6th Armoured Division. A patrol led by Lieut. P. R. **July 16**
Freyberg approached close enough to Monte Luco to learn from civilians that the Germans had withdrawn under this double pressure, and the 24th Guards Brigade were once more able to advance. The 3rd Coldstream took the first leap ahead, and when the Grenadiers received their orders to pass through them to the hills beyond, one of their officers wrote gloomily: "It looks as though we shall have to tramp to Florence along the back of the Chianti Mountains." He was not mistaken. During the next fortnight the Grenadiers climbed higher and higher, far from the villas and sleepy villages one associates with the neighbourhood of Florence, far from the comforts and acclamations of a liberated town.

Their first bound, to a hill-top beyond the Coldstream, was not
difficult; but on the next day No. 4 Company (Major C. B. Frederick) **July 18**
were sent off at first light to climb in turn Monte Torricella and Monte Majone (two thousand six hundred and sixty feet). It was a test of endurance more than of tactical skill, for the steep slopes were covered with thick undergrowth, and when the Guardsmen arrived exhausted at the top the few Germans were taken completely by surprise, and abandoned even their wireless set, which continued to broadcast frantic German messages to the Grenadiers until the batteries ran down. While the South African tanks boldly tackled the appalling slopes of the mountain to support them, Nos. 1 and 3 Companies pushed on through the brambles and boulders to Points 768 and 777. No supplies reached them that night, but at least they were spared a battle once they reached their objectives, and sat for three days on

1944 their lonely summits undisturbed even by shell fire. Looking east, the
view embraced the Prato Magno, and the whole length of the Arno
Valley from Arezzo to Pontassieve; looking west and north, the horizon was confined by a closer range of hills, particularly by the two
heights of Monte San Michele and Monte Domini. The former was
July 22 captured by the 1st Scots Guards, who obtained from its summit the
Brigade's first sight of Florence; the latter on the next day by the
July 23 Coldstream Guards. Both these battles were watched by the Grenadiers from their great height above the valley, and then it was once
again their own turn to leapfrog their companies northwards along the
mountain-spine.

The ridge which now faced them, and to which they gave their name, ran south to north in ascending terraces, thickly wooded except at its upper end. Grenadier Ridge was a sharply sloping massif, a huge breakwater flung up from the rumpled mass of hills around it. Colonel Gordon-Lennox planned to attack it step by step, by company after company, consolidating each gain before continuing to the next, but without ever relaxing the momentum gained by the initial successes; however tired the men might be, it would save them casualties to press on while the enemy were still off their balance. This was the chief lesson taught by the months of fighting which the Battalion had experienced.

July 24 The first phase, carried out by No. 1 Company at night, cleared the
approaches to the main objective by the capture of Point 621. Very
July 25 early the next morning Nos. 2 and 3 Companies were brought up in
lorries and advanced at dawn towards Casa Rugliano, where they met the first German outpost. No. 2 Company (Capt. D. B. Fergusson, M.C.) struggled up the hill through gorse bushes and field wire to attack the house. Their company signallers suddenly disappeared into a disused well, from which they emerged two hours later, bruised and battered, but with the wireless still intact. Two platoons carried out the attack, and half a dozen Germans surrendered quietly, but when Lieut. T. A. Jones, commanding the third platoon, was called up to join the others he stepped on a mine and was so badly wounded that his leg was later amputated. No. 3 Company (Capt. W. J. L. Willson, D.S.O.) were shielded by smoke shells during their attack, but they too lost an officer, Lieut. R. F. Sanderson, who was wounded by a grenade when he ran towards a group of Germans. These men then surrendered. "Capt. Willson," records one account of this skirmish, "made two of the prisoners take up the mines on the road, and sent off the third through the smoke to shout to his comrades to come down off the high ground beyond, but this man came back empty-handed," thinking, no doubt, that he was under strict orders to return himself.

How vividly does this small incident reveal the difference in outlook between the British soldier and the German! 1944

By this time the tanks of the Pretoria Regiment had caught up with the Grenadiers, and preceded them by two hundred yards up the next slope, plunging through the bushes, as one Guardsman remarked,

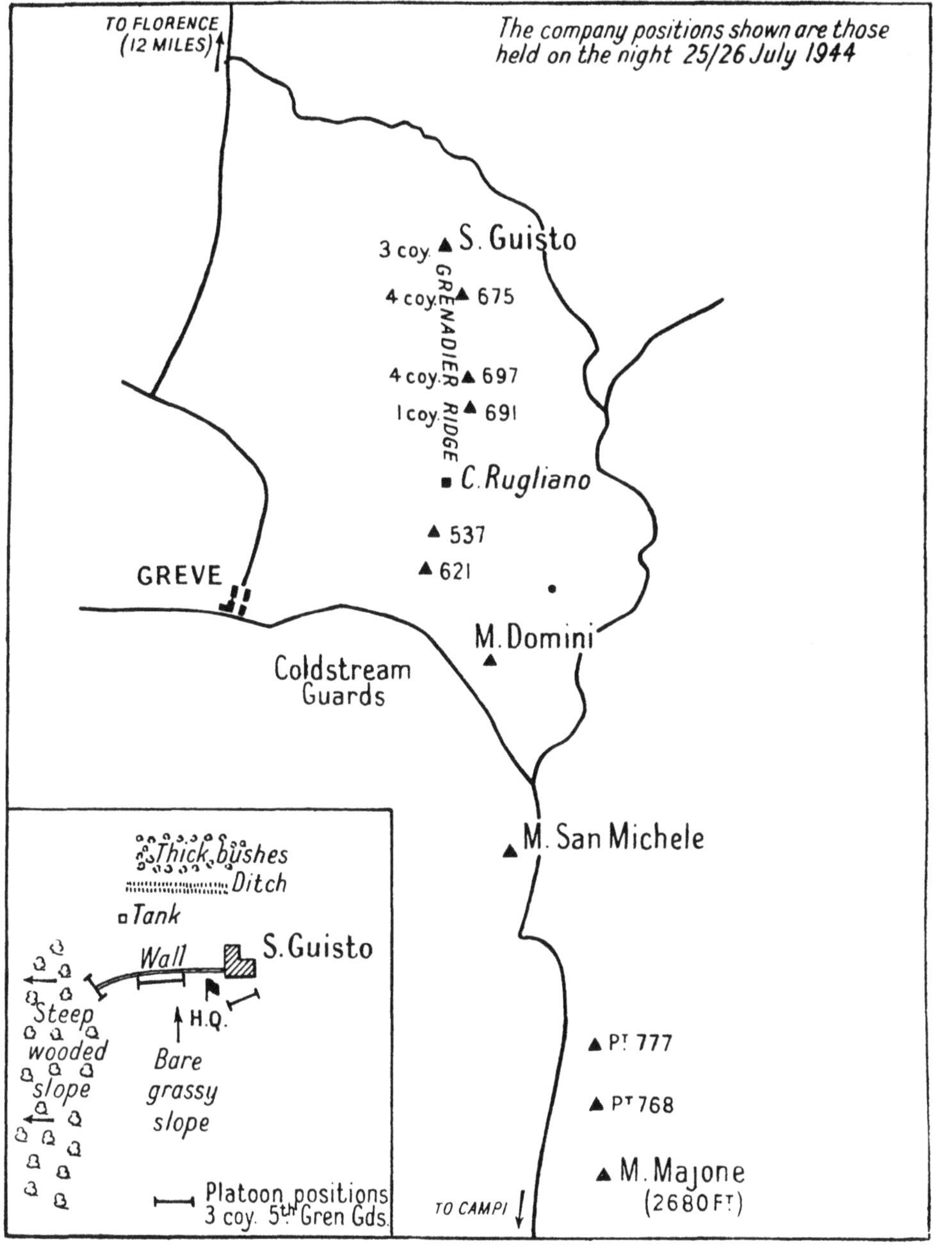

GRENADIER RIDGE

1944 "like mountain goats." On Point 697 the Germans turned to rally, but were swept aside by the tanks, which continued in the heat of the afternoon to overcome physical obstacles in a manner which would have astonished the designer of the Sherman no less than the Germans whom they encountered. A startled voice, trespassing by chance on the British wireless wave-length, was heard to shout: "Achtung! Achtung! Vier Panzer!" ("Look out! Look out! Four tanks!"). In the evening the Grenadiers were ordered to occupy the remainder of the ridge. No. 3 Company took the lead, and emerged from the woods to find that the final stretch ran along a hump of short, crisp grass which conveniently deadened their footsteps. The farm at San Guisto was deserted except for a single South African tank which had arrived there before them. They dug themselves in among the farm buildings and along a low wall (see inset plan). The other companies, supported by companies of the Scots Guards, were extended in a long tail behind them as far as the Battalion's starting point, for the ridge was too narrow to allow more than a single company to straddle any part of it, and the Battalion's lines of communication were open on both sides.

July 26 At dawn the Germans strongly counter-attacked San Guisto. The forward platoon of No. 3 Company had just come back to the wall from a ditch in front of the farm when two Italians emerged from the bushes and warmly embraced Capt. Willson and Lieut. Williams. This was a Judas kiss, for immediately afterwards Germans opened fire from the bushes and retreated only when they had set the tank ablaze and the Grenadiers had disclosed all their positions. The men had no sooner finished their breakfasts than the Germans attacked again, this time with two companies. The bullets and grenades flew for one and a half hours between the ditch and the wall—the Germans were too close to our own men to risk calling for artillery fire, though the Scots Guards carrier platoon gave them valuable support from behind—and at the moment when the Grenadiers were running seriously short of ammunition the Germans cut their losses and withdrew, leaving behind them twenty rifles and two machine guns. It was a great achievement, for which the brilliant leadership and personal courage of Capt. Willson were in no small way responsible. With fifty-eight men No. 3 Company had held off a hundred and fifty of the enemy and lost few men themselves either in the battle or in the heavy shelling which followed. Lieut. Williams was twice wounded, once by a German grenade and once by mortar fire.

No. 1 Company relieved No. 3 Company that night, but the Battalion were not again attacked. The enemy were now more concerned with the British advance on either side of Grenadier Ridge—

with Brigadier Heber-Percy's 12th Brigade on the east side and the 1944
South African Armoured Brigade on the west. The 5th Battalion
looked down upon their battles, watched the German guns firing
below them, and the long column of tanks winding through Greve.
Twenty-four hours later the danger of counter-attack had passed, and July 27
the Battalion left their mountain for the last phase of the advance to
Florence.

The Germans dragged out the battle to its bitter end, fighting all
the more fiercely as the mountains dropped away into gentler hills,
where every small swelling in the ground was capped by a pink-and-
white villa, and in place of the endless pine forests there were small
olive groves or a curving avenue of cypresses. For five days the Grena- July 26-
diers waited uneasily while others fought for the possession of Strada. Aug. 1
As soon as it was captured by the 12th Brigade they advanced once
more between Strada and Impruneta; but the tanks, which had been
undefeated by the mountains, at last met their match in the walled
terraces of the intensely cultivated and densely populated region
round Florence, and were confined to the close network of roads and
lanes, facing the risk of a German anti-tank gun round every corner.
Nos. 1 and 4 Companies made some progress between the two towns,
but the Battalion lost several men from shell fire (among them Lieut.
G. W. Lamb, who was wounded), and were halted in the evening
short of Impruneta. The next morning they found its shattered streets Aug. 3
deserted, and passed through to occupy without opposition a group
of hills on the far side. This was the limit of their present advance. The
Coldstream went ahead, and then the Scots Guards overtook the Aug. 4
Coldstream to occupy positions a mile south of the Arno, from where
they sent patrols to the southern bank and looked across the water at
the Germans on the far shore. The Grenadiers did not enter Florence,
but one of their officers who went forward to gaze upon the city wrote
this record of his impressions:

> "It is a very strange sight. It seems quite deserted when you look down from the hills. There is no movement in the streets, no smoke, no sound, no traffic. Nobody has hung up their washing, there are no children at the street corners, the windows are shuttered. It lies—the platitude so exactly fits the impression it made upon me—it lies at the feet of its conquerors: quiet, motionless, pink, lovely and dignified. . . . Afterwards I went down to the part of the city which lies south of the river. I looked across the broken bridges to the Uffizi and the square which contains the David and the Perseus. I saw an old woman waving her handkerchief in what she rightly imagined to be the direction of the Allied armies, *ripae ulterioris amore*. If all my other experiences in this war were obliterated from my mind, this is the moment which I should choose to remember."

CHAPTER IX

THE NORTHERN APENNINES

3RD AND 5TH BATTALIONS

1

THE GOTHIC LINE

Strength and weakness of the Gothic Line—General Alexander's intentions—The line breached by Eighth Army at Pesaro—Role of Fifth Army

1944 STRANGE and much-exaggerated reports about the Gothen Stellung, or Gothic Line, had begun to spread among the rank and file of both the German and the Allied armies before either of them had come within a hundred miles of the hills where it lay. In those days the German prisoners would refer to it as the "Grüne Stellung," the Green Line; and Allied intelligence reports would loosely describe it as the Pisa—Rimini Line. Its exact course, plotted from air photographs, had long been known, and upon the small-scale maps of Italy which had hung for months past in British and American headquarters the Gothic Line had been marked in deep-blue chinagraph pencil, cutting across the peninsula from coast to coast. It followed the southern escarpment of the Apennines where they swung round in a quarter-circle to divide the Plain of Tuscany from the Plain of Lombardy. Two years had been spent upon the construction of its defences. Thousands of Italian civilians had been forced to labour upon them side by side with German overseers from the *Organisation Todt*. Concrete, wire and mines had been lavishly expended; and within recent months the villages within the defence zone had been cleared of their populations, the trees cut down to open up firing lanes for the machine guns, and the whole vast complex put into a state ready for immediate occupation. There, the German infantryman was told, he would at last find rest and complete security: the Allies would require months of preparation before they dared to attack it, and then they would fail.

The weakness of the Gothic Line lay in its very elaboration. It had been constructed long before it was known how many troops would

be available to man it, so that when the German divisions eventually 1944
settled in there were too many emplacements for them to hold, and many blind spots were left in the defences. In those positions which had been built a year or more before, the concrete had crumbled, the wire and mines had grown rusty, the dug-outs had fallen in or become water-logged, and the elaborate camouflage had turned so brown with age that it merely drew attention to what it was intended to conceal. Furthermore, among the thousands of Italian workmen many had had the courage to construct here and there a loophole from which it was impossible to fire a machine gun, or to make the only exit from a dug-out lead outwards in full view from the south. The German battalions were therefore disappointed by what they found, but at least they did not expect the Allies to attack immediately. This was exactly General Alexander's intention. Division by division the Eighth Army had been swung over to the Adriatic coast, so that when they approached Pesaro, the eastern terminus of the Gothic Line, they were not only hot on the heels of the enemy but held ready an overwhelming force to break through the concrete and the wire before the Germans had time to settle in behind them. The Eighth Army were immediately successful. In less than two days they had penetrated the Gothic Line and were heading for Rimini. In the messes and at Sept.
innumerable conferences there was already talk of the new encirclement of the German Army, of the race for the Po, even of the Brenner Pass and Southern Austria.

Shortly afterwards the reaction set in. North of Pesaro the exhausted divisions had a slow and hard fight to reach Rimini, and the Germans remained solidly in their Gothic positions facing the Fifth Army. Part of the line had indeed been forced, but beyond it there was no clean break-through, only a bulge. At the same time, the weather began to deteriorate rapidly, and the Allies felt keenly the loss of those French and American divisions which had been taken from Italy for the invasion of Southern France. Nevertheless, the Eighth Army offensive was barely relaxed, and the Fifth Army were also ordered to penetrate the Gothic Line on a broad front north of Florence, with the object of drawing off German reserves from the Eighth Army, and opening up direct communications with them across the fifty-mile-wide strip of mountains which divided the valley of the Arno from the valley of the Po. It was in these operations, in these hills, that both the 1st and 24th Guards Brigades were engaged during the coming winter of 1944-45.

2

THE 5TH BATTALION: THE ARNO AND THE GOTHIC LINE

The front line on the Arno at San Miniato—The river crossed by the 24th Guards Brigade unopposed—Pursuit to Pistoia—Close contact with the Gothic Line—The enemy abandon the line—Great Allied optimism

1944 From the 6th to the 22nd of August the 24th Guards Brigade had been at rest in the neighbourhood of Siena. On their return to the **Aug. 24** front they relieved part of the 85th American Division on a sector of *See Map p. 496* the Arno, between Empoli and San Miniato. The whole South African Division came under the command of the IV American Corps. So secret was this relief that the officers of the Brigade were dressed in American uniforms when they went forward to make their reconnaissance of the new positions. "It was not therefore surprising," reads the Brigade's War Diary, "that the Brigade Commander, dressed as an American private, first class, should have found himself somewhat at a disadvantage on encountering behind a bush the Army Commander, General Mark Clark, who was also spying out the land." Nor were the local Italians deceived for one moment. The 5th Battalion of the Grenadiers arrived at San Miniato to find that tactful civilian hands had already replaced the Stars and Stripes by a Union Jack, and that the walls of the houses were stamped with the welcome "Viva Grenadieri."

The Battalion occupied the flat ground between the river banks and the ridge on which stood San Miniato. It was thickly cultivated and speckled with small houses, the Arno itself lying almost invisible in its deep channel. All the tracks leading to the river were strewn with mines, and on the south bank the Germans had left one or two patrols, following their normal practice of holding both banks of a defended river line. During the first few days the Brigade lay quietly at watch without attempting to do more than discover the positions of the German strong-points on the south bank, and to prevent the infiltra-**Aug. 28** tion of their patrols towards the main San Miniato Ridge. One evening Lieut. H. E. Dunlop was suddenly seized by a German patrol as he was walking round his company positions, and was killed when he attempted to escape. Then there came a change in Allied policy. The Arno Line was known to be no more than a temporary delaying position, and already there were signs that the Germans were preparing to abandon it for their main Gothic defences. The South African

Division was therefore ordered to cross the river as soon as it was 1944
certain that only a thin German screen was left on the north bank, and
to pursue the enemy towards Pistoia. Although there was no question
of a full-scale attack, it was important to reconnoitre immediately for
fords and bridging sites so that when the time came the pursuit would
not be delayed. Each battalion sent many patrols to gain this information. For the Grenadiers, the most remarkable was the patrol led by
Lieut. J. E. M. Conant, who found, after several trials, a place where Aug. 30
the river-bottom was firm and pebbly, and the water not more than
waist-deep. He himself waded to within five yards of the north bank,
and, though the moon was full and high, and he could hear the enemy
talking, he returned undetected with his invaluable information. On Aug. 31
the next night the Germans withdrew along the whole front.

In the morning the 3rd Coldstream and 1st Scots Guards both sent Sept. 1
strong forces over the river, to find no more than a few German
stragglers, who had thought it preferable to remain behind, and the
Engineers worked all night to clear the approaches to the ford and
build a low-level bridge across the Arno. At dawn both were completed, and the Grenadiers passed across the river in their lorries to Sept. 2
take up the pursuit, with No. 3 Company (Major E. B. M. Vaughan)
as the advance guard to the whole Brigade. At Lazzaretto they took
nine isolated prisoners, and then continued, with No. 4 Company
(Major C. B. Frederick) in place of No. 3 Company, to the town of
Lamporecchio, which was likewise captured without even the necessity for the Guardsmen to dismount from their lorries. However, the
civilian population who came out to welcome them were sent scurrying for shelter by a German artillery concentration which descended
on the town at the moment of the Grenadiers' entry, and ten Guardsmen were wounded. By evening the whole Battalion were tactically
deployed in the hills round Lamporecchio.

Others then continued the pursuit towards Pistoia, notably the tanks
of the South African Armoured Brigade, which ranged over that fertile country between the Arno and the mountains like a cavalry screen
in seventeenth-century warfare. It was a leisurely, almost bloodless,
pursuit. The main German forces had retired in one bound from the
Arno to the Gothic Line, leaving a troop of artillery here, a couple of
machine guns there, to give us warning of their presence and themselves warning of our approach; but there was little fighting. Even
Pistoia was liberated by its own Partisans, and when the 12th South Sept. 8
African Motor Brigade made a formal entry into the city they found
that only two thousand of its twenty thousand inhabitants had remained, and rival bands of Partisans, as in the days of Guelph and
Ghiberline, roamed its deserted streets. The Grenadiers made them- Sept. 5-11

1944 selves comfortable in the villas round Lamporecchio, where they found a hatred for the Germans and an affection for the Allies more marked than they had encountered elsewhere in Italy. With time on their hands, they were able to arrange cinema shows, concerts by the Regimental Band, and day excursions to Florence. They were not only very contented but extremely optimistic. The main assault on the Gothic Line on either side of the Futa Pass was now imminent, and other divisions were to bear the brunt of the attack. The South African Division were officially informed that they must remain fresh for the pursuit across the Po Valley.

When the 5th Battalion moved up from Lamporecchio to Monsummano (where Kesselring had had his headquarters during the retreat
Sept. 12-17 from Rome) they were still in reserve to the other battalions of the 24th Guards Brigade, but could now clearly see ahead of them the high escarpments and deep ravines over which the Gothic Line had been constructed. Already the Coldstream and Scots Guards had left the plain for the lower slopes, where tanks were quite useless and the infantry depended for their supplies on strings of mules and twisting, slippery jeep tracks. On the 11th of September a Scots Guards patrol had come across the first six-foot-thick barbed-wire entanglements of the outer defences, and point by point the leading battalions began to edge their way up the mountains until they were facing the main Gothic Line at a distance of a thousand yards and at nearly three thousand feet above sea-level. German opposition had greatly stiffened. Although there were already heavy shelling and sharp, short-range patrolling by both sides, the Brigade were ordered to advance to even closer contact with the line, and to exert upon it maximum pressure short of actual attack. At this stage the 5th Grenadiers were
Sept. 19 moved up into the mountains on the right of the Scots Guards, about three miles north-west of Pistoia, with Nos. 3 and 4 Companies in the most advanced positions. Their arrival in this sector coincided with the relief of a weak German division by the formidable 16th S.S. Division, who immediately made their presence known by fierce patrols through the thick woodlands. However, they were not allowed to remain long enough to disturb the Grenadiers very greatly, for the Allied penetration of the Gothic Line, fifteen miles away to the east, had forced on the German High Command the decision to withdraw
Sept. 23 from almost its entire length. At the first sign of the withdrawal No. 1 Company of the Grenadiers (Major Hon. F. M. Legh) occupied without resistance the hill overlooking Piazza, where hitherto patrols had always been met by the most stubborn defence, and Lieut. R. R. B. Kitson investigated the ground farther ahead without finding any enemy. The S.S. Division had not melted completely away. When

Lieut. A. J. G. Harris led a careful patrol up Route 66 beyond Piazza 1944
he was severely wounded by a sudden burst of fire, and later died of Sept. 24
his wounds. This had been no more than a light rearguard and the next
day the Grenadiers were able to pass through the wire and mines to Sept. 25
occupy without a fight the concrete pillboxes of the Gothic Line itself.
They entered the village of Cireglio, where all the houses had been
blown down to block the road, and heard the thud of German demolitions for many miles ahead. From this time onwards the Battalion
lost all touch with the enemy. While some of the men satisfied their
curiosity by close examination of the much-vaunted defences, Lieut.
P. C. Holt took a patrol nearly four miles ahead to Campo Tizzoro, Sept. 27
and while he was searching a small-arms factory in that town the
board of directors suddenly appeared and invited the entire patrol to
sit down to luncheon. They returned to the Battalion very much later
that night.

For the Guards Brigade to continue the pursuit in this direction
would only mean that the South African Division would be split by a
high intervening range of hills, for already their Motor Brigade had
advanced some miles through the Gothic Line up Route 6620, which
offered the Division better opportunities for exploitation than Route
66. The latter was therefore handed over to a light anti-aircraft regiment (one of the many which were now converted into infantry for
lack of German aircraft to shoot at), and the 24th Guards Brigade
came down from their mountains to camps outside Pistoia. The pene- Sept. 28
tration of the Gothic Line, though very exhausting in its later stages,
had been less costly than they had feared, and the Grenadiers in
particular were left fairly fresh for the pursuit to Bologna. The optimism of the Fifth Army was still very high. They felt that once the
watershed of the Apennines had been surmounted they would be
attacking down a favourable slope, and the maps showed long, green
fingers reaching out to welcome them to the valley of the Po. This was
a most mistaken impression. They soon discovered that the strength
of the Gothic Line lay not so much in its prepared defences as in
the interminable series of natural positions, ridge after ridge, which
lay behind it. The Germans had every opportunity to recover, and
Bologna was not in fact captured until seven months later.

3

THE 3RD BATTALION: MONTE PESCHIENA AND MONTE BATTAGLIA

Breaching of the Gothic Line at Monte Peschiena—Interlude on the Upper Arno—Armoured divisions fighting in rain and mountains—1st Guards Brigade take over Monte Battaglia from the Americans—Conditions of great hardship—A German attack beaten off with surprising results—First sight of the Alps

1944 While the 5th Battalion had been clawing their way to the summit of the mountains above Pistoia, the 3rd Battalion had also been making their contribution to the dismemberment of the Gothic Line.
Sept. 3-9 They had obtained their first sight of the line from the hills at Borselli, above Pontassieve. It was not at first a period of great activity, for the Germans were clearly about to withdraw of their own accord; and just as the 6th South African Division had been allowed, indeed ordered, not to over-exert themselves in anticipation of sterner tasks ahead, so too the 6th British Armoured Division were poorly suited by their equipment, training and organization to embark on operations in steep mountains and were encouraged to reserve their strength for the rapid advance which was expected to follow the German collapse. The South Africans had their eyes on Bologna: the 6th Armoured on Forli. Between the two divisions lay the main weight of the Fifth Army's infantry, mainly American troops, who in the middle of September were launched against the centre of the Gothic Line astride the Futa Pass. As it turned out, not only were the South Africans immediately involved in the consequences of this battle but, to an even greater extent, the 6th Armoured Division as well. By the end of the autumn progress had become so slow, and the strain on Allied resources so great, that first the infantry brigades of armoured divisions and later their actual tank crews, fighting as infantry, were employed in a manner which they had little expected when Allied plans and tactics were first discussed in August.

The 3rd Battalion's approach to the Gothic Line, however, was as simple as the 5th Battalion's. Discovering one morning, without great
Sept. 10 surprise, that the Germans had withdrawn from the hills between Pontassieve and Consuma, they followed them with patrols up the Sieve Valley towards Dicomano. The foremost patrol, the spearhead of the entire XIII Corps, was led by Lieut. R. Neville, and he reported with some disgust that the Italians were making fools of his men by seeking them out among the hedgerows to present them with bottles

of wine and bouquets of flowers, "being unable to understand why we 1944
were creeping so furtively about the countryside." Italian optimism was, for once, quite justified. Dicomano was found shattered but quite clear of enemy, and the further advance of the 1st Guards Brigade met no opposition until they reached a point within a few hundred yards of the Gothic Line itself. The Grenadiers, based upon the hills immediately east of Dicomano, patrolled as far as the lower slopes of Monte Falterona, while the Coldstream leap-frogged their companies into the heart of the hills immediately north of the town. The Welsh Guards, to everyone's astonishment, actually penetrated the Gothic Line itself at the point where the formidable defences covered the road to San Godenzo. They were quite deserted. The reason for this strange withdrawal was soon discovered. The Germans had found that the positions which had been so carefully prepared for them were most unsatisfactory. There were far too many entrenchments for their weakened and extended battalions to hold, the majority of them were almost derelict, and they were poorly sited half-way down a slope which was dominated by the hills already in British hands. So they rightly decided to concentrate their forces at the top of the mountain, the watershed between the Arno and the Po. It was called Monte Peschiena.

Although the attack on the Futa Pass was progressing very well, the American Corps badly needed support on their right flank, and in addition the Eighth Army were most anxious that an attack on Forli should be launched from the south, not only to loosen their own front but to open up an alternative supply route to the Po Valley. The Dicomano—Forli road lay entirely within the sector of the 6th Armoured Division, and this road was overlooked for a great part of its length by the ridge of which Monte Peschiena (three thousand five hundred feet) was the dominating height. The 1st Guards Brigade were therefore ordered to capture the hill. There were two possible approaches to its pyramidical peak, each of which followed a long, curving spur, meeting like horns at the summit: the northern spur was allotted to the Welsh Guards; the southern to the Grenadiers.

The 3rd Battalion tackled their long ascent in two stages, in order to give the men time for rest half-way up the mountain and to build up behind them the supplies which they would need for the final
assault. On the first day No. 4 Company (Capt. A. K. C. Nation) Sept. 15
established themselves astride the southern spur, and Lieut. C. A. Scarisbrick led a patrol towards the summit. They captured a prisoner, whose information would have been invaluable, but were obliged to shoot him and retire hurriedly when the Germans opened fire at
close range; Lieut. Scarisbrick himself was wounded. On the second Sept. 16

1944 day No. 1 Company (Major T. S. Hohler, M.C.) and No. 2 Company (Major D. V. Bonsor, M.C.) advanced as far as a hollow just below the summit, where they had time to dig three-foot trenches before their positions were detected and heavily mortared. Two patrols went forward that night, led by Lieuts. J. Lyttleton and H. G. Nisbett, and, though their evidence was slightly contradictory, it was correctly assumed that the Germans were still in firm possession of the watershed. The Welsh Guards by this time had closed to equivalent positions on the northern spur. Sept. 17 At 9 in the morning No. 3 Company of the Grenadiers (Capt. J. S. M. Pearson-Gregory) advanced alone to the final assault. Lieut. J. Penn's platoon, leading the company, found themselves in the middle of an enemy section before either British or Germans fully realized it, and in the close-quarter fighting which followed Lieut. Penn seized a German machine gun intact and L./Cpl. Chriscoli, M.M., killed two Germans and captured five of the company's nine prisoners. Having beaten off two German patrols, Lieut. Penn moved his platoon forward to a point just west of the summit, from where artillery spotters were able to direct their gun fire on to the reverse slopes and break up any German attempts to counter-attack. The Battalion's task was completed. They had topped the watershed, and, though the enemy had not yet abandoned the hill entirely, but shared the long summit with the Grenadiers, the Gothic Line had been broken in yet another place, and the Battalion were able to hand over to other troops a most favourable starting point for fresh advances.

Until the end of September the 1st Guards Brigade were again temporarily detached from the 6th Armoured Division, and sent round to plug a gap in the line on the east side of the Prato Magno, Sept. 19-27 under the direct command of the X Corps. Driving as far south as Arezzo, down the long road which had been their axis of advance during the past two months, the Grenadiers turned north along the narrow, silvery stream of the Upper Arno and found adequate billets in the village of Chitignano. Here they remained in reserve to the other two battalions of the Brigade, who faced the Gothic Line in the neighbourhood of the great Franciscan Monastery of La Verna, one of the few stretches of the line which the Germans had not yet abandoned. It was a wild, remote part of the Central Apennines, the scene of Dante's early exile and Saint Francis's retirement, and from the highest hills sprang the head-waters of the Arno, the Tiber, and those many lesser streams which flow into the Adriatic south of the Po. Neither the Germans nor the Allies had ever contemplated heavy fighting in those hills. The X Corps were at that time a scratch formation of many independent battalions and brigades, strung together in a thin line of outposts, and its commander, General McCreery, was about to take over command of the Eighth Army, leaving Brigadier Scott, Commander of the 1st Guards Brigade, in charge of the Corps. The Welsh and Coldstream Guards had the satisfactory experience of once again probing through the Gothic Line defences when the Germans withdrew, but the Grenadiers never moved from Chitignano. Their sternest trial of the whole campaign was about to come. 1944

The 6th Armoured Division were still advancing very slowly beyond Monte Peschiena up the road to Forli, delayed by strong German forces who found themselves in country ideal for defence, but even more by the destruction of the only available road. Not only were the bridges and culverts blown to pieces but at every sharp bend, at every cutting, the road had been sliced clean away by explosives, leaving a precipitous glacis of rock and rubble which was barely distinguishable from the virgin hillside. The sappers, by a great feat of military engineering, managed to repair the road from San Godenzo to the watershed in about ten days, and the 61st and Armoured Brigades of the Division climbed over the pass to begin their long descent to Forli. At first it was a race for the capture of the town between the 6th Armoured Division coming from the south-west and the Eighth Army advancing up the plain from the south-east. Two misfortunes then made the former's effort almost hopeless. In the first place, the weather finally broke, and the rain, lashing those hill-tops day after day, made it quite impossible for the tanks to move off the few hard roads. In the second place, the available force of infantry, who despite their recent hardships might have struggled on through the rocks and mud, was reduced to one single brigade by the sudden cancellation of the 1st Guards Brigade's return to the Division. The latter were ordered to move direct from Arezzo to another part of the front twelve miles west of the Forli axis. It was then that the 3rd Grenadiers first heard the name of Monte Battaglia. Sept. 30

The Gothic Line was now a thing of the past. The whole front had shifted to the centre of the band of mountains which divided Northern from Central Italy, and astride each of the many river valleys which eventually broadened out into the Plain of Lombardy were slung one Allied division and one German division, facing each other across a No Man's Land of an average width of half a mile. Ultimately it was the valley floors, or the roads which followed them, which were of greatest importance, but the key to the valleys was the highest ground on either side. Monte Battaglia was one such key, one of the most important in the whole front, dividing the valley of the Santerno from the valley of the Senio. The stunted, ruined castle by which it was

1944 crowned dominated not only its own immediate surroundings but the whole tossing mass of hills. It had been visible from the summit of Monte Peschiena: it was still visible seven months later when the Battalion found themselves in the neighbourhood of Imola. It was indeed appropriately named "Battle Mountain," its little medieval castle bearing witness to the tactical importance which for centuries had been attached to it.

The approach to Battaglia from Firenzuola was by a minor road which had been constructed for local, peasant, traffic, and even had the bridges not been blown away nor its surface scarred with bombs and shells, the thin tarmac would never have withstood for long the passage of the heavy German and American convoys at a time of year when the rain spread over it a film of mud, and the later frosts crumbled what remained. Yet there was no alternative to this road. Gangs of engineers worked throughout the winter to keep it in reasonable repair: every half-mile or so there was a Bailey bridge slung across a chasm, and wrecks by the roadside or far below in the river-bed, showed what a price had been paid in war material and men's lives to maintain the flow of supplies. About five miles from Battaglia wheeled transport could go no farther. Here the infantry left their lorries, and, accompanied by porters and mules, they climbed the track leading up the mountain-side. By the incessant rainfall and continual passage of men and mules, the tracks had been turned into glaciers of liquid mud. Men's boots, however tightly laced, would be pulled away from their feet; fully loaded mules would belly inextricably in the morass and be shot where they lay; and even as far back as Brigade Headquarters the Brigade Major, Major J. D. Buchanan, was so firmly embedded in the mud that it took twenty-five minutes to dig him out. From this point forward, a distance of three miles, it sometimes took ten hours for the supply train to reach Battaglia and return. An Indian muleteer expressed what they all felt, man and beast, by the patient understatement: "Mule tired; me very unhappy."

At Battaglia itself the conditions were even worse than on its approaches. For the last mile the track ran along the knife-edge of a causeway so narrow that in places there was room only to stand with feet astride upon it, and with their machine guns and mortars the Germans could bring every yard of it under fire. The small castle hill lay at the northern extremity of the causeway. Within the castle itself there was room for only part of one platoon, the remainder of the Battalion being grouped round the inside of a bowl lying at its foot, or strung back at intervals along the causeway. Plotted on a map, the Battalion's position therefore had the shape of a tadpole, the castle hill forming the head, the causeway the tail. The Germans were lying

on the far side of the hill and on two spurs which ran out at right angles **1944**
from it. Both British flanks were completely open, nor was there anything to prevent German patrols attacking the causeway at any point they chose, so cutting the tail from the head. This meant, of course, that no company ever felt safe from direct attack or encirclement, and that the mules and porters, the Battalion Headquarters and medical posts, which normally count on a greater degree of security, were continually exposed to exactly the same danger as the companies. The rain and mortar fire were unceasing. The American regiment whom the Guards Brigade relieved had been losing casualties at the rate of a hundred a day, and even during the first reconnaissance of the position
Capt. J. S. M. Pearson-Gregory, M.C., was badly wounded. By day the **Oct. 3**
men lay in open slit trenches, soaked to the skin, and surrounded by water-logged shell-holes, sopping blankets, stunted trees shorn off shoulder-high by shrapnel, rusting ration tins, and the corpses of German and American dead which could not be buried while the shell fire was so intense. The night brought them little rest, for it was then that the supply trains were struggling forward, German fire was redoubled, and German companies might at any moment be creeping up to launch a violent attack. Six or seven times they had been repulsed, but still they seemed determined to regain the hill.

The Grenadiers took over from the Americans, with No. 1 Com- **Oct. 4/5**
pany (Major T. S. Hohler, M.C.) and No. 4 Company (Major V. A. P. Budge) in the foremost positions under the castle hill, where after a few days they were relieved by the other two companies (Major D. V. Bonsor, M.C., and Capt. D. I. Rollo, M.C.). Colonel Nelson soon decided that no man could be expected to remain and fight in such conditions for more than seventy-two hours at a stretch. For the first week the 3rd Grenadiers endured greater misery than any to which they had been exposed in Italy. They lost an average of ten men a day from shell fire, and were saved from casualties as heavy as the Americans' only by holding the line with fewer men and digging deeper trenches.
Among these casualties were two officers: Lieut. J. Lyttleton, who **Oct. 10**
was hit in the back as he stepped from his trench under the castle hill and died soon afterwards from his wounds; and Capt. R. A. Kennard, who was wounded.

The night before, Battalion Headquarters itself had come under direct attack. A salvo of German shells descended upon the house, wounding Lieut. T. E. Streatfeild-Moore and the Intelligence Officer, Lieut. Hon. J. D. Berry, the latter so severely that he also died before he could be carried back to the road. While the survivors, including the Commanding Officer, Colonel Nelson, were doing their best to care for the wounded and to restore the broken signal wires, a German

1944 patrol attacked the house, killed the sentries, flung grenades through the window, and could have done even more damage if they had pressed home their raid. Lieut. M. H. Jenkins and ten other ranks were wounded. A grenade which fell under the table at which Colonel Nelson was sitting did not explode.

On the very next night the Germans launched their most violent assault of all.

From an operation order captured during the ensuing battle it was learned that three German battalions were to have taken part in the attack, approaching the causeway and Battaglia Castle from three different directions. Their ultimate object was to "occupy the enemy maintenance route, and hold the objectives against any counter-attacks"—in other words, to cut the causeway about half a mile south-west of the castle and isolate the two Grenadier and one Welsh Guards companies which lay inside the castle bowl. From the start the German attack was grossly mismanaged: two of their three battalions did not advance at all; the third, which at least made an attempt to
Oct. 11 carry out its orders, completely failed. Shortly after 4 a.m. No. 1 Company of the Grenadiers (Major Hohler), who held the western approaches to the castle hill, were attacked by about a hundred Germans. The main weight of the attack fell on the platoon commanded by Sergt. J. Sibbald, D.C.M., and it was due to the courageous action of a single man in the leading section, Gdsm. R. Wood, M.M., that the attack was repulsed. The man lying next to him was killed at short range, and when Wood started to fire back, his Bren gun jammed after a few rounds. "He picked up the gun," reads his citation, "and knocked the leading German over the head, stunning him. He struck the next one with his fists, and when four other Germans attempted to rush the trench, Wood hurled grenades at them at five yards' range, and continued to throw anything he could lay his hands on," including, adds another account, his web equipment. The Germans started to retreat, but had not gone many yards when they touched off the beehive mines which the sappers had laid across the track. The set-back and the casualties which they had inflicted saved the Grenadier castle companies from any further molestation. The main danger was that the causeway should be cut behind them.

In the valley lying west of the causeway a Welsh Guards patrol were overrun, leaving nothing between the Germans and the British headquarters but a detachment of Grenadier 3-inch mortars who had been firing in support of No. 1 Company. They were commanded by Sergt. A. Goult, D.C.M. They continued to fire until the Germans approached within range of a grenade, and then took to their lighter weapons to ward off a hand-to-hand attack, one German approaching close enough to try to wrench a mortar from its base-plate. Farther west a Welsh Guards platoon held their own against an entire enemy company, but a considerable German force managed to climb the western slopes of the causeway and attacked Colonel Nelson's Headquarters which he shared with the regimental aid post. ("It is not too easy," remarked the Commanding Officer, "to command a battalion with a telephone in one hand and a revolver in the other.") The Germans gained only a very temporary foothold, as not only had their commander lost control of his force and his own sense of direction but the whole floor of the valley and slopes of the causeway were covered by a very heavy bombardment directed by Major B. M. Knox, M.C., of the Ayrshire Yeomanry. At dawn the Germans withdrew in confusion, some of them back to the safety of their start line, but over seventy of them to the inadequate shelter of a small cottage lying at the bottom of the causeway slope. This cottage became the focus of every British weapon within range. 1944

> "Within a short time," reads a contemporary account, "a white flag was seen to appear from the cottage chimney, pushed up from inside at the end of a long pole, and a German soldier emerged from the house and approached the forward company of the Welsh Guards. He brought not a message of surrender, but simply a request for time to evacuate the German wounded. We granted half an hour's amnesty for this purpose, and declared that we would totally destroy the cottage at the end of that period if all the occupants had not decided to surrender. For three-quarters of an hour not a movement was seen, not a casualty was brought out. We decided to open fire when the full hour had elapsed. A few minutes later the Germans began to stream out of the cottage without their weapons, fluttering handkerchiefs and bits of white paper. We assembled them on the causeway and counted one officer and seventy-five men. Our own casualties, in the whole Brigade, were thirteen."

Later, in the German officer's diary which was found in the cottage, the Grenadiers read this passage: "The English foot-slogger completely lacks aggressiveness: he is in fact a coward who only tries to achieve success with the support of his heavy weapons."

After this costly failure (of which General Sir H. C. Loyd, Commanding the Brigade of Guards, had himself been a witness), the enemy abandoned their attempts to retake Battaglia. The shell fire decreased, even the weather slightly improved, and by the frequent relief of forward companies the Grenadiers were given some respite from this unenviable position. For a time Major P. H. Lort-Phillips took over command from Colonel Nelson. The Germans, under the pressure of Allied advances up the Santerno and Senio Valleys, at last withdrew two miles north of Battaglia, and No. 2 Company (Major Oct. 24

1944 Bonsor) sent forward patrols to occupy Point 621. The melancholy
Oct. 26 castle now became little more than a reserve area, and two days later the Brigade came down to the comparative safety of the Santerno Valley.

The congestion and appalling state of the main supply route prevented the Battalion from returning to Florence, and among the poor entertainments which could be provided nearer the front we read of a lecture by a War Office delegate on "Schemes for the Release of the Armed Forces," which can hardly have given much hope or consolation to these weary, rain-soaked men. At the end of October they were once more under orders to occupy another block of mountains, east of their Battaglia position, overlooking the valley of the Senio.

Nov. 4-17 It was fortunately a quiet sector, where the main problems were problems of supply. So serious indeed were they—the very mules being known to drop dead from exhaustion on their arrival at a forward company—that the Grenadiers deliberately withdrew to a
Nov. 8 shorter line, leaving behind them nests of booby-traps and trip-flares which the Germans thought it inadvisable to reconnoitre. The No Man's Land was left wide and bleak, and patrolling was of little urgency.

The first snow of the year fell on the 9th of November. A Grenadier wrote in a letter of that date:

> "I climbed an enormous mountain [this, though censorship regulations forbade him to say so, was Monte Battaglia]. There was nothing higher than myself for miles around. I looked down on a crumpled white quilt of snow-covered foothills, and beyond was the great northern plain, with German lorries sometimes visible scurrying up and down the Via Emilia. I could see little groups of villas and farmhouses in that plain which, if all goes well, we may occupy before the winter is out, for even the squalid mountain chalets which some of us are lucky enough to occupy at the moment were not designed for winter visitors. But that was not all I saw. You may not believe it—I saw the Alps. Though they are nearly one hundred miles away, there they stood up above the mist which covered the Po basin, clear-cut on the horizon, with blue shadows down one side and sharp, serrated edges. I was so excited that I have rushed back to write you a special letter about it."

Nov. 5 Field-Marshal Alexander himself visited the Brigade in their new positions, but on that day the Alps were hidden by a screen of clouds.

4

THE 5TH BATTALION: MONTE CATARELTO AND MONTE SOLE

Advance through the mountains towards Bologna—The Grenadiers attack a German S.S. division on Monte Catarelto—Projected attack on Monte Sole several times postponed—The Grenadiers capture an outlying spur of Monte Sole—The offensive halted

After the breaching of the Gothic Line at Monte Peschiena, until 1944
the end of the winter, the 3rd Battalion were never called upon to capture fresh ground; in each successive position their role was to hold, sometimes against bitter counter-attacks, the hill-tops which had been won by others or voluntarily evacuated by the enemy. The 5th Battalion, on the other hand, were several times engaged in the attacks by which the 6th South African Armoured Division were slowly forcing their way up the road leading from Prato to Bologna. Along both routes the tanks of the armoured divisions were almost useless; occasionally they could be used to fire from the road like field guns at targets far above them in the hills. Otherwise every battle was a tussle of infantry against infantry, artillery against artillery. So it was in the Battle of Monte Catarelto, the first serious engagement in which the 5th Battalion were involved since leaving the Arno.

Having patrolled through the Gothic Line north-west of Pistoia, the 24th Guards Brigade were switched from Route 66 to the minor road, Route 6620, leading northwards from Prato. Already the 11th South African Armoured Brigade had progressed more than a third of the way up this road towards Bologna, and it was uncertain whether the Germans would attempt to make a serious stand south of the plain. Then suddenly the line tightened. The enemy had skilfully judged the moment when the first Allied effort was spent and when the demolitions, the rain and the narrowing valleys were making their communications over the Apennine passes extremely precarious. Monte Battaglia was one bastion of this new line: Monte Catarelto another.

It lay to the east of the road, just north of Castiglione, a wooded ridge rising to two thousand five hundred feet, overlooking a long
stretch of the valley to the south. The 1st Scots Guards were moved up Sept. 28
through Castiglione to the tail of the ridge, with orders to clear it as far as the highest point, Point 707, while the 3rd Coldstream advanced an equivalent distance on the left of the road, and the Grenadiers were held in reserve ready to pass through to the next bound, several

1944 miles to the north. It was an ambitious plan, based on ignorance of the true German strength; but the fortunate capture of a German marked map showed the Scots Guards that Point 707, far from being the position of the usual light rearguard, was held by an entire battalion of the 16th S.S. Division. The attack was therefore postponed to give them time to elaborate their preparations. The first phase was very successful. The Germans retired from an intermediate height on the approach of the Scots Guards, and concentrated round Point 707 itself, allowing the Guardsmen to advance to within a few hundred yards of the summit before checking them with a curtain of fire. The two Scots Guards companies dug in on either side of the crest. During the night the right-hand company were left immune from direct attack, but the left-hand company were gradually surrounded on all but one side and so weakened that it became impossible for them to
Oct. 1 renew their own attack. Brigadier Clive therefore withdrew the Scots Guards to the intervening position half-way up the ridge, and called upon the 5th Grenadiers to complete the capture of the hill. To give the Battalion more room for manœuvre, he also withdrew the other Scots Guards company, so that the Grenadiers started their attack with a firm base but with the knowledge that the whole hill ahead was held very strongly by first-rate troops who had already been heartened by success.

Oct. 2 At 4.30 the next morning the Grenadiers began to advance through a film of mist and rain which hid their objectives, deprived them of observed artillery support, and for hours on end put their light wireless sets out of action. No. 2 Company (Capt. D. B. Fergusson, M.C.) led the attack on the right, and No. 3 Company (Major E. B. M. Vaughan) were on the left; the other two companies followed behind in reserve. It was a stiff advance up slippery, wooded banks; in places the men were obliged to swing themselves up by clutching at the wet tree trunks and search for firm footholds among the undergrowth and roots. Under cover of mist and a heavy barrage, both companies advanced to about the same point which had been reached by the Scots Guards two days before, and there they too were halted, and dug in. In No. 2 Company Lieut. M. J. W. Cassy was killed and Capt. Fergusson wounded; in No. 3 Company Lieut. J. A. Nugent was wounded and died a short time afterwards in enemy hands. Nothing further was gained that day, but Colonel Gordon-Lennox moved forward No. 1 Company (Capt. F. M. Legh) to a position behind No. 2 Company, proposing to deliver a final assault in the morning. The
Oct. 3 Germans withdrew during the night, probably on account of the heavy casualties they had already suffered, for when the Grenadiers occupied Point 707 they found thirty German corpses round the summit, and a

conservative estimate put their total losses at two hundred and fifty 1944 men. Lagaro was occupied by the Battalion's carriers, and the village of Ripoli by Lieut. P. C. Holt's platoon.

The capture of Monte Catarelto opened the way for the II American Corps, who were operating on the right of the Division, on the main axis of Route 65, to bound forward another five miles to Mon- Oct. 9 zuno. In step with this new advance the Grenadiers were able to move up to the wedge of hills lying between the Sambro and Setta Valleys, and a week later to positions near the river bank immediately south Oct. 16 of Monte Sole, a name which remained linked with their own until the day came, four months later, when the 5th Battalion were withdrawn for the last time from active operations. On the right bank of the Setta the ground was clear of enemy as far as the immediate approaches to Monte Sole, but on the opposite bank a long chain of formidable heights, dividing the Setta from the Reno Valley, remained to be captured one by one before the projected assault on Sole could even begin. On the 7th of October the 3rd Coldstream captured Monteacuto, on the 13th the 12th South African Brigade captured Monte Stanco; on the 23rd the last heights of Monte Salvaro fell to the Kimberley Regiment, and on the next day Monte Termine to the Scots Guards. During all this time the Grenadiers on the floor of the valley and on its opposite slopes were deliberately spared the heavy fighting in which the rest of the Brigade and the Division were involved, for the Battalion were reserved for the crucial phase of the Brigade's coming attack. Yet only in comparison with the hardships endured by the troops on the upper levels could it be claimed that the Grenadiers enjoyed a period of relief. The Battalion were usually drenched in rain or enveloped in mist; the enemy were very confident and very watchful, and held most of the commanding ground, from which they regularly bombarded every Allied position below them. And over the heads of the Battalion hung the grim prospect of the attack on Monte Sole. Long before the capture of Monte Termine Grenadier patrols went out to search for crossing places over the River Setta and to scare German outposts from the farms and villages at the mountain's foot. Among the officers who led these patrols were Lieuts. J. E. M. Conant, J. G. Owen, C. M. Wheatley, A. J. Savill, M.C., H. W. Freeman-Attwood and R. R. B. Kitson.

The immediate preliminary to the attack on Monte Sole was the *See Inset Plan p.496* capture of a lower ridge, Point 501, which rose sharply from the north bank of the river. The Battalion were faced by a most unpleasant task. Not only would it be necessary for them to ford the Setta before lining up for their advance, but the opposite slope was steeper than any they had yet encountered, and Point 501 was believed to be very strongly

1944 held. Even after they had gained it, scarcely one-quarter of their task would be accomplished. The Battalion were therefore much relieved
Oct. 25 by the arrival of a German deserter on the morning of the attack, an eighteen-year-old who considered that he had suffered enough from shortage of food and the intensity of shell fire, and volunteered the information that his company had evacuated Point 501 for "winter positions" on the upper slopes of Monte Sole, leaving behind no more than a single section. This news was confirmed by a patrol led by Lieut. A. J. Savill to Point 501. Though in the pitch darkness he was not certain how far he had been, he had found no sign of the enemy. The Grenadiers' artillery support was therefore cancelled, and just after dark No. 3 Company (Major Vaughan) forded the river just west of La Quercia. The other companies followed them. Though the water was no more than ankle-deep during the early part of the night, the rain raised the level to three feet before the last company was across, and one Guardsman was swept away and drowned. Arriving on the north bank, cold and wet but still optimistic, No. 3 Company formed a shallow bridgehead, and at about 5.30 a.m. Nos. 1 and 4 Companies began their ascent. On the east slope of Point 501, No. 1 Company established themselves without difficulty. On the summit of the ridge No. 4 Company found five miserable Germans asleep in their slit trench—the section of which the deserter had spoken.

Oct. 31 Though they did not then know it, the Battalion had reached the farthest limit of their autumn offensive. At the end of October the Fifth Army Commander, General Mark Clark, decided that his troops were too exhausted, and his supply difficulties too great, to continue immediately; among other projects, the attack on Monte Sole was postponed for at least a month.

5

THE OFFENSIVE HALTED

Comparison of the 3rd and 5th Battalions' positions during the winter of 1944-45—Mud and snow—Declining morale of the Germans—The Santerno Valley—The 5th Battalion's attack on another spur of Monte Sole—Both Guards Brigades withdrawn for rest

For five months, from November, 1944, to April, 1945, the Fifth Army remained in static positions on a line drawn across the northern rim of the Apennines. In the last few miles they were defeated by the mountains which they saw dying away before them into the enormous

Plain of Lombardy. Bologna was little more than ten miles away from 1944 the farthest limit of their advance, and yet they no longer had the strength to attack. There were many reasons. The Italian command had been depleted of troops for the operations in North-West Europe and the South of France; those who remained were largely deprived of reinforcements to bring their battalions up to full strength, and they were tired out by the continual effort since the Cassino offensive in May; through some miscalculation they were short of ammunition for their guns; the weather had reduced the Apennine passes to such a state that it was barely possible to supply even static forces, while the Germans, with their short run-in from the plain, had no such difficulties. Finally, all along the front the way forward was blocked by natural bastions on which the Germans formed their winter line. The grain of the hills, which hitherto had run parallel to the Allied advance, now ran counter to it, and in the Vena del Gesso (Vein of Chalk) separating the Senio from the Santerno, in Monte Grande, which formed the apex of the whole Fifth Army's line, and in Monte Sole, the Germans held three key-points which the Allies could not bypass, and could capture only by an expenditure of men and ammunition which they could not at the moment afford. The Eighth Army were little better off in the plain. They prolonged their offensive into December, by which time they reached the River Senio between Faenza and Ravenna, and were then halted for the same reasons—their own exhaustion and the strength of the enemy positions. During the winter of 1944-45 Field-Marshal Alexander's forces were therefore split between the hill and the plain, the boundary between his Armies coinciding approximately with the junction between the two. The Fifth Army envied the Eighth their easy communications, their freedom from mountain climbing; the Eighth Army envied the Fifth the "natural drainage," the cool, clean air, and the wide observation of their hills. In truth, neither the plain nor the mountain was preferable to the other as a scene of winter warfare.

Between November and February both the 3rd and 5th Battalions occupied positions facing two of the three bastions mentioned above: the 3rd lay in turn upon the heights of Monte del Verro and Monte Penzola, overlooking the Santerno Valley and opposite the Vena del Gesso; the 5th occupied the southern slopes of Monte Sole. In detail their experience varied greatly, but in atmosphere there were many common factors between them which can be summarized before examining separately the conditions in which the two Battalions fought and lived.

The Italian campaign had lost the world's attention. The Arnhem adventure, the German counter-offensive in the Ardennes, and the

1944 crossing of the Rhine had pushed the Italian news to the bottom of the back page. The troops were well aware of this, and their own interest in the campaign began to wane. They were isolated in their separate valleys—few men in the 3rd Battalion, for example, had ever heard the name of Monte Sole, which meant everything to the 5th Battalion—and what concerned them most were the characteristics of the particular part of the particular hill which they were ordered to hold. What was the condition of the tracks—stone, mud or ice? How steep were they? How many hours to the nearest metalled road? Any "casas" (houses), however ruinous? Could you move about in daylight? How long a period in the line must they do at a stretch? And the enemy—were they the patrolling type, or the sit-back-and-shell type? Where were the minefields, the nearest platoons on the right and left, the closest German outpost?

Of all the answers to these questions the one which the Guardsmen came to dread most was that the tracks were very muddy. They knew that this meant that they would be permanently soaked and filthy from the waist downwards, and that supplies would be erratic and reliefs exhausting. To the uninformed public mud was no longer news, and they reserved their sympathy for the time when photographs began to appear of soldiers sitting in snow-bound trenches. Yet frost and snow were exactly what the men most desired. Frost immediately froze the tracks into their original condition, snow filled in the potholes, and until the thaw once more liquefied the surface mud, walking was not only possible but on bright, sunlit days after a fresh fall of snow highly exhilarating. Snow is far less wetting than rain: a greatcoat and a pair of Army boots are enough to keep it off the inner clothing, and it can be built up in amateur igloos as a shield against the wind. More than that, it was actually a protection against the enemy. "German shells," wrote an officer, "do not go off when they fall in soft snow. They just go whe-e-e-o-o-o-o—poof." And the crunching of heavy boots through the surface crackle not only gave warning of the approach of German patrols but showed by their tracks the next morning exactly whence and whither they had come. So with the onset of regular frosts in December the lives of the troops began to brighten. The hills looked strange and vast, but there was a cleanliness about them, a new vigour.

How did they spend their time? In daylight there was very little to do, very little movement was possible to keep themselves warm, there was little contact with the outside world, little fresh to discover in the familiar landscape ahead. Not more than one or two sentries from each platoon were necessary to keep a watch ahead, and the remainder huddled into their trenches and blew into life small petrol fires on which they would boil themselves cups of tea. At night, especially in the early part of the night, there was much more activity. It was then that the mule trains arrived with their rations and their mail, that the patrols went out, that new minefields were laid or old ones taken up; that the Germans stepped up their artillery and machine-gun fire ("It was like a jungle," wrote a Grenadier, "the animals start baying at nightfall"), and from several miles behind the front line Allied searchlights, reflected from the cloud-base, cast upon the snowfields the light of an artificial moon. Sometimes there was a family of Italian civilians to be evacuated from their farm in No Man's Land; or a German patrol dog came close enough to be shot; or a shower of propaganda leaflets fluttered down upon the trenches. So they waited day after day, in great discomfort but in no great danger, and finally, after a week, or perhaps a fortnight, the Battalion would be relieved by others, and slip quietly out of their trenches, wind in long, black files down the mountain tracks to the road, and there find the lorries which took them back over the passes to the comfort of the Arno Valley. The 5th Battalion normally returned for their rest periods to Prato; the 3rd to Greve, south of Florence. 1944

For the Germans there were comparatively few such periods of relief, poorer rations, heavier shell fire, and the greater strain which resulted from their knowledge of the course of the war elsewhere in Europe, and the fear that at any moment, at any point in the long line, the Allies might renew their attack in Italy. Yet the majority withstood their hardships with fortitude. Of the attitude of the German soldier at this time a Grenadier wrote:

> "Since Tunisia there has been a rise of about ten per cent. in the number of pure-German deserters, but not more. When they come in, either as deserters or as genuine prisoners, they all maintain, probably in self-defence, that the morale of their comrades is as poor as their own. You can see for yourself that they are badly dressed and shod compared to our own men, that they are hungry, frightened and depressed. There is scarcely a full-blooded Nazi among them: not one who will speak out loud and bold that he believes that a German victory is still possible. The letters from home which they carry say: 'Pray God that it will all end soon: we cannot stand this bombing much longer; Tommy was over again tonight.' On the evidence of these letters you might say that the will to win had softened. But, after all, what matters to us are the skill and courage with which the front-line soldier fires his machine gun at the troops who attack him. There is some loss of skill noticeable since 1943: there is certainly no loss of courage."

The 3rd Battalion, during these four winter months, occupied a very typical sector of the line. From Monte Verro or Monte Penzola

1944 they looked down the widening length of the Santerno Valley to the distant roof-tops of Imola. The Battalion were stuck, first by the mud, later by the decision to abandon further operations, and it was tantalizing for them, on bright, calm evenings, to see how close to their own position seemed the searchlights and gun-flashes of the Eighth Army's Senio line. It was like a bag or drawer which would not close because of some obstruction which it was beyond their power to remove. The
Nov. 29- Battalion first held the hill of Monte Verro, a barren ridge to which
Dec. 8 the only approach was along a causeway of the same type which they had found at Monte Battaglia, soon reduced by the nightly strings of mules to a knee-deep, glutinous morass, in which men and beasts wallowed and even lost their lives. Thirty per cent. of the stores sent up never reached their destination, and the forward companies were soon drawing their water from the very shell-holes. Some of the mules, complained Capt. J. G. Milln (who throughout the autumn and winter was the Battalion's chief muling officer), "were no bigger than Great Danes," and their spindly legs were no match for the pools of liquid mud on the causeway. They sank up to their girths, died from exhaustion, or were shot. Once again the passage of this causeway was made under mortar and machine-gun fire, and only in the absence of any direct German attack was Verro preferable to Battaglia. Among their most serious losses was a fine Grenadier, C.S.M. Flannagan, of No. 1 Company, who was killed by a mortar bomb on the 3rd of December.

Dec. 5 After the capture of Monte Penzola by the 2nd Coldstream Guards, and the failure of the 61st Brigade's attack on the village of Tossignano, which lay in the centre of the Vena del Gesso, further offensive operations were abandoned until the spring. The 3rd Grenadiers took it turn and turn about with the 2nd Lothians and 2nd Rifle Brigade to hold the pinnacle and ridge of Monte Penzola, each battalion remaining in the line for about ten days. Four times the Grenadiers returned
Dec. 25 from Greve to Monte Penzola. They spent Christmas Day upon its slopes, heard the strains of hostile carolling, of "Tannenbaum" and "Die stille Nacht," float eerily across the snow, and when the Germans rang the bells of Tossignano to celebrate the common festival they replied with the bells of Fontanelice. They ate their Christmas dinners
Dec. 29 four days late, at Greve.

1945 In the New Year the Battalion were switched for a short period to the opposite side of the Santerno Valley, where they had the welcome cover of the houses of Fontanelice, and of the farms lying between Fontanelice and Borgo. Borgo itself was occupied by a platoon of Italian Partisans, operating with British weapons and under British command, and forming a block across the valley floor. There were patrol clashes and machine-gun duels across the waste of snow, spas-

modic artillery fire (Lieut. R. O. H. Crewdson was one of the few **1945**
casualties), and a trickle of prisoners from the German side; but there **Feb. 5**
were no attacks, no battles. For the last time the Grenadiers climbed the two-thousand-four-hundred-foot peak of Penzola, where the final slopes were so steep and icy that each man had to haul himself up by a rope, and for the last time, in the middle of February, they came
away to Greve. The Battalion were not again within sound of gun fire **Feb. 15**
for two months, until the snow had melted, the spring had come, and Alexander's Armies were once again on the march, this time within sight of final victory.

The 5th Battalion meanwhile had been fighting their last battles on **1944**
the slopes of Monte Sole. All through the months of November and December the 24th Guards Brigade (now commanded by Brigadier M. D. Erskine, D.S.O.) had been preparing for their major attack on the summit of that formidable mountain, and though the operation was eventually postponed to coincide with the spring offensive and then carried out by other troops, the Guardsmen were never free from the strain of anticipating what would certainly be a most costly battle, and at one moment were within thirty-six hours of embarking upon it. While they waited the men were not idle. They employed every hour of darkness to feel their way forward with patrols up the lower slopes of Monte Sole; they made firm the bases north of the River Setta which they had already captured; they dumped large stores of ammunition in the forward posts; and by the careful questioning of civilians and prisoners they obtained a detailed estimate of the opposition they would have to overcome. The ridge of Monte Sole was unapproachable along most of its length, being faced on its southern side by a cliff which was proof against infantry as well as tanks. But at its south-western end the ridge opened out into a wide triangle, formed by the three peaks of Abelle, Caprara and Sole itself. (See inset map, page 496.) This was the only feasible approach, and all the patrolling and all the preliminary attacks were conceived with the intention of making it more secure. After several postponements it seemed certain that the main attack would take place on the night of the 6th of December, but it was first necessary to establish a foothold on the greater part of the lower foothills. As has already been described, the 5th Battalion had gained the tail of the left-hand spur (Point 501) by their attack of the 26th of October. They were now ordered to capture equivalent positions on the right-hand spur, by seizing Points 445 and 476. The way would then be open for the attack on the first main German outpost at Casa Fudella.

Lieut.-Colonel P. T. Clifton, D.S.O. (who had succeeded Colonel

1944 Gordon-Lennox in command of the Battalion on the 1st of November), planned to use two companies for the night attack on Point 445,
holding the others in close reserve. At first all went well. No. 3 Com-
Dec. 1 pany seized Point 431 without difficulty, and Lieut. R. F. Sanderson
led his platoon forward to capture the outcrop known as "The Rock,"
a few hundred yards south of Point 445. Meanwhile, No. 2 Company
(Capt. P. H. A. Burke) were approaching Point 445 from the north-
east. They were almost within striking distance when shells from their
own artillery fell short in the middle of the company, causing several
casualties. Simultaneously the German machine guns opened fire from
Point 445 down lanes between the trees, and when the men stepped off
the track into the undergrowth they found it thickly strewn with mines.
Capt. Burke and Lieut. J. G. Owen were both wounded. Lieut. C. M.
Wheatley then pressed on with two platoons to within fifty yards of
Point 445, but the mines, the machine guns and the very steep banks
were too much for them, and they were withdrawn to Point 429. The
Italian stretcher-bearers attached to the Battalion did splendid work
in evacuating the many casualties. It was too late to renew the attack
Dec. 2 from a fresh direction, but on the next night the Battalion made a
second attempt which was no more successful and no less gallant.
This time No. 4 Company (Capt. G. W. Chaplin, M.C.) made a frontal
attack on Point 445 from the south, while No. 2 Company moved
round in a left-hand sweep to occupy Point 476. No. 2 Company were
successful after a stiff climb across the ravine, and, though a mortar
bomb caused a large number of casualties in their company headquarters, Point 476 was occupied without resistance. There they
waited, in a strong position above and behind Point 445, for the
result of No. 4 Company's attack. This failed. Capt. Chaplin, a fear-
less officer who had given the Battalion great service in Africa and
Italy, was killed by a machine-gun bullet, and there were eighteen
other casualties in the company, including Sergt. G. Simmonds, M.M.,
both of whose legs were blown off. They were meeting exactly the
same difficulties which had halted No. 2 Company the night before—
mines, a close network of German machine guns, steep, wooded slopes
and a bright moon which showed up every movement. They were
withdrawn under C.S.M. Fisher to the Rock, and No. 2 Company on
Point 476 were left isolated and with too little time before dawn to
attack southwards. They were therefore also withdrawn, and the
Battalion did not again renew their attack. They returned to Prato
Dec. 4 for a short period of rest.

The main attack on Monte Sole was not finally cancelled by General Mark Clark until the end of December, and the 24th Guards Brigade remained upon its lower slopes until the middle of February. Unlike

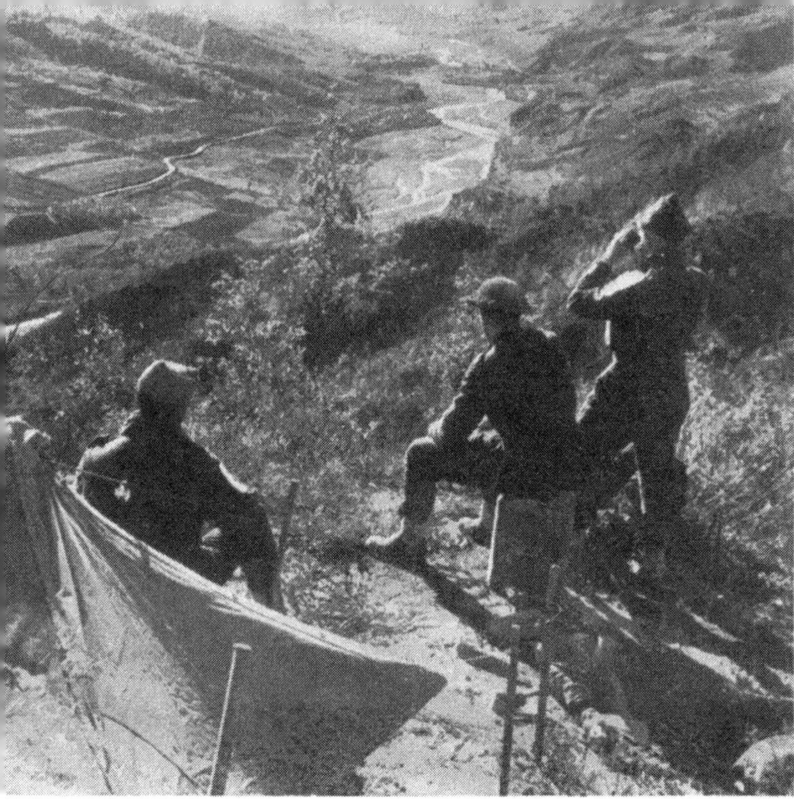

The 5th Battalion overlooking the valley of the River Setta, Northern Apennines.

Fontanelice, in the Santerno Valley, Northern Apennines, Winter 1944-1945.

Crown copyright

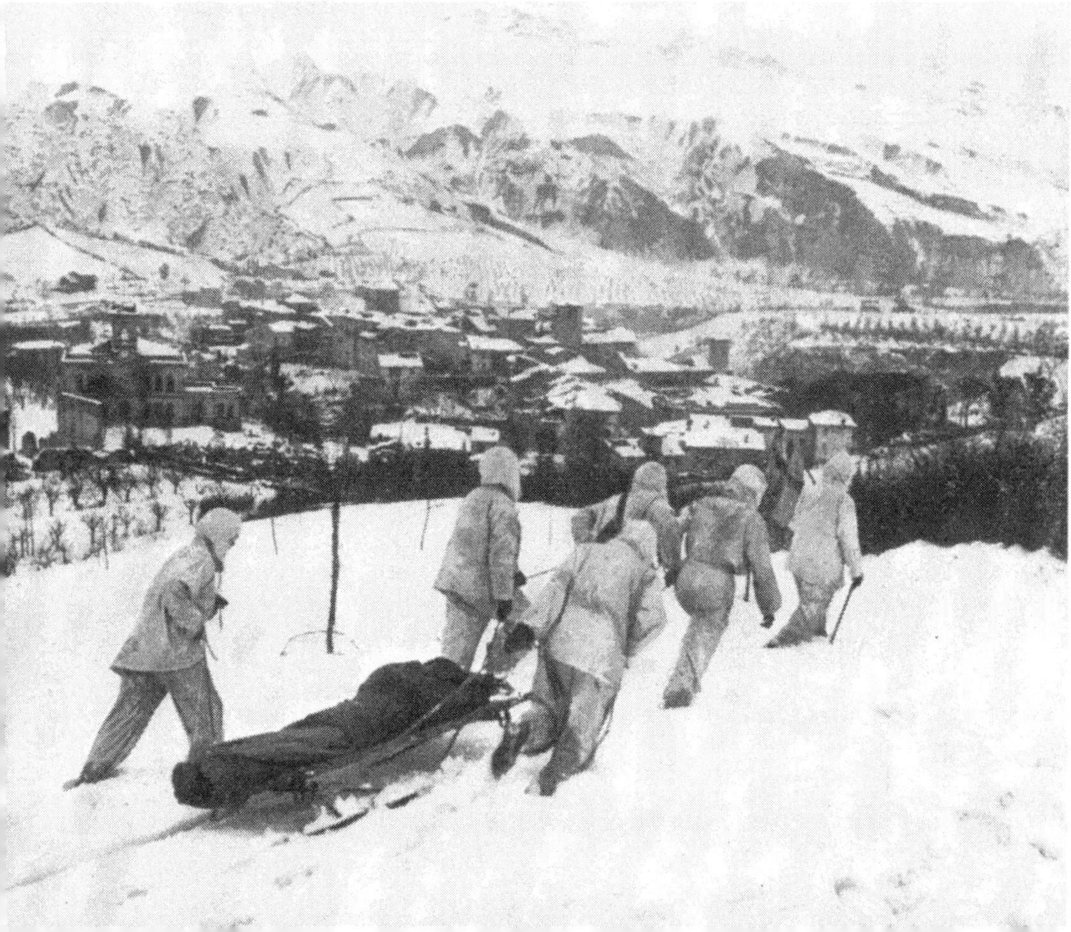

the 3rd Battalion, who at least dominated their own group of hills and were able to look across a wide intervening stretch of No Man's Land, the 5th were crowded upon the narrow shelf north of the Setta, overlooked at close range by the Germans on the peaks above them. For four miles to the south the approach road was under German fire and observation, and even Brigade Headquarters was within full view of Monte Sole. But the nearer one approached the front line the more chance there was of remaining undetected. This was because the foothills were well wooded and crinkled into folds and gullies where a whole company could remain hidden. There were two main sectors, which were held in rotation by two of the three Guards battalions while the third either returned to Prato for rest or, when the threat of German counter-attack was most acute, retired only a short distance down the valley to remain in close support and dig reserve lines of trenches. The first of the Sole sectors was based upon La Quercia and included Points 501 and 505 as the advanced company locality. The platoons were well entrenched in soft clay, and limited movement was possible behind the convex slope, but the enemy were only a few hundred yards away at Casa Fudella, and the tracks were always liable to be smothered suddenly by shells or cut by German patrols. The general verdict of platoon commanders was: "Not so bad, once it froze." The second sector was based on the hamlet of Gardaletta and included Point 429 and the Rock; Point 445 remained in enemy hands. The Rock was an excellent platoon position, for the soft sandstone could be carved into deep and sheltered trenches, and, though the shelling in this sector was much heavier than at Point 501, the only officer to be wounded by shell fire after the New Year was Lieut. J. B. Kidston. The approach to Point 429 was extremely steep and difficult to climb without a rope when the temperature fell below freezing point, and it was not improved by the habit of the Italian porters of sliding down on empty petrol cans. Countless patrols were sent out from both sectors against an enemy (first the 16th S.S. Division, and later the 4th Parachute Division) who had few equals for skill and courage in the entire German Army. Of these patrols there is space to mention only three. One consisted of L./Cpl. Hamer and one Guardsman, who crept up to San Giovanni di Sopra in broad daylight and hurled grenades into a room occupied by a German section. The second, on the 1st of January, was a fierce raid led by Lieut. H. W. Freeman-Attwood against Casa Fudella. And on the third, one of the very last to be sent out from the Sole sector, Lieut. V. E. Naylor-Leyland was wounded.

1945 Jan.-Feb.

The 24th Guards Brigade were finally relieved by the American 135th R.C.T. Though the Guardsmen looked with envy at the winter

Feb. 18

1945 equipment which the Americans brought with them, they were thankful to see the last of Monte Sole. For many of them it was also the last they saw of active service in the field. Their only regret was that their departure meant their separation from the 6th South African Armoured Division, after nine months of the most friendly and fruitful co-operation in many battles and over many hundreds of miles. A most generous tribute to the Brigade was paid by the Divisional Commander, Major-General W. H. E. Poole, D.S.O., in forwarding to Field-Marshal Alexander a cheque for five thousand pounds, contributed by all ranks of the Division towards the rebuilding of the Guards' Chapel at Wellington Barracks. "It is a token," he said, "of the tremendous admiration which we South Africans have for the unsurpassed courage and fighting qualities of His Majesty's Brigade of Guards, and in honoured memory of their fallen." In their replies the senior Guardsmen in Italy and at home showed that they felt no less warmly about the South Africans.

6

SPOLETO, AND THE DISBANDMENT OF THE 5TH BATTALION

Feb. 19 Both the 1st and 24th Guards Brigades, from their respective sectors of the front, returned to join hands at Spoleto, between Rome and Perugia, and here after a lapse of time faint echoes began to reach them of the life they had just left behind—that Point 501 had been raided, that Fontanelice had again been heavily shelled. But now at last they were both comfortably housed in one of the loveliest towns of the loveliest valley in Italy, undamaged by war, in perfect weather, within easy reach of Rome, and with opportunities for entertainment and relaxation such as neither Battalion had enjoyed since landing in Italy over a year before. The 3rd and 5th Battalions, hitherto almost strangers to each other, shared the Caserna Minervio at Spoleto—it was the first time that the 3rd Battalion had been in barracks since Aldershot in 1939—and, though the long rooms were draughty, and huge Fascist signs yelled at them from the walls "The humble and sacred duty of commanding is second to the glories of obedience," the union of the two Battalions was very happy, and cemented by common parades in the main square, by evening parties, and by long discussions of their past and future.

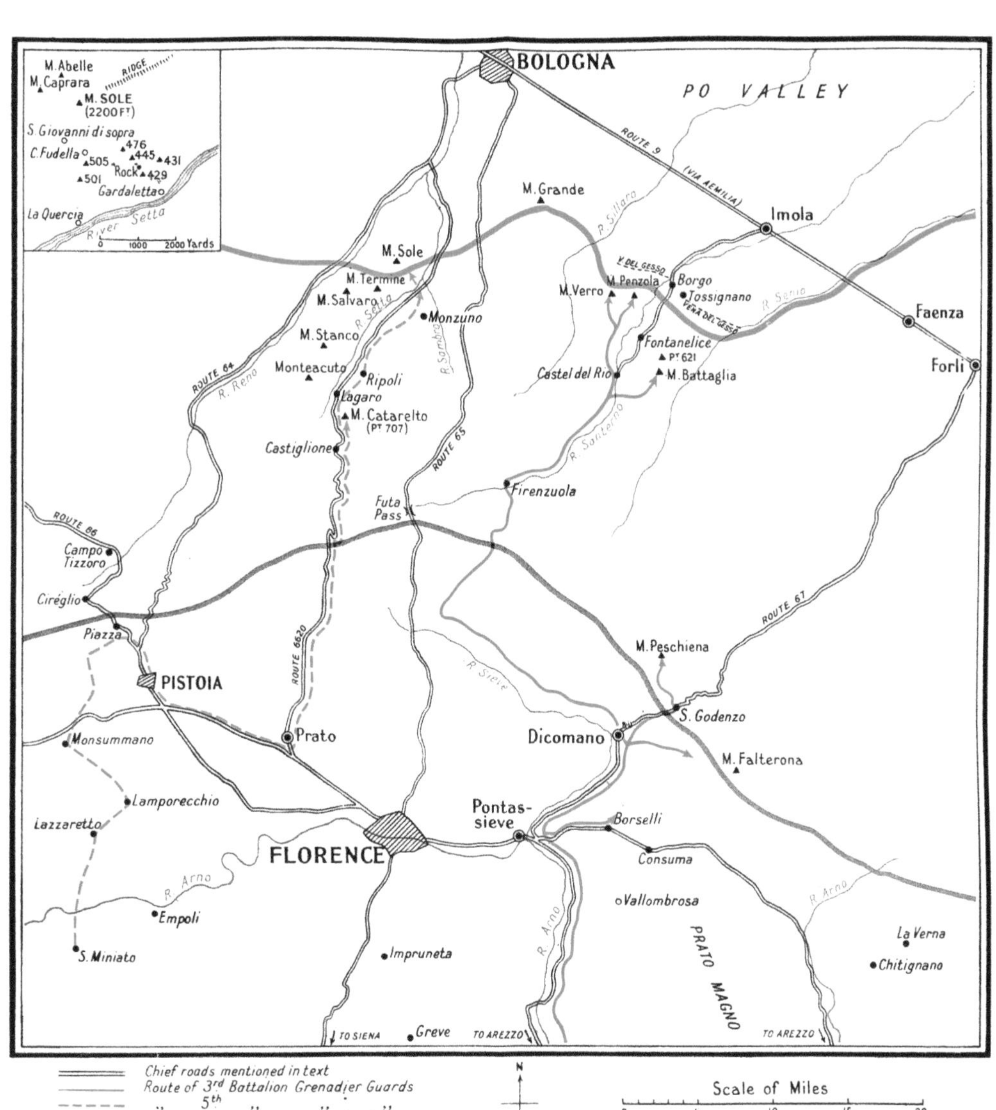

Face page 496

THE GOTHIC LINE

The reason for the withdrawal and concentration of the two Guards 1945
Brigades was to carry out a long-projected reorganization. Casualties and lack of reinforcements had already made necessary the disbandment of the 6th Battalion. The 5th were now to follow. From those who had been abroad the longest in both the 3rd and 5th Battalions five hundred men were selected to return home to England under the command of Lieut.-Colonel E. J. B. Nelson, D.S.O., M.C. Of the fresher men, a new 3rd Battalion was formed under the command of Lieut.-Colonel P. T. Clifton, D.S.O.; and two companies of the remaining Grenadiers were sent to the I.R.T.D. (which was commanded with great skill through the campaign by Lieut.-Colonel G. C. Harcourt-Vernon, D.S.O., O.B.E., M.C.) as reinforcements to the 3rd Battalion. At the same time, the 2nd and 3rd Battalions of the Coldstream Guards came to similar arrangements, the latter returning home. The two Guards Brigades then emerged in this form:

1ST GUARDS BRIGADE
(Brigadier G. L. Verney, D.S.O.)
3rd Battalion Grenadier Guards.
3rd Battalion Welsh Guards.
1st Battalion The Welch Regiment.

24TH GUARDS BRIGADE
(Brigadier M. D. Erskine, D.S.O.)
2nd Battalion Coldstream Guards.
1st Battalion Scots Guards.
1st Battalion The Buffs.

The 5th Battalion, bearing little resemblance to its original self, left Mar. 11
Spoleto for Naples as soon as the change-over was complete and
embarked a week later on a Dutch ship with the 3rd Coldstream Mar. 19
Guards. Field-Marshal Alexander himself came on board in Naples harbour to bid them good-bye. After a slow but happy voyage, calling
at Malta, Algiers and Gibraltar, they docked at Birkenhead and were April 1
taken to Chelsea Barracks, London, from where all the men went on a three weeks' leave. When they reassembled it was only to wind up
the Battalion formally at a parade at Wellington Barracks, which was May 7
inspected by the Colonel of the Regiment, H.R.H. Princess Elizabeth. It was the eve of the end of the war in Europe. Four days later the
5th Battalion was officially disbanded. May 11

CHAPTER X

THE LAST PHASE IN ITALY

3RD BATTALION

1

THE BEGINNING OF THE FINAL OFFENSIVE

Training and reorganization on the Adriatic coast—Strategic plan for the final offensive—The 6th Armoured Division strike through the Argenta Gap—Grenadiers cross the Fosso Cembalina, the last compact German line in Italy—The German collapse begins—The Grenadiers ordered to force a crossing of the River Po

1945 IN North-Western Europe three battalions of the Grenadier Guards were with the British Second Army as it struck into the heart of Germany; but in Italy only one, the 3rd Battalion, now remained. They had been the first Grenadiers to engage the enemy on the southern shores of the Mediterranean; they had seen the climax of the Tunisian surrender; and now, having fought their way up half the length of the Italian peninsula, they ended the war still in the forefront of the Allied armies, crossing the frontier into Austria on the very day which was celebrated as Victory Day in most of the countries of the world. It was a splendid close to their long exertions. Without paying the penalty in heavy casualties they were once again present at the most historic moments of the campaign—at the crossings of the Rivers Po and Adige, at the link-up with Tito's Partisans advancing westwards from Yugoslavia, and at the surrender of the German armies in Southern Austria. Just as they had been the first Guardsmen to encounter the enemy, then so fresh and audacious, on the Maginot Line in 1940, so now it was their Brigade, the 1st Guards Brigade, which exchanged the last shots with a tattered German rearguard at Caporetto in the Southern Alps, when fighting in the rest of Europe had all but ceased.

At the end of the last chapter the story of the 3rd Battalion was carried as far as their reorganization at Spoleto, where the 5th Battalion transferred to the 3rd some two hundred officers and men. An intake on this scale requires some digestion: all but a few platoons found themselves commanded by a new officer, every section was composed of men whose only links were the traditions of their Regiment and a general similarity of past experience. Colonel Clifton had no more than five weeks in which to mould his Battalion into a fighting force. A beginning was made at Spoleto with drill parades and communal entertainment, and then the 1st Guards Brigade moved across to Fermo, near the Adriatic coast, where the combination of plain and river, mountain and sea, gave them the opportunity to train for any type of fighting which the future might still hold in store. These were happy days at Fermo. The battle front was far to the north; the countryside was undamaged by the swift passage of the Eighth Army during the previous summer, and was now restored to its farmers and the strolling population of a Central Italian town. The spring weather remained unbrokenly serene. The Grenadiers were made very welcome, for they impinged but little on the life of Fermo, and their association with the Italians was of the type which Italians most enjoy. They would play the local teams at football; at dusk the Drums of the Battalion would beat "Tattoo" and "Retreat" in the piazza, watched from the surrounding arcades by a great crowd of spectators, linked arm in arm, and softly beating time to the music, which they regarded as a symbol of liberation and not a symbol of defeat. There were closer, more intimate, contacts. It is true that the ten-year-old son of the house where the officers were lodged remarked: "The Germans are serious, the Americans frivolous, and the English tedious," but other judgments were less severe. Many Guardsmen entered Italian homes as guests, and several proposals resulted, though no actual marriages. There was, however, a convent in the neighbourhood which housed a colony of small illegitimates, the offspring of Italian girls and British prisoners of war who, despite incarceration at Ascoli, had evidently secured for themselves considerable freedom of action. "I know I shouldn't say so," whispered the Mother Superior, "but I do so love them all."

1945

Mar. 16

The long days of training, of shooting in the sunny hills, of wireless exercises and discussions on armoured tactics, need no detailed description. But it should be emphasized that not more than half a dozen officers in the whole Brigade had any knowledge of the forthcoming Italian offensive until the morning of the very day on which it opened. Many believed that the armies in Italy had no further contribution to make to the defeat of Germany, and that the victory in Europe would find them faced on the River Senio and in the Northern Apennines by an undefeated German force which would become lamely involved in the general surrender. It was indeed arguable that as the main role of Alexander's 15th Army Group was merely to prevent the twenty-five German divisions in Italy from operating elsewhere, the risks of a

1945 full-scale offensive outweighed its advantages. Numerically the opposing forces were almost equal, but the Germans had on their side the benefits of ground—the difficult mountain country in the west, and the chain of rivers and canals in the low-lying valley of the Po. To break through these formidable barriers would certainly be costly: yet not to attempt it would be a waste of the most experienced fighting force which the Allies possessed. The decision was taken. At 10 a.m. on the 9th of April, nine hours before the start of the attack, Brigadier Verney assembled his senior officers in an upper room in Fermo. Before them they saw a vast wall map of the country between the Northern Apennines and the Po, a broad red line marking the present front, and behind it a branching network of blue, the rivers and canals on which the Germans had already prepared successive lines of defence. "The 15th Army Group," began the Brigadier, "is about to destroy the German Army south of the Po."

April 9 In outline the strategic plan was this. The New Zealanders, the Poles and the Indians of the Eighth Army attacked across the River Senio between Ravenna and Faenza, and after an initial success which exceeded all their hopes they linked and widened their bridgeheads, overrunning one German line after another, to create within a few days a broad salient which welled out over the plain like a limp mainsail suddenly filling with wind. The Santerno was crossed, Imola captured, and at the moment when the Germans began to fear for their communications between Bologna and their winter line in the Apennines, the American Fifth Army also attacked, captured Monte Sole as one of their first objectives, and then headed northwards for Bologna itself. The German line at this stage was unbroken. There was great pressure, but no breach. They had, on the other hand, already exhausted all but their minimum reserves in countering the first attacks, and they foresaw as keenly as did the Allies that if they could not stem the offensive immediately, or at least conduct a slow and orderly retreat, they would find their army cut up into small pockets, their communications in danger, and their withdrawal across the Po a matter of very great difficulty. All the bridges over that river had long since been demolished by the Allied air forces, and their elaborate system of ferries and floating bridges, which had been just sufficient for the German supply traffic, was unlikely to stand the sudden strain of transporting their entire army from the south bank to the north—unless time was on their side.

It was therefore plain that the Allies must at all costs maintain their pressure, and gather their strength to strike decisively into the flank of what became, after the fall of Imola, the German bridgehead south of the Po. On its eastern flank there was only a limited stretch of country

where tank attack was possible. At its southern end were the Apen- **1945**
nines, at its northern end the great salt-water lagoon of Lake Cam- *See Map p. 524*
machio, and between these two natural obstacles was a wide area which the Germans had flooded by breaching the banks of the Reno. The Eighth Army were left with two possible approaches. The first was the broader, southern, route immediately north of the Imola—Bologna road; and the second a narrow isthmus of dry land between Lake Cammachio and the northern limit of the floods. This was known as the Argenta Gap. Clearly there was a greater risk, but a greater prize to be expected, from an attempt to force the Argenta Gap than from a thrust farther south, and until he saw how the battle developed the Commander-in-Chief, General McCreery, was unwilling to commit himself to one or the other. He had but one mobile division in reserve, the 6th Armoured Division; it would not be launched, he said, "until I can see daylight ahead," and meanwhile it must hold itself in readiness until a glimmer appeared, either in the direction of Argenta or in the direction of Bologna. The most careful plans were made for both contingencies.

The Grenadiers, as part of the 6th Armoured Division, moved up
from Fermo, through Ancona and Rimini, and across the Rubicon, **April 11**
to a concentration area near Forli, just south of the Bologna road. "We lay among the first foothills of the Apennines," reads a contemporary account, "from where we would watch the endless columns of supply lorries moving in a steady stream towards the front; and by night we would see the searchlights illuminating the still-distant battlefield, the flash of guns, and the aircraft flares dropping and dripping slowly through the sky." They waited a week, debating the Bologna—Argenta problem in the light of hourly reports from the front; and
then suddenly the decision was made. The Division received its defin- **April 18**
ite, immediate orders. It was to move to a new concentration area north-west of Ravenna, and break through the Argenta Gap in the general direction of Ferrara. "That night," continues the same account, "there was an atmosphere of keen expectancy, almost of jubilation, in the 1st Guards Brigade. After two months' rest, and ten days' waiting while others fought, the 6th Armoured Division was keyed up to a great pitch of energy and excitement, knowing full well that they were the last reserves of the Eighth Army, and now it was their privilege to reap the fruits of the victory already won by the infantry. . . . The plain facts were evident to every man."

While the 3rd Grenadiers waited in the fields around Argenta, indolently watching the columns of prisoners trudging back down the road, and the aircraft of both sides turning circles in the sky, the tanks of the Division cleared the northern edge of the floods, and fanned out

1945 across country in eager anticipation of a clear run to the River Po. They were disappointed. Instead of entering the battle with a flying start they found themselves battling for minor road junctions and the crossings over small canals. The country was very thick and close, broken by water-courses over which no bridges remained, and the highest ground in the whole plain was the thirty-foot crest of the long banks bordering the Reno, which stood up above the vineyards like the ramparts of a vast Iron Age camp. The tank commander, whose vision was limited to a few yards by the clinging tendrils of the vines and the brittle boughs of olive trees brushing against his turret, was no match for the German lurking in the undergrowth with a bazooka. He could not see his fellows; he could only with great difficulty read his map. The sense that he was lost, blinded, hemmed in by water, and in continual danger took the edge off his first enthusiasm. The tanks made slow progress, and it became necessary to call up the infantry to beat the fields and orchards for pockets of Germans, to marshal the prisoners, and finally to secure crossing places over the canals which the Engineers could bridge and where the tanks could later pass. It was in this way that the Grenadiers first became involved in the Battle of the Po.

See Map **p. 510** A dozen miles north-west of Argenta there was one canal, slightly larger than the others, called the Fosso Cembalina. As usual, all its bridges had been blown up, leaving a continuous water-filled obstacle like a moat, and on its western bank the Germans were strongly entrenched, determined to make amends for their loss of the Argenta Gap by holding this new line to the last. It is a frequent and remarkable occurrence in warfare that suddenly one particular feature of the ground, the sector of a battalion or even of a single company, becomes the key to the operations of an entire Army. Already in previous chapters we have seen examples of this in Hammam Lif in Tunisia, and in the Gully at Anzio; and here again, at the Cembalina Canal, a tremendous importance was attached to a quick break-through. Beyond the canal the German columns retreating from Bologna were pouring back across the Po; their flanks were unguarded, and if the thin screen was once pierced the 6th Armoured Division could throw their whole weight upon the mass of vehicles and men. As Brigadier Verney put it in a special message addressed to all ranks of the Brigade: "The success of tonight's attack will set the seal on what may prove to be a decisive victory"; and so it turned out, in a sense truer than even he then realized, for the Cembalina was the last continuous defence line which the Germans were capable of organizing in Italy.

April 21 Already the 1st Battalion of the Welch Regiment had reached the

southern bank of the canal, and the 17th/21st Lancers, by brilliant 1945
use of an earthen causeway, had struck beyond it to capture the village of Poggio Renatico, six miles in rear of the German front line. This splendid exhibition put new heart into the whole Division, and evidence of the enemy's declining morale came with the desertion to the Welch Regiment of a complete German platoon. But the far bank of the Cembalina was still strongly held, and it became even more necessary than before to breach the German line in a new place, so that the narrow corridor through which the Lancers had passed would not be cut behind them and their *coup de main* turned into disaster. The Welch were ordered to capture a bridgehead some five hundred yards deep three miles east of the Reno; the 3rd Grenadiers were then to pass through and beyond them to seize the village of San Bartolomeo. For the Grenadiers there was therefore an uneasy period of waiting—waiting for news of the Welch attack, waiting for their own orders to advance, and during this time, as they hugged the meagre shelter of a few ditches, they suffered the majority of their casualties from German mortar fire. The Welch Regiment were successful, spread out in a thin screen on the north bank of the canal opposite the site of a demolished bridge; but the night was so dark and the vegetation so thick, that they could not prevent a few German machine gunners creeping back to the canal bank and spraying the bridge site with bullets at the moment when the Grenadiers began to cross. Nos. 1 and 4 Companies (Majors E. C. Russell and W. J. L. Willson, D.S.O.) were the first to run the gauntlet of their fire, crossing by the rubble of the broken bridge, and they were followed shortly afterwards by Nos. 2 and 3 Companies (Major S. E. Bolitho, M.C., and Capt. G. G. H. Marriott, M.C.), who doubled in ones and twos, by the light of a blazing farmhouse, across a floating kapok bridge. The only officer to be hit was Lieut. E. J. S. Rollo, of No. 4 Company.

On the north bank the Battalion did not wait to reassemble, nor even to search out the enemy machine guns or the exact positions of the Welch Regiment. They advanced immediately up either side of the road, paying little attention to their open flanks, for they were concerned only with driving as deep a wedge as possible, and splitting open the German defences by exploiting the line of least resistance—the standard tactics which had so often met with success in the past. They met little opposition. There was one house on the left of the road where Sergt. Jones's platoon eliminated a German section by throwing grenades through the window, and two or three tracked vehicles were heard moving about ahead of them. When the leading companies halted on the line of a second and smaller canal just short of San Bartolomeo, the impression began to grow that the Germans had

1945 already decided to withdraw: a prisoner, indeed, declared emphatically that his whole unit had been ordered back to the Po, and some of the Grenadiers even heard the German non-commissioned officers calling the roll of their platoons before they marched off.* There was no time to intercept their retreat. When Nos. 2 and 3 Companies entered San Bartolomeo ("with such speed that the advance almost developed into a race") they found it in ruins, the fires caused by our bombing already dying down, and the only Germans dead Germans. Patrols were sent off in every direction, and, though they collected five prisoners, there was no threat of counter-attack. When the tanks of
April 22 the Derbyshire Yeomanry thundered through at dawn the Grenadiers were settling down to boil their tea for breakfast.

The honours of the next two days went to the tanks of the 26th Armoured Brigade which were at last able to range at will over a wide expanse of country and strike into the unprotected flank of the German columns, while the Derbyshire Yeomanry raced almost unopposed round the outskirts of Ferrara to reach the southern bank of
April 23 the Po. The Germans were in a state of terrible confusion. Their supply trains were divorced from their fighting troops, their stragglers were cut off in hundreds by the branching columns of British tanks or waylaid by the ubiquitous Italian Partisans. If they managed to reach the river it was only to find its banks choked by earlier arrivals, and the actual passage would have to be braved under a rain of shells and bombs. The air was thick with the smoke of burning lorries, and the countryside strewn with their wrecks. Everywhere there were packs of roving horses turned loose by the Germans at the river bank, and parties of weary soldiers trudging northwards to swim the river or to give themselves up to the first British troops who appeared. For, whereas the Allies were exultant, comparatively fresh, well organized and with no doubts about what was expected of them, the Germans were beginning to feel that the end was near. One of their corps commanders, Graf von Schwerin, who had declared in a recent order of the day "We shall do our duty as military honour demands," now gave up the struggle and surrendered with his staff near Ferrara, saying openly that the position was hopeless. The Grenadiers, who had been moved up during the afternoon to guard a series of undemolished bridges west of Ferrara, reported that they were being surrounded by Germans on all sides "extremely anxious to give themselves up," and by 6 p.m. they had collected two hundred and twenty prisoners, "including a Chinaman, in a large straw hat, and four Mongols."*

*These men were in fact natives of Eastern Russia. Having been taken prisoner at Stalingrad, they were forced to serve in the German Army. Their second captivity at the Po was therefore liberation.

Field-Marshal Alexander visited the Grenadiers and spoke to some 1945 of their prisoners. "He appeared delighted," says the War Diary, "at this evidence of the enemy's complete defeat south of the Po"; but it is doubtful whether even the Supreme Allied Commander was at this stage entirely confident that the German collapse was complete, or that they were incapable of re-forming their line on the Po, the Adige or in the southern passes of the Alps. Great as was the evidence of material destruction, there was a feeling of slight disappointment in the Allied camp. Italian civilians reported that the Germans had undoubtedly been able to ferry much equipment and a great number of men across the river—the total of prisoners amounted so far to only twenty thousand instead of the hundred thousand that had been expected—and when the Derbyshire Yeomanry and the first Grenadier patrols peered cautiously across the stream they could see German helmets moving about the trenches on the far bank. On Brigadier Verney's instructions our guns remained quite silent, in order to give the impression that no more than patrols had reached the Po in this sector, and that the crossing was to be attempted farther east, north of Ferrara.

That very afternoon the Brigadier was called to the Headquarters of the 6th Armoured Division, and at a conference which was attended in its opening stages by the Field-Marshal himself, the 1st Guards Brigade were ordered to cross the Po with the minimum of delay, and within the present boundaries of the Division. The 3rd Grenadiers were selected to lead the assault.

2

THE PO AND THE ADIGE

The setting and the plan for the assault across the Po—A fleet of amphibious vehicles—The assault is completely successful—Advance between the Po and the Adige—The break-up of the German armies on the Adige

Although the operation was later postponed by twenty-four hours, Colonel Clifton was left with very little time in which to perfect his complicated arrangements, and began his final co-ordinating conference only two hours before the first wave of assault craft left the southern bank of the Po. The Battalion were about to carry out an operation of a type which they had never before attempted: they were using equipment which they had never hitherto seen, some of which, indeed, was now being used for the first time in the Italian

1945 campaign. They were crossing a river as wide as the Rhine. In what strength its northern bank was defended they did not know, but they could fear only the worst. Privately, the medical services were warned to prepare for three hundred casualties in the Grenadier Battalion alone.

The plan which was evolved during the thirty-six hours left for preparation turned entirely upon the peculiar formation of the channel of the River Po. The flood waters, as with every major river and canal in this plain, were contained within twenty-five-foot artificial banks, or "lévées," leaving a one-hundred-foot ledge on the southern side which shelved gently down to the water's edge. These lévées were too steep to allow vehicles to mount them except at those points where the Germans had constructed approach roads leading diagonally across the banks down to their ferry piers. It so happened that one such ferry had been in use by the Germans between the villages of Palantone on the south bank and Gaiba on the north, on the extreme left of the Divisional sector. Though the ferry boat itself had been beached on the far side and the decking of the landing stages had been dismantled, the approach road was still in good repair, and capable of carrying the heavy amphibious assault craft. Branch tracks led off the road from the top of the lévée, across the ledge and down to the river, affording fairly easy access to the water. Furthermore, six hundred yards down-stream there was a hard bank of sand on the far side which was suitable for the landing of the amphibious tanks. The river at this point was one thousand five hundred feet broad, nine feet deep, and running at a speed of about five knots.

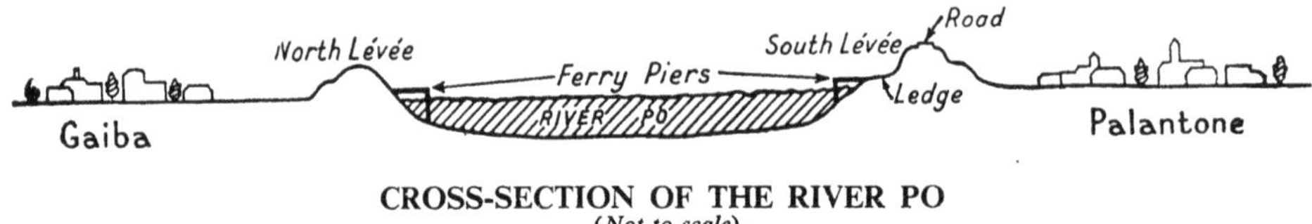

CROSS-SECTION OF THE RIVER PO
(Not to scale).

The scene was thus described by one of the Grenadier officers who went forward at dawn to reconnoitre the crossing site:

April 24 "We found a house in Palantone which just overtopped the southern lévée, so we woke up the Italian householder and made him take us up to a bed room on the top floor. The shutters were closed when we entered the room, but he told us that he had always been in the habit, at about this hour in the morning, of throwing them wide open and shaking out his blankets. We told him to carry on with this performance while the rest of us stood well back in the darkness of the room. This he did, and through the aperture of the open window we caught our first sight of the River Po. It was a swift, silver stream, broader

Air Ministry

The River Po, at the point where it was crossed by the 3rd Battalion, north-west of Ferrara.

The village on the north bank is Gaiba, the village in the bottom left-hand corner is Palantone. Between the two is the German ferry crossing, and on the right is the sandbank where the D.D. tanks landed.

> than any of us had imagined, broader even than the Thames in Central London, and lined on both banks by rows of poplars gently stirring in the breeze. We could see no sign of the Germans on the far bank; by crouching low down by the window-sill we could just make out the pier of the ferry, and it seemed deserted. Beyond the northern lévée the country was dense with trees, through which emerged, here and there, the roof-tops and the campanile of Gaiba. It was only after a few minutes that any of us observed the most striking feature of the whole scene. 'Do you see what I see?' said J—— suddenly. We all looked at where he was pointing, and there on the far horizon we saw unmistakably a line of hills, a hard, blue outline against the morning sky. They were the Alps." 1945

Such was the setting of the Grenadiers' assault on the Po. Their plan was simple. At 1 a.m. on the 25th of April they were to cross the river at Palantone at the same time as the New Zealanders crossed two miles up-stream at Ficarolo, and once they had established independent bridgeheads on the north bank they were to link up inland and advance side by side to the Adige. For their assault the Grenadiers were allotted seven Fantails, a new type of lightly armoured amphibious craft which ran overland on the same tracks which propelled them in the water; fifteen dukws, likewise amphibious but not armoured; and to support them a squadron of D.D. tanks manned by the 7th Hussars (these were of the normal Sherman type but fitted with inflatable canvas skirts which gave them buoyancy in about nine feet of water). This large convoy, or fleet, assembled in the fields round Palantone under the control of a naval commander. A single concentration of German artillery or mortar fire would have done immense damage. It was not encouraging to see the local inhabitants desert their village and begin to burrow fiercely under the river banks for protection against the expected bombardment. But none came, and it is now certain that the enemy remained entirely unaware of our preparations, just as we remained unaware of his. Though the Germans were little more than five hundred yards away, they had no means of discovering what was happening across the river. They had no aircraft, the lévée hid from them all but the roofs and tree-tops on the British side, and no Italian informer was given the chance to cross over and sound the alarm.

As zero hour approached, the noise of coughing engines, of bulldozers grinding up the road, of the non-commissioned officers shouting, and of the men scrambling with their equipment up the high, metal sides of the Fantails became uncontrollable. Shortly before 1 a.m. the leading Grenadier companies mounted the ramp to the top of the southern lévée. Their intentions could no longer be concealed. For a distance of several hundred yards the road ran eastwards along April 25

1945 the top of the lévée before turning north down to the water's edge, and the whole armada was poised for a few minutes in full view from the far bank, silhouetted by the moonlight and aircraft flares—a slow procession of labouring vehicles packed with troops, like a frieze depicting the mechanical apparatus of war. With the exception of a few dukws which were bulldozed bodily into the water, the assault craft crossed the sandy ledge and slipped easily into the river.

Up to this moment not a single shot had been fired. Away to the left they could hear the barrage supporting the simultaneous crossing of the New Zealanders. Part of the barrage overlapped the left of the Battalion's sector and lifted off the far bank only just before No. 4 Company landed. But the Grenadiers themselves were relying less on shot and shell than on silence and surprise. It was a great moment in their history. As they sped across that swift, moonlit stream the hearts of many were in their mouths lest suddenly they should be illuminated by a hundred flares, the water criss-crossed with tracer bullets, and the boats repelled from the steep, grassy banks of the northern side by every type of close-range weapon in the German armoury. Their fate was very different. Instead of three hundred casualties they suffered no more than three—and one of those by an accident. As they crossed the water a single machine gunner opened fire from the northern bank and the bullets ricocheted so wide of the assault craft that they scarcely seemed to be the target aimed at; there was also an explosion, perhaps of a mortar bomb, alongside one of the Fantails, but it did no damage. Otherwise there was no sign of opposition. No. 1 Company (Major E. C. Russell) were the first to touch down: Lieut. J. B. Hosegood's platoon were in the lead, and the first British soldier to jump ashore on the northern bank of the Po was Gdsm. Doggett. No. 4 Company (Major W. J. L. Willson, D.S.O.) followed immediately afterwards, and the two companies together swarmed over the northern lévée and down into the dark fields around Gaiba. The beachmaster, Lieut. J. Tayleur, set his two hurricane lamps at the side of the northern pier as a signal to those on the home shore that the crossing had been completely successful.

They found three frightened Germans on the north bank, one of whom was killed, but inland they progressed a long way before making any further contact with the enemy. Gaiba was deserted, its entire population huddled in a great barn, from which they emerged a hot and grateful crowd when the Guardsmen unexpectedly flung back the doors. In a house at the top end of the village a complete German dinner, still hot from the oven, was found on the table, and a few shadowy German patrols were seen making off into the darkness. Only No. 3 Company (Major G. G. H. Marriott, M.C.) found any core of resistance against which they could use their weapons. 1945 This was several hundred yards down-stream in the direction of Stienta, where a compact group of Germans had dug themselves into the lévée. Eleven of them were killed, six taken prisoner, and many others wounded, while the Grenadier company suffered but a single casualty in exchange.

Behind them the remainder of the 1st Guards Brigade, the 3rd Welsh Guards and the 1st Welch Regiment, were ferried across the river, and by the middle of the morning the Brigade held a secure bridgehead reaching from Stienta to the point beyond Gaiba where No. 4 Company had linked up with the New Zealanders. The river was now alive with ferry craft. Tanks were floated across on improvised rafts, storm-boats whipped to and fro like fireflies, and the more ponderous dukws panted backwards and forwards with supplies of food and ammunition, of which ten tons were unloaded on the northern bank under the eye of D./Sergt. Wood, D.C.M. There was almost no interference with this regatta by German shell fire, still no sign of counter-attack, and the Grenadiers were able to patrol deeper and deeper inland without seeing more than a few grey-clad figures scurrying behind a hedge. Where *were* the Germans? Was this the best use they could make of the greatest river in Italy? How was it to be explained that they had left the northern bank virtually undefended?

The stories of the first prisoners, confused as they were, were pieced together to provide an intelligible answer to these questions, and to show what remarkably good fortune the Grenadiers had enjoyed.

> "The regular German division which had been withdrawn across this sector of the Po," reads a contemporary intelligence report, "was in no fit condition to remain in the line, and its place had been hurriedly filled by two scratch formations which had only recently been brought down from the north-east of Italy. One of these battalions had been given a sector of some six or seven miles to hold pending the arrival of the others, and could do no more than man a thin line of slit trenches spaced at intervals of three to four hundred yards along the northern lévée. On the evening of the 24th of April the fresh troops began to arrive in the area, and to concentrate in company groups a mile or so north of the river. At that moment we attacked. The isolated machine gun which fired blindly into the river was one of the original posts: the scattered groups which the Grenadiers began to meet inland were part of the other formation. They had arrived in darkness after a long march, and, being completely at sea in unfamiliar surroundings, and out of touch with their own troops in front, they were quite unprepared for battle.
>
> "The next morning the enemy commander began to collect his wits, and determined to throw back the British bridgehead. He ordered a battalion to attack our right flank with the support of six Tiger tanks.

1945 The attack, which had as its objective the northern terminus of the ferry crossing, was to have begun at 11 a.m. on the 25th, the very hour at which the Brigadier was holding an Order Group with the commanding officers on the northern bank of the lévée. To arrange the final details, the German commander sent a sergeant-major to the headquarters of the neighbouring battalion. On his way there this man was captured by Italian Partisans and handed over to us, to whom he spilled the whole story. The attack did not materialize, perhaps on account of the lack of liaison between the units taking part. We should have had to fight hard to repel it, as at that hour we had no more than three battalions of infantry across the river, supported by about twenty tanks and a handful of anti-tank guns."

By the afternoon of the 25th a sufficient force had been assembled on the northern shore for the Brigade to leave the security of their bridgehead and strike across the fifteen-mile-wide corridor which separates the Po from the Adige. The first experiment was made by Lieut. P. G. H. Hedley-Dent with a patrol of three D.D. tanks and twenty men. They occupied the village of Cura without difficulty, and captured among a batch of half a dozen prisoners a liaison officer from the headquarters of the German Tenth Army, who was carrying valuable information and documents, with neither of which he was in the least reluctant to part. At midnight the Battalion doubled the depth of the bridgehead at a single bound by advancing to Canda, where a bridge was blown up by the German rearguard in the faces of No. 4 Company. But such was the exhilaration born of this easy pur-
April 26 suit that no mere hole in the road was enough to stop them. Two Grenadier platoons scrambled across the rubble and set off for the Adige on a fleet of bicycles, commandeered from the Italians by the Intelligence Officer, Lieut. Hon. J. B. Norton, M.C. One of these patrols, under Lieut. R. J. G. Candlish, bicycling gaily up a country lane, saved the bridge at Rasa and took prisoner the twelve Germans who had been left behind to blow it up. The other reached the outskirts of Lendinara, which they decided, reluctantly, was still too strongly held to be seized by a handful of bicyclists. It was captured the next day by the Welsh Guards, and the New Zealanders surged up on their left flank to the banks of the Adige. The Grenadiers, in this carefree and yet decisive manner, had fired their last shots of the Second German War.

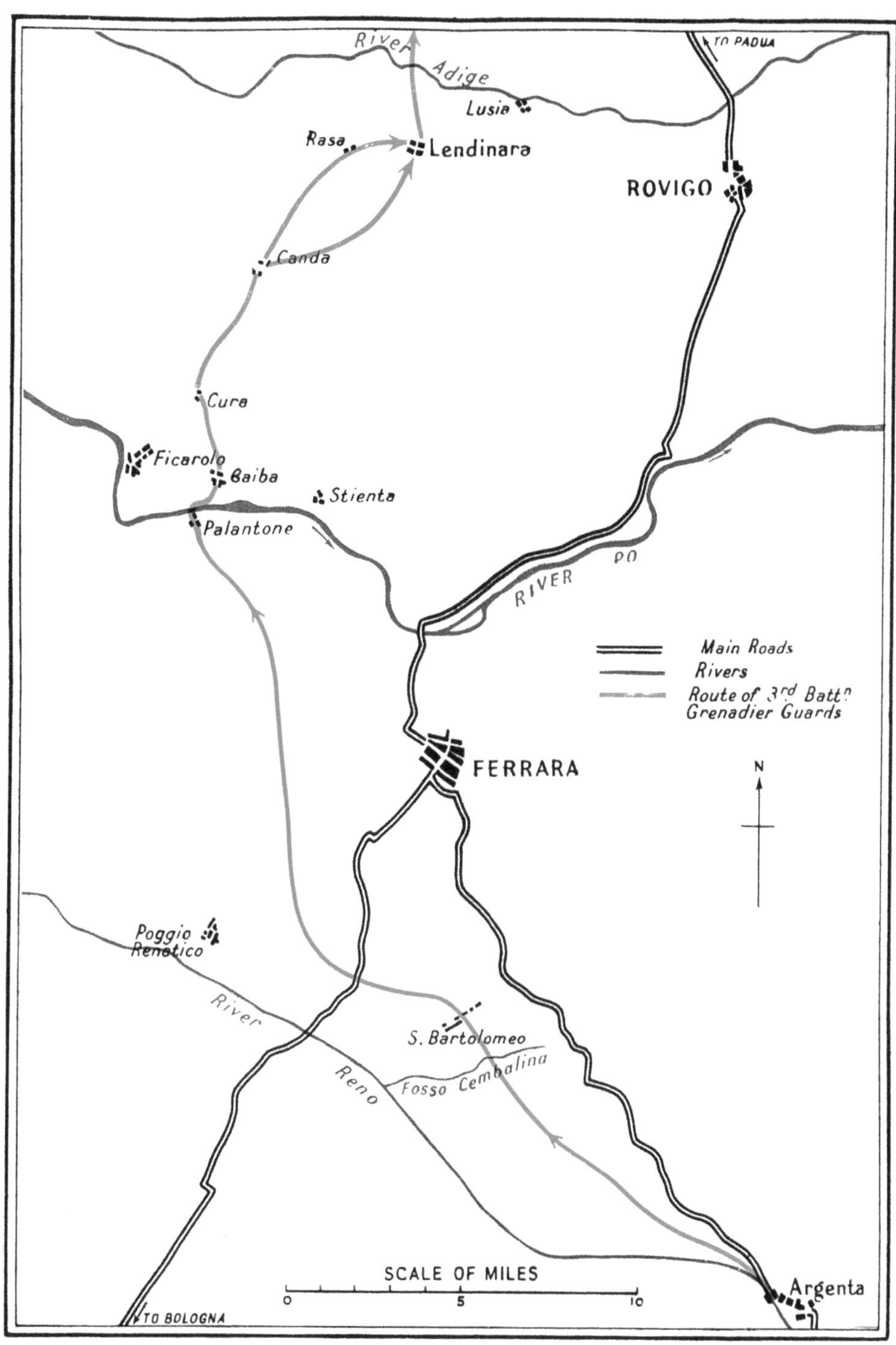

THE PO AND THE ADIGE

3

THE END OF THE ITALIAN CAMPAIGN

The 6th Armoured and New Zealand Divisions continue the advance alone through Padua towards Trieste—All German resistance crumbles when the Italian Partisans block the Alpine passes—Grenadiers hear of the German capitulation at Cividale, six hours after the armistice had come into force—Link-up with the Yugoslav Partisans causes a serious diplomatic embarrassment—A communication from the German Commander-in-Chief

From the top of the campanile at Lendinara it was possible to see at **1945**
a glance the whole graveyard of the Eastern German Army. In the foreground, on the southern bank of the Adige, a furious battle was in progress: for, although Lendinara and Rovigo were both captured, a large German force was trapped between the two towns around Lusia, and was attempting to hold off the British attacks while their vehicles crossed the river by a pontoon bridge.

> "One's attention," wrote a Grenadier, "was immediately caught by the sight of at least a hundred enemy motor and horsed vehicles collected on the top and at the foot of the southern floodbank of the Adige, halted in long, immovable convoys, frantically trying to disperse into the fields, or edging slowly down the approaches to the pontoon bridge by which they hoped to make a last-minute get-away. This was the last time our loyal friends the Ayrshire Yeomanry fired their guns: it was their best target of the war. They concentrated their fire on the bridge itself, directed by an artillery spotting aircraft hovering over the river, and finally scored sufficient direct hits upon it to cut the bridge in half. It floated down-stream a blazing wreck, leaving on the southern bank a vast quantity of material which could be dealt with at our leisure. The Germans who survived and who could swim, jumped into the water and swam across. The remainder had no choice but to surrender."

This was not all. Far beyond the Adige, on the northern horizon, a *See Map p.* **524**
cloud of dust was seen rising from the foot of the Alps as a column of American tanks raced eastwards from Verona. The Fifth Army had crossed the Po in the centre of the northern Italian plain, and while part had swung west to overrun the region of Milan and Turin the remainder skirted the Alps to outflank the Adige Line and seal the German escape routes. The Germans on the Adige were not aware of this. They regarded their passage of the river as their last major obstacle before reaching the security of their Alpine fortress. They did not know, as the Grenadiers in Lendinara now knew, that the Americans were already behind them, and that the entrance to every Alpine pass was closed against them by brigades of Italian Partisans.

1945 Even so, the finality of the German debacle was not yet apparent to the Allies. Our front-line troops had under-estimated the effectiveness of the Partisans' sudden intervention, and it was rumoured that the four best and most mobile German divisions had received orders to abandon their fellows in the plain and make with all speed across the Austrian or Yugoslav border. From a glance at a relief map it was clear that in the north-eastern corner of Italy only a relatively narrow strip of plain is left between the mountains and the sea—a strip, moreover, which is crossed by a series of rivers, the Brenta, the Piave, the Tagliamento and the Isonzo, all of which had afforded the Allies in the First German War a series of natural delaying positions, and in the closing stages of this war were likely to give the enemy a similar advantage.

The Germans had lost North-West Italy for good: the Fifth Army were reaping their reward in unopposed pursuit. So remote and rapid was their progress that the Grenadiers were obliged to rely upon B.B.C. reports for their information now that the Americans had swung right out of their own orbit of operations; they followed the campaign, like any civilians, on maps printed in the newspapers or torn out of school atlases. But the north-eastern corner, their own corner, was a different matter. Had the Eighth Army the strength to pursue, had they the whole width of the Lombardy Plain in which to deploy, they felt that it might be possible to bring the campaign to a decisive close. They had neither. It would be many days before the Po and the Adige could both be spanned by bridges strong enough to carry tanks, and communications were so stretched that it was proving difficult to supply even those few divisions which were already across. In the 6th Armoured Division the whole of the Armoured Brigade was stranded south of the Po.* Were the armoured cars and the handful of Derbyshire Yeomanry tanks which had been floated across on rafts sufficient to worry the German rearguards off the series of rivers which remained ahead? And what would happen when they reached the Alps?

It seemed at first that the 1st Guards Brigade would have no share either in the final triumphs or in the final setbacks of the campaign. The New Zealanders had crossed the Adige almost alone, and the 6th Armoured, in the R.A.F. term which had penetrated the Army's vocabulary, were "grounded," excluded from further operations by

*There had been a slight miscalculation over the question of the Po bridges. It had been expected that the 56th Division, operating north-east of Ferrara, would be the first to reach and cross the Po, and most of the bridging equipment had been moved into their sector. When the 6th Armoured Division crossed, it was found impossible to switch the bridging to the Gaiba sector. The New Zealanders laid a floating bridge at Ficarolo, but it was too weak to carry tanks.

the bottleneck at the crossings of the two great rivers. The Grenadiers 1945 at Lendinara were merely ordered to clear the neighbouring farms and villages of German stragglers, and Brigadier Verney, in an address given in the local cinema, forecast that the Brigade's active April 29 participation in the war had come to a close.

It was therefore with mixed feelings that they received in the early hours of the next morning a telephone message of great urgency ordering them to cross the Adige and press on with all speed in the direction of Padua. In general the change of plan was welcomed. Although it involved the postponement of their rest and leave, and though they knew that a large part of any fighting which remained would fall on their own shoulders, the prospect was improved by the news that German opposition had crumbled away in a most remarkable manner. The New Zealanders, covering sixty miles in twenty-four hours, had passed through the German "Venetian Line" without a fight, had entered Padua, and on the evening of the 29th had captured Venice. There was no indication that greater trouble awaited them farther east, but the New Zealanders now asked for support: they needed the co-operation of a parallel column on their left flank, to sweep the area between Padua and Udine as far north as the mountains, while their own Division continued by the coastal road to Trieste. Thus it was that of all the divisions in the Eighth Army only two, or more strictly, one and two-thirds, remained in the field: the New Zealand Division, and the 1st Guards Brigade and the 61st Brigade of the 6th Armoured Division. A great responsibility and a great experience were to devolve upon them both.

All that day the lorries followed the excellent road which led April 30 through the heart of the Venetian Plain, past the Palladian villas and the orchards. Padua, which had been liberated by its own Partisans two days before, was still in a state of great excitement. The population crowded round the British lorries as they waited to take their turn to cross the Brenta bridge, while down the other side of the street marched long columns of German prisoners, slouching through a sudden shower of rain. The Battalion reached Noale, fifteen miles beyond, before halting for the night. They were still many miles behind the New Zealanders and the 61st Brigade. Nor did they catch them up the next day, though they drove another forty-five miles May 1 through Treviso to Sacile, a small village in the foothills between the Piave and the Tagliamento. They arrived to find the church bells pealing and the streets thronged with Partisans, celebrating simultaneously the Allied victory and their own reunion with their families after months of self-imposed exile in the hills. The Partisans were made responsible for scouring the Alpine valleys for German stragglers. Except

1945 for the Welsh Guards, who went to Vittorio Veneto, the Guards Brigade never left the plain, waiting like patient shepherds for the thousands of prisoners to be driven down to them from every crevice in the mountains into the makeshift pens which lined the main road.

May 2 They continued eastwards, crossing the swollen waters of the Tagliamento by a minor bridge which had been left unblown, and reached the town of Udine, which the 61st Brigade had entered the evening before. All this time there was no fighting, scarcely any danger, scarcely any need for the most elementary precautions against surprise. At the crossing of the Tagliamento a few rounds from an unlocated German gun had fallen wide of the convoy—they were the last shots to be fired at the Grenadiers during the war—but for the rest it was merely a matter of driving farther and farther east, cheered by the Italian cottagers from their doorsteps, changing and refolding their maps every two or three hours, and searching the air for wireless messages from the vanguard and from the flanking columns on right and left as they skirted the mountains and the sea. But there were two vital reports which did not reach them until later. They did not know as they approached Udine that, fifteen miles beyond, at the small town of Cividale, a battalion of Yugoslav Partisans were awaiting their arrival. Nor did they know that representatives of the German High Command had signed an instrument of surrender at Field-Marshal Alexander's Headquarters at Caserta, and that an armistice was to come into force at noon that very day, the 2nd of May, 1945.

The first to enter Cividale were the 1st Battalion of the Welch Regiment, who at this last moment had taken the lead from the 61st Brigade. Later in the afternoon two companies of the Grenadiers were ordered up from Udine to relieve the Welch, so that the latter could continue northwards to Caporetto. It was in Cividale, at 9 p.m. that evening, that the Grenadiers heard on the civilian wireless the news of the Caserta capitulation. It was taken calmly. They already found themselves involved in a political tangle which required all their attention, and for several days caused them great anxiety. It was no occasion for rejoicing.

The friction in Cividale arose from the fact that, quite suddenly, three separate forces, the Italian Partisans, the Yugoslav Partisans and the British Eighth Army, were brought face to face over the corpse of their common enemy. Until now all of them had been fighting for a single end, the defeat of the German Army in Italy; until now not one of the three had actually encountered either of the other two. It was in a way a misfortune that the hour of their juncture should coincide with the armistice, leaving them with no common object to pursue; and that the place of their juncture should be on the confines of that very territory which for many years had been in dispute between two of the three peoples concerned, the Yugoslavs and the Italians. At Cividale the first on the scene had been the Italian Partisans. It was they who on the previous day had liberated their own town, and collected the five hundred German prisoners whom the Grenadiers found basking in a sunny field just outside. The next to arrive were the Yugoslav battalion. Without delay, and paying scant attention to the Italian Partisans, they not merely occupied all the chief buildings and filled the streets with motley and often disorderly bands of young soldiers of both sexes: they also began to replace the Italian Tricolor by the Red Star of the Yugoslav Partisan Army, helped themselves liberally to the Italian food supplies, and printed a proclamation which declared that Cividale was under Yugoslav military control, and that all food, clothing and military equipment was to be handed over to them intact. In effect, the Italians were to be immediately disarmed, and their contribution to their own liberation, their claims to settle the affairs of their own town, would pass virtually unacknowledged. Cividale was already in danger of becoming a Yugoslav protectorate. **1945**

It was at that moment that the British arrived. The Italian Mayor of the town appealed to Colonel Clifton to arbitrate between them and see that justice was done. If the proclamation were posted up, said the Mayor, he feared that serious riots might break out. At an immediate meeting with the Yugoslav commander, Colonel Clifton extracted a promise that the proclamation would not be posted until they had had a fuller discussion on the next day. Nevertheless, the walls the next morning were found placarded with these same provocative decrees, and when the conference assembled at the Town Hall **May 3** there was a large and excitable crowd waiting to see on which side the British would use their influence. Brigadier Verney steered a calm and central course, emphasizing that it was no business for soldiers to decide what should be the ultimate fate of Cividale: all that concerned them was some working arrangement whereby all the soldiers were adequately lodged and the civilians adequately fed; it was not a matter of prestige: it was a matter of co-operative organization.

The dispute was by no means settled at the two conferences, but a breathing space was gained, grievances ventilated, and an open breach at least postponed. Although the Yugoslav proclamations remained on the walls of Cividale, the Italians tacitly disregarded them. The Italian flag was once more unfurled, flanked on one side by the Red Star, on the other by the Union Jack. The soldiers of the three

1945 nations patrolled, still fully armed, through the streets, eyeing each other with curiosity more than hostility. Slowly, and with infinite tact, the Grenadiers began to gain a moral ascendancy. Their appearance, the amount and quality of their equipment, their good temper and friendliness, made a great impression upon the Yugoslavs as well as on the Italians, and the Battalion's prestige was raised still higher at a public performance by their Drums on the second afternoon. Surrounded by a large crowd of Italians, and watched from distant windows by the Yugoslavs, the drummers climbed out of their lorry in a far corner of the piazza, shook into perfection the creases in their trousers and hitched their white belts into exact alignment. The crowd waited expectantly. The drummers took up their positions under the far colonnade, and at a signal from the Drum-Major swept up the length of the square, marching and playing with such effortless elegance, symbols of such deep-rooted discipline and tradition, that the crowd burst into prolonged applause, and even the Grenadiers in the crowd, to whom this was no new experience, felt a sudden lump swell into their throats. It was a tremendous triumph. "A Guardsman," says the War Diary, with unusual primness, "who was seen walking out with one of the Yugoslav female soldiers, put the finishing touch to a difficult day."

In their concern over the local situation the Grenadiers had had every reason to forget the Germans. In Cividale itself there were many hundreds of obedient prisoners who were gradually passed back into the cages of Central Italy, and the Grenadiers evacuated a local hospital of its German patients, many of whom were found to be malingerers of several weeks' standing.

With the wider problems raised by the capitulation, the Battalion had little to do. It was an interesting situation. The enemy who controlled the north-eastern passes of the Alps had recently been transferred from the command of von Vietinghoff, the Commander-in-Chief in Italy, to the command of von Loehr, who was in charge of troops in Southern Austria and Northern Yugoslavia. The latter claimed that he was not bound by the Caserta agreement, and refused to withdraw his men behind the Italo-Austrian frontier. They remained stubbornly across the deep valleys between Caporetto and Tarvisio, blowing up all the bridges within reach, and sending an occasional envoy under a white flag to deliver a note of defiance.

Unwilling as they were to reopen hostilities in the difficult country of the Alpine watershed, the Eighth Army seemed to have no alternative. A heavy weight of artillery was hurriedly assembled; a fleet of bombers stood in readiness. But the unofficial truce was once more prolonged, and at 6 p.m. on the 7th of May a German general called

Felmy arrived at the road block north of Caporetto with a note signed 1945
by General Loehr in person. It read as follows:

"I authorize General Felmy to represent me with the Allied High Command in the Mediterranean, to discuss certain matters which I have indicated to him.—(*Signed*) LOEHR, Lieutenant-General, Headquarters, South-East."

On arrival at the British Corps Headquarters Felmy announced that in view of Admiral Doenitz's general order to the German forces to cease fire, British troops would be allowed to enter Austria unopposed. Indeed, now that the responsibility for general surrender was removed from their shoulders on to those of their Supreme Commander, the Germans were only too anxious that the British should occupy as large a part of Austria as possible before the Russians and Yugoslavs overran the entire country. From the Eighth Army they seemed to expect more lenient treatment.

4

THE OCCUPATION OF SOUTHERN AUSTRIA

The Grenadiers cross the Italo-Austrian frontier on VE Day, 8th May, 1945—Celebration in Villach of the end of the war with Germany—Problems raised by the occupation of Villach—Attitude of the German soldiers and civilians—Diplomatic tension caused by the Yugoslav claims to Carinthia—The 1st Guards Brigade at Klagenfurt—The Brigade return to the United Kingdom

By the process of elimination which began at the River Po, the only troops available to undertake an immediate occupation of Southern Austria were the two infantry brigades of the 6th Armoured Division. They therefore lost no time in assembling behind the Austrian frontier, and the dawn was scarcely yet discernible when the Grenadiers May 8
set out from Cividale. For the first time in many weeks their lorries began to climb steeply. Above the drone of their engines they heard again the rush of a mountain torrent; they looked upwards towards the serrated knife-edge which formed the frontier between Italy and Yugoslavia, and downwards upon a thick blanket of grey mist covering the valley of the Isonzo. The villages were still asleep, the Red Star of Marshal Tito's Army swaying wetly from the wooden balconies. As they entered the zone where the three international boundaries converge and the population is mixed in blood and tradition, they observed that the architecture was no longer purely Italian: it was Alpine, with high roofs matching the gradient of the surrounding

1945 hills, and long eaves sweeping over the upper windows like beetling eyebrows. The lorries climbed up and up round the hairpin bends of the Predil Gorge, past block-houses and barracks and memorials erected during the campaign of 1917, over the last Bailey bridge to be built across an Italian stream, and down into Tarvisio, the frontier town, where Italian and Austrian notices hung side by side. It was now 7 o'clock on the morning of the 8th of May—Victory Day throughout the Western world.

For two hours the Battalion remained halted in Tarvisio, while four miles ahead of them, in the customs house at Thoerl, General Murray, Commander of the 6th Armoured Division, arranged with a German officer the final details of the British entry into the German Reich. There was no hitch. The great striped pole which hung across the road was slowly raised to point upwards into the sky, and the leading armoured cars of the 6th Armoured Division passed from Italy into Austria, and continued driving eastwards hour after hour until they met the advanced elements of the Russian Army south of Graz. At 9.45 a.m. the Welsh Guards led the 1st Guards Brigade across the frontier, and an hour later the Grenadiers also crossed. German soldiers were still lounging against the customs house, watching with apparent indifference the passage of the unending convoy. At one point two German tanks covered the road with empty, drooping guns, and groups of uniformed figures stood at every farmhouse door, outside every village inn. There was no overt hostility in their faces: many of the civilians were even welcoming; bunches of lilac were thrown into the passing lorries, lace handkerchiefs waved from upper windows, and an eager crowd of Austrian peasants would gather round any vehicles halted at the wayside. Suddenly a group of cheering and more familiar figures streamed across the road, clamouring in English for news of home. They were our own prisoners, released that morning by their Austrian guards.

The Guards Brigade went no farther than Villach, the first large town within the Austrian border. Here they were ordered to establish a temporary military government, pending the arrival of the expert administrators who for the past two years had been studying the special problems of Austria. We entered the country as conquerors: yet, in the words of Field-Marshal Alexander's first proclamation to the Austrian people: "The Allies affirm their agreement that Austria shall be liberated from German domination, and their wish to see her re-established in freedom and independence." The emphasis during the first few days was on the fact of conquest more than on the suggestion of liberation. Our troops were forbidden to fraternize with the Austrians: the flag of the old Austrian Republic, which was found

Photo: Brigadier Verney

1st Guards Brigade enter Caporetto.

On the last day of the Italian Campaign, 2nd May, 1945, the flag of the Yugoslav Partisans hangs against the house in the background. The armistice came into force at 12 noon, but the news had not yet reached the forward troops by 5 p.m., when this photograph was taken, and a battle was still in progress on the far side of the village.

The 3rd Battalion hoist the British flag at Villach, Austria, on V.E. Day, 8th May, 1945.

The mountains in the background form the frontier between Austria and Yugoslavia.

Photo: Brigadier Verney

floating from every building, was hauled down on British orders, and 1945
at a ceremony attended by the Corps Commander, General Keightley, the Grenadiers raised the Union Jack over the artillery barracks which they had occupied. It was now dusk. At a dozen wireless sets scattered through the camp small groups of Guardsmen listened to Winston Churchill's announcement of the end of the war with Germany: already the bulk of the Battalion were standing guard over key-places inside and outside the town. Again there was no time for celebration.

Their orders were to prevent the movement of all but the essential civilian traffic, to protect food and petrol dumps from pillage, and to direct German soldiers, thousands of whom were still wandering about at liberty, into main concentration areas where they could be disarmed and put under guard. Major E. C. Penn, M.C., took his company to occupy the railway stations, where trains from all parts of Austria were still arriving to disgorge German wounded, civilian refugees, and even German military stores. To check the resulting congestion in Villach, the railway lines were cut outside the town by charges of gun-cotton. For the moment it was of first importance to establish order, to freeze, as it were, the existing situation, before they could turn their heads to the revival of a normal civilian life.

Gradually, with the co-operation of German officers, the scattered and bewildered soldiers whom the end of the war had overtaken in Villach were herded into great cages on its outskirts. The main cage was put under the control of the Grenadiers, with Lieut. J. W. Harkness as resident commandant, but the internal organization of the camp was left to the Germans themselves. Though sufficiently docile, they showed little initiative. They would lie about all day, idling and sunbathing, their attitude to their British guards being one of servility more than of hostility or shame. Their officers would come for orders and advice on matters which were well within their own powers and capacities to solve. With few exceptions, they seemed to regard the capitulation as a mere transference of authority. In their dealings with the British they would venture thin jokes and offer limp cigarettes: there would be appeals to "honour among soldiers." In talking of the past they would attempt to kindle discussions about phases of the Italian campaign, only to see their efforts flicker under the damp wood of British reserve, and then die. In talking of the future they were most concerned about the date of their own demobilization (as though the teams could disperse now that the game were ended); and already there were sly references to Anglo-Russian rivalries. It was not an impressive attitude; but it was convenient: they gave little trouble.

Far more serious were the differences of opinion which arose, and

1945 daily grew more grave, between the British and their Yugoslav allies. Already at Cividale the Grenadiers had seen at first hand how Tito's Army had ambitions which were not satisfied by the defeat of Germany and the liberation of their own country. The Partisans demanded tangible recompense for their years of suffering: they aimed at supreme political power in Yugoslavia, which they soon achieved and which was no concern of ours; but they also claimed territorial reparations from Italy and Austria, for which they were not prepared to wait until the matter was discussed at a peace conference. Both claims were based on the presence in Venezia Giulia and in the Austrian province of Carinthia of a minority of Serbian nationals who had been ill-treated by the Fascists and the Nazis, and for whom the hour of liberation was now at hand. That both provinces were under British control, that both contained a majority of Italian or Austrian nationals, in no way tempered the Yugoslav claims. Just as Udine, with its purely Italian population, had been included in the first claim to Venezia Giulia, so Villach and Klagenfurt, both undeniably Austrian, were to be swept bodily within the new borders of the Yugoslav State. "The Yugoslav Army," ran the proclamation which they posted up throughout the province, "has entered Carinthia in order to clean the land once and for all time of Nazi criminals and guarantee the Slovenian and Austrian people a truly popular democracy, freedom and prosperity in the new, victorious and powerful Greater Yugoslavia. We hereby make known that throughout the whole of liberated Carinthia the military authority of the Yugoslav Army has been established."

This proclamation and the flood of propaganda literature by which it was supported were introduced into Carinthia by Yugoslav soldiers who did not set foot inside Austria until some days after the arrival of the Eighth Army. At Villach there had been no challenge to the authority of the 1st Guards Brigade. But when the Brigade moved
May 12 farther east to the area between Klagenfurt and the River Drava, they found that every village had its section, every small town its platoon, company or battalion of Yugoslav Partisans, who were issuing orders in contradiction to those of the British Military Government, while from across the border the Belgrade radio directed a stream of inflammatory reports which represented the Slovene minority as oppressed by new tyrants—the British. It was a most uneasy situation. The Guardsmen were told that there was no intention to allow British authority in our zone of Austria to be overridden; that it was our business to hold the ring, to keep the peace, while the Yugoslav claims were discussed at a diplomatic level; at all costs we must avoid incidents which might prejudice the success of these discussions. But by

the time these generalities had filtered down to the actual Guardsman 1945 on sentry at Grenadier Bridge over the Drava River, he was little wiser about what specific action was expected of him. Was he to prevent further Yugoslav convoys from crossing the bridge, or was he not? If not, was he to shoot at them when they insisted on passing? Should he allow the Partisans to help themselves to the vast piles of discarded German equipment? What was he to do when civilians, even Slovenes, came and begged for British protection against looting bands of Yugoslavs? All these questions were settled on the spot by subalterns and non-commissioned officers, acting as best they could on their own judgment of what was fair and politic. They did not help the Partisans —indeed, they put every obstacle in their path, short of shooting at them: a tank would conveniently "break down" across a main railway line; the decking of a bridge would be found in need of urgent repairs. But in their personal dealings with Partisans the Grenadiers treated them with friendly firmness, like English policemen at a football match. "Come on now, sonny," they would say to a young Croat as he started to drive off an abandoned German tank, "you don't want to go playing about with that old thing." And though not a word was intelligible to the Croat, and not a threatening gesture was made by the Guardsmen, the tank would remain where it was.

It was not always as easy as that. As one of the last areas to be occupied by the Allied armies, the province of Carinthia had become the sump of Europe, into which had drained the prisoners, criminals, refugees and stragglers of many nations and many armies. Their rivalries persisted long after the official armistice. Their lack of homes and of any means of sustenance forced them either to appeal for help to the British or to live by pillaging the local peasantry. But of all the various groups, the Axis army which had fought in Yugoslavia caused the greatest anxiety. The following message, received from Headquarters, 6th Armoured Division, gives a good idea of the scale of the problem which confronted the 1st Guards Brigade:

> "Three hundred thousand Germans and two hundred thousand May 14 Croats, the greater part of them armed, are moving across the Yugoslav border, although they have all nominally surrendered to Tito. They have with them sufficient rations for not more than forty-eight hours, and are accompanied by thirty thousand horses and two thousand motor vehicles. The Eighth Army have been urgently asked for a decision whether we are to accept the surrender of these forces, or oblige them to return to Yugoslavia. Pending the decision they will be held south of the Drava."

These men, it must be understood, had never fought against the British. For many years they had been waging implacable warfare in

1945 the mountains of Yugoslavia, and, though it might seem a matter of small importance which particular Ally should now accept their surrender, the Yugoslavs felt strongly that these prisoners belonged to them. About thirty thousand of them did in fact find their way into a cage which the Grenadiers hurriedly set up at Viktring, south of Klagenfurt. The next day a lorry full of Tito's Partisans drove very fast down the road leading through the camp and opened fire on a group of German officers sitting outside the Grenadier guard tent. Nobody was hit, and the lorry escaped, but as a result of this and similar incidents relations between the British and the Partisans became very strained indeed. "Jug" (an inevitable abbreviation which soon appeared even in official documents)—Jug armoured cars would prowl round the countryside; propaganda newspapers containing vitriolic anti-British articles, printed the day before in Ljubljana, would be smuggled across the frontier in shopping baskets; the streets of Klagenfurt itself were paced nightly by rival patrols. One Grenadier platoon, deep and high in the mountains on the frontier itself, shared the Loibhl Pass customs house with a platoon of Partisans, each keeping strictly to the rooms of their own side of the frontier. They waited anxiously for a settlement to be announced from Belgrade: it seemed that at any moment one more frontier incident, a single slip by a hot-headed non-commissioned officer, might lead to very serious consequences indeed. Eventually the settlement was reached. Marshal Tito agreed to withdraw from Carinthia but not
May 21 from Venezia Giulia, and with the departure of the last Partisan lorry, the disappearance of the last Red Star, the Grenadiers could at last recognize the existence of a peace which had been formally declared a fortnight before.

With time to look around them they discovered that they were in a part of Europe which had much to offer to tired and victorious campaigners. A chain of long lakes sparkled at the bottom of each valley, and on their shores there were villas, chalets, hotels and bathing spas which before the war had been the summer resorts of the Viennese and were now requisitioned by the Eighth Army as billets for their men. Never in Africa or Italy had they seen better. It was not only that their accommodation was comfortable, the countryside pleasant and almost untouched by the war: they also found waiting for them the apparatus of a vast adult playground. On the lakes there were speed-boats and small yachts, water-skis, surf-boards, racing eights; and on land there were golf courses, tennis courts, the pick of the German Army horses on which to ride through the woods; fishing, climbing and shooting. The Grenadiers, the bulk of whom were billeted on the shores of the largest lake, the Wörther See, were so happy that even the offer of a free holiday on the Lido at Venice could tempt 1945 few away from Austria. There was only one advantage which Italy enjoyed over Austria. With the Austrians the men were still forbidden to fraternize; and, though at first the Guardsmen turned obedient cold shoulders to the blandishments of a friendly and decorative population, the order was growing increasingly unpopular, and was in fact lifted soon after the Grenadiers left the country.

Of their allies, the Americans, French and Russians, who occupied zones of Austria contiguous to that of the Eighth Army, the Guards Brigade saw little, for their present duties seldom took them far from the happy shores of their own lakes. There was, however, one meeting with the Russians which fittingly closed the Battalion's overseas service. A British military mission was setting out for Vienna to discuss the division of the city into three zones which the three Great Powers were later to occupy. They took with them a party of ten Grenadiers under the charge of Sergt. J. Sibbald, D.C.M., whose duties were to mount a guard over the temporary British Headquarters. They carried out this task with such success that the Viennese gathered in crowds to watch the Grenadiers on sentry drill; and at a dinner given in honour June 15 of the British mission a Russian marshal proposed a toast in these words: "To the gallant British Guardsmen, the best soldiers in the British Army, the smartest soldiers in the world."

In the last week of June, between the end of the German War and the end of the Japanese War, the two Guards Battalions of the 1st Guards Brigade were ordered to return to the United Kingdom and prepare for service in the Far East. The Commander of the Eighth Army came in person to bid them farewell, and officers and men took their leave of their many friends in the 6th Armoured Division, with whose fortunes they had linked their own two and a half years before, at the Kasserine Pass in Tunisia. Early the next morning, as the long June 29 convoy of lorries drove westwards across the Divisional boundary, the Grenadiers and Welsh Guards found General Murray standing with his staff at the roadside, and behind them, raised on the grass verge, was a vast mailed fist, flanked for the occasion by their own two emblems, the grenade and the leek: beneath was written, "Good-bye and Good Luck."

Two days later the Battalions were back on the Adriatic coast, at Fano, where they spent another month waiting, hot and dusty and July 1-28 impatient, until the arrangements for their homeward journey were completed. Some flew in Liberator bombers direct from Foggia to England; others took the long sea route through the Straits of Gibral-

1945 tar. By the second week in August the 3rd Battalion were reunited in their own country. The end of the Japanese War made their participation in the Far Eastern campaigns unnecessary, and the 3rd Battalion, radically reconstituted, were sent to Palestine.

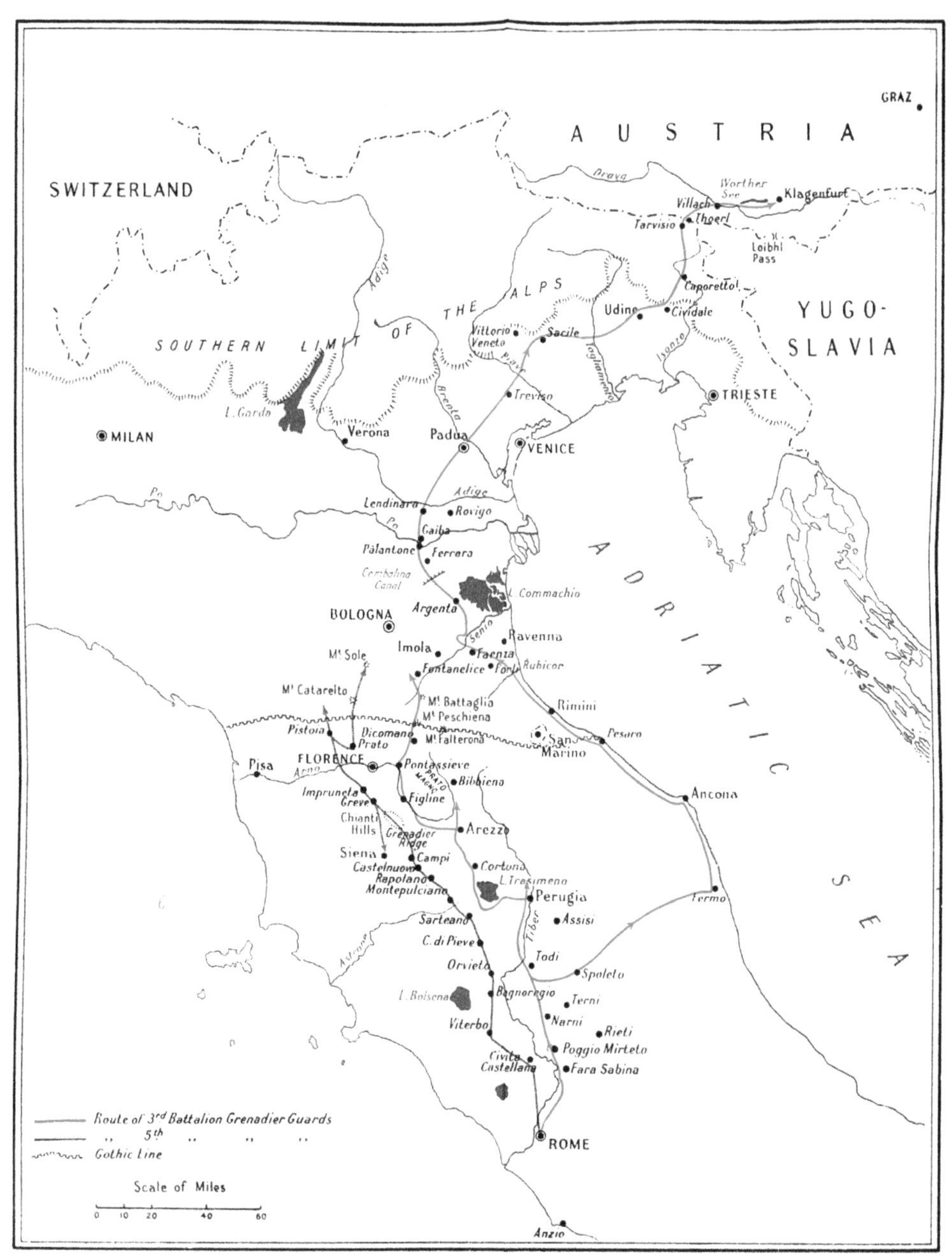

NORTHERN ITALY

Face page 524

APPENDIX I

REGIMENTAL HEADQUARTERS; THE TRAINING AND HOLDING BATTALIONS

REGIMENTAL HEADQUARTERS

THE Headquarters of the Regiment remained in London throughout the war. For the first five years they occupied their traditional offices in Bird Cage Walk, and when these were badly damaged on Sunday, the 18th of June, 1944, by the same flying bomb which destroyed the Guards' Chapel with heavy loss of life,* they found a new home at 25 Buckingham Gate, a commodious set of rooms which they continued to occupy until June, 1948.

During the six war years there were four Lieutenant-Colonels of the Regiment, and four Regimental Adjutants. A complete list will be found in Appendix VI, from which it will be seen that the partnership which extended over the major part of the war, from 1941 to 1945, was that between Colonel J. A. Prescott and Major A. H. Penn. It was they who fostered the expansion of the Regiment, they who sent in turn six Battalions overseas, and kept them supplied with reinforcements; and they to whom the major credit is due for maintaining, during those vital years, the unity of the Regiment, the balance between their far-flung Battalions, and those amicable relationships with the War Office, the families of serving Grenadiers, and their own Commanding Officers, on which the happiness and standards of the Regiment ultimately depend.

Of all the problems which the successive Lieutenant-Colonels had to face, the question of man power was the most acute. At first it was not too difficult. With the inflow of reservists and recruits it was immediately possible to put three Battalions into the field, with large reserves in the Training and Holding Battalions, and a pool of reinforcements overseas. Nor was it difficult to find men of the right calibre and height (which never fell below a minimum of 5 ft. 9 in. through the war) to form the 4th, 5th and 6th Battalions in the course of 1940 and 1941. But thereafter, as Battalions went overseas and suffered heavy casualties, and as the expanding Army found itself in competition for new men with industry and the other Services, the Grenadiers were reduced so low that they were unable to maintain the original number of Battalions. The 6th Battalion were withdrawn from active service early in 1944; the 5th Battalion a year later: and, though the remaining four Battalions saw the end of the war on the field of battle, they were scraping the bottom of the bin for their last reserves.

It never became necessary for the Brigade of Guards, as it was for many regiments of the line, to absorb from outside whole companies which retained their regimental identity; but within the Brigade certain adjustments were necessary to maintain the Battalions at fighting strength, such as the temporary inclusion of a company of Grenadiers in the 3rd Battalion Welsh Guards, and the transformation into Guardsmen of many men of the Royal Air Force Regiment. Thus in the end the Grenadiers were a smaller Regiment than in the middle years of the war, but they were undiluted. Four of their six Battalions were intact. Employed outside the Regiment, Grenadiers were scattered over the width of the world—a Guardsman, perhaps, acting as servant to a General in Syria, an officer detached to the Scilly Islands to train falcons for the interception of German carrier pigeons—and so on, endlessly. As all these men were still held on the paper establishment of the Regiment, it was often difficult to convince the War Office that the Regiment's fighting strength was as low as those at Regimental Headquarters knew to be the truth.

---

*Four Grenadier officers and eleven other ranks were killed in this disaster. The officers were Lieut.-Colonel The Lord Edward Hay, Major D. H. B. Thornton, Capt. L. E. G. Wall (and his wife) and Capt. G. D. Kemp-Welch.

There were other difficulties. It was necessary to estimate, with little knowledge of the future operational commitments of Battalions which were often thousands of miles away from London, what their separate casualty rates were likely to be six months ahead, and to have reinforcements available for them at the right place, at the right time, and with the correct proportions of officers, non-commissioned officers and men. On the whole, the forecasts were remarkably accurate. Casualties in infantry battalions were slightly under-estimated: casualties in armoured battalions slightly over-estimated; and the losses in rifle companies were higher than had been expected in proportion to the losses among specialists. But it is a measure of the success of the planning in London that at the end of the war there were only two officers trained for armoured warfare who remained unabsorbed into a field Battalion.

Second only to the problems of man power, Regimental Headquarters was concerned with the supply of information to the families of serving Grenadiers. "Both of us," wrote the parents of a missing officer, "have been greatly impressed and touched by the trouble which has been taken to find out everything possible. I can find no words to express our gratitude. I do not think that a History of the Regiment would be quite complete without some indication of your goodness to people in our position." It was the same with countless others. After every major engagement a list of casualties was circulated as soon as possible to the families of all the men engaged. Details of the action, and the progress of the wounded, were likewise personally communicated as soon as they were available. And at intervals a News-Letter gave the background to the Battalions' activities overseas. Major Penn himself maintained an enormous volume of personal correspondence. Mrs. A. F. L. Clive, the wife of the Commanding Officer, issued a 6th Battalion News-Letter until security regulations made it impossible to continue. Mrs. C. R. Britten, as Chairman, and Mrs. H. St. L. Stucley, as Secretary, of the Grenadier Guards Relief Committee throughout the war, organized an unbroken chain of correspondence between the women relatives of Grenadier officers and men. This intimate association between Regimental Headquarters and the families of serving Grenadiers did much to ease the strain of war and absence; and those who gave their time to this work cannot now feel that their efforts went without reward.

One further innovation sponsored by Regimental Headquarters, perhaps the most important in the domestic history of the Regiment during the war, yet not directly connected with the war, was the appointment of H.R.H. Princess Elizabeth as Colonel of the Regiment. The Duke of Connaught, who had been Colonel since 1904, died on the 23rd of February, 1942, at the age of 91. Few members of the Regiment could remember a time when he had not been their Colonel, and his death left a gap which it was not easy to fill. The suggestion that Princess Elizabeth should be invited to take his place was one which met with immediate acclaim from the entire Regiment. She was then approaching her sixteenth birthday, and her acceptance of the appointment marked her first emergence from private life. Her birthday was celebrated by a parade of detachments from all eight Battalions of the Regiment at Windsor Castle on the 21st of April, 1942, and it was then that the Princess, accompanied by the King and Queen, took her first salute from her new Regiment. Thereafter, as the pages of this History have shown, her interest in the Regiment's activities and welfare was unflagging. She inspected each of the Battalions individually before their departure for overseas, or after their return; and, although her public responsibilities began to grow as the war progressed, she retained for her Grenadiers an affection of which every Guardsman was gratefully proud.

THE TRAINING AND HOLDING BATTALIONS

Once a recruit had been accepted by the Regiment, his training went through several distinct stages before he was considered fit for service in a field Battalion. He would spend his first eight weeks (later extended to sixteen) at the Guards Depot, where he absorbed those essentials of drill and discipline which stamp a Guardsman with a style he will never lose. He then passed to the Training Battalion for a thorough grounding in field tactics and weapon training. It was then that the men were sorted out, according to their different abilities and preferences, and the current demand for reinforcements, into those destined for the armoured Battalions and those destined for the infantry. From the Training Battalion the young Guardsman might pass for a period to the Holding Battalion, but more often, and especially in the later stages of the war, he would go direct to a service Battalion or, in the case of the tank Battalions, to the Guards Armoured Training Wing.

The officers were trained and selected in much the same way. For the first year after the outbreak of war those applying for commissions in the Regiment would go direct from civil life to Sandhurst, and thence, if acceptable on their performance as officer cadets, as second-lieutenants to the Training Battalion. In the later war years potential officers would spend a preliminary two months at the Guards Depot, and would undergo exactly the same training and discipline as a Guardsman, before passing on to Sandhurst. This was a most successful innovation on the practice of the 1914 war. A young officer would never forget, through his own, sometimes bitter, experience, exactly what he was asking of his men in terms of time and drudgery.

THE TRAINING BATTALION

The Training Battalion was formed at Victoria Barracks, Windsor, very shortly before the outbreak of war, and remained there until its official disbandment on the 1st of August, 1946. During these seven years, seven hundred and fifty officers and fifteen thousand other ranks passed through its gates, some to return a second and a third time. During the waiting years, when the inflow of new men was heavier than the demand for reinforcements to service Battalions, more than three thousand men, as well as a permanent staff of the Auxiliary Territorial Service, were concurrently on the Windsor establishment.

There was naturally not room enough for this vast number in Victoria Barracks itself. The Battalion had offshoots in nearly every street of the town: one thousand five hundred men were encamped on the race-course at Kempton Park; and on orders from London District many detachments were stationed at "vital points" in the neighbourhood of Windsor and London. At one time the Training Battalion were finding guards for all the Thames bridges between Kew and Maidenhead, for the Headquarters of Fighter Command, Bomber Command and Coastal Command, and for the aerodromes at Heathrow, Hendon, Langley, Hanworth and Smith's Lawn. Kempton Park itself was the main internment camp for German civilians trapped in England at the outbreak of war, and later for the Italians. All these duties, which demanded tact and firm control, were carried out by raw recruits, who fitted in, as best they could, their own training for active service.

There is unfortunately no space to describe these manifold activities in greater detail. But there was one duty, unique in the history of the Regiment, which should not pass unrecorded. Soon after Dunkirk, when the Royal Family moved to Windsor Castle, a company of the Training Battalion, commanded over a long period by Major G. P. Philipps, C.V.O., were given the privilege of guarding the Castle in close proximity to Their Majesties. The company lived in the Royal Mews, constructed a network of slit trenches which circled the inner and outer wards, and maintained a system of patrols along the river banks and actually within the spacious corridors of the Castle itself. Their main object was to defend the Castle against surprise attack by enemy parachutists, and in the event of an overpowering invasion of England, to escort the Royal Family to the King's private aerodrome at Smith's Lawn, itself under the guard of another Grenadier detachment. Their adventures throughout several years were few, and for the officers and men of the Windsor Castle Company the chief memory is of the personal interest and kindness constantly shown to them by the Royal Family.

THE HOLDING BATTALION

In April, 1940, the bulk of the Kempton Park detachment was moved to Wellington Barracks in London to form the Holding Battalion. In the early years the Battalion had three main functions. The first was to form a secondary pool of reinforcements; the second, to mount King's Guard and other public duties in rotation with other battalions of the

Brigade; and the third was to provide guards for the inner defences of London, at Whitehall, Downing Street, the War Office and Westminster. These duties, and the lack of suitable areas within easy reach, made the Holding Battalion unsuitable for the training of recruits. As the war progressed, the Battalion was therefore filled by older soldiers who were temporarily employed, by drafts from disbanded service Battalions, and by those who were convalescing from wounds or serious illness. If Victoria Barracks, Windsor, was the Regiment's nursery, Wellington Barracks was its waiting room and hall. In November, 1943, the Holding Battalion was disbanded and its place taken by the Westminster Garrison Battalion, which was composed of detachments from the three senior regiments of the Brigade of Guards.

APPENDIX II

ALPHABETICAL LIST OF OFFICER CASUALTIES, 1939-1945

LEGEND

The following legend is used:

KA	Killed in Action.
KPW	Killed while Prisoner of War.
KAS	Killed on Active Service.
DW	Died of Wounds.
DPW	Died while Prisoner of War.
DWPW	Died of Wounds while Prisoner of War.
DIAS	Died of Injuries on Active Service.
DAS	Died on Active Service.
W	Wounded.
WPW	Wounded and taken Prisoner of War.
WPWE	Wounded, taken Prisoner of War, and Escaped.
WBA	Wounded, Battle Accident.
PW	Prisoner of War.
PWE	Escaped as Prisoner of War.
PDW	Presumed Died of Wounds.

Name	*Casualty*	*Battalion*	*Date*	*Place*
Abel Smith, Capt. R. E.	KA	3	21/ 5/40	River Escaut (B.E.F.)
Adair, Lieut. D. A. S.	KA	6	10/11/43	M. Camino
Addison, Lieut. P. L. G.	W	6	6/12/43	M. Camino
Akroyd, Lieut. M. B.	W	1	3/ 9/44	Pont-a-Marcq
Alexander, Lieut. N. W.	PW	1	27/ 9/44	Heesch
Alington, Capt. P. C. W.	DW	6	24/ 9/43	Salerno
Allsopp, Capt. J. R.	KA	6	17/ 3/43	Mareth Line
Alston-Roberts-West, Major W. R. J.	KA	3	21/ 5/40	River Escaut (B.E.F.)
Angus, Capt. A. D.	W	3	18/ 6/44	Perugia
Anthony, Major J. E.	KA	5	25/ 1/44	Anzio
Ardee, Capt. Lord	W	6	6/12/43	M. Camino
Aubrey-Fletcher, Lieut. L. P. ..	WPW	3	28/ 5/40	Ypres-Comines Canal (B.E.F.)
Baillie, Capt. S. E. H.	PW	S.A.S.	23/ 8/44	France
Baker, Major N. E. W.	W	1	3/ 9/44	Pont-a-Marcq
" " "	W	1	14/ 9/44	Escaut Canal (N.W.E.)
" " "	W	1	27/ 9/44	Heesch
" " "	W	1	30/ 3/45	Aalten
Baring, 2/Lieut. P.	KA	3	19/ 5/40	Ninove (B.E.F.)
Barry, 2/Lieut. J. A.	KA	1	3 /8/44	Drouet
Bastard, Lieut. J. R.	W	3	4/ 2/43	Dj. Mansour
Bayley, Lieut. M. S.	W	1	30/ 3/45	Aalten
Berry, Lieut. Hon. J. D.	DW	3	10/10/44	M. Battaglia
Bevan, 2/Lieut. O. D.	KA	2	29/ 5/40	Furnes (B.E.F.)
Birchall, Lieut. T. H. (Can., loan) ..	W	1	31/ 3/45	Groenlo
Boles, Lieut. K. C.	WBA	1	22/ 7/44	Cagny
Bolitho, Capt. S. E.	W	3	25/ 4/43	Dj. Kournine

Name	Casualty	Battalion	Date	Place
Bond, Lieut. D. W. D.	W	3	19/12/42	Medjez el Bab
„ Capt. „	PW	3	26/ 8/44	Florence
Bonham-Carter, Lieut. M. R. ..	PWE	6	17/ 3/43	Mareth Line
Boult, Lieut. F. C.	KA	5	3/ 5/43	Dj. Bou Aoukaz
Boulton, Lieut. D. D.	KA	5	7/ 2/44	Anzio
Boyd, 2/Lieut. A. N.	KA	3	21/ 5/40	River Escaut (B.E.F.)
Boyd, Lieut. J. R.	KAS	2	3/ 9/43	United Kingdom
Brabourne, Lieut. Lord	WPW	6	17/ 3/43	Mareth Line
„ „ „	KPW	6	15/ 9/43	N. Italy
Braybrooke, Lieut. Lord	KA	3	23/ 1/43	Bou Arada
Brennand, Lieut. N. J.	W	1	6/ 9/44	N.W.E.
Brinckman, Capt. R. N.	WPWE	3	27/ 5/40	Ypres-Comines Canal (B.E.F.)
Britten, Major P. C.	W	6	25/ 1/44	Minturno
Brocklebank, Lieut. J. R. A. ..	W	6	25/ 9/43	Salerno
„ „ „ ..	KA	6	8/11/43	M. Camino
Bromley, Major R. H.	W	1	3/ 8/44	Drouet
Brooke, Lieut. B. J. D.	KA	6	11/ 3/43	Medenine
Brown, Capt. I. A. M.	KA	6	9/ 9/43	Salerno
Bruce, Lieut. C. J.	DIAS	H.Q., 5 Gds. Amd. Bde.	6/ 4/45	Germany
Buchanan, Lieut. A. G.	KA	6	17/ 3/43	Mareth Line
Buchanan, Lieut. H. A. D.	PWE	Commandos	11/ 8/42	M.E.
Buchanan, Lieut. P. A.	W	3	10/ 6/44	Poggio Mirteto
Bull, Major G. H.	DW	2	20/ 6/40	B.E.F.
Burke, Capt. P. H. A.	W	5	1/12/44	M. Sole
Butler, Major T. P.	WPWE	6	17/ 3/43	Mareth Line
Buxton, Capt. J. G. F.	KA	5	23/ 4/43	Dj. Bou Aoukaz
Cannan, Capt. J. A.	W	4	7/ 8/44	Estry
„ „ „	W	4	22/ 2/45	Goch
Canning, Lieut. Hon. V. S. de R. ..	W	5	25/ 1/44	Anzio
„ „ „ „ ..	KA	5	6/ 5/44	River Sangro
Carey, Lieut. R. G.	W	5	17/ 2/45	M. Sole
Carter, Lieut. H. H.	KA	5	27/ 4/43	Dj. Bou Aoukaz
Cassy, Lieut. M. J. W.	KA	5	2/10/44	M. Catarelto
Chaplin, Capt. G. W.	KA	5	2-3/12/44	M. Sole
Cholmondeley, Lieut. H. P. G. ..	KA	6	7/11/43	M. Camino
Clark, Lieut. A. D. N.	W	5	27/ 4/43	Dj. Bou Aoukaz
Clark, Capt. R. C. R. M.	W	2		B.E.F.
Clark, Lieut. R. F. B.	W	3	6/ 8/44	Arno Valley
„ „ „	WBA	3	10/ 2/45	Fontanelice
Clifton, Capt. P. T.	W	3	21/ 5/40	River Escaut (B.E.F.)
Clive, Lieut.-Colonel A. F. L. ..	W	6	17/ 3/43	Mareth Line
Clive, Major M. G. D.	KA	5	1/ 5/43	Dj. Bou Aoukaz
Collie, Lieut. A. MacR.	WBA	4	2/ 3/45	Germany
Collie, Lieut. E. D.	WPW	5	7/ 2/44	Anzio
Colvin, Major R. B. R.	W	2	1/ 6/40	Dunkirk (B.E.F.)
Conville, Lieut. M. N.	W	5	25/ 6/44	River Astrone
Cook, Major E. T.	DW	6	8/11/43	M. Camino
Cook, Lieut. P. H.	W	2	3/ 4/45	Gilderhaus
Cooper, Lieut. M. A. R. R.	W	3	28/ 5/44	M. Grande
Corbett, Lieut. Hon. J. P.	KA	2	18/ 7/44	Cagny
Corbett, Lieut. Hon. T. A.	W	1	23/ 9/44	Uden
„ „ „ „	W	1	19/ 4/45	Hamburg-Bremen Autobahn
Cornelius, 2/Lieut. V. E.	W	Holding Bn.	30/ 5/40	Dunkirk (B.E.F.)

Name	Casualty	Battalion	Date	Place
Courage, Lieut. A. J.	W	5	21/ 4/43	Medjez el Bab
" " "	KPW	5	7/ 2/44	Anzio
Crewdson, Lieut. R. O. H.	W	6	30/ 1/44	Minturno
" " "	W	3	13/12/44	Fontanelice
Crompton-Roberts, Lieut. R. ..	KA	3	27/ 5/40	Ypres-Comines Canal (B.E.F.)
Cubitt, Lieut. V. B.	KA	3	27/ 6/44	Perugia
Daniel, Lieut. J. K.	W	2	3/ 4/45	Bentheim
Davenport, Lieut. A. J. R.	W	4	22/ 4/45	River Elbe
Denny, Lieut. J. F. L.	WBA	1	19/ 7/44	Cagny
de Rougemont, Lieut. R. C. I. ..	DW	3	11/12/42	Medjez el Bab
Drake, Lieut. R. M.	KA	6	10/ 9/43	Salerno
Duncan, Lieut. J. A. C.	DW	1	30/ 3/45	Aalten
Dunlop, Lieut. B. E.	KA	5	17/ 4/43	Medjez el Bab
Dunlop, Lieut. H. E.	KA	5	28/ 8/44	S. Miniato
Durham, Lieut. N. J. R. J.	KA	6	17/ 3/43	Mareth Line
Earle, Capt. C.	W	3	28/ 5/40	Ypres-Comines Canal (B.E.F.)
Edward-Collins, Lieut. R. F. ..	W	2	27/ 7/44	Caen
" " " " ..	W	2	25/ 9/44	Heesch
Egerton, Capt. S. J. L.	W	5	27/ 4/43	Dj. Bou Aoukaz
Eliott, Lieut. Hon. M. R. V. ..	W	4	5/11/44	Meijel
Ellison, Lieut.-Colonel P. J. M. ..	W	R. Sussex R.		B.E.F.
Etherton, Capt. R. R.	W	4	8/ 4/45	Wunsdorf
Evelyn, Major P. G.	PDW	6	17/ 3/43	Mareth Line
Faber, Lieut. T. H.	W	3	28/ 5/44	M. Grande
Fairbairn, Capt. S. G.	DAS	H.Q., L'nd'n District	19/ 1/43	London
Fairbanks-Smith, Lieut. E. F. ..	W	1	31/ 3/45	Eibergen
Farebrother, Lieut. H.	DW	3	19/ 6/44	Perugia
Farquharson, Lieut. N. S.	W	1	30/ 4/45	Sandbostel
Fergusson, Capt. D. B.	W	5	2/10/44	M. Catarelto
Fergusson-Cuninghame, Lieut. J. A.	W	H.Q., 5 Gds. Amd. Bde.	4/ 8/44	Normandy
Fielden, Lieut. J. N.	DW	2	21/ 9/44	Nijmegen
Fitzalan-Howard, Lieut. Hon. Martin	W	2	11/ 8/44	Viessoix
Fitzroy, Lieut. Lord Oliver	KA	4	7/ 8/44	Estry
Forbes, Lieut. The Master of ..	W	3	21/ 5/40	River Escaut (B.E.F.)
Ford, Major C. G.	KA	5	28/ 1/44	Anzio
Frank, Lieut. Sir Howard, Bt. ..	KA	2	11/ 9/44	Escaut Canal (N.W.E.)
Frederick, Major C. B.	W	5	25/ 6/44	River Astrone
Frederick, Lieut. J. C.	KA	5	19/ 4/43	Medjez el Bab
Freeman, Lieut. R.	W	5	21/ 4/43	Medjez el Bab
" Capt. "	W	5	4/ 2/44	Anzio
Freeman-Attwood, Lieut. H. W. ..	WBA	5	1/ 7/44	Montepulciano
Freyberg, Lieut. P. R.	PWE	5	7/ 2/44	Anzio
Fryer, Lieut. F. C. H.	W	2	12/ 9/44	Escaut Canal (N.W.E.)
Gage, Lieut. Q. H. M.	W	5	4/ 2/44	Anzio
Garton, Lieut. A. C.	WBA	5	9/ 8/43	Tunis
Gascoigne, Major J. C.	W	4	6/10/44	Nederweert
Gerard, Major R. C. F.	WBA	H.Q., Gds. Amd. Div.	6/11/44	Rhineland
Gibbs, Capt. Hon. V. P.	KA	1	20/ 9/44	Nijmegen
Gidley-Kitchin, Lieut. G. C. B. ..	W	4	7/ 8/44	Estry

Name	Casualty	Battalion	Date	Place
Giffard, Lieut. P. R. de L.	W	3	2/ 8/44	River Arno
Glyn, Capt. J. P. R.	W	6	6/12/43	M. Camino
Gordon, Major A. J. E.	W	6	17/ 3/43	Mareth Line
Gordon-Lennox, Lieut.-Colonel G. C.	W	5	26/ 1/44	Anzio
Gore-Browne, Capt. T. A.	W	5	25/ 1/44	Anzio
„ „ „ „	WPW	5	7/ 2/44	Anzio
Goschen, Brigadier W. H.	KA	H.Q., 4 Inf. Bde.	6/ 5/44	Burma
Goss, Capt. R. J. V.	KA	6	17/ 3/43	Mareth Line
Grant, Major Sir Arthur L., Bt. ..	KA	2	18/ 7/44	Cagny
Gray, Lieut. A. H.	W	4	27/ 2/45	Weeze
Grazebrook, Lieut. C. N.	KA	6	17/ 3/43	Mareth Line
Grazebrook, Capt. M. W.	W	6	30/ 1/44	Minturno
Greenall, Lieut. P. B. M.	KA	1	20/ 9/44	Nijmegen
Grey, Capt. G. C., M.P.	KA	4	30/ 7/44	Caumont
Gurney, Lieut. A. J.	WPW	5	28/ 1/44	Anzio
Gwyer, Lieut. G. C. F.	W	1	31/ 5/40	Furnes (B.E.F.)
„ Capt. „	DW	6	24/ 3/43	Mareth Line
Haden, Lieut. W. C.	KA	6	17/ 3/43	Mareth Line
Hamilton-Russell, Lieut. Hon. G. L.	DW	3	2/ 6/40	B.E.F.
Hanbury, Major H. C.	W	6	8/12/43	M. Camino
„ „ „	W	6	30/ 1/44	Minturno
Harding, Lieut. A. R.	W	2	3/ 4/45	Gilderhaus
„ „ „	W	2	29/ 4/45	Sandbostel
Harding, Lieut. G. R. H.	KA	5	28/ 1/44	Anzio
Hargreaves, Lieut. J. M.	KA	5	25/ 1/44	Anzio
Harkness, Lieut. J. W.	W	3	28/ 5/44	M. Grande
Harris, Lieut. A. J. G.	DW	5	25/ 9/44	Gothic Line
Hay, Lieut.-Colonel Lord Edward ..	KA	Westminster Garrison	18/ 6/44	Guards' Chapel
Henshaw, Lieut. B.	KA	6	7/11/43	M. Camino
Hermon, Capt. J. V.	KA	6	11/ 9/43	Salerno
Hervey-Bathurst, Lieut. B. A. F. ..	W	6	7/11/43	M. Camino
Heywood, Capt. A. G.	W	2	3/ 9/44	Brussels
Heywood-Lonsdale, Major R. H. ..	W	4	30/ 7/44	Caumont
Hodson, Lieut. C. C. P.	W	5	24/ 6/44	River Astrone
Hogarth, Major J. U.	DAS	Serving with Band	19/ 7/44	Narni
Hohler, Capt. T. S.	W	5	26/ 1/44	Anzio
Holland, Capt. A. T. A.	W	5	9/ 2/44	Anzio
Hovell, Lieut. E. M.	W	6	16/ 3/43	Mareth Line
Howard, Capt. R. M. C.	W	6	10/11/43	M. Camino
Huggins, Lieut. J. H. W.	W	1	18/ 7/44	Cagny
Humphreys, Lieut. R. W.	W	1	18/ 7/44	Cagny
Huntington, Lieut.-Colonel A. C. ..	KA	5	9/ 2/44	Anzio
Huntington, Lieut. T. W.	KA	6	7/12/43	M. Camino
Hussey, Lieut. M. J.	WPW	5	7/ 2/44	Anzio
Inchbald, Lieut. A. I.	DW	H.Q., 201 Gds. Bde.	6/12/43	M. Camino
Ingram, Major M. W.	WBA	H.Q., 43 Div.	10/ 7/44	Normandy
Jeffreys, Capt. C. J. D.	KA	2	28/ 5/40	Furnes (B.E.F.)
Jenkins, Lieut. M. H.	W	3	10/10/44	M. Battaglia
Johnston, Lieut. J. F. D.	W	4	21/ 4/45	River Elbe
Johnstone, Capt. N. D. M.	WPW	5	7/ 2/44	Anzio
Joly, Lieut. R. B.	W	1	13/ 8/44	Vire
„ „ „	KA	1	30/ 3/45	Aalten

Name	Casualty	Battalion	Date	Place
Jones, Lieut. A. N. V.	KA	2	10/ 4/45	Eggermuhlen
Jones, Capt. J. A. P.	W	2	18/ 7/44	Cagny
Jones, Lieut. T. A.	W	5	25/ 7/44	Grenadier Ridge (Italy)
Kemp-Welch, Capt. G. D.	KA	M.O.I. (S.P.)	18/ 6/44	Guards' Chapel
Kennard, Capt. R. A.	W	3	10/10/44	M. Battaglia
Keyser, Lieut. C. T.	W	5	27/ 4/43	Dj. Bou Aoukaz
Kidston, Lieut. J. B.	W	5	23/ 1/45	M. Sole
Kingsford, Lieut. M. G. R.	DW	5	14/ 6/44	Bagnoregio
Kingsmill, Lieut.-Colonel W. H. ..	W	6	14/ 9/43	Salerno
King-Smith, Lieut. R. G.	W	5	12/ 7/44	Campi
Kinsman, Lieut. A. H. I.	WPWE	L.R.D.G.	15/ 1/43	M.E.
Lamb, Lieut. G. W.	W	5	2/ 8/44	Impruneta
Lane-Fox, 2/Lieut. J. H.	W	3	28/ 5/40	Ypres-Comines Canal (B.E.F.)
„ „ Capt. „	W	1	22/ 7/44	Cagny
Lascelles, Lieut. Viscount	WPW	3	18/ 6/44	Perugia
Lascelles, Lieut. J. F.	W	1	10/ 8/44	La Bottrie
Lawrence, Lieut. D. A. L.	W	6	24/ 9/43	Salerno
Lee, Major R. T.	KA	H.Q., 7 Gds. Bde.	8/ 3/41	London
Leeke, Lieut. R. H.	DW	Att. 3 W.G.	7/ 8/44	River Arno
Letcher, Lieut. R. P.	W	1	13/11/44	Gangelt
Llewellyn, Lieut. M. R. G.	W	5	12/ 7/44	Campi
Lloyd, Lieut.-Colonel J. A.	KA	2	28/ 5/40	Furnes (B.E.F.)
Loch, Lieut. Hon. S. D.	W	1	3/ 9/44	Pont-a-Marcq
„ Capt. „ „	W	1	31/ 3/45	Aalten
Longman, Lieut. R. S.	PW	5	7/ 2/44	Anzio
Lowe, Lieut. W. R. C. E. C.	W	1	6/ 9/44	Belgium
Lowry-Corry, Capt. M. W.	W	6	23/ 1/44	Minturno
Lumley-Savile, Lieut. Hon. H. L. T.	W	3	18/ 6/44	Perugia
Luttrell, Lieut. H. R. F.	KA	5	28/ 1/44	Anzio
Lyttleton, Lieut. J.	DW	3	11/10/44	M. Battaglia
Lyttleton, Lieut. J. A.	DW	5	24/ 2/44	Anzio
Maclean, Lieut. P.	W	3	4/ 2/43	Dj. Mansour
„ „ „	W	3	6/ 5/43	Medjez el Bab
„ Capt. „	KA	3	20/ 2/44	M. Ornito
McEwen, Lieut. J. N.	WPW	1	2/ 8/44	Arclais
Magill, Lieut. D. S.	W	4	18/ 4/45	Uelzen
Margetson, Lieut. N. S. T.	KA	6	16/ 3/43	Mareth Line
Marriott, Lieut. G. G. H.	W	5	27/ 4/43	Dj. Bou Aoukaz
Marriott, Capt. M. R. R.	DW	2	4/ 5/45	Zeven
Marriott, Capt. R. H. M.	W	1	2/ 8/44	Drouet
Marshall-Cornwall, Lieut. J. G. ..	KA	4	30/ 7/44	Caumont
Martin, Lieut. R. J.	W	5	23/ 4/43	Dj. Bou Aoukaz
„ „ „	W	H.Q., 24 Gds. Bde.		Italy
Meyrick, Lieut. P. J. O.	KA	6	24/ 9/43	Salerno
Micklem, 2/Lieut. G. H.	W	2	1/ 6/40	Furnes (B.E.F.).
Miller, Major W. E. P.	W	5	25/ 1/44	Anzio
Minnette-Lucas, Lieut. I. C. ..	KA	4	4/ 4/45	Minden
Misa, Lieut. H. F.	KA	2	11/ 8/44	Viessoix
Moller, Lieut. J. A.	KA	2	19/ 9/44	Nijmegen
Moller, Lieut. J. C.	KA	1	9/ 4/45	Dalum
Monteith, Capt. R. H.	DIAS	4	23/ 3/45	Rhineland
Murdoch, Lieut. R. C.	W	3	28/ 5/44	M. Grande

Name	*Casualty*	*Battalion*	*Date*	*Place*
Naylor-Leyland, Lieut. V. E. ..	W	5	3/ 2/45	M. Sole
Needham, Lieut. A. E. P.	W	5	25/ 1/44	Anzio
Needham, Capt. F. J. R. P.	W	3	4/ 2/43	Dj. Mansour
Nelson, Major E. J. B.	W	3	24/ 2/43	Kasserine Pass
" " "	W	5	25/ 1/44	Anzio
" Lieut.-Colonel E. J. B. ..	W	3	21/ 6/44	Perugia
Norman-Barnett, Major C. W. ..	W	5	4/ 5/43	Dj. Bou Aoukaz
Northumberland, Lieut. Duke of ..	KA	3	21/ 5/40	River Escaut (B.E.F.)
Nugent, Lieut. J. A.	KA	5	2/10/44	M. Catarelto
Nugent, Lieut. P. E. C.	KA	5	27/ 4/43	Dj. Bou Aoukaz
Ogilvie, Lieut. B. M.	W	5	26/ 4/43	Dj. Bou Aoukaz
Oldfield, Lieut. C. C. B.	W	6	6/ 4/43	Wadi Akarit
" " "	W	5	7/ 7/44	Campi
Orme, Capt. J. A.	W	5	10/ 2/44	Anzio
" " "	W	5	11/ 6/44	Bagnoregio
Owen, Lieut. J. G.	W	5	1/12/44	M. Sole
Owen, Lieut. R. J.	W	4	27/ 2/45	Weeze
Pakenham, Major H. D. W. ..	DW	2	2/ 6/40	Furnes (B.E.F.)
Parker, Lieut. T. O.	WBA	1	21/ 3/45	Gennep
Palau, Lieut. G. B.	W	1	2/ 8/44	Normandy
Parr, Lieut. R. P.	KA	6	30/ 1/44	Minturno
Pearson-Gregory, Lieut. J. S. M. ..	PWE	3	26/ 8/44	Florence
" " " " ..	W	3	3/10/44	M. Battaglia
Philpott, Lieut. (Qrmr.) E. V. ..	WBA	3	7/10/44	M. Battaglia
Pike, Lieut. D. E.	KA	1	5/ 3/45	Kapellern
Potter, Capt. G. E. W.	W	2	31/ 5/40	Furnes (B.E.F.)
Prescott, Lieut. P. G. A.	W	2	20/ 4/45	Heeslingen
Pritchard, Lieut. H. E.	KAS	2	11/ 3/43	England
Radford-Norcop, Capt. P. J. C. ..	DW	3	14/ 7/40	U.K. Wounded, River Escaut (B.E.F.), 21/5/40.
Ramsay, Capt. A. A. D.	W	3	24/ 4/43	Dj. Kournine
Rawlings, Lieut. P. G.	KA	2	23/ 7/44	Caen
Raynor, Lieut. A. P. St. C.	W	1	19/ 7/44	Cagny
Reeves, Lieut. T. C.	DWPW	1	24/ 4/45	Zeven
Renton, Lieut. J. E.	W	6	13/ 2/44	Minturno
Reynell-Pack, Lieut. H.	KA	3	21/ 5/40	River Escaut (B.E.F.)
Ridpath, Lieut. M. D.	KA	6	9/ 9/43	Salerno
Ridpath, Lieut. T. G.	KA	6	17/ 3/43	Mareth Line
Robertson, Major P. A. S.	W	1	22/ 7/44	Cagny
Robson, Capt. W. M.	W	1	3/ 4/45	Bentheim
Rocke, Lieut. G. F.	W	4	5/11/44	Meijel
Rogers, Lieut. R. D.	W	5	27/ 4/43	Dj. Bou Aoukaz
Rolleston, Lieut. S. C.	W	4	1/11/44	River Elbe
Rollo, Lieut. D. I.	WPWE	3	4/ 2/43	Dj. Mansour
Rollo, Lieut. E. J. S.	W	3	22/ 4/45	Fosso Cembalina
Rowan, Lieut. R. C.	W	6	17/ 3/43	Mareth Line
Rowley, Capt. J. F.	PW	3	26/ 8/44	Florence
Ruggles-Brise, Lieut. T. O.	KA	2	18/ 7/44	Cagny
Rutland, Capt. Duke of	W	1	3/ 4/45	Bentheim
Ryan, Lieut. A. R. B.	KA	2	9/ 4/45	Dalum
Ryott, Lieut. D. B.	W	1	30/ 4/45	Sandbostel

Name	Casualty	Battalion	Date	Place
Sainsbury, Lieut. O. M.	W	6	10/11/43	M. Camino
" " "	KA	6	30/ 1/44	Minturno
Saltoun, Lieut. The Master of ..	Missing	6	9/ 2/44	Minturno
Sanderson, Lieut. R. F.	W	5	25/ 7/44	Grenadier Ridge (Italy)
Savill, Lieut. A. J.	W	6	29/ 1/44	Minturno
Scarisbrick, Lieut. C. A.	W	3	15/ 9/44	Gothic Line
Scott, Lieut. J. W.	W	2	27/ 9/44	Heesch
Selby, Capt. R. W.	W	H.Q., Gds. Amd. Div.	22/ 8/44	Normandy
Sewell, Lieut. G. R. M.	W	2	7/10/44	Grave
Seymour, Lieut. J. E.	W	1	14/ 5/40	Louvain (B.E.F.)
Shephard, Lieut. J. H. G.	W	5	16/ 2/44	Anzio
Shephard, Lieut. P. le R.	KA	5	27/ 4/43	Dj. Bou Aoukaz
Sidney, Major W. P., V.C.	W	5	8/ 2/44	Anzio
Sloan, Lieut. J. K. W.	KA	6	17/ 3/43	Mareth Line
Smith, Major O. W. D.	W	3	28/ 5/40	Ypres-Comines Canal (B.E.F.)
Snell, Lieut. C. V. I.	KA	5	27/ 6/44	River Astrone
Stanley, Major H. F.	W	1	20/ 9/44	Nijmegen
Stiff, Lieut. N. G. J. H.	W	1	3/ 9/44	Pont-a-Marcq
Stokes-Roberts, Lieut. G. R. ..	KA	6	22/ 1/44	Minturno
Stourton, Lieut. Hon. C. E.	W	2	1/ 9/44	Albert
Strang-Steel, Lieut. J. M.	KA	6	16/ 3/43	Mareth Line
Streatfeild-Moore, Lieut. T. E. ..	W	3	10/10/44	M. Battaglia
Stucley, Major L. R. C.	DAS	H.Q., 201 Gds. Bde.	16/ 9/43	North Africa (taken ill at Salerno)
Sumner, Lieut. J. B.	W	4	6/ 8/44	Estry
Surtees, Lieut. R. V. N.	W	1	30/ 4/45	Sandbostel
Swift, Capt. I. R. K.	W	4	24/ 1/45	Maastricht Appendix
Talbot, 2/Lieut. R. E.	KA	1	27 /9/44	Heesch
Thomas, Lieut. R. D. D.	KA	3	2/ 8/44	River Arno
Thorne, Major G.	W	1	20/ 9/44	Nijmegen
Thorne, Lieut. P. F.	W	3	28/ 5/40	Ypres-Comines Canal (B.E.F.)
Thornton, Major D. H. B.	KA	H.Q., L'nd'n District	18/ 6/44	Guards' Chapel
Thwaites, Lieut. T. A.	W	6	9/ 9/43	Salerno
" " "	KA	5	12/ 6/44	Bagnoregio
Trenchard, Lieut. Hon. H.	KA	6	16/ 3/43	Mareth Line
Trimmer-Thompson, Lieut. C. E. A.	KA	6	17/ 3/43	Mareth Line
Tufnell, Lieut. H. J.	KA	6	11/ 3/43	Medenine
Tyser, Lieut. A.	W	1	11/ 8/44	Viessoix
Utterson-Kelso, Lieut. J. P.	KA	2	11/ 8/44	Viessoix
Vaughan, Lieut. E. B. M.	W	6	17/ 3/43	Mareth Line
" Capt. "	W	6	9/ 9/43	Salerno
" Major "	W	5	14/12/44	M. Sole.
Vereker, 2/Lieut. Hon. C. S. ..	DAS	H.Q., 7 Gds. Bde.	27/ 2/41	England
Verney, Lieut. H. A.	W	4	9/ 8/44	Estry
Vivian, Lieut. A. G.	PW	6	17/ 3/43	Mareth Line
" " "	KPW	6	15/ 9/43	N. Italy
Voeux, Major Sir W. R. de B. des, Bt.	W	H.Q., Airborne Div.	16/11/42	North Africa

Name	Casualty	Battalion	Date	Place
Voeux, Lieut.-Colonel Sir W. R. de B. des, Bt.	DW	156 Para. Regt.	19/ 9/44	Arnhem
Wace, Lieut. J. R. S.	W	6	8/11/43	Salerno
Wall, Capt. L. E. G.	KA	Westminster Garrison	18/ 6/44	Guards' Chapel
Way, Major A. G.	W	3	28/ 5/44	M. Grande
Wedderburn, Lieut. D. M. A. ..	PW	5	26/ 1/44	Anzio
Westmacott, Lieut. I. R.	W	1	20/ 9/44	Nijmegen
Westmacott, Capt. R. V. C.	W	H.Q., 24 Gds. Bde.	30/ 1/45	Italy
Whatman, Capt. J. D.	W	5	12/ 7/44	Campi
Wheatley, Lieut. C. M.	W	6	12/11/43	M. Camino
Whitley, Lieut. P. N.	W	2	2/ 8/44	Drouet
Wiggin, Lieut. J. H.	PW	6	17/ 3/43	Mareth Line
Wigram, Capt. Hon. F. C.	KA	6	11/ 9/43	Salerno
Williams, Lieut. C. I. M.	W	5	26/ 7/44	Grenadier Ridge (Italy)
Wills, Lieut. C. O. M.	KA	3	4/ 2/43	Dj. Mansour
Wills, Lieut. Hon. E. R. H.	W	3	4/ 2/43	Dj. Mansour
Wilson, Lieut. W. D.	KA	H.Q., 150 Inf. Bde.	4/42	M.E.
Winch, Lieut. A. D.	KA	4	24/ 1/45	Maastricht Appendix
Wodehouse, Lieut. A. B.	W	1	2/ 8/44	Drouet
Wollaston, Lieut. H. W.	W	4	7/ 8/44	Estry
Yuill, Lieut. A. E.	W	P.W. Sub-Mission	17/12/44	Greece

APPENDIX III

LIST OF FATAL CASUALTIES AMONG OTHER RANKS, 1939-45

LEGEND

The following legend is used:

KA .. .. Killed in Action.
KPW .. .. Killed while Prisoner of War.
KAS .. .. Killed on Active Service.
DW .. .. Died of Wounds.
DPW .. .. Died while Prisoner of War.
DWPW .. .. Died of Wounds while Prisoner of War.
DIAS .. .. Died of Injuries on Active Service.
DAS .. .. Died on Active Service.

An asterisk indicates an approximate date.

Number	*Name and Rank*	*Casualty*	*Battalion*	*Date*
2621156	Abbott, L./Cpl. P.	DW	6	17/ 9/43
2613615	Aby, Sergt. F.	DAS	1	12/ 9/42
2617410	Acock, Gdsm. C.	KA	3	5/ 2/43
2619775	Adcock, Gdsm. R.	KA	5	9/ 2/44
2619914	Ainger, Gdsm. W.	DW	5	20/12/44
6398344	Attfield, Gdsm. A.	KA	2	1/ 6/40
2622972	Anderson, Gdsm. H.	DW	1	2/ 9/44
2618650	Ash, Gdsm. H.	KA	6	17/ 3/43
2616216	Ashford, Gdsm. R.	DAS	3	15/ 6/43
2622271	Axon, Gdsm. A.	KA	2	3/ 8/44
2616256	Armitage, L./Sergt. A.	KA	6	9/ 9/43
2618190	Archer, Gdsm. E.	DW	5	26/ 1/44
2623355	Ancombe, Gdsm. D.	KA	4	30/ 3/45
2621187	Allam, L./Sergt. A.	KA	6	8/11/43
2622047	Asbury, Gdsm. L.	KA	6	17/ 3/43
2615075	Appleton, Gdsm. D.	KA	6	17/ 3/43
2622522	Allseybrook, Gdsm. F.	KA	6	17/ 3/43
2620823	Andrews, Gdsm. G.	KA	5	9/ 2/44
2616586	Ashley, Gdsm. P.	KA	H.Q., 1 G.B.	7/12/44
2617553	Arliss, Gdsm. T.	KA	5	27/ 4/43
2621529	Ayres, Gdsm. G.	KA	5	23/ 4/43
2616496	Allen, Gdsm. R.	KA	1	16/ 5/40
2616861	Aston, Sergt. D.	DW	4	13/10/44
2617890	Ayscough, Sergt. C.	DW	4	6/11/44
2625809	Alvey, Gdsm. J.	KA	1	31/ 3/45
2620142	Atkins, Gdsm. A.	DW	5	1/ 3/44
2615445	Arthurs, L./Cpl. D.	KA	1	2/ 6/44
2616840	Ansett, Gdsm. V.	DW	3	27/ 5/40
2621727	Ash, Gdsm. C.	KA	1	27/ 9/40
2617603	Atkinson, Gdsm. H.	KA	3	28/12/42
2620565	Atkin, Gdsm. D.	DW	5	27/ 4/43
2607409	Aldridge, C.S.M. C.	KA	1	1/ 6/40
2615899	Archer, Gdsm. A.	DAS	3	5/ 8/43
2613216	Atherton, Gdsm. J.	KA	3	21/ 5/40
2623393	Aslin, Gdsm. J.	KA	4	23/ 1/45
2623864	Atkins, L./Cpl. F.	KA	1	29/ 4/45
2613283	Anlezark, Gdsm. C.	KA	1	3/ 9/44
2622470	Allam, Gdsm. W.	KA	1	11/ 8/44

Number	Name and Rank	Casualty	Battalion	Date
2614561	Ballard, Gdsm. R.	KA	2	18/ 7/44
2616328	Bartlam, Gdsm. J.	KA	2	6/ 4/45
2618346	Bailey, L./Cpl. W.	KA	6	10/ 3/43
2620815	Barker, Gdsm. W.	KA	6	22/ 9/43
2623627	Baldwin, Gdsm. K.	DW	1	4/ 4/45
2622354	Barsby, Gdsm. J.	KA	2	20/ 4/45
2616710	Barfoot, Gdsm. E.	KA	2	18/ 7/44
2619970	Basnet, Gdsm. F.	KA	5	26/ 1/44
2622912	Barclay, Gdsm. F.	DW	3	18/ 9/44
2623157	Banton, Gdsm. T.	KA	6	6/12/43
2610923	Baker, Sergt. W.	KA	2	23/ 7/44
14223900	Barker, Gdsm. G.	DW	5	9/ 2/44
2623007	Bailey, L./Cpl. F.	KA	1	29/ 4/45
2564654	Badder, L./Sergt. E.	DW	1	3/11/44
2619186	Barnes, Gdsm. P.	DW	XIV	10/ 1/45
2615582	Bateman, Gdsm. L.	KA	6	11/ 9/43
2613348	Bakehouse, Gdsm. J.	DW	3	26/ 5/40
2616906	Backshell, L./Sergt. O.	KA	3	5/ 2/43
2613556	Barton, Gdsm. A.	KA	3	28/ 5/40
2612976	Banks, Sergt. R.	KA	3	5/ 2/43
2614133	Baker, L./Sergt. A., D.C.M.	KA	1 Commando	22/ 1/45
2621203	Baldwin, Gdsm. B.	DWPW	6	16/ 4/43
2617999	Baker, L./Sergt. G.	KA	5	23/ 4/43
2615008	Ball, Gdsm. C.	KA	1	16/ 5/40
2614105	Bailey, L./Cpl. A.	KA	6	17/ 3/43
2620695	Bates, Gdsm. T.	KA	6	17/ 3/43
2622286	Benson, Gdsm. A.	KA	6	17/ 3/43
2622238	Beswick, Gdsm. G.	KA	6	17/ 3/43
2620431	Bray, Gdsm. G.	KA	6	17/ 3/43
2617514	Bailey, Gdsm. C.	DAS	1	9/ 7/42
2622451	Bailey, L./Cpl. J.	KA	2	28/ 7/44
2622434	Barber, Gdsm. E.	DW	1	10/10/44
2619435	Barker, Cpl. R.	DAS	3	15/ 6/43
2619397	Bagshaw, Gdsm. J.	KA	6	10/ 9/43
2612698	Barratt, Gdsm. T.	KA	1	2/ 4/40*
2621721	Beverley, Gdsm. A.	DW	6	12/11/43
2616030	Bell, Gdsm. R.	DW	1	3/ 8/44
2622391	Bennett, Gdsm. A.	KA	2	27/ 7/44
2717859	Beal, Gdsm. F.	KA	1	27/ 9/44
2620731	Berry, Gdsm. G.	KAS	4	29/ 6/42
2621540	Beale, Gdsm. G.	KA	6	9/11/43
2617184	Beale, Gdsm. F.	KA	3	28/12/42
2615238	Bennett, L./Sergt. H.	DAS	6	11/ 1/43
2617255	Beecham, Gdsm. L.	KA	3	31/12/42
2622194	Bean, Gdsm. J.	KA	2	4/ 8/44
2623944	Bell, Gdsm. A.	KA	1	3/ 9/44
2616576	Bennett, Sergt. G.	KA	1	3/ 9/44
2622462	Berry, Gdsm. R.	DAS	1	21/10/43
2624572	Bennett, Gdsm. W.	KA	1	7/ 1/45
2621121	Benson, Gdsm. J.	DW	5	25/ 1/44
2612832	Beech, Gdsm. H.	DW	3	19/ 6/44
2615048	Belshaw, Gdsm. J.	KA	1	3/ 4/45
2614311	Beale, Sergt. F.	KA	2	5/ 3/45
2619042	Bearpark, Gdsm. N.	KA	6	9/12/43
2615924	Bentley, Gdsm. E.	KA	X List	29/ 5/40*
2615775	Bennett, Gdsm. W.	DAS	3	26/ 2/40
2618466	Belshaw, Gdsm. R.	KAS	4	20/10/40
3652644	Bellis, Gdsm. H.	KA	3	28/ 5/40
2624227	Best, Gdsm. R.	DAS	G.A.T.W.	8/ 9/40
2614763	Beech, L./Cpl. A.	KA	6	24/ 9/43
2618462	Bennett, Gdsm. J.	KA	5	27/ 1/44

Number	Name and Rank	Casualty	Battalion	Date
2622026	Bell, Gdsm. J.	KA	6	9/ 9/43
2621161	Begley, Gdsm. T.	KA	3	11/10/44
2614517	Bell, Gdsm. T.	KA	3	11/10/44
2617103	Betteridge, Gdsm. C.	KA	3	9/10/44
2619349	Burns, Gdsn. J.	KA	6	17/ 3/43
14220893	Bebbington, Gdsm. B.	KA	6	7/11/43
2620813	Bennett, L./Cpl. L.	KA	6	8/11/43
2621471	Birkin, Gdsm. C.	KA	5	30/10/44
2621188	Birch, Gdsm. M.	KA	3	20/ 6/44
2617155	Badger, L./Cpl. W.	KA	3	28/ 5/44
2616405	Bianchil, Sergt. S.	KA	3	28/ 5/44
2616140	Buckingham, L./Cpl. R.	KA	3	28/ 5/44
2616790	Bishop, Gdsm. L.	DW	XI List	9/10/43
829098	Birch, Gdsm. H.	KA	1	31/ 5/40*
2616128	Blackmore, Gdsm. A.	KA	6	8/11/43
2617736	Blanchard, Gdsm. R.	KA	6	11/ 9/43
2623797	Bland, Gdsm. K.	DW	5	25/ 6/44
2613418	Blower, L./Cpl. W.	DW	2	31/ 5/40*
2625816	Blythe, Gdsm. J.	KA	1	5/ 3/45
2622793	Bleach, Gdsm. F.	KA	5	19/ 7/44
2615042	Blaskett, C.S.M. F.	KA	5	27/ 4/43
2618884	Blewitt, L./Sergt. P.	DW	5	8/ 2/44
2617685	Blake, Sergt. G.	KA	4	5/11/44
2618423	Blenkarn, Gdsm. R.	KA	5	28/ 4/43
2622152	Bottomley, L./Cpl. W.	DW	5	22/ 2/44
2624294	Bodfish, Gdsm. C.	KA	1	27/ 9/44
2615209	Bond, L./Sergt. H.	KA	5	8/ 2/44
2614268	Box, Gdsm. W.	KA	2	30/ 5/40*
14681736	Bowers, Gdsm. E.	KA	1	23/ 9/44
2620119	Bowers, Gdsm. L.	KA	1	11/ 8/44
2617261	Bower, L./Cpl. A.	KAS	W.G. Bn.	18/ 6/44
2624532	Bowen, Gdsm. F.	KA	1	3/ 9/44
2621472	Boulton, Gdsm. J.	DAS	XIV	28/ 4/43
2622330	Boulton, Gdsm. H.	DWPW	6	11/ 2/44
2616613	Booth, L./Cpl. G.	KA	6	26/ 5/44
2618801	Bolton, Gdsm. J.	DAS	4	13/ 9/44
2621834	Bourne, Gdsm. A.	DW	5	20/12/44
2621395	Botterill, Gdsm. C.	DW	6	8/11/43
2620237	Bottrell, Gdsm. G.	KA	3	8/10/44
2618266	Bostock, Gdsm. R.	KAS	4	20/10/44
2626020	Boldero, Gdsm. J.	DAS	Depot	8/12/44
2618682	Bowler, Gdsm. M.	KA	4	30/ 7/44
2619824	Bonser, Gdsm. A.	KA	5	27/ 4/43
14582184	Booth, Gdsm. E.	KA	6	31/ 1/44
14702883	Brown, Gdsm. W.	DW	1	7/ 1/45
2614982	Brownlee, Gdsm. J.	DW	1	1/ 8/44
2615517	Bradney, Gdsm. R.	DAS	1	19/ 5/43
2620462	Broughton, Gdsm. S.	KAS	W.G. Bn.	18/ 6/44
2615316	Brown, Gdsm. G.	KA	3	21/ 5/40
2623856	Bowes, Gdsm. W.	DW	1	3/ 8/44
2614577	Bryant, Gdsm. J.	KA	2	31/ 8/44
2619638	Brown, Gdsm. L.	KA	5	2/ 8/44
2615265	Breen, Sergt. A.	KA	1	29/ 4/45
2620604	Bragger, Gdsm. C.	DW	6	12/ 9/43
2623229	Broad, Gdsm. C.	KA	2	10/ 9/44
2625561	Brown, Gdsm. F.	DW	3	25/ 3/45
2619566	Brewer, L./Cpl. H.	KA	1	20/ 9/44
4857849	Bramwill, Gdsm. D.	KA	5	27/ 3/43
2614614	Brown, Gdsm. A.	DW	6	12/ 9/43
2621728	Bayliss, Gdsm. K.	DW	6	22/ 9/43
2620221	Brown, Gdsm. J.	KA	6	10/12/43

Number	Name and Rank	Casualty	Battalion	Date
3447800	Brown, L./Cpl. W.	KA	1	3/ 9/44
6201592	Browne, Gdsm. D.	DW	1	1/ 6/40*
2616198	Browne, Gdsm. H.	KA	1	1/ 2/40*
2622089	Brocklebank, Gdsm. J.	DW	6	1/ 5/43
2615314	Bradley, Gdsm. W.	DW	3	27/ 5/40
2615183	Browning, L./Cpl. C.	KA	6	10/ 9/43
2625161	Brown, Gdsm. S.	DW	1	11/ 4/45
2616018	Bridle, Gdsm. C.	KA	1	1/ 6/40*
2616234	Brown, Sergt. B.	KA	6	17/ 3/43
2614424	Brown, Sergt. L.	DW	1	20/ 9/44
2615328	Brimilconbe, L./Sergt. A.	KA	3	19/ 5/40
2618868	Brewin, Gdsm. W.	DW	3	14/10/44*
2614462	Bradbury, Gdsm. C.	DAS	2	16/ 9/39
2623057	Brighton, Gdsm. C.	DW	6	13/ 9/43
2619679	Birkin, L./Sergt. R.	DW	6	29/ 1/44
2615299	Brighton, L./Sergt. J.	DW	6	30/ 1/44
2612605	Brandrick, Gdsm. A.	KA	6	30/ 1/44
2621267	Brookshank, Gdsm. J.	KA	6	30/ 1/44
2620027	Brown, Gdsm. R.	KAS	Depot, Chelsea	27/ 9/40
4104749	Bridgwater, Gdsm. J.	KA	3	8/ 3/44
2619479	Brett, L./Sergt. J.	KA	3	10/ 6/44
2622139	Brooks, Gdsm. N.	KA	5	23/ 4/43
2621724	Byron, Gdsm. R.	KA	5	23/ 4/43
2622254	Bradley, Gdsm. A.	DW	6	7/11/43*
2619724	Brownlow, Gdsm. J.	KA	5	4/ 5/43
2616663	Brown, Gdsm. W.	DW	2	10/ 4/45
2614989	Bradbury, Gdsm. S.	KA	3	21/ 5/40
2620767	Brasted, L./Sergt. P.	KA	6	11/ 9/43
2623580	Brookes, Gdsm. J.	DW	5	11/11/44
6297229	Brown, Gdsm. J.	KA	4	23/ 1/45
2613956	Brewer, Gdsm. R.	KA	1	1/ 6/40*
2620340	Brown, Gdsm. K.	KA	6	9/11/43
2623301	Brown, Gdsm. F.	KA	6	24/ 9/43
2623509	Burton, Gdsm. D.	KA	5	9/ 2/44
2613952	Buckley, Gdsm. T.	KA	1	1/ 6/40*
2617996	Burton, Gdsm. A.	KA	5	27/ 4/43
2618871	Buckerfield, Gdsm. P.	KA	1	27/ 9/44
2623361	Butler, Gdsm. F.	KA	5	8/ 2/44
2621153	Bulcock, Gdsm. T.	DW	5	10/ 2/44
2615528	Butterfield, L./Cpl. R.	DAS	1	13/11/41
2612364	Bunce, C.Q.M.S. G.	DW	1	30/ 5/40
2620369	Buckett, Gdsm. T.	KA	6	8/ 4/44
2610921	Bushrod, Gdsm. C.	DAS	2	14/ 4/42
2613488	Burnett, L./Cpl. W.	KA	3	21/ 5/40*
2722906	Burke, Gdsm. D.	DW	6	7/ 2/44
2613138	Buckley, L./Cpl. W.	KA	3	21/ 5/40
2617587	Burton, Gdsm. R.	KA	1	23/ 9/44
2616656	Bunting, Gdsm. R.	KA	257 C.D.S.	4/ 8/44
2613225	Bugg, Gdsm. W.	KA	2	31/ 5/40*
2609951	Butler, C.S.M. J.	KA	2	1/ 6/40
6286759	Button, Gdsm. G.	KA	3	21/ 5/40
2614959	Bywater, L./Sergt. D.	KA	1	11/ 8/44
2624251	Byrne, Gdsm. D.	DW	3	26/ 6/44
2620816	Cartwright, Gdsm. F.	KA	5	28/ 1/44
2617201	Carruthers, Gdsm. J.	KA	3	28/12/42
2623137	Carpenter, Gdsm. A.	KA	6	31/ 1/44
2621007	Cable, Gdsm. R.	KA	6	8/ 4/44
2616121	Cass, L./Sergt. G.	KA	XI	5/11/43
2613030	Cassford, P.S.M. A.	DW	3	29/ 5/40

Number	Name and Rank	Casualty	Battalion	Date
2615410	Cawthray, Gdsm. F.	KA	2	31/ 5/40*
823356	Caley, Gdsm. G.	KA	3	21/ 5/40
873182	Carter, Gdsm. J.	KA	3	21/ 5/40
2615676	Carlan, Gdsm. D.	KA	4	5/11/44
2616671	Calvert, Gdsm. W.	KA	5	4/ 5/43
2622816	Carver, Gdsm. H.	KA	2	9/ 4/45
2621942	Canning, Gdsm. G.	DAS	1	11/ 6/43
2624469	Cave, Gdsm. J.	KAS	W.G. Bn.	18/ 6/44
2624041	Catteral, Gdsm. R.	DW	1	4/ 9/44
2625744	Cann, Gdsm. F.	DW	1	11/ 4/45
2619780	Cammack, L./Sergt. L.	DW	5	13/ 7/44
2620319	Canning, L./Sergt. J.	DW	5	25/ 1/44
2622276	Cartwright, Gdsm. J.	KA	5	5/ 5/43
2613348	Cattermole, Gdsm. A.	KA	3	21/ 5/40
2612356	Carrick, Sergt. J.	DW	5	13/ 7/44
2617766	Checkly, L./Cpl. E.	KA	6	24/ 9/43
2031751	Chifney, L./Cpl. K.	DW	5	12/ 6/44
2617566	Chell, Gdsm. A.	KA	5	26/ 1/44
2615398	Chapman, L./Cpl. G.	KA	3	8/11/44
2615800	Chapman, Gdsm. W.	KA	3	21/ 1/40
862719	Charter, Gdsm. T.	KA	1	1/ 6/40
2619510	Charnock, Gdsm. E.	KA	3	5/ 2/43
2616729	Challacombe, L./Cpl. G.	KA	5	23/ 4/43
2614706	Chandler, Gdsm. H.	KA	2	1/ 6/40*
2621998	Charlton, Gdsm. W.	KA	6	17/ 3/43
2617267	Chipchase, Gdsm. J.	DW	1	7/ 1/45
2618825	Christmas, Gdsm. L.	DW	5	26/ 6/44
2621576	Churchill, Gdsm. B.	KA	6	9/ 9/43
2623882	Charlton, L./Cpl. D.	KA	1	3/ 9/44
2619737	Chapman, Gdsm. J.	KA	5	29/ 8/44
2620834	Christopher, Gdsm. A.	KA	3	10/ 6/44
2622163	Chapman, L./Sergt. R.	DW	1	3/ 4/45
2614197	Clay, Sergt. G.	KA	2	27/ 9/44
2622421	Clements, Gdsm. E.	DW	6	27/ 9/43
2621023	Clarke, Gdsm. H.	KA	3	22/ 4/44
2732808	Clarke, Gdsm. S.	KA	6	31/ 1/44
2621317	Clayton, Gdsm. G.	DW	6	11/11/43
2624289	Clayton, Gdsm. R.	DW	1	19/ 1/45
2620912	Clarke, Gdsm. W.	KA	2	13/ 4/45
2615948	Clarke, Gdsm. B.	KA	6	17/ 3/43
2624475	Clayton, L./Cpl. H.	KA	1	29/ 3/45
14220897	Clough, Gdsm. H.	KA	4	6/ 8/44
2619320	Clarke, Gdsm. S.	KA	1	22/ 7/44
2616159	Clogg, Gdsm. A.	KA	6	17/ 3/43
2612110	Clarke, Gdsm. A.	KA	1	2/ 6/40*
6344525	Clarke, Gdsm. C.	KAS	Holding Bn.	10/ 5/41*
2621692	Clough, L./Sergt. N.	KA	6	31/ 1/44
2620229	Cole, Gdsm. H.	KA	6	30/ 1/44
2622619	Cope, Gdsm. R.	KA	5	27/ 4/43
7691232	Conroy, Gdsm. C.	KA	1	5/ 9/44
2623697	Cokayne, Gdsm. F.	KA	1	26/ 9/44
2615581	Corbett, Gdsm. J.	DAS	Training Bn.	3/ 8/42
2615902	Cosser, Gdsm. D.	DW	3	28/ 5/40
2618327	Cotterill, Gdsm. T.	DW	5	7/ 5/43
2618164	Cotterell, Gdsm. L.	DW	6	23/ 9/43
2619699	Coram, Gdsm. J.	DAS	5	27/ 5/43
2617871	Cowen, Gdsm. F.	DW	5	1/ 2/44
2612042	Cooper, Gdsm. A.	KAS	E.R.E. 21/A.G.	20/ 2/44
2621482	Cort, Gdsm. F.	DW	6	17/ 3/43
2621141	Cook, Gdsm. H.	DW	6	13/ 9/43
2612948	Cole, Gdsm. T.	KA	2	20/ 9/44

Number	Name and Rank	Casualty	Battalion	Date
2611778	Cossins, L./Sergt. H.	KA	6	7/11/43
2618808	Cooking, Gdsm. J.	KA	3	11/ 2/44
2613101	Cooper, L./Sergt. W.	KA	5 G.A.B.	1/ 8/44
2620812	Cooper, L./Sergt. L.	KA	XIV	6/ 8/44
2619529	Cook, L./Cpl. W.	KA	6	17/ 3/43
2618863	Cooper, Gdsm. P.	KA	6	10/ 9/43
2622037	Cooke, L./Cpl. R.	DW	3	16/ 8/44
2623595	Coles, Gdsm. R.	KA	5	26/ 1/44
2614746	Couchman, Gdsm. R.	KA	5	25/ 7/44
2620710	Cottle, L./Cpl. R.	KA	6	4/12/43
2616260	Cottrell, Gdsm. A.	KA	3	21/ 5/40
2617112	Cooch, L./Cpl. D.	KA	6	8/11/43
2618869	Cook, L./Cpl. R.	KA	5	23/ 4/43
5047810	Cooper, L./Cpl. S.	KA	1	31/ 5/40*
2618085	Cockton, L./Cpl. J.	KA	5	30/ 4/43
2611193	Cox, Sergt. S.	KA	6	24/ 3/43
2615649	Cook, Gdsm. J.	KA	1	1/ 6/40*
2616101	Cole, Gdsm. S.	DW	2	22/ 5/40
2619698	Copperthwaite, Gdsm. W.	KA	1	10/ 9/44
2616235	Cook, Gdsm. R.	KA	3	21/ 5/40
2623068	Cooper, Gdsm. R.	KA	2	18/ 7/44
2622812	Cook, L./Cpl. S.	KA	4	4/ 4/45
2612974	Cooper, L./Sergt. J.	KA	2	4/ 8/44
2618934	Cox, L./Sergt. G.	KA	1	3/ 4/45
2622082	Cockings, Gdsm. L.	KA	3	26/ 5/44
2615831	Cornall, Gdsm. R.	KA	1	31/ 5/40*
2619814	Collishaw, Gdsm. W.	DW	5	26/ 1/44
2616165	Creswell, L./Sergt. F.	KA	6	25/ 9/43
2613459	Cracknell, Gdsm. S.	DW	3	27/ 5/40
2621903	Crossley, Gdsm. C.	DAS	3	5/ 8/43
2623947	Croucher, Gdsm. P.	KA	1	3/ 8/44
2624105	Crouch, Gdsm. C.	DAS	Training Bn.	19/ 5/44
14498932	Crofts, Gdsm. A.	KAS	W.G. Bn.	18/ 6/44
2613023	Critchlow, Gdsm. G.	KA	2	16/ 5/40
2621791	Crewe, L./Cpl. A.	DW	6	22/ 1/44
2611246	Crooks, Gdsm. R.	KA	201 G.B.	4/12/43
2624120	Craven, Gdsm. R.	KA	1	27/ 9/44
2616787	Crosby, Gdsm. R.	KA	1	13/ 8/44
2617526	Crooks, Gdsm. D.	DW	2	22/ 9/44
2622833	Cullen, Gdsm. B.	KA	6	31/ 1/44
2622457	Curry, Gdsm. P.	KA	6	9/11/43
2621946	Curtis, Gdsm. C.	KA	5	27/ 3/43
2610501	Cutler, C.S.M. W.	DW	2	31/ 5/40*
2615159	Cupper, L./Sergt. A.	DW	6	3/10/43
14499452	Curry, Gdsm. E.	KAS	W.G. Bn.	18/ 6/44
2623752	Cupit, Gdsm. G.	DW	XIV	26/ 5/44
2621545	Curryer, Gdsm. E.	KA	6	17/ 3/43
2617239	Darby, Gdsm. W.	DW	5	20/ 7/44
2614722	Davis, Gdsm. J.	DW	XIV	29/ 1/44
2618787	Davenport, Gdsm. F.	DAS	"Y" List	30/12/43
2619701	Davies, Gdsm. L.	KA	6	17/ 3/43
2619613	Davey, Gdsm. R.	KA	6	15/10/43
2623578	Davies, Gdsm. R.	KA	XIV	10/ 2/44
2621972	Downs, Gdsm. J.	DPW	3	15/ 5/43
2616201	Davis, Gdsm. D.	KA	5	30/ 4/43
2623920	Daldry, L./Cpl. E.	KA	5	25/ 6/44
2622447	Davis, Gdsm. H.	KA	5	25/ 6/44
2620550	Davies, L./Cpl. A.	KA	3	29/ 5/44
2614439	Davis, Gdsm. F.	DAS	6	11/ 1/44
2623517	Davis, Gdsm. H.	KA	1	11/ 8/44

Number	*Name and Rank*	*Casualty*	*Battalion*	*Date*
2617509	Davies, Gdsm. H.	KA	5	26/ 1/44
2620692	Davies, Gdsm. A.	KA	5	25/ 1/44
2620241	Davis, Gdsm. A.	KA	6	10/ 9/43
2619700	Davies, Gdsm. L.	KA	6	16/ 3/43*
799178	Davies, Gdsm. A.	KA	6	13/11/43
2621631	Davies, L./Cpl. P.	KA	5	17/ 4/43
2614362	Dawson, L./Cpl. H.	KA	2	3/ 6/40
2615726	David, Sergt. W.	KA	2	27/ 7/44
2612102	Davies, Gdsm. G.	KA	6	5/12/43
2620036	Davies, L./Sergt. E.	KA	5	26/ 7/44
2614946	Daniels, Gdsm. D.	KA	3	21/ 5/40
5882360	Denton, Gdsm. H.	KA	XIV	15/ 7/44
6607559	Deferm, Gdsm. S.	KA	2	20/ 5/40
557505	Dexter, L./Cpl. H.	KA	3	21/ 5/40
2616397	Denny, Gdsm. T.	KA	6	8/11/43
2623067	Dear, Gdsm. W.	KA	2	3/ 8/44
2618303	Denny, Gdsm. C.	KA	5	28/ 4/43
2619657	Denton, L./Sergt. L.	DW	5	28/ 4/43
2621695	Devall, Gdsm. A.	KA	5	25/ 6/44
2623256	Dean, Gdsm. R.	KA	3 Commando	6/ 6/44
2623941	Dennis, L./Sergt. L.	KA	1	9/ 4/45
2618671	Delaney, L./Sergt. W.	KA	5	27/ 6/44
2617610	Dean, Gdsm. W.	KA	5	22/ 9/44
2617852	Dench, Gdsm. A.	KA	XI	5/10/43
2620988	Davies, Gdsm. H.	KA	5	27/ 4/43
2618162	Dewey, Gdsm. E.	KA	6	10/ 9/43
2611998	Dicken, Gdsm. B.	DW	1	21/ 7/44
2625419	Dixon, Gdsm. R.	DW	1	11/ 4/45
2613212	Diamond, Gdsm. P.	KA	3	6/10/44
2610908	Ditchett, Gdsm. E.	KA	3	21/ 5/40
2613568	Doyle, Gdsm. W.	KA	3	21/ 5/40*
2616282	Dove, Gdsm. R.	DAS	"Y" List	9/ 9/43
2624811	Down, Gdsm. R.	DW	1	23/ 9/44
2622024	Douglas, Gdsm. J.	KA	6	17/ 3/43
2617911	Dolphin, Gdsm. J.	KA	5	25/ 1/44
2618213	Doughty, L./Sergt. J.	DWPW	6	9/11/43
2611284	Dobson, Gdsm. J.	KA	3	28/ 5/40
2624557	Draper, Gdsm. A.	DW	XIV	26/ 9/44
2619077	Draycott, L./Sergt. W.	KA	1	20/ 9/44
2617961	Drew, L./Sergt. H.	KA	5	25/ 1/44
2617917	Draper, Gdsm. H.	KA	3	22/ 1/43
2623705	Dryden, Gdsm. G.	KA	5	9/ 2/44
2622336	Drage, Gdsm. C.	DW	5	19/ 7/44
2615003	Draycott, Gdsm. G.	KA	3	19/ 5/40
2611693	Dryden, Sergt. C.	KA	3	19/ 5/40
2625678	Drane, Gdsm. F.	DW	1	8/ 2/45
2615635	Draycott, Gdsm. J.	KA	2	1/ 6/40
2625582	Dudgeon, Gdsm. R.	KA	3	22/ 4/45
831680	Du-Feu, Gdsm. L.	KA	1	11/ 8/44
2616382	Dunett, Gdsm. F.	KA	6	16/ 5/43
769279	Durdle, Gdsm. T.	KA	3	28/ 5/40
2615556	Dutton, Gdsm. W.	KA	3	21/ 5/40
2618813	Dye, Sergt. E.	KA	4	23/ 1/45
2623534	Eason, Gdsm. P.	DW	5	28/ 6/44
4193347	Eaton, Gdsm. P.	KA	2	10/ 4/45
2616286	Eaton, L./Sergt. S.	KA	1	3/ 9/44
2619925	Eastwood, Gdsm. W.	KA	5	25/ 6/44
2616082	Easton, L./Cpl. F.	KA	3	28/ 5/40
3782765	Eastwood, Gdsm. J.	KA	5	25/ 7/44
2622433	Ecclestone, Gdsm. G.	KA	1	3/ 9/44

Number	Name and Rank	Casualty	Battalion	Date
2619767	Edgley, Gdsm. L.	KA	2	3/ 9/44
46835	Edge, Gdsm. N.	DW	2	14/ 6/40
2616253	Edwards, L./Sergt. J.	KA	6	17/ 3/43
2616602	Edwards, L./Cpl. A.	KA	2	9/ 8/44
2623149	Elliot, Gdsm. A.	DW	6	24/ 8/43
2612045	Eggleston, Gdsm. J.	KA	2	29/ 5/40
4857983	Eggington, Gdsm. T.	KA	1	1/ 6/40
2614925	Ellerington, L./Cpl. W.	KA	3	21/ 5/40
2616544	Elway, Gdsm. W.	KA	2	28/ 4/45
2623773	Ellis, Gdsm. C.	KA	2	19/ 9/44
2622845	Elliot, Gdsm. J.	KA	3	11/10/44
2621579	Elcome, Gdsm. F.	KA	5	11/ 6/44
2619656	Ellison, Gdsm. J.	DW	6	18/ 3/43
2617141	Emerson, L./Sergt. F.	KA	5	4/ 2/44
5381648	Entwisle, Sergt. M.	DW	6	17/ 3/43
2614742	Evans, Gdsm. R.	DW	3	27/ 1/43
2613366	Evason, Sergt. J.	KA	6	10/ 9/43
2612838	Evans, Gdsm. H.	KA	1	1/ 6/40
2620788	Everin, L./Sergt. S.	DW	2	3/12/44
2617457	Fairweather, L./Cpl. R.	KA	5	2/10/44
2618927	Farr, Gdsm. J.	KA	5	23/ 4/43
2621664	Fairclough, Gdsm. H.	KA	6	17/ 3/43
2623718	Faithful, Gdsm. H.	KA	1	2/ 8/44
2613320	Falls, Gdsm. J.	KA.	1 G.B.	18/ 5/40
2622282	Fairbrother, Gdsm. J.	KA	6	16/ 9/43
2614298	Farnworth, L./Cpl. G.	KA	1	12/ 8/44
2610986	Fagg, L./Sergt. F.	DW	5	12/ 6/44*
2622121	Fairclough, Gdsm. W.	DAS	5	17/ 6/43
2622719	Faulder, Gdsm. A.	DW	3	10/ 6/44
2623277	Fairclough, Gdsm. J.	KA	6	29/ 1/44
2623466	Finch, Gdsm. A.	DAS	5	28/ 8/43
2617905	Finney, L./Sergt. J.	KA	2	11/ 8/44
2621070	Finney, Gdsm. J.	DAS	5	13/ 9/43
2623748	Finch, L./Cpl. E.	KA	2	3/ 9/44
2613303	Flannagan, C.S.M. W.	DW	3	3/12/44
5836337	Fordham, Gdsm. J.	DW	5	26/ 7/44
2621319	Fleming, Gdsm. G.	KA	6	9/ 9/43
2618855	Fletcher, Gdsm. D.	KA	5	26/ 4/43
2623396	Floyd, Gdsm. D.	KA	5	11/ 6/44
3712394	Fletcher, L./Sergt. A.	KA	3	29/ 7/44
2619396	Foster, Sergt. T.	KA	5	29/ 4/43
2616908	Forrester, L./Sergt. R.	DW	5	25/ 1/44
2616742	Fox, Gdsm. T.	KA	2	10/ 4/45
2613879	Ford, Gdsm. H.	DW	5	13/ 6/40
2615600	Fortune, Gdsm. R.	DPW	3	27/ 1/43
2612702	Folder, Sergt. D.	KA	2	4/ 8/44
2616754	Fowler, Gdsm. E.	KA	1	11/ 8/44
2620886	Foxley, L./Sergt. J.	DAS	5	18/ 3/43
2621163	Forrester, Gdsm. T.	DAS	Holding Bn.	25/ 6/41
2618938	Frith, Gdsm. J.	DW	1	17/11/44
14680864	French, Gdsm. G.	DW	1	3/11/44
1066403	Frewin, P.S.M. W.	DPW	3	22/ 6/40
6102628	French, Gdsm. A.	KA	6	17/ 3/43
2615001	France, L./Sergt. J.	KA	6	10/ 9/43
2612088	Fuller, Gdsm. A.	KA	1	30/ 3/45
2616413	Fussey, Gdsm. R.	DW	2	1/ 6/40
2624121	Gates, Gdsm. D.	DAS	2	12/ 1/45
2623456	Garner, Gdsm. R.	KA	4	14/10/44
2622768	Gamble, Gdsm. H.	DAS	Training Bn.	11/ 6/42

Number	Name and Rank	Casualty	Battalion	Date
2622046	Gale, L./Cpl. C.	DW	6	13/ 9/43
2620496	Gardner, Gdsm. A.	KA	5	21/ 4/43
2616343	Gardner, Gdsm. J.	DW	1	1/ 9/44
2618050	Gale, Gdsm. G.	DAS	3	23/ 4/41
2612111	Gash, Gdsm. W.	KA	3	21/ 5/40
2618534	Gardner, Sergt. H.	KA	4	21/ 4/45
2619728	Gardener, Gdsm. H.	KA	5	27/ 4/43
2622616	Gammell, Gdsm. K.	DW	6	24/12/43
2611838	Garrod, L./Sergt. B.	KA	5	27/ 3/43
2622432	Gerrard, L./Sergt. T.	KA	1	3/ 9/44
2619437	Gent, L./Cpl. E.	KA	2	12/ 9/44
2613824	Gee, Gdsm. J.	DPW	"S" List	3/11/41
5182911	George, Gdsm. R.	DW	3	28/ 5/40
2621493	Gell, L./Cpl. J.	DW	5	6/ 7/44
2622526	Gilbert, L./Cpl. J.	DAS	Training Bn.	18/ 5/43
2613606	Gibbs, Gdsm. F.	DW	3	27/ 5/40
2620910	Gillies, Gdsm. A.	DAS	4	2/ 8/42
2619784	Gilliver, Gdsm. R.	DW	5	28/ 4/43
2621533	Gifford-England, L./Cpl. S.	KA	201 G.B.	4/12/43
2616849	Gilbert, Gdsm. J.	DW	X List	28/ 5/40
2616827	Gosnay, Gdsm. J.	DAS	1	8/ 2/43
2623369	Goodman, Gdsm. P.	KA	2	10/ 4/45
2617321	Goulding, Gdsm. E.	KAS	2	29/ 6/42
2615305	Goodlad, Sergt. J.	DW	3	28/ 5/44
2624903	Gould, Gdsm. R.	KA	1	5/ 3/45
2622477	Golby, Gdsm. L.	KA	5	12/ 6/44
2613175	Goodman, L./Cpl. H.	KA	2	20/ 4/45
2613711	Goodman, L./Cpl. J.	DW	2	31/ 5/40*
2616928	Gooch, L./Cpl. A.	KA	6	11/ 9/43
2615217	Goodwin, Gdsm. G.	KA	3	18/ 6/44
2622863	Greenhalgh, L./Cpl. T.	KA	5	28/ 1/44
2608035	Grey, Gdsm. J.	DAS	XIV	1/ 3/43
2616174	Gregory, Gdsm. G.	DAS	"Y" List	2/ 4/41
2620926	Grayson, Gdsm. S.	KA	5	27/ 4/43
4802756	Grimsdell, Gdsm. A.	KA	2	25/ 9/44
14673759	Gridley, Gdsm. F.	KA	1	27/ 9/44
2623615	Graves, Gdsm. M.	DW	5	12/ 6/44
2617972	Grundy, L./Cpl. W.	KA	3	10/ 6/44
2617543	Greenwood, Gdsm. A.	KA	4	3/11/44
2618831	Green, Gdsm. F.	DW	5	20/ 7/44
2616215	Grandfield, Gdsm. L.	KA	3	21/ 5/40
2624254	Grant, Gdsm. D.	DAS	Depot	13/ 9/43
2620795	Green, Gdsm. C.	DW	4	4/ 8/44
2623039	Grewcock, Gdsm. G.	DW	6	26/10/43
4535420	Greaves, Gdsm. F.	DW	6	10/10/43
2618562	Griffin, Gdsm. E.	KA	5	23/ 4/43
2619883	Griffin, Gdsm. J.	KA	5	27/ 4/43
2617390	Grose, Gdsm. W.	KA	2 Commando	28/ 3/42
2621985	Gray, L./Cpl. T.	DW	5	27/ 4/43
2616023	Green, Gdsm. F.	DW	1	10/ 5/40*
2624423	Greenwood, Gdsm. D.	DW	4	7/ 4/45
2622549	Grindley, Gdsm. R.	KA	5	27/ 4/43
2619881	Graham, Gdsm. H.	DW	6	8/10/43
2621489	Granby, Gdsm. J.	DW	6	17/ 3/43*
2621643	Green, Gdsm. C.	DW	5	28/ 3/43
2621489	Granby, Gdsm. L.	KA	6	17/ 3/43
2623981	Green, Gdsm. H.	KA	2	29/ 4/45
2611534	Green, Gdsm. M.	KA	6	17/ 3/43
2619379	Green, Gdsm. W.	KA	6	17/ 3/43
2614515	Grogan, Sergt. T.	KA	6	28/ 1/44
2622561	Gunn, Gdsm. G.	DAS	5	12/ 6/43

Number	Name and Rank	Casualty	Battalion	Date
2619742	Harris, L./Cpl. F.	KA	6	31/ 1/44
2611158	Hammond, Gdsm. S.	KA	6	9/11/43
2617057	Hambleton, Sergt. H.	KA	6	17/ 3/43
2626500	Harvey, Gdsm. R.	DAS	Depot	19/ 2/45
2620752	Harley, Gdsm. R.	KA	6	30/ 1/44
2619540	Hartley, L./Sergt. R.	KA	6	17/ 3/43
2622803	Hards, L./Sergt. F.	DW	5	7/ 2/44
2622170	Hatton, Gdsm. J.	KA	2	10/ 4/45
2621337	Hardy, Gdsm. G.	KA	3	8/ 3/44
2622272	Hartley, L./Cpl. H.	KA	5	10/ 2/44
2622953	Hall, Gdsm. K.	DW	3	24/ 4/43
2621029	Hazlehurst, Gdsm. W.	DW	3	5/ 2/43
2615954	Hawkins, Gdsm. H.	KA	3	21/ 5/40
2612039	Hancock, Gdsm. J.	KA	2	31/ 5/40*
2615104	Hall, L./Cpl. C.	DW	5	20/ 2/44
2614623	Hadgett, Cpl. A.	DW	5	8/11/44
2611470	Hamer, Gdsm. W.	KA	3	9/ 8/44
2612418	Hayes, Gdsm. S.	KA	3	21/ 5/40
2615053	Hall, Sergt. G.	DW	1	10/ 9/44
2615486	Haddon, Gdsm. L.	KA	6	27/ 1/44
2615361	Hazlegrove, Gdsm. T.	DW	5	25/ 1/44
2620851	Hambleton, Gdsm. T.	KA	6	31/ 1/44
2622212	Harper, L./Sergt. M.	KA	5	30/10/44
2625784	Hardy, Gdsm. M.	KA	1	29/ 4/45
2620986	Harlow, Gdsm. V.	DW	6	17/10/43
5176858	Haynes, Gdsm. W.	KA	6	6/12/43
2622402	Harvey, L./Cpl. G.	KA	5	27/ 7/44
2617087	Harris, Gdsm. J.	KA	5	2/ 8/44
2622781	Harrison, Gdsm. J.	KA	5	26/ 7/44
2622065	Hallam, Gdsm. R.	KA	6	17/ 3/43
2618616	Hawksworth, Gdsm. G.	KA	5	26/ 1/44
2615680	Harriman, Gdsm. T.	KA	6	10/ 9/43
2612299	Hancock, Gdsm. W.	DW	5	3/11/44
2622802	Hallsworth, L./Sergt. H.	KA	1	5/ 9/44
2621419	Haylor, Gdsm. P.	KA	6	21/ 9/43
2612826	Hancock, Gdsm. W.	DW	2	31/ 5/40*
11408360	Hague, Gdsm. H.	DW	1	23/ 4/45
2624437	Hackman, L./Cpl. B.	DW	1	27/ 9/44*
2624945	Hayler, Gdsm. W.	DW	1	3/ 4/45
2617893	Harper, L./Sergt. S.	KA	1	13/ 8/44
2621230	Hargrave, L./Cpl. F.	DAS	Training Bn.	21/ 4/42
2622960	Hall, Gdsm. L.	KA	5	19/ 7/44
14220377	Haill, Gdsm. W.	KA	5	2/ 1/45
2623088	Harman, Gdsm. F.	DW	6	10/ 9/43
2620643	Hardy, Gdsm. W.	DW	5	4/ 2/44
2615360	Hayes, Gdsm. F.	KA	S.S. Unit	27/12/41
2616062	Hartley, Gdsm. J.	KA	2	1/ 6/40*
2622266	Harris, Gdsm. W.	KA	5	12/ 7/44
2619829	Hampson, Gdsm. A.	KA	5	30/ 4/43
2622607	Harmsworth, Gdsm. R.	KA	6	17/ 3/43
878433	Haigh, Sergt. W.	KA	3	21/12/44
2613354	Hardy, Gdsm. W., M.M.	DW	3	27/ 5/40
2613779	Harris, L./Cpl. R.	DW	3	28/ 5/40
2623768	Hamblin, Gdsm. G.	KA	1	20/ 9/44
2615211	Hastings, L./Sergt. J.	KA	1	28/11/44
2617370	Hammond, Gdsm. W.	KA	6	17/ 3/43
2617483	Hall, L./Cpl. S.	KA	4	6/ 8/44
2624817	Haizelden, Gdsm. A.	DW	1	13/11/44
2624157	Herridge, Gdsm. R.	KA	2	10/ 4/45
2622914	Hemstock, Gdsm. H.	KA	5	9/ 2/44
2615242	Hewitt, L./Cpl. H.	DPW	3	19/ 8/40

Number	Name and Rank	Casualty	Battalion	Date
2619572	Herring, L./Cpl. L.	KA	6	17/ 3/43
2615345	Heffernan, Sergt. P.	KA	1	22/ 9/44
14279266	Herman, Gdsm. R.	KA	4	6/ 8/44
2613699	Headland, L./Sergt. T.	DAS	8 Commando	27/ 8/41
2612555	Hewitt, Gdsm. A.	DW	3	10/ 6/40
2623753	Henshaw, Gdsm. J.	KA	2	3/ 9/44
2618527	Hendrick, Gdsm. T.	KA	5	26/ 4/43
2615523	Hemming, Sergt. S.	KA	2	18/ 7/44
2619287	Hearn, Gdsm. C.	KA	6	22/ 1/44
2615027	Hesketh, Gdsm. H.	DW	6	5/10/43
2611126	Hewitt, Gdsm. H.	DAS	Training Bn.	14/ 9/44
2612343	Herbert, C.S.M. S.	KA	3	5/ 2/43
2624024	Hicks, Gdsm. H.	KA	2	10/ 4/45
2610868	Hicks, P.S.M. R.	KA	3	21/ 5/40
2615895	Hillman, Gdsm. R.	KA	4	14/ 8/44
2618058	Hicks, L./Sergt. E.	KA	6	29/ 1/44
2622211	Hirons, Gdsm. C.	KA	3	5/ 2/43
2616495	Hill, Sergt. I.	DW	3	16/ 9/44
2616230	Higgins, Gdsm. W.	DW	5	8/ 7/44
6283699	Hill, Gdsm. G.	KA	1	3/ 9/44
2614645	Hill, L./Cpl. E.	KA	2	12/ 9/44
2612016	Hilson, Sergt. T.	KA	2	1/ 6/40
2615767	Hilson, Gdsm. F.	KA	6	6/12/43
2622785	Howes, Gdsm. C.	DAS	Training Bn.	11/ 6/42
2623135	Holt, Gdsm. G.	DW	2	24/ 7/44
3527184	Holding, L./Sergt. J.	DAS	Depot	26/10/39
2622168	Hough, L./Sergt. F.	KA	2	3/ 9/44
2613846	Hooper, Gdsm. D.	KAS	W.G. Bn.	18/ 6/44
2621503	Holmes, Gdsm. W.	KA	6	17/ 3/43
147115	Howell, Sergt. H.	KA	5	9/ 2/44
2617379	Hodgson, Gdsm. D.	DW	6	22/ 9/43
2623224	Howarth, Gdsm. F.	KA	4	5/11/44
2616676	Homer, Gdsm. D.	KA	5	1/ 5/43
2617023	Houghton, Cpl. A.	KA	5	30/ 4/43
2613137	Hope, Gdsm. J.	DW	3	27/ 5/40
2615399	Howe, Gdsm. W.	KA	3	21/ 5/40
2617100	Holmes, Gdsm. G.	KA	3	5/ 2/43
2621430	Hook, Gdsm. W.	KA	5	30/ 1/44*
2614788	Horsman, Gdsm. L.	KA	3	31/12/42
2617031	Hodgson, Gdsm. F.	DW	3	26/ 1/43
2624188	Howes, Gdsm. H.	KA	1	3/ 9/44
2616751	Hodson, L./Cpl. C.	KA	1	13/11/44
2625114	Horrex, Gdsm. A.	KA	1	30/ 3/45
2609470	Hoare, P.S.M. A.	KA	1	15/ 5/40*
2611288	Hope, Gdsm. C.	KAS	Holding Bn.	10/ 5/41*
2614992	Holland, Sergt. P.	KA	1	26/ 9/44
2623943	Holland, Gdsm. D.	KA	1	11/ 8/44
2621551	Hobbs, Gdsm. A.	KA	6	17/ 3/43
2617323	Horrocks, Gdsm. T.	KA	6	17/ 3/43
2618814	Howland Gdsm. R.	KA	6	25/ 4/43
2618434	Hodge, Cpl. H.	KA	5	27/ 4/43
2615985	Holman, Gdsm. T.	KA	5	26/ 7/44
2615259	Howarth, Gdsm. J.	DW	1	29/ 5/40
2619365	Humphries, Gdsm. G.	KA	6	31/ 1/44
2617412	Hutt, L./Cpl. D.	KA	3	29/ 5/44
2618353	Hunter, L./Cpl. F.	KA	5	7/ 7/44
2617433	Hughes, Gdsm. R.	DW	3	22/ 2/43
2623673	Hunt, Gdsm. J.	KA	3	24/10/44
2617750	Hunt, Gdsm. J.	DW	6	4/ 3/43
2614938	Hull, Gdsm. H.	KA	3	30/ 5/40
2620919	Hudson, Gdsm. E.	DPW	5	17/ 7/44

Number	Name and Rank	Casualty	Battalion	Date
2614384	Hudson, L./Cpl. H.	DAS	4	16/10/42
2615233	Hughes, L./Sergt. A.	DAS	1	10/ 6/43
2615483	Hutson, L./Cpl. J.	KA	1	30/ 5/40
2609628	Hunt, L./Sergt. G.	KA	4	14/ 8/44
2615506	Hudson, L./Cpl. J.	KA	3	21/ 5/40
2616379	Hunt, L./Cpl. W.	KA	5	23/ 2/44
2618056	Hunt, Gdsm. A.	DW	5	11/ 6/44
2620388	Hyam, Gdsm. J.	DW	5	24/ 4/43
2615212	Hyde, Gdsm. F.	KA	3	30/ 5/40*
2619119	Hyde, Gdsm. C.	KA	5	27/ 6/44
2621433	Ingram, Gdsm. F.	DAS	6	24/ 2/44
2611658	Instone, L./Cpl. H.	DAS	Training Bn.	6/ 3/45
2615815	Irwin, Gdsm. R.	KA	2	3/ 6/40
2615890	Irons, L./Sergt. H.	KA	3	28/ 5/44
2621909	Iliff, Gdsm. R.	KA	5	12/ 6/44
2623644	Jakeways, Gdsm. V.	KA	1	3/ 9/44
2613579	Jarrold, Gdsm. C.	DW	3	22/ 5/40
2621509	Jaques, Gdsm. G.	KA	5	28/ 1/44
2615914	Jarvis, Gdsm. T.	KA	2	1/ 6/40*
2622760	Jackman, Gdsm. W.	DW	5	1/ 9/44
2622401	Jackson, Gdsm. G.	DW	5	25/ 1/44
2612556	Jay, Cpl. J.	KA	3	21/ 5/40
2619504	Jackson, L./Sergt. S.	DW	5	26/ 7/44
789403	Jackson, L./Sergt. F.	DW	5	23/ 4/43
4104505	James, Gdsm. A.	KA	3	20/ 2/43
2613361	Jenkinson, P.S.M. A. S.	KA	3	21/ 1/40
2619726	Jeffries, Gdsm. A.	KA	6	25/ 9/43
2616862	Jewkes, Gdsm. J.	DW	1	31/ 5/40*
2620597	Jeffs, Gdsm. W.	DW	5	22/ 9/44
2619013	Johnson, L./Cpl. E.	DAS	H.Q., 6 G.T.B.	26/ 9/44
2615668	Jennings, Gdsm. J.	KA	6	8/11/43
2621405	Johnson, Gdsm. N.	KA	6	7/11/43*
2622830	Johnson, Gdsm. I.	KA	6	10/11/43
2620158	Johnson, Gdsm. P.	KA	6	8/11/43
2621422	Jonas, Gdsm. A.	KA	6	17/ 3/43
2614786	Jones, Gdsm. F.	DW	2	1/ 6/40*
2622792	Jones, Gdsm. E.	KA	3	15/ 7/44
2625028	Jones, Gdsm. S.	DAS	G.A.T.W.	21/ 2/45
2618257	Jones, L./Sergt. S.	KA	5	2/10/44
2616408	Jones, Gdsm. W.	DAS	Training Bn.	12/ 3/42
2623242	Jones, Gdsm. K.	KA	1	11/ 8/44
2620217	Jones, Gdsm. W.	KA	6	30/ 1/44
2620460	Jones, Gdsm. L.	KA	6	30/ 1/44
2618134	Johnson, L./Sergt. A.	DAS	4	29/ 9/43
2621669	Jones, Gdsm. E.	DPW	5	7/ 4/45
2617874	Jones, Gdsm. L.	KA	3	6/ 3/44
2617705	Johnson, Gdsm. R.	KAS	Holding Bn.	13/10/40
2617186	Jones, Gdsm. R.	KA	3	8/11/44
5881020	Jones, Gdsm. A.	DW	2	1/ 6/40
2617981	Jones, Gdsm. G.	DAS	Training Bn.	13/ 6/42
2622512	Jones, Gdsm. G.	DW	3	19/ 6/44
2615656	Johnson, Sergt. R.	DW	1	3/ 9/44
2614861	Johns, Sergt. S.	KA	3	21/ 5/40
2612957	Jones, Gdsm. J.	KA	5	19/ 7/44
2623293	Johnson, Gdsm. A.	KA	4	6/ 8/44
2613339	Johnson, Gdsm. A.	KA	3	21/ 5/40
2613723	Jones, Gdsm. S.	KA	3	31/12/42

Number	Name and Rank	Casualty	Battalion	Date
2621627	Judge, L./Cpl. E.	KA	6	22/ 1/44
2625840	Judd, Gdsm. B.	DW	1	18/ 5/45
2614533	Jull, L./Sergt. A.	KA	3	18/ 6/44
2618602	Jukes, Gdsm.F.	DW	6	4/ 5/43
2624323	Justice, Gdsm. I.	KA	5	28/ 9/44
2617441	Kay, Gdsm. W.	KA	6	31/ 3/43
2612803	Kennedy, Gdsm. J.	DW	1	28/ 9/44
11000166	Kerr, Gdsm. E.	KA	3	28/12/42
6464769	Kettle, L./Cpl. W.	KA	1	27/ 9/44
2618557	Kemish, Gdsm. F.	KAS	Depot, Chelsea	27/ 9/40
2626868	Kempster, Gdsm. C.	KA	3	4/ 9/44
2612195	Keen, Gdsm. G.	KA	6	16/ 5/43
2612234	Keeley, Gdsm. E.	KA	2	30/ 5/40
2622203	Kelly, Gdsm. J.	KA	5	24/ 6/44
2622395	Kent, Gdsm. K.	KA	2	4/ 8/44
2614887	Keeling, L./Cpl. T.	KA	3	18/ 3/43
2620088	Kelly, Gdsm. A.	KA	5	4/ 2/44
4983931	Key, Gdsm. H.	KA	5	19/ 7/44
6202660	Keeble, Gdsm. A.	DW	X List	21/ 5/40
2616659	Keeling, Gdsm. W.	KA	5	21/ 4/43
2617746	Keeling, Gdsm. A.	KA	6	7/12/43
2617929	Kirk, Gdsm. J.	DW	5	28/ 2/44
2624017	King, Gdsm. D.	KA	3	9/10/44
2618873	Killoran, Gdsm. A.	KA	5	5/ 7/44
6010028	Kilford, Sergt. R.	KA	2	3/ 8/44
2613194	Kilsby, Gdsm. F.	DW	5	22/ 7/44
2619139	Kimpton, Gdsm. R.	KA	1	3/ 8/44
2615082	Kiddy, Gdsm. C.	DW	X List	31/ 5/40*
2619926	King, L./Cpl. F.	KA	1	6/11/44
2617962	King, L./Cpl. J.	KA	6	17/ 3/43
2621389	Knapp, L./Cpl. T.	KA	6	17/ 9/43
2624337	Knapp, Gdsm. G.	DW	1	1/ 4/45
2615991	Lay, Gdsm. J.	KA	2	10/ 4/45
2621701	Lafferty, Gdsm. P.	KA	5	27/ 4/43
2611810	Law, Gdsm. J.	KA	6	12/ 6/44
2612889	Lambert, Gdsm. A.	KA	6	23/ 9/43
2620029	Layton, L./Sergt. M.	KA	2	5/ 3/45
2621744	Lawrence, Gdsm. H.	DIAS		12/ 1/41
2621603	Lawrence, Gdsm. A.	DW	5	9/ 2/44
2619323	Langdon, Gdsm. E.	KA	5	2/ 2/44
2612635	Laycock, Sergt. W.	DW	6	21/ 3/43
2612986	Ladds, L./Cpl. D.	KA	2	13/11/44
2609719	Law, Gdsm. W.	KA	XIV	6/ 8/44
2623059	Lawty, Gdsm. W.	KA	6	23/10/43
2612204	Laird, C.S.M. J.	KA	6	17/ 3/43
2622108	Lane, Gdsm. P.	KA	3	9/10/44
2620923	Lawes, Gdsm. R.	DW	5	7/ 3/44
2615228	Lawrence, Sergt. A.	KA	5	9/ 2/44
2618894	Lang, Gdsm. N.	KA	5	25/ 6/44
2623040	Lanbert, Gdsm. C.	KA	5	12/ 6/44
2622018	Lance, L./Cpl. G.	KA	6	10/11/43
3518163	Latham, Sergt. W.	DAS	1	2/ 9/43
2623073	Lenton, Gdsm. A.	KA	6	10/11/43
2617070	Lee, L./Cpl. A.	KA	5	26/ 1/44
2620867	Leach, Gdsm. W.	KA	5	21/ 4/43
2617650	Leather, Gdsm. J.	KAS	Holding Bn.	7/11/40
2619151	Leather, Gdsm. W.	DW	5	7/ 4/43

Number	Name and Rank	Casualty	Battalion	Date
2615888	Lee, L./Cpl. W.	DW	2	31/ 5/40*
2613094	Lees, L./Sergt. G.	KA	6	30/ 1/44
2619705	Lear, Gdsm. F.	KA	4	5/11/44
2614448	Lewis, L./Sergt. R.	KA	2	18/ 7/44
2617158	Lewis, Gdsm. J.	KA	2 Commando	28/ 3/42
2619099	Lee, Gdsm. E.	KA	6	10/11/43
2621671	Lever, Gdsm. E.	DAS	6	11/10/43
2617922	Lloyd, L./Cpl. A.	KA	3	5/ 2/43
2619018	Lloyd, L./Cpl. D.	KA	4	5/ 8/44
2619053	Lloyd, Gdsm. J.	DW	6	12/12/43
2621383	Lloyd, L./Sergt. F.	KA	4 Commando	20/ 6/44
2622331	Lineker, Gdsm. W.	DW	1	27/ 9/44
2618259	Little, L./Cpl. B.	KA	4	21/ 4/45
2617050	Lindsey, Gdsm. H.	DAS	6	6/12/42
820757	Lindsay, Gdsm. H.	DW	3	23/ 5/40
2622343	Liversidge, Gdsm. R.	KA	257 C.D.S.	25/ 9/44
2614860	Little, Gdsm. H.	KA	3	21/ 5/40
2621889	Liddiard, Gdsm. L.	KA	6	30/ 1/44
2622966	Lindoff, Gdsm. B.	DW	6	15/10/43
2614096	Lines, Gdsm. R.	DW	3	19/ 5/40
2611995	Lines, Gdsm. R.	KA	2	3/ 9/44
2612213	Lindley, Gdsm. T.	KA	3	21/ 5/40
2611339	Little, L./Sergt. W.	DW	3	15/ 9/44
2619789	Lock, Gdsm. F.	KA	5	27/ 4/43
2620009	Lowe, Gdsm. S.	KA	5	2/10/44
2615107	Lord, Gdsm. J.	KA	3	7/ 5/43
2620715	Lucock, Gdsm. J.	KA	6	14/ 3/43
2611424	Lyons, Gdsm. D.	DWPW	3	13/10/40
5726099	Marshallsay, L./Cpl. S.	KA	2	9/ 4/45
2614486	Maggs, Sergt. E.	KA	1	1/ 6/40
2619906	Maides, Gdsm. W.	KA	5	27/ 3/43
2623048	Mallard, Gdsm. T.	DAS	Training Bn.	9/ 7/44
2612426	Mace, Gdsm. W.	DAS	4	6/ 8/44
2615350	Marriott, Gdsm. C.	DW	3	29/ 5/40*
2616914	Maslen, Sergt. R.	KA	6	4/12/43
2614679	Mace, Gdsm. J.	KAS	2	16/ 9/39
2614656	Matthews, L./Sergt. F.	DW	5	12/ 7/44
2625014	Mander, Gdsm. A.	DW	1	3/ 4/45
2616309	Mason, Sergt. N.	DW	1	1/ 8/44
2620209	May, Gdsm. R.	KA	5	3/ 2/44
2621526	Maybury, Cpl. J.	KA	4 Commando	18/ 1/45
2617467	Mason, L./Cpl. E.	DW	5	2/ 5/43
2618238	Maher, Gdsm. M.	KA	6	7/10/43
2624402	MacDonald, Gdsm. J.	KA	XIV	28/ 5/44
2616074	Mann, Cpl. H.	KA	5	21/ 4/43
2618846	Mawdsley, Gdsm. W.	DW	4	11/ 8/44
2621617	Matthews, Gdsm. E.	KA	5	4/ 2/44
2615471	Marmont, L./Sergt. A.	KA	2	11/ 8/44
2615074	Mannion, Gdsm. W.	DW	3	27/ 5/40
2617495	Mawson, Sergt. G.	DW	5	25/ 6/44
2621439	Mayne, Gdsm. R.	KA	5	21/ 4/43
2623436	Mason, Gdsm. W.	DW	6	10/ 9/43*
2618761	May, Gdsm. S.	DW	6	7/11/43*
2615736	Marks, Gdsm. E.	KA	2	18/ 7/44
2616465	Marshall, Gdsm. B.	KA	5	11/ 6/44
2617628	Madden, Gdsm. J.	DW	3	5/ 2/43
2620100	Mackenzie, Gdsm. P.	KA	5	25/ 1/44
2621952	McCrone, Gdsm. J.	KA	5	30/ 4/43
2623475	McDonald, Gdsm. E.	DW	5	14/ 5/44
2616711	Meredith, Sergt. W.	KA	2	3/ 9/44
2617131	Merrett, Gdsm. A.	KA	3	8/ 3/44

Number	Name and Rank	Casualty	Battalion	Date
2613344	Meade, Gdsm. W.	KA	3	21/ 5/40
2613657	Mercer, L./Sergt. N.	KA	5	12/ 6/44
2621324	Mercer, Gdsm. F.	KA	3	7/ 5/43
2620094	Merry, Gdsm. J.	KA	6	10/11/43
2623086	Meek, Gdsm. F.	KA	5	26/ 7/44
2622849	Mitchell, Gdsm. E.	KA	2	18/ 7/44
2615340	Millward, L./Sergt. A.	KA	3	24/12/42
2612089	Milton, L./Cpl. F.	DW	2	1/ 6/40
2616020	Miller, Gdsm. S.	KA	1	3/ 8/44
2617724	Miles, Gdsm. T.	KA	5	11/ 6/44
2621813	Miller, Gdsm. L.	KAS	Depot	11/ 1/41
2622002	Mitchell, L./Cpl. E.	KA	6	10/ 9/43
2612482	Miller, P.S.M. J.	DW	2	12/ 6/40
910177	Millard, Gdsm. J.	KA	5	17/ 4/43
4272340	Morgan, Gdsm. R.	KA	6	17/ 3/43
2619961	Moakes, L./Cpl. A.	KA	6	17/ 3/43
2610453	Moughton, C.S.M. W.	DAS	"Y" List	18/ 1/44
2622755	Moore, Gdsm. J.	KA	6	21/ 9/43
2623236	Moore, Gdsm. H.	KA	6	15/10/43
2617028	Moore, Gdsm. N.	DW	3	12/ 3/44
2614522	Monks, Gdsm. C.	KA	XIV	26/ 5/44
2613442	Moring, L./Sergt. G.	KA	3	28/ 5/40
2617156	Molyneux, Gdsm. J.	KA	3	28/ 5/44
2615993	Moultrie, L./Cpl. W.	DW	XI List	1/12/43
2613178	Mountford, Sergt. H.	KA	5	7/ 7/44
2623065	Moore, Gdsm. G.	DW	5	12/ 6/44
783275	Morris, Gdsm. A.	KA	3	28/ 5/40
2619409	Morgan, Gdsm. F.	KA	1	8/ 8/44
2616273	Moss, L./Sergt. T.	KA	1	8/ 3/45
2616365	Moran, Gdsm. J.	KA	1	24/ 5/40
2617565	Murray, Gdsm. T.	KA	3	5/10/44
2615098	Murrell, Gdsm. R.	DAS	1	12/ 9/40
2615967	Murcott, L./Cpl. J.	KA	1	1/ 6/40*
2619278	Muskett, Gdsm. H.	KA	6	7/11/43
841527	Murton, Gdsm. V.	KA	6	6/12/43
2619233	Murray, Gdsm. W.	KA	5	28/ 4/43
2616006	Nadin, L./Sergt. W.	KA	6	21/ 1/44
2623455	Newsome, Gdsm. J.	KA	2	19/ 9/44
2625453	Neal, Gdsm. H.	DAS	Training Bn.	28/ 3/45
2616211	Neale, Gdsm. B.	KA	3	21/ 5/40
2622946	Newsham, Gdsm. B.	DW	3	12/ 2/44
2619004	Newson, L./Sergt. S.	KA	5	12/ 6/44
2621651	Newell, Gdsm. F.	DW	3	21/12/44
2622329	Nicholls, Gdsm. A.	KA	6	17/ 3/43
2613387	Nippierd, Gdsm. N.	DW	5	11/ 6/44
2618204	Nicholls, Gdsm. R.	DW	6	28/ 3/44*
2620709	Nixon, Gdsm. J.	KA	6	17/ 3/43
2621368	Norminton, L./Sergt. J.	KA	6	17/ 3/43
2621802	Norman, L./Sergt. E.	KA	5	17/ 4/43
2619454	Noakes, Gdsm. W.	DW	3	31/12/42
2620397	Norton, Gdsm. W.	KAS	W.G. Bn.	18/ 6/44
2621801	Norman, Gdsm. V.	KA	5	27/ 4/43
2622100	Oakley, L./Cpl. A.	DW	4	5/ 8/44
2619242	O'Brien, Gdsm. A.	KA	6	11/ 9/43
2622876	O'Grady, Gdsm. J.	KA	2	23/ 4/45
2615994	O'Grady, Gdsm. C.	KA	5	1/12/44*
2623403	Oliver, Gdsm. L.	DW	5	28/ 9/44

Number	Name and Rank	Casualty	Battalion	Date
2616097	O'Monaghan, Gdsm. D.	DW	1	15/ 5/40
2613279	O'Neill, Gdsm. B.	DW	6	11/10/43
2619598	Orbell, L./Sergt. W.	KA	6	11/ 9/43
2619201	Oswell, L./Sergt. W.	DW	3	30/ 3/44
2615731	Osborne, Sergt. R.	DW	2	10/ 4/45
2612438	Otter, Gdsm. F.	KA	5	27/ 1/44
2614697	Overton-Davies, L./Sergt. C.	KA	1	18/ 7/44
2623169	Overton, Gdsm. A.	KA	2	25/ 9/44
2623190	Owen, Gdsm. J.	DW	2	24/ 7/44
2613926	Owen, Gdsm. M.	DW	5	17/ 2/44*
4104302	Owens, Gdsm. R.	KA	1	29/ 5/40
2620461	Page, Gdsm. G.	KA	5	17/ 4/43
2611950	Panting, L./Sergt. A.	KA	3	28/ 5/44
2614026	Parker, Gdsm. R.	DW	2	30/ 5/40
2619211	Parker, L./Cpl. A.	KA	6	10/11/43
2618275	Page, Gdsm. A.	KA	6	30/ 1/44
2626674	Parker, Gdsm. C.	DAS	Training Bn.	13/ 4/45
2619575	Parker, Gdsm. L.	KA	5	28/ 1/44
2615818	Parry, L./Cpl. R.	KA	5	3/ 2/44*
2623950	Pash, Gdsm. G.	KA	1	20/ 9/44
2617619	Palmer, Gdsm. A.	KA	5	12/ 6/44
2616708	Partridge, Gdsm. L.	KA	1	11/ 8/44
2618170	Pattison, Gdsm. F.	DW	3	12/ 6/44
2623092	Patton, L./Cpl. K.	KA	6	30/ 1/44
2621407	Pash, Gdsm. R.	KA	2 Commando	13/ 9/43
2622355	Parkin, Gdsm. W.	KA	4	5/ 8/44
2609789	Payne, Sergt. A.	DAS	Training Bn.	24/ 2/44
2624967	Page, Gdsm. F.	KA	1	31/ 3/45
2618577	Partington, Gdsm. E.	KA	5	27/ 7/44
2618408	Parkinson, Gdsm. A.	DW	5	22/ 6/44
2622039	Payne, L./Cpl. E.	DW	5	29/11/44
2615230	Parrott, L./Sergt. A.	KA	1	1/ 6/40*
2620729	Partridge, Sergt. W.	KA	1	24/ 2/45
2615847	Peterson, Gdsm. D.	DW	XIV	20/ 2/44
2617421	Pease, Gdsm. S.	KA	6	10/ 9/43
2624409	Pepperall, Gdsm. D.	KA	1	30/ 3/45
2625019	Perry, Gdsm. J.	KA	1	11/12/44
2616901	Perkins, Gdsm. W.	DAS	3	20/ 9/40
2620274	Perkins, Gdsm. V.	KA	5	4/ 2/44
2620640	Pearson, Gdsm. F.	KA	5	29/ 4/43
2622308	Perry, Gdsm. J.	KA	6	17/ 3/43
2622828	Pell, L./Cpl. G.	KA	2	18/ 7/44
2620680	Pearce, Gdsm. W.	DAS	Holding Bn.	11/ 5/41
2616423	Peterson, L./Sergt. E.	DW	5	1/ 5/43
2621707	Peers, L./Cpl. N.	DAS	6	24/ 2/44
2613424	Perkins, Gdsm. S.	DAS	2	16/ 9/39
2614425	Peat, Gdsm. G.	KA	2	1/ 6/40
2614470	Percival, Sergt. W.	DW	1	31/ 5/40*
2621360	Phillips, Gdsm. G.	KA	6	17/ 3/43
2623053	Phelps, Gdsm. J.	KA	5	2/ 8/44
2621807	Phillipps, Gdsm. W.	KA	3	6/10/44
2621798	Philpot, Gdsm. E.	KA	6	17/ 3/43
5045807	Pickerill, Gdsm. L.	KA	3	19/ 2/44
2623620	Pilgrim, L./Cpl. N.	KA	5	29/10/44*
2616040	Pilbro, Gdsm. F.	KA	5	17/ 1/45
2613533	Pinkney, Gdsm. A.	DW	3	4/ 6/40*
2620426	Pimlott, Gdsm. D.	KA	5	30/ 4/43
2617207	Pickering, Gdsm. S.	DPW	5	22/ 3/45
2615784	Pinder, L./Sergt. F.	KA	3	10/ 6/44

Number	Name and Rank	Casualty	Battalion	Date
5047729	Plant, Gdsm. G.	KA	6	17/ 3/43
2622344	Plummer, Gdsm. J.	KA	1	11/ 8/44
2624247	Power, Gdsm. M.	KA	XIV	20/ 6/44
7021442	Porteus, Gdsm. F.	KA	5	5/ 2/45
2617868	Pollard, Gdsm. E.	DW	3	26/12/42*
2618224	Potter, Gdsm. R.	KA	2	10/ 9/44
2620924	Pollard, Sergt. H.	DW	6	13/ 9/43
2616889	Portsmouth, Gdsm. E.	KA	3	28/ 5/40
2618060	Poole, Gdsm. W.	DW	5	10/ 2/44
2615854	Poole, Gdsm. D.	DW	1	5/ 9/44
2619177	Poyser, Gdsm. J.	DW	5	4/ 5/43
2612419	Porter, Gdsm. C.	KA	3	19/ 5/40
2614931	Powell, Gdsm. C.	DW	3	27/ 5/40
2621751	Port, Gdsm. E.	KA	5	2/ 8/44
2615401	Proctor, Gdsm. S.	KA	5	30/ 4/43
2623817	Price, Gdsm. W.	KA	3	9/10/44
2622120	Prescott, Gdsm. W.	KA	6	22/ 1/44
2623233	Priest, Gdsm. J.	KA	6	30/ 1/44
2617820	Pritchard, Gdsm. J.	KAS	Holding Bn.	16/11/40
2622124	Preston, Gdsm. H.	DW	6	17/ 3/43
2620213	Prior, Gdsm. H.	KA	6	17/ 3/43
2624349	Pritlove, Gdsm. A.	KA	3	24/10/44
2616514	Preston, L./Cpl. E.	KA	2	27/ 7/44
2616893	Puckett, Gdsm. A.	DW	3	30/ 5/44
2622088	Pugh, L./Cpl. W.	DW	4	23/ 1/45
2613961	Pye, Sergt. T.	KA	1	21/ 7/44
2620974	Pye, Gdsm. H.	KA	5	4/ 5/43
14499977	Quirk, Gdsm. S.	DW	2	30/11/44
2623360	Rawson, Gdsm. D.	KA	2	25/ 9/44
2621815	Rainey, L./Cpl. P.	KA	6	17/ 3/43
2618244	Randle, Gdsm. C.	KA	5	9/ 2/44
2623701	Rainford, Gdsm. R.	DAS	Training Bn.	8/ 5/43
2622248	Rakes, L./Cpl. L.	DW	5	3/ 5/43
2621031	Ramsden, Gdsm. C.	KA	6	10/ 9/43
2622905	Rawlings, Gdsm. T.	KA	5	9/ 2/44
2622148	Ratcliffe, Gdsm. H.	KA	5	2/ 8/44
2618675	Randle, L./Cpl. G.	KA	5	27/ 4/43
2614730	Radley, Cpl. D.	DAS	3	15/ 6/43
2612123	Reynolds, Gdsm. W.	KA	1	3/ 9/44
2613997	Reardon, Gdsm. G.	KA	3	28/ 5/40
2623577	Reeve, Gdsm. R.	KA	1	29/ 4/45
2617819	Reardon, Gdsm. A.	KA	5	26/10/44
2616252	Reddish, Gdsm. R.	KA	1	1/ 6/40*
2613551	Reynolds, Gdsm. E.	KA	3	21/ 5/40
2619216	Reynolds, Gdsm. R.	DW	6	17/ 3/43*
2614440	Reynolds, L./Cpl. J.	KA	2	20/ 5/40
2616239	Reddington, Gdsm. T.	KA	5	28/ 4/43
2619255	Rhodes, Gdsm. J.	DAS	5	27/ 1/45
2620991	Rhodes, Gdsm. G.	KA	6	17/ 3/43
2616983	Rhodes, L./Cpl. J.	DW	3	8/ 3/43
2619981	Rigg, Gdsm. J.	DW	2	5/ 8/44
2624351	Ribbins, Gdsm. L.	DW	1	1/10/44
2615321	Rimmell, L./Sergt. A.	KA	3	21/ 5/40
4077354	Richards, Gdsm. A.	KA	6	29/ 1/44
2620486	Riggal, Gdsm. S.	DAS	"Y" List	19/ 5/41
2614724	Riches, Gdsm. D.	KA	3	21/ 5/40
2623171	Richards, Gdsm. J.	KA	2	18/ 7/44
2616265	Richards, Gdsm. M.	DW	5	7/ 5/44

Number	Name and Rank	Casualty	Battalion	Date
2619400	Richardson, Gdsm. J.	DAS	6	27/ 7/42
1612655	Richardson, Gdsm. A.	KA	1	12/10/44
2619239	Richardson, Gdsm. G.	KA	1	20/ 9/44
2613497	Rigby, Sergt. J.	DAS	5	25/ 5/43
2615046	Richardson, Gdsm. R.	KA	5	25/ 6/44
2622181	Rigby, Gdsm. W.	KA	1	14/ 9/44
2619562	Rixon, Gdsm. L.	KA	5	28/ 4/43
2616802	Riding, Gdsm. K.	KA	3	28/ 5/40
2615396	Roberts, Gdsm. T.	KA	5	26/ 1/44
2619196	Robinson, Gdsm. S.	KA	2 Commando	28/ 3/42
2611976	Rowlands, Gdsm. W.	KA	3	21/ 5/40
2615721	Rosenberg, Gdsm. J.	KA	3	28/ 5/40
2624744	Roughton, Gdsm. N.	KA	2	10/ 4/45
2611290	Route, L./Cpl. P.	KAS	Holding Bn.	16/11/40
2620754	Ross, Gdsm. A.	KA	3	10/10/44
2618229	Rodwell, Gdsm. J.	KA	3	5/ 2/43
2615808	Roulstone, Gdsm. L.	DW	2	24/ 5/40
2609961	Roberts, Sergt. E.	DW	2	1/ 6/40
2623139	Robinson, Gdsm. H.	KA	2	25/ 9/44
2620074	Robinson, Cpl. L.	KA	5	27/ 4/43
2623056	Robinson, Gdsm. W.	KA	6	30/ 1/44
2623096	Robertshaw, Gdsm. A.	KA	4	30/ 7/44
2613868	Robinson, Gdsm. F.	DPW	X List	10/ 3/41
2619629	Robinson, L./Cpl. G.	KA	6	9/11/43
2620677	Rose, Gdsm. W.	KA	6	8/11/43
2611636	Roberts, Gdsm. W.	DW	11 B.D.	31/ 5/40
2615169	Roden, Gdsm. A.	KA	6	17/ 3/43
2611397	Rosson, L./Sergt. H.	KA	3	27/ 6/44
2617663	Robinson, Gdsm. W.	KA	5	9/ 2/44
2616605	Robinson, Gdsm. F.	KAS	2	29/ 6/42
2623197	Roe, Gdsm. L.	KA	5	11/ 6/44
2615653	Roberts, L./Cpl. E.	KA	3	25/ 5/40
2616508	Rowley, Gdsm. A.	KA	2	20/ 5/40
2622527	Rolfe, Gdsm. J.	DW	3	13/12/42*
2619391	Roe, Gdsm. A.	DAS	5	25/ 9/43
2616053	Rudkin, Gdsm. C.	KA	6	17/ 3/43
2621148	Rumley, Gdsm. R.	KA	6	10/ 9/43
2614815	Rubie, Gdsm. R.	KA	3	31/ 5/40
2624293	Rule, Gdsm. A.	KA	4	27/ 2/45
2618112	Russell, Gdsm. T.	KA	3	22/ 2/44
2617949	Russ, Gdsm. J.	KA	1	11/ 8/44
1652944	Rudge, Gdsm. W.	DW	1	7/10/44
2624006	Russell, Gdsm. H.	KA	1	20/ 9/44
865667	Russell, Gdsm. G.	KA	6	23/ 9/43
2617174	Ryan, Gdsm. D.	KA	6	17/ 3/43
2612065	Rush, Cpl. A.	DAS	3	16/ 6/43
2615207	Ryder, Sergt. J.	DPW	3	25/ 7/40
2623407	Rynenberg, Gdsm. I.	KA	6	21/ 9/43
2620429	Saunders, L./Sergt. A.	KA	3	11/10/44
2617888	Sansom, L./Cpl. E.	KA	5	26/ 1/44
2618139	Sarson, L./Sergt. G.	KA	6	17/ 3/43
2619101	Sault, Gdsm. E.	KA	2	31/ 8/44
2617327	Saunders, Gdsm. I.	DW	3	10/ 6/44
2622465	Scothern, Gdsm. S.	DW	5	28/ 4/43
2620107	Scrutton, Gdsm. G.	KA	6	10/11/43
2617005	Staton, Gdsm. G.	DAS	1	18/ 3/43
2606637	Scriven, L./Sergt. R.	DAS	Training Bn.	28/ 1/45
2618132	Scholes, L./Sergt. J.	DW	6	10/ 9/43
2618994	Scott, Gdsm. S.	DW	4	23/ 3/45
2621363	Scott, Gdsm. S.	KA	5	12/ 7/44

Number	Name and Rank	Casualty	Battalion	Date
2621033	Scrivener, Gdsm. G.	DW	6	18/ 3/43
2618962	Scott, Gdsm. A.	KA	4	5/ 8/44
2620687	Searson, Gdsm. R.	KA	5	17/ 2/45
2615232	Shaw, L./Sergt. H.	KA	6	16/ 3/43*
2618424	Shelley, Gdsm. A.	DAS	5	14/ 9/43
2619176	Shaw, Gdsm. W.	DPW	5	30/ 3/45
2623623	Shutler, Gdsm. W.	KA	5	8/ 8/44
2045689	Shaw, Gdsm. J.	KA	1	31/ 5/40*
2624626	Short, Gdsm. S.	KA	1	27/ 9/44
3527915	Shirriff, Gdsm. K.	KA	1	1/ 6/40
2616866	Snape, Gdsm. G.	KA	3	28/12/42
2621679	Shine, Gdsm. R.	KA	5	27/ 6/44
2611417	Sheppard, C.Q.M.S. E.	KA	1	1/ 6/40
2622174	Shaw, Gdsm. A.	KA	2	21/ 9/44
2622837	Shrimpton, L./Cpl. D.	KA	3	26/ 6/44
2605448	Sheather, R.S.M. C.	KA	1	1/ 6/40
2620448	Sheehy, Gdsm. M.	KA	5	7/ 2/44*
2613559	Shinton, Gdsm. H.	KA	1	27/ 9/44
2618468	Snape, Gdsm. E.	DW	6	5/12/43
2618195	Short, Gdsm. S.	KAS	4	20/10/40
2620591	Siddorn, Gdsm. J.	DAS	Training Bn.	16/ 3/41
2612557	Sinfield, Sergt. C.	DAS	Holding Bn.	25/ 6/40
2616653	Simpkin, Gdsm. H.	DPW	1	4/ 6/40
2619676	Simmonds, Sergt. G., M.M.	DW	5	15/ 2/45
2611159	Simpson, Gdsm. A.	DAS	2	16/ 9/39
2619631	Sidders, Cpl. F.	DAS	XIV	28/10/43
2614335	Sidley, L./Cpl. R.	KA	1	8/ 3/45
2615015	Simpson, Gdsm. J.	KA	3	31/12/42
2615978	Simmonds, L./Cpl. J.	DW	2	20/ 7/44
2610918	Simpson, Gdsm. L.	KA	5	27/ 4/43
2618853	Slater, Gdsm. F.	KA	5	7/ 2/44*
2621146	Slater, Gdsm. H.	DAS	Training Bn.	8/ 3/44
2622967	Slater, Gdsm. H.	KA	1	17/11/44
2623550	Slade, Gdsm. R	KA	6	30/ 1/44
2612498	Smith, L./Sergt. W.	KA	1	31/ 5/40
2618522	Smith, L./Cpl. R.	KA	1	3/ 8/44
2613833	Smith, Gdsm. H.	KA	5	7/ 4/43
2618499	Smith, Gdsm. G.	KA	5	23/ 4/43
2617092	Smith, Gdsm. T.	DW	5	23/ 4/43
2614837	Smith, Gdsm. E.	KA	3	20/ 5/40*
2080854	Smart, L./Sergt. R.	KA	3	19/ 2/44
2617159	Smith, Gdsm. T.	KA	6	7/11/43
2618443	Smith, Gdsm. R.	KA	6	9/11/43
2623173	Smith, Gdsm. A.	KA	2	11/ 8/44
14499377	Smith, Gdsm. J.	KAS	W.G. Bn.	18/ 6/44
2620104	Smith, Gdsm. C.	KA	257 C.D.S.	15/ 9/44
2621055	Smith, Gdsm. B.	KA	H.Q., G.A.D.	21/ 7/44
2618953	Smith, L./Sergt. G.	KA	5	9/ 5/44
2620405	Smith, Gdsm. F.	KA	6	6/12/43
2620541	Smith, Gdsm. E.	KA	3	28/ 5/44
5040930	Smith, L./Cpl. F., M.M.	DAS	Training Bn.	20/12/42
2614476	Smith, Sergt. G.	DAS	5	24/ 3/43
2620258	Smith, L./Cpl. A.	DW	5	13/ 7/44
2615407	Smith, Gdsm. C.	KA	201 G.B.	4/12/43
2622374	Smith, Gdsm. J.	KA	4	6/ 8/44
2608592	Smith, Gdsm. C.	KA	3	19/ 5/40
2623437	Snowden, Gdsm. G.	KA	1	1/ 9/44
5046864	Snow, Gdsm. J.	KA	1	3/ 8/44
2611045	South, Gdsm. S.	KA	6	8/11/43
2615277	Sorry, Gdsm. C.	DW	3	11/ 7/44
2614331	Southern, Gdsm. T.	KA	1	1/ 6/40*

Number	Name and Rank	Casualty	Battalion	Date
2622221	Sowerby, Gdsm. J.	DW	24 G.B.	27/10/44
2616650	Sobey, Gdsm. R.	KA	5	25/ 1/44
2618940	Soane, L./Sergt. E.	KA	5	23/ 4/43
2617300	Southern, Gdsm. E.	DPW	3	19/12/42*
2623544	Southby, Gdsm. R.	KA	3	28/ 5/44
2614889	Soar, Gdsm. A.	KA	5	4/ 2/44
2622359	Spencer, L./Cpl. L.	KA	6	7/11/43
4858330	Spencer, L./Sergt. W.	KA	6	9/11/43
4858097	Spencer, L./Sergt. A.	KA	5	7/ 4/43
2621364	Spencer, Gdsm. J.	KA	6	10/ 5/43
2615249	Spratt, Gdsm. T.	KA	XIV	30/ 1/44
2616459	Spence, Gdsm. J.	KA	6	25/ 9/43
2623174	Speed, Gdsm. T.	KA	4	5/11/44
2615590	Spence, Gdsm. G.	DPW	3	24/ 4/44
2621568	Square, Gdsm. H.	KA	6	17/ 3/43
2622295	Sutton, Gdsm. A.	KA	6	10/11/43
2620611	Stockdale, Gdsm. G...	DAS	5	1/ 5/45
2623468	Standige, Gdsm. S.	KA	4	30/ 3/45
2624020	Stevens, Gdsm. A.	KA	4	21/ 4/45
2616152	Stephens, Gdsm. W.	KA	3	6/ 9/44
2619392	Stretton, Gdsm. E.	KA	6	21/ 9/43
2616280	Sturdy, Sergt. V.	KA	6	24/ 9/43
2620987	Stevens, Gdsm. J.	KA	6	6/12/43
2622686	Styles, Gdsm. L.	KA	1	30/ 3/45
2618568	Stevens, L./Sergt. A...	KA	4	6/ 8/44
2621411	Stevens, L./Cpl. G.	KA	5	30/10/44
2615759	Stacey, Gdsm. J.	KA	2	3/ 9/44
2622051	Sturman, Gdsm. A.	KA	6	17/ 3/43
2622877	Stevens, Gdsm. E.	KA	5	28/ 4/43
2619549	Stiles, L./Cpl. L.	KA	5	23/ 4/43
2620177	Strothard, Gdsm. W.	KA	5	26/ 1/44
2620371	Steel, Gdsm. V.	KAS	Holding Bn.	17/ 4/41
2615606	Stanfield, L./Cpl. V...	DAS	5	28/ 9/44
2622010	Stonehouse, Gdsm. E.	DW	XIV	26/ 6/44
869841	Steel, L./Cpl. T.	DAS	1	14/10/41
2618277	Stout, Gdsm. T.	DW	5	19/ 7/44
2619828	Stretton, Gdsm. J.	KA	2	9/ 4/45
2607827	Stokes, R.S.M. L.	KA	2	5/12/44
2623351	Stonehouse, Gdsm. R.	DW	6	29/ 1/44
2622998	Sutton, Gdsm. R.	KA	5	10/ 2/44
2621593	Swain, Gdsm. E.	KA	5	10/ 2/44
2622213	Swindell, Gdsm. F.	KA	5	11/ 6/44
992520	Swallow, Gdsm. J.	KA	5	26/ 1/44
2616493	Swan, L./Sergt. F.	KA	1	31/ 3/45
2618872	Swinnerton, Gdsm. S.	KA	6	16/ 3/43*
2615112	Syson, Sergt. A.	KA	3	28/ 5/44
2612729	Swallow, L./Cpl. W.	DW	3	27/ 5/40
2616535	Spiers, L./Sergt. J.	DW	1	8/ 3/45
2616695	Smith, L./Sergt. F.	DW	1	3/ 8/44
2616392	Sheppard, Gdsm. F.	KA	2	20/ 5/40
2616029	Simpson, Gdsm. F.	DW	1	20/ 9/44
2618251	Taylor, Gdsm. H.	KA	5	26/ 6/44
2613692	Taylor, Gdsm. A.	KA	"X" List	15/ 5/40
2620755	Taylor, Gdsm. P.	DW	5	3/ 8/43
7955216	Taylor, Gdsm. R.	KA	4	13/10/44
2617973	Taylor, Gdsm. W.	KA	3	20/ 6/44
2621388	Tapping, Gdsm. A.	KA	6	17/ 3/43
2614300	Taylor, Gdsm. H.	KA	6	22/ 1/44
2620746	Taylor, Gdsm. G.	KA	5	28/ 9/44
6342225	Taylor, L./Sergt. F.	KA	2	16/ 8/45

Number	Name and Rank	Casualty	Battalion	Date
2621390	Tarling, Gdsm. J.	DW	2	4/10/44
2617873	Taylor, L./Cpl. A.	DAS	Holding Bn.	28/ 9/40
2617361	Taylor, Gdsm. J.	KA	6	17/ 3/43
2617532	Terry, Gdsm. J.	DAS	2 Troop, Commando 8	29/ 8/40
2607483	Teece, D./Sergt. T.	KA	1	30/ 5/40
2620562	Thickpenny, Gdsm. J.	KA	6	12/ 9/43
2621605	Thrower, Gdsm. L.	KA	6	24/ 9/43
2616697	Thompson, Gdsm. E.	DW	3	21/ 5/40
2621401	Thomas, Gdsm. W.	DPW	XI M.E.	8/ 7/43
2617593	Thompson, Gdsm. G.	KA	5	12/ 6/44
2614143	Thomas, L./Sergt. R.	KA	5	2/ 9/44
2613660	Theobald, Sergt. H.	KA	1	3/ 8/44
2617741	Thornhill, Gdsm. D.	KA	1	3/ 8/44
2620282	Thornton, Gdsm. H.	KAS	Training Bn.	18/ 6/44
2624734	Thomas, Gdsm. G.	KA	1	3/ 9/44
2617849	Thomas, L./Sergt. E.	DW	5	28/ 4/43
2613734	Thomas, L./Sergt. E.	KA	XIV	26/ 7/44
2625804	Thomas, Gdsm. S.	KA	1	30/ 3/45
2623650	Thompson, Gdsm. E.	DW	XIV	23/ 6/44
2615224	Thompson, Gdsm. W.	KA	1	31/ 5/40*
2616626	Thorne, L./Cpl. F.	KA	4	30/ 7/44
2618392	Thompson, L./Cpl. G.	KA	4 Commando	10/ 6/44
2619474	Tibbits, Gdsm. G.	KA	H.Q., 24 G.B.	25/ 6/44
2624357	Timson, Gdsm. B.	KA	2	3/ 4/45
2612970	Tingle, Gdsm. G.	KA	2	29/ 5/40
2613248	Titmus, Gdsm. J.	KA	3	21/ 5/40
2615611	Titley, Gdsm. J.	DW	5	12/ 2/44
2615958	Tomlinson, L./Cpl. H.	DAS	3	5/ 8/43
2624797	Tompkins, Gdsm. P.	KA	1	30/ 3/45
2622615	Tomlinson, Gdsm. G.	KA	1	27/ 9/44
2614627	Treeby, Sergt. A.	KA	3	8/ 4/44
2617732	Trowles, L./Cpl. G.	DW	5	5/ 5/43
2615530	Truswell, Gdsm. C.	KA	40 R.H.U.	2/ 1/45
2616831	Tuffs, Gdsm. A.	KA	3	5/ 2/43
2620927	Tulk, Gdsm. J.	KAS	Depot, Chelsea	27/ 9/40
2612157	Turner, Gdsm. J.	KA	3	21/ 5/40
6607946	Turner, L./Sergt. G.	KA	5	20/ 3/43
2620662	Tunnicliffe, Gdsm. L.	DW	5	5/10/44
2606370	Turton, D./Sergt. N.	KAS	W.G. Bn.	18/ 6/44
2622865	Tunaley, Gdsm. K.	DW	5	7/ 7/44
69671	Twitty, Gdsm. T.	DW	6	24/ 1/44
2623946	Tyrell, Gdsm. L.	DW	3	10/ 8/44
2623546	Tyler, Gdsm. F.	DW	5	11/ 2/44
2617896	Vaughan, Gdsm. G.	DW	3	5/10/44
2618286	Vasey, L./Sergt. J.	KA	3	4/ 2/43
2615267	Vanschalkwyk, Gdsm. N.	KA	1	29/ 5/40
2617530	Vine, Gdsm. J.	DAS	6 G.T.B.	24/10/44
2615754	Vincent, L./Cpl. R.	KA	2	18/ 7/44
2612591	Vincent, Gdsm. F.	KA	1 G.B.	18/ 5/40
2612202	Vickers, Gdsm. F.	KA	3	16/ 9/44
2616924	Virgo, L./Cpl. J.	KAS	2	29/ 6/42
2616002	Viggars, L./Cpl. G.	KA	5	9/ 2/44
2616078	Walters, L./Cpl. L.	KA	1	15/ 5/40*
2622060	Wake, Gdsm. E.	DAS	5	31/ 3/43
2620364	Waite, Gdsm. C.	DW	1	11/ 8/44
2615178	Wakefield, Gdsm. R.	KA	1	11/ 8/44

Number	Name and Rank	Casualty	Battalion	Date
2620747	Walters, Gdsm. J.	DW	4 Commando	6/ 6/44
2617846	Waring, L./Sergt. H.	KA	3	5/ 2/43
2617339	Watkins, Gdsm. W.	DW	XIV	30/ 1/44
2618526	Walton, Gdsm. G.	KA	2 Commando	28/ 3/42
2611402	Walker, Gdsm. C.	DW	3	31/ 5/40
2620351	Walmesley, Gdsm. F.	KA	6	17/ 3/43
2619968	Wallace, Gdsm. W.	DW	5	29/ 5/43
2617716	Wadsworth, L./Cpl. E.	KA	4	6/ 8/44
2616522	Watts, Gdsm. R.	KA	5	7/ 2/44*
2618819	Warham, Gdsm. R.	DW	5	27/ 1/44
2614661	Wakeford, Sergt. R.	KA	2	20/ 9/44
2620786	Watson, L./Sergt. G.	KA	5	7/ 7/44
2622118	Wareham, Gdsm. A.	KA	2	25/ 9/44
2615077	Walker, Gdsm. F.	KA	1	1/ 6/40
2619971	Walsh, L./Cpl. A.	DAS	3	5/ 8/43
2616433	Waghorn, Gdsm. J.	DW	1	1/ 8/44
2617780	Wainwright, Gdsm. S.	KA	3	5/ 2/43
2614321	Waters, C.S.M. K.	KA	3	2/ 8/44
2616548	Waterhouse, Gdsm. J.	DAS	1	19/ 5/43
2620509	Walshe, Gdsm. R.	KA	5	6/ 2/44
2623690	Walker, Gdsm. D.	DW	1	28/ 9/44
2613830	Warden, Sergt. H.	KA	6	17/ 3/43
2622624	Webb, Gdsm. E.	KA	5	27/ 4/43
2622261	Westhead, Gdsm. G.	DW	6	12/ 4/44
2615694	Webster, Gdsm. G.	DW	6	24/ 9/43
2617346	Weatherby, Gdsm. T.	DW	5	23/ 4/43
2615738	Weems, L./Sergt. E.	KA	2	3/ 4/45
2613069	Wentworth, L./Cpl. W.	KA	3	21/ 5/40
2613670	Webster, L./Cpl. L.	KA	1	1/ 6/40*
2616244	Webb, Gdsm. G.	DW	1	31/ 5/40*
2617739	Weaver, L./Cpl. G.	KA	4	8/ 4/45
2615268	Webster, Sergt. A.	DAS	E.R.E.	23/ 7/44
2613423	Westlake, Gdsm. L.	KA	3	4/ 2/43
2616017	Welch, Gdsm. J.	KA	1	13/ 8/44
2614971	Weeks, L./Cpl. J.	KA	6	17/ 3/43
2615190	Westby, Gdsm. G.	KA	3	24/ 2/43
2624193	Weaver, Gdsm. D.	KAS	W.G. Bn.	18/ 6/44
2620154	West, Gdsm. H.	KA	5	28/ 4/43
2622729	Whittle, L./Sergt. F.	KA	1	31/ 3/43
848953	White, Sergt. K.	KA	4	3/11/44
2614847	Whittaker, Gdsm. H.	DW	3	4/ 8/44
2619055	Wheeler, L./Cpl. K.	KA	4	5/11/44
2621951	White, Gdsm. C.	KA	5	27/ 4/43
2620598	Whittaker, Gdsm. J.	KA	4 Commando	19/ 8/42
5382558	White, L./Cpl. E.	DW	6	9/ 5/43
2616066	Whelpdale, Gdsm. L.	DW	2	21/ 5/40*
2621507	White, Gdsm. G.	KA	6	17/ 3/43
2622634	Willsher, Gdsm. E.	KA	3	28/ 5/44
2618680	Winstanley, Gdsm. L.	KA	3	15/ 7/44
2614494	Wilkes, Gdsm. A.	KA	1 G.B.	10/ 6/40
2616118	Williams, Gdsm. H.	DW	1	28/ 7/44
2618770	Wilkins, L./Cpl. T.	KA	4	4/ 4/45
2619428	Williams, Gdsm. A.	KA	1	5/ 8/44
2618151	Wingate, Gdsm. G.	KA	5	27/ 4/43
2615927	Wigglesworth, Gdsm. R.	DW	3	1/ 6/40
2614075	Wigley, Gdsm. M.	DW	1	31/ 5/40*
2614981	Wild, Gdsm. J.	KA	5	8/ 2/44*
2615127	Williams, Sergt. F.	KA	1	5/ 3/45
2621465	Wilson, Gdsm. A.	KA	6	16/ 3/43
2614943	Williams, Gdsm. J.	KA	3	31/ 5/40
2620148	Williams, Cpl. J.	DAS	3	15/ 6/43

Number	Name and Rank	Casualty	Battalion	Date
4799063	Wiles, L./Cpl. J.	KA	1	1/ 6/40
2615755	Wilson, Gdsm. W.	KA	4	6/ 8/44
2621987	Wilson, Gdsm. D.	KA	5	27/ 4/43
2618845	Willis, L./Sergt. F.	KA	6	17/ 3/43
2618603	Winstone, L./Cpl. L.	KA	4	30/ 3/45
2613638	Wilson, Gdsm. T.	DW	1	4/ 6/40
2611633	Woodward, Gdsm. H.	KA	2	1/ 6/40*
5499840	Woodley, L./Cpl. S.	KA	3	30/ 5/40
2613135	Woods, Gdsm. C.	KA	1	1/ 6/40
2623538	Woodhouse, Gdsm. J.	KA	2	10/ 4/45
2616401	Woolerton, Gdsm. R.	DW	5	4/ 5/43
2619266	Wood, L./Sergt. C.	DW	6	8/10/43
2612532	Wood, Gdsm. G.	KA	6	17/ 3/43
5333815	Wooders, Gdsm. W.	KA	2	1/ 6/40*
2614140	Worrall, Gdsm. J.	KA	2	16/ 5/40
2615819	Woof, Cpl. F.	DW	2	29/ 7/44
2617045	Worthington, Gdsm. C.	KA	3	10/ 2/44
2620032	Worthington, Gdsm. A.	KA	5	25/ 7/44
2622357	Woolford, Gdsm. E.	DAS	"Y" List	30/ 9/43
2618922	Wright, Gdsm. H.	KA	2	11/ 8/44
2615834	Wray, Gdsm. C.	KA	1	30/ 4/45
2621300	Wright, Gdsm. K.	DW	5	3/ 7/44
2619208	Wright, Gdsm. F.	KA	2	12/ 9/44
2614438	Wright, Gdsm. W.	KA	2	29/ 5/40*
2620721	Wright, Gdsm. C.	KA	6	7/11/43
2623732	Wright, L./Cpl. L.	KA	1	5/ 3/45
2619003	Wright, Gdsm. A.	KA	XIV	28/ 4/43
2616158	Young, L./Sergt. E.	DAS	Training Bn.	12/ 6/42
2616362	Youngman, Gdsm. C.	KA	"X" List	1/ 6/40*
2619973	Yates, Gdsm. H.	DW	6	22/ 9/43

APPENDIX IV

CONSOLIDATED CASUALTIES—OFFICERS AND OTHER RANKS 1939-1945

OFFICERS

	K	*DW*	*K or D in captivity*	*M*		*W*	*PW*
1st Battalion	7	1	1	0	..	39	3
2nd Battalion	15	4	0	0	..	19	0
3rd Battalion	12	6	0	0	..	37	7
4th Battalion	6	0	0	0	..	18	0
5th Battalion	22	3	1	0	..	47	9
6th Battalion	29	4	2	1	..	29	6
Others	12	3	0	0	..	10	3
	103	21	4	1	..	199	28

Total Killed, Died and Missing: 129.

Total Wounded and Prisoners of War: 227.

Combined Total: 356.

OTHER RANKS

	K	*DW*	*K or D in captivity*	*M*		*W*	*PW*
1st Battalion	142	54	0	0	..	636	13
2nd Battalion	106	28	0	0	..	283	15
3rd Battalion	154	57	2	0	..	496	122
4th Battalion	43	8	0	0	..	112	0
5th Battalion	193	86	4	0	..	855	284
6th Battalion	193	57	0	0	..	585	179
	831	290	6	0	..	2,967	613

Total Killed, Died and Missing: 1,127.

Total Wounded and Prisoners of War, 3,580.

Combined Total: 4,707.

APPENDIX V

DECORATIONS AND AWARDS

Victoria Cross

	Gazetted
2614910 L./Cpl. H. Nicholls	30/ 7/40
Major W. P. Sidney	30/ 3/44

PART ONE—OFFICERS

ORDER OF THE BATH

COMPANION OF THE BATH

Major-General A. H. S. Adair, D.S.O., M.C.	29/ 3/45
Lieut.-Colonel P. G. S. Gregson-Ellis, O.B.E.	14/ 6/45

ROYAL VICTORIAN ORDER

COMMANDER OF ROYAL VICTORIAN ORDER

Major A. H. Penn, M.C.	1/ 1/46
Major G. P. Philipps	1/ 1/46

ORDER OF THE BRITISH EMPIRE

KNIGHT COMMANDER

Lieutenant-General F. A. M. Browning, C.B., D.S.O.	1/ 1/46

COMMANDER

Lieut.-Colonel P. D. Miller, O.B.E	20/ 9/45

OFFICERS

Lieut.-Colonel P. G. S. Gregson-Ellis	9/ 7/40
Lieut.-Colonel W. H. Diggle, D.S.O., M.C.	3/ 9/40
Lieut.-Colonel. C. R. Gerard, D.S.O.	2/ 6/43
Lieut.-Colonel P. D. Miller	23/ 9/43
Lieut.-Colonel C. Earle	23/ 9/43
Major G. F. Turner, M.B.E., D.C.M.	8/ 6/44
Lieut.-Colonel J. A. Goschen	24/ 8/44
Colonel C. G. Keith, M.C.	1/ 2/45
Colonel R. P. Fleming	14/ 6/45
Major G. E. Shelley	14/ 6/45
Lieut.-Colonel G. C. FitzH. Harcourt-Vernon, D.S.O., M.C.	28/ 6/45
Lieut.-Colonel A. M. Stern	28/ 6/45
Major Hon. B. Pleydell-Bouverie	13/12/45
Lieut.-Colonel A. W. Acland, M.C., T.D.	24/ 1/46
Lieut.-Colonel A. S. Hanning	24/ 1/46
Lieut.-Colonel H. E. E. Ault	13/ 6/46

MEMBERS

	Gazetted
Capt. P. W. Marsham	9/ 7/40
Lieut. (Qrmr.) R. S. Walker	9/ 7/40
Major N. D. M. Johnstone	26/12/41
Lieut. (Qrmr.) T. W. Garnett	2/ 6/43
Major A. W. H. Grant	2/ 6/43
Major G. E. Pike	23/ 9/43
Lieut. J. F. Prideaux	14/10/43
Lieut. D. I. Rollo	15/ 6/44
Capt. A. G. Howland-Jackson	21/12/44
Major Viscount Errington	1/ 2/45
Major D. W. Heneage	1/ 2/45
Major Hon. F. F. G. Hennessy	1/ 2/45
Capt. R. A. Paget-Cooke	19/ 4/45
Lieut. (Qrmr.) E. V. Philpott	19/ 4/45
Major J. G. S. Gammell	21/ 6/45
Capt. N. Nicolson	28/ 6/45
Capt. A. R. Taylor	28/ 6/45
Major R. H. Whitworth	20/ 9/45
Capt. J. D. Buchanan	20/ 9/45
Major J. P. T. Boscawen	11/10/45
Capt. D. V. Bendall	13/12/45
Lieut.-Colonel A. E. C. Taylor	13/12/45
Major G. F. R. Hirst, M.C.	1/ 1/46
Lieut. (Qrmr.) E. R. Randall	24/ 1/46
Capt. P. R. Colville	24/ 1/46
Major R. C. F. Gerard	24/ 1/46
Major D. J. Beaumont-Nesbitt	13/ 6/46

DISTINGUISHED SERVICE ORDER

Lieut.-Colonel A. H. S. Adair, M.C.	27/ 8/40
Major R. N. Brinckman	8/ 8/41
Lieut.-Colonel G. C. Gordon-Lennox	8/ 7/43
Major A. F. L. Clive, M.C.	22/ 7/43
Lieut.-Colonel A. G. W. Heber-Percy	23/ 9/43
Brigadier J. A. Gascoigne	27/ 1/44
Lieut.-Colonel W. H. Kingsmill, M.C.	27/ 1/44
Capt. R. M. C. Howard	23/ 3/44
Major Sir Hugh J. F. S. Cholmeley, Bt.	20/ 7/44
Major T. P. Butler	3/ 8/44
Capt. W. J. L. Willson	7/12/44
Lieut.-Colonel E. H. Goulburn	21/12/44
Lieut.-Colonel J. N. R. Moore	1/ 3/45
Lieut.-Colonel E. J. B. Nelson, M.C	10/ 5/45
Major G. E. Pike, M.B.E.	10/ 5/45
Lieut.-Colonel Lord Tryon	10/ 5/45
Major I. J. Crosthwaite	21/ 6/45
Lieut.-Colonel P. H. Lort-Phillips	28/ 6/45
Lieut.-Colonel P. T. Clifton	23/ 8/45
Lieut.-Colonel C. Earle, O.B.E.	24/ 1/46
Colonel R. B. R. Colvin	20/ 7/46

BAR TO DISTINGUISHED SERVICE ORDER

	Gazetted
Lieut.-Colonel A. F. L. Clive, D.S.O., M.C.	20/ 7/44
Brigadier E. H. Goulburn, D.S.O.	1/ 3/45
Lieut.-Colonel A. G. W. Heber-Percy, D.S.O.	26/ 4/45
Lieut.-Colonel P. H. Lort-Phillips, D.S.O.	12/ 7/45

MILITARY CROSS

Major A. F. L. Clive	9/ 7/40
2/Lieut. J. A. P. Jones	9/ 7/40
Lieut. R. Crompton-Roberts	11/ 7/40
Capt. W. H. Kingsmill	20/12/40
Major R. N. Brinckman, D.S.O.	30/ 9/41
Lieut. D. W. D. Bond	11/ 2/43
Major K. E. M. Tufnell	4/ 5/43
Major A. Heywood-Lonsdale	22/ 7/43
Lieut. G. G. H. Marriott	22/ 7/43
Major C. W. Norman-Barnett	22/ 7/43
Major A. J. E. Gordon	19/ 8/43
Lieut. W. S. Dugdale	23/ 9/43
Capt. E. J. B. Nelson	23/ 9/43
Lieut. G. R. Stokes-Roberts	27/ 1/44
Major H. C. Hanbury	24/ 2/44
Major G. E. W. Potter	24/ 2/44
Capt. J. D. Whatman	23/ 3/44
Capt. Hon. M. F. Fitzalan-Howard	6/ 4/44
Lieut. G. W. Chaplin	15/ 6/44
Capt. T. S. Hohler	15/ 6/44
Capt. Lord Stanley	15/ 6/44
Capt. M. W. Grazebrook	29/ 6/44
Major E. C. W. M. Penn	29/ 6/44
Lieut. J. E. Renton	29/ 6/44
Lieut. The Master of Saltoun	29/ 6/44
Lieut. J. A. Fergusson-Cuninghame	19/10/44
Capt. A. D. Angus	7/12/44
Lieut. D. I. Rollo, M.B.E.	7/12/44
Capt. A. G. Way	7/12/44
Lieut. C. I. M. Williams	7/12/44
Major N. E. W. Baker	21/12/44
Major F. J. C. Bowes-Lyon	21/12/44
Major J. C. Gascoigne	21/12/44
Lieut. Hon. J. R. B. Norton	21/12/44
Lieut. P. G. A. Prescott	21/12/44
Lieut. J. Penn	8/ 2/45
Major R. H. Bromley	1/ 3/45
Capt. Lord Carrington	1/ 3/45
Capt. J. B. Currie	1/ 3/45
Lieut. G. R. Merton	1/ 3/45
Capt. J. W. Neville	1/ 3/45
Major H. F. Stanley	1/ 3/45
Lieut. D. B. Fergusson	8/ 3/45
Lieut. G. F. Rocke	22/ 3/45
Lieut. Hon. S. D. Loch	29/ 3/45

	Gazetted
Lieut. R. J. McCallum	12/ 4/45
Lieut. Hon. L. G. H. Russell	12/ 4/45
Lieut. P. R. Freyberg	19/ 4/45
Lieut. M. Stoop	7/ 6/45
Capt. R. R. Etherton	21/ 6/45
Major A. M. H. Gregory-Hood	21/ 6/45
Major C. E. H. Villiers	21/ 6/45
Major D. V. Bonsor	28/ 6/45
Lieut. A. J. Savill	28/ 6/45
Lieut. A. MacR. Collie	12/ 7/45
Major R. H. Heywood-Lonsdale	12/ 7/45
Lieut. J. N. R. Hearne	12/ 7/45
Major J. Tufnell	12/ 7/45
Major Hon. G. N. C. Wigram	12/ 7/45
Lieut. J. F. D. Johnston	2/ 8/45
Major S. E. Bolitho	23/ 8/45
Major G. Thorne	11/10/45
Capt. R. Ritchie	15/11/45
Lieut. J. W. Harkness	13/12/45
Lieut. Hon. T. A. Corbett	24/ 1/46
Major B. A. Johnston	24/ 1/46
Capt. S. C. Rolleston	24/ 1/46
Capt. J. H. Wiggin	21/ 2/46
Lieut.-Colonel A. E. H. Villiers	4/ 4/46
Major H. A. D. Buchanan	18/ 4/46

BAR TO MILITARY CROSS

Capt. J. A. P. Jones, M.C.	19/10/44
Major N. E. W. Baker, M.C.	1/ 3/45
Major F. J. C. Bowes-Lyon, M.C.	1/ 3/45
Major A. M. H. Gregory-Hood, M.C.	12/ 7/45

MENTIONED IN DESPATCHES

Capt. G. R. Westmacott, D.S.O.	23/ 7/40
Lieut. E. W. S. Ford	23/ 7/40
Capt. E. J. B. Nelson	23/ 7/40
Brigadier G. E. C. Rasch, C.V.O., D.S.O.	23/ 7/40
Lieut.-Colonel P. J. M. Ellison	20/12/40
Capt. Hon. M. F. Fitzalan-Howard	20/12/40
Major W. H. Goschen	20/12/40
Lieut. G. C. F. Gwyer	20/12/40
Capt. C. J. D. Jeffreys, M.V.O.	20/12/40
Lieut.-Colonel J. A. Lloyd	20/12/40
Capt. Earl of Munster	20/12/40
Major G. E. Pike	20/12/40
Lieut.-Colonel J. A. Prescott	20/12/40
Major O. W. D. Smith	20/12/40
Major L. S. Starkey	20/12/40
Capt. J. Trotter	20/12/40
Brigadier A. H. S. Adair, D.S.O., M.C.	29/ 4/41
Capt. A. D. Dodds-Parker	26/ 9/41
Capt. P. W. Marsham, M.B.E.	26/ 9/41

	Gazetted
Major R. N. Brinckman, D.S.O.	30/ 9/41
Lieut. J. F. Prideaux	30/12/41
Capt. A. G. Way	23/ 9/43
Capt. J. D. Buchanan	23/ 9/43
Major M. G. D. Clive	23/ 9/43
Lieut. G. W. Chaplin	23/ 9/43
Lieut. T. H. Faber	23/ 9/43
Lieut. D. B. Fergusson	23/ 9/43
Major A. C. Huntington, M.V.O.	23/ 9/43
Lieut. B. M. Ogilvie	23/ 9/43
Capt. R. C. Riseley	29/ 3/43
Capt. A. M. Stern	23/ 9/43
Capt. P. le R. Shephard	23/ 9/43
Major G. F. Turner, M.B.E., D.C.M.	23/ 9/43
Major T. P. Butler	15/ 6/44
Lieut. M. R. Bonham-Carter	15/ 6/44
Lieut. J. Tayleur	24/ 8/44
Major S. E. H. Baillie	24/ 8/44
Lieut.-Colonel Sir William R. de B. des Voeux, Bt.	24/ 8/44
Capt. R. C. Rowan	24/ 8/44
Capt. A. R. Taylor	11/ 1/45
Capt. D. Willis	11/ 1/45
Capt. A. D. Angus	11/ 1/45
Major P. C. Britten	11/ 1/45
Lieut. Hon. V. S. de R. Canning	11/ 1/45
Major E. W. S. Ford	11/ 1/45
Lieut. H. W. Freeman-Attwood	11/ 1/45
Lieut.-Colonel G. C. Gordon-Lennox, D.S.O.	11/ 1/45
Lieut. R. G. King-Smith	11/ 1/45
Lieut. R. H. Leeke	11/ 1/45
Major W. E. P. Miller	11/ 1/45
Capt. N. Nicolson	11/ 1/45
Major G. E. Pike	11/ 1/45
Lieut. (Qrmr.) B. H. Pratt	11/ 1/45
Capt. B. A. F. Hervey-Bathurst	15/ 3/45
Lieut. P. N. Whitley	22/ 3/45
Major-General A. H. S. Adair, D.S.O., M.C.	22/ 3/45
Capt. P. R. Colville	22/ 3/45
Major J. G. S. Gammell	22/ 3/45
Major Sir Arthur L. Grant, Bt.	22/ 3/45
Lieut.-Colonel J. N. R. Moore, D.S.O.	22/ 3/45
Lieut. (Qrmr.) E. R. Randall	22/ 3/45
Capt. J. D. W. Stobart	22/ 3/45
Major J. Trotter	22/ 3/45
Major G. F. Turner, M.B.E., D.C.M.	22/ 3/45
Major W. H. Goschen	5/ 4/45
Lieut. Colonel Lord Tryon, D.S.O.	10/ 5/45
Lieut. M. G. T. Webster	10/ 5/45
Lieut. Hon. T. A. Corbett	10/ 5/45
Lieut.-Colonel G. R. de Beer	10/ 5/45
Major Hon. M. F. Fitzalan-Howard	10/ 5/45
Lieut. D. A. C. Rasch	10/ 5/45
Capt D. V. Bendall	19/ 7/45
Lieut. W. S. Dugdale	19/ 7/45
Capt. P. R. de L. Giffard	19/ 7/45

	Gazetted
Lieut. W. H. D. Heaton-Armstrong	19/ 7/45
Lieut. M. H. Jenkins	19/ 7/45
Capt. G. H. Micklem	19/ 7/45
Major R. L. M. Lawes	2/ 8/45
Major G. Thorne	9/ 8/45
Lieut. A. D. Winch	9/ 8/45
Major-General A. H. S. Adair, C.B., D.S.O., M.C.	9/ 8/45
Lieut. R. F. Edward-Collins	9/ 8/45
Major A. M. H. Gregory-Hood, M.C.	9/ 8/45
Lieut. J. F. D. Johnston, M.C.	9/ 8/45
Colonel C. G. Keith, O.B.E., M.C.	9/ 8/45
Colonel R. S. Lambert, M.C.	9/ 8/45
Lieut.-Colonel Sir William R. de B. des Voeux, Bt.	20/ 9/45
Major M. S. B. Vernon, M.V.O.	23/ 9/45
Capt. R. Ritchie	27/ 9/45
Capt. H. W. Wollaston	8/11/45
Lieut. A. R. Harding	8/11/45
Capt. R. Steele	8/11/45
Capt. I. R. K. Swift	8/11/45
Capt. M. Dawson	8/11/45
Lieut.-Colonel C. M. F. Deakin	8/11/45
Major H. J. Gould	8/11/45
Lieut. J. W. Harkness	29/11/45
Major C. E. Irby, M.C.	29/11/45
Major Hon. F. M. Legh	29/11/45
Capt. D. V. Bendall	29/11/45
Lieut. R. O. H. Crewdson	29/11/45
Capt. A. M. Denny	29/11/45
Major C. B. Frederick	29/11/45
Lieut.-Colonel A. G. W. Heber-Percy, D.S.O.	1945
Lieut. A. J. Courage	22/ 3/46
Lieut. R. C. Taylor	4/ 4/46
Major T. F. C. Winnington	4/ 4/46
Major P. A. Walker	4/ 4/46
Major A. G. Heywood	4/ 4/46
Major R. S. A. Hardy	4/ 4/46
Capt. J. Howe	4/ 4/46
Colonel C. G. Keith, O.B.E., M.C.	4/ 4/46
Capt. R. P. Letcher	4/ 4/46
Lieut. J. R. M. Rocke	4/ 4/46
Major-General A. H. S. Adair, C.B., D.S.O., M.C.	4/ 4/46
Capt. W. T. Agar	4/ 4/46
Lieut. (Qrmr.) J. E. Bolton	4/ 4/46
Lieut. A. N. Breitmeyer	4/ 4/46
Capt. (Qrmr.) F. E. J. Carver	4/ 4/46
Capt. M. A. Cooke	4/ 4/46
Lieut.-Colonel G. R. de Beer	4/ 4/46
Major Viscount Errington	4/ 4/46
Lieut. F. C. H. Fryer	4/ 4/46
Capt. E. F. Fairbanks-Smith	4/ 4/46
Lieut.-Colonel E. H. Goulburn, D.S.O.	4/ 4/46
Capt. R. V. C. Westmacott	23/ 5/46
Capt. R. C. Wilson	23/ 5/46
Capt. A. E. Yuill	23/ 5/46
Major Hon. D. S. T. B. Dixon	23/ 5/46

	Gazetted
Capt. J. B Hosegood	23/ 5/46
Lieut. G. W. Lamb	23/ 5/46
Capt. R. A. T. G. Meyrick	23/ 5/46
Capt. A. E. P. Needham	23/ 5/46
Major E. F. Oliver	23/ 5/46
Major E. F. Stern	23/ 5/46
Lieut. T. E. Streatfeild-Moore	23/ 5/46

CERTIFICATES FOR MERIT, GALLANTRY AND GOOD SERVICE

CERTIFICATE OF MERIT

Lieut.-Colonel C. M. Dillwyn-Venables-Llewelyn, M.V.O. .. .. ..
Lieut. (Qrmr.) B. H. Pratt 1942
Lieut. (Qrmr.) T. W. Garnett 1943

COMMANDER-IN-CHIEF'S CERTIFICATE FOR GALLANTRY

Lieut. M. Dawson 1944
Lieut. J. B. Sumner 1944

COMMANDER-IN-CHIEF'S CERTIFICATE FOR GOOD SERVICE

Lieut. G. W. Howarth 1944
Lieut. J. R. M. Rocke 1944

FOREIGN DECORATIONS AND AWARDS

UNITED STATES OF AMERICA

SILVER STAR

Lieut.-Colonel E. J. B. Nelson, M.C. 28/12/44

BRONZE STAR

Lieut. J. Tayleur 1945
Lieut.-Colonel P. D. Miller, C.B.E. 1946

LEGION OF MERIT

Colonel J. L. Campbell 4/ 4/46

FRANCE

LEGION OF HONOUR

Major-General A. H. S. Adair, C.B., D.S.O., M.C. 1945

CROIX DE GUERRE WITH PALM

Major-General A. H. S. Adair, C.B., D.S.O., M.C. 1945

CROIX DE GUERRE WITH GILT STAR

Major I. J. Crosthwaite 1945
Major G. F. Turner, O.B.E., D.C.M. 1945
Capt. M. Dawson 1945

CROIX DE GUERRE WITH SILVER STAR

Lieut. F. J. Jefferson 1945

Gazetted

BELGIUM

OFFICER OF THE ORDER OF LEOPOLD WITH PALM

Colonel R. S. Lambert, M.C. 1945

CROIX DE GUERRE, 1940, WITH PALM

Colonel R. S. Lambert, M.C. 1945
Lieut.-Colonel Lord Tryon, D.S.O. 1945
Lieut.-Colonel Sir John L. Gilmour 1945

CHEVALIER OF THE ORDER OF LEOPOLD II

Lieut.-Colonel Lord Tryon, D.S.O. 1945

CHEVALIER OF THE ORDER OF THE CROWN WITH PALM

Lieut.-Colonel Sir John L. Gilmour 1945

CHEVALIER OF THE ORDER OF LEOPOLD II WITH PALM

Major H. G. C. Illingworth 1945

CROIX DE GUERRE WITH PALM

Major H. G. C. Illingworth 1945

HOLLAND

KNIGHT COMMANDER OF THE ORDER OF ORANGE NASSAU WITH SWORDS

Brigadier E. H. Goulburn, D.S.O. 28/ 5/46

PART TWO—OTHER RANKS

MILITARY CROSS

2612933 R.S.M. F. Dowling 21/12/44
2612943 R.Q.M.S. J. Oldfield 11/10/45

ORDER OF THE BRITISH EMPIRE

MEMBERS

2606109 R.S.M. H. Robinson 30/12/41
2609368 O.R.Q.M.S. F. Booth 26/ 5/42
2609380 R.S.M. A. Douglas 2/ 6/43
2604909 R.Q.M.S. W. Lavers, D.C.M. 31/12/43
2608107 R.Q.M.S. T. Scott 2/ 6/44
2610100 R.Q.M.S. J. Atkinson 21/12/44
2609294 R.S.M. W. Hagell 21/12/44
5328437 R.S.M. E. Miness 29/12/44
2607683 R.Q.M.S. W. Reed .. ..
2610922 W.O.II C. Reeve 13/12/45
2610258 R.S.M. A. Warburton 13/12/45
2605738 W.O.II W. Stubbs 1/ 1/46
2609814 R.S.M. B. Deakin 1/ 1/46

Gazetted

BRITISH EMPIRE MEDAL

2612035	Sergt. S. Watling	21/ 9/43
2615198	Sergt. F. Roscoe	21/ 9/43
3448414	L./Sergt. A. Howarth	21/ 9/43
2614873	Sergt. A. Hallows	20/ 9/45
2615214	Sergt. H. Williams	20/ 9/45
2615248	Sergt. E. Boyers	13/12/45
2614932	Clr.-Sergt. T. W. Sherratt	9/ 1/46
2613182	W.O.II A. Peters	9/ 1/46
2611726	Sergt. E. Scott	9/ 1/46
2612226	L./Sergt. G. Brown	4/ 6/46
2618069	Sergt. A. Cottam	4/ 6/46

DISTINGUISHED CONDUCT MEDAL

2613030	P.S.M. A. Cassford	11/ 7/40
2611848	P.S.M. H. Wood	27/ 8/40
2615150	L./Sergt. N. Bullock	27/ 8/40
867330	Sergt. H. Mitchell	22/10/40
2614780	Sergt. J. Wood	22/10/40
2615873	Sergt. J. Weston	21/10/41
2616748	L./Cpl. J. Byrne	6/ 4/43
2614133	L./Cpl. A. Baker	22/ 4/43
2617752	L./Cpl. F. Walmsley	30/ 4/43
2614185	Sergt. S. Delebecque	17/ 8/43
2613643	Sergt. J. Harrison	17/ 8/43
2616563	L./Sergt. F. Fletcher	21/ 3/44
2022288	D./Sergt. G. Armstrong	13/ 6/44
2620559	L./Sergt. H. Hough	13/ 6/44
2614627	Sergt. A. Treeby	27/ 6/44
2615284	C.S.M. C. Feebury	3/ 8/44
2615794	Clr.-Sergt. J. Spiller	5/12/44
2613675	Sergt. G. Wilcox	21/12/44
2613912	Sergt. P. Robinson	1/ 3/45
2613804	Gdsm. W. Meadows	1/ 3/45
2613330	Sergt. L. Berresford	1/ 3/45
2615057	Sergt. J. Sibbald	6/ 3/45
2612007	Sergt. A. Goult	6/ 3/45
2618220	L./Cpl. V. Garner	19/ 6/45
2619843	L./Sergt. C. Harwood	23/ 8/45
2627280	Sergt. A. McCree	23/ 8/45
2616015	Sergt. R. Wood	24/ 1/46

MILITARY MEDAL

2614519	Sergt. G. Osborne	9/ 7/40
2615595	Gdsm. J. Kosbab	9/ 7/40
2613550	Gdsm. W. Maund	23/ 8/40
2613354	Gdsm. W. Hardy	20/12/40
2612864	C.S.M. F. Aston	19/ 8/41
5382080	Gdsm. H. Collett	4/11/41
2617252	C.S.M. G. Barnes	24/ 2/42
4141633	Sergt. D. Kershaw	3/11/42
2617533	L./Sergt. R. Bennett	3/11/42

		Gazetted
2617725	L./Sergt. G. Rose	3/11/42
2619513	Gdsm. G. Fairclough	5/ 1/43
2615840	Gdsm. F. Waller	30/ 4/43
2620306	L./Sergt. C. Wilkes	6/ 7/43
2620010	Gdsm. H. Heseltine	6/ 7/43
2621138	L./Cpl. R. Taylor	20/ 7/43
2611610	Sergt. E. Smith	17/ 8/43
2621074	L./Cpl. W. Aden	17/ 8/43
2612147	Gdsm. A. Clark	24/ 8/43
2617665	L./Sergt. R. Holmes	10/ 9/43
2620979	Gdsm. W. Davies	21/ 9/43
2618357	Gdsm. C. Hoyle	21/ 9/43
2617867	Gdsm. W. Sargeant	21/ 9/43
2617187	Gdsm. T. Seale	21/ 9/43
2619341	Cpl. W. Westripp	23/ 9/43
2620077	L./Sergt. J. White	16/11/43
2620294	Sergt. H. Pollard	23/11/43
5834230	L./Cpl. L. Bozeat	23/11/43
2618485	L./Sergt. T. Morely	25/ 1/44
2618253	Gdsm. W. Butterworth	25/ 1/44
2621363	Gdsm. S. Scott	22/ 2/44
2614175	L./Sergt. V. Buck	21/ 3/44
2618001	L./Sergt. D. Nixey	21/ 3/44
2615780	L./Cpl. J. Edwards	21/ 3/44
2620673	Gdsm. R. Higgs	21/ 3/44
2618923	Gdsm. F. Smith	21/ 3/44
2617414	Gdsm. S. Taylor	21/ 3/44
2616841	Gdsm. E. Worley	21/ 3/44
2615140	L./Sergt. J. Stacey	25/ 4/44
2618478	Sergt. R. Williams	13/ 6/44
2619676	Cpl. G. Simmonds	13/ 6/44
2618589	L./Sergt. J. Wilkinson	13/ 6/44
2619757	L./Cpl. R. Shirley	13/ 6/44
2620653	Gdsm. W. Heath	13/ 6/44
261396	Gdsm. R. Stratton	13/ 6/44
2623394	Gdsm. W. Thorman	13/ 6/44
2612922	Gdsm. S. White	13/ 6/44
5045681	Sergt. A. Bartram	27/ 6/44
2612263	L./Cpl. J. Walsh	27/ 6/44
2615068	Gdsm. H. Butcher	27/ 6/44
2623066	Gdsm. T. Murphy	27/ 6/44
2608829	Gdsm. R. Porter	27/ 6/44
2609443	R.Q.M.S. C. Hutchinson	18/ 7/44
2616491	Cpl. J. Anchor	3/10/44
2616227	L./Sergt. E. Lister	19/10/44
2623408	Gdsm. P. Gregory	19/10/44
2622769	Gdsm. W. Palmer	19/10/44
2609784	Sergt. J. Howe	26/10/44
2614321	C.S.M. K. Waters	5/12/44
2613477	Sergt. F. Lovett	5/12/44
2613036	L./Sergt. E. Benton	5/12/44
2614198	L./Sergt. W. Grandfield	5/12/44
2617369	L./Sergt. J. Wardle	5/12/44
2623583	L./Cpl. C. Wellings	5/12/44
2617477	Gdsm. A. Atkinson	5/12/44

		Gazetted
2620020	Gdsm. J. Downing	5/12/44
2623062	Gdsm. A. Drake	5/12/44
2617559	Gdsm. W. Eaton	5/12/44
2620662	Gdsm. L. Tunnicliffe	5/12/44
2617417	Gdsm. A. Hill	21/12/44
2614409	Sergt. W. Armstrong	21/12/44
2620788	L./Sergt. S. Everin	21/12/44
2612594	L./Sergt. P. Kinsella	21/12/44
2619464	L./Cpl. R. Stenhouse	21/12/44
2615634	L./Cpl. W. Leese	21/12/44
2616117	L./Sergt. D. Wright	4/ 1/45
2621991	L./Sergt. A. Hill	8/ 2/45
2614073	Gdsm. J. Foster	8/ 2/45
2623478	L./Cpl. R. Green	8/ 2/45
2621950	L./Cpl. J. Chriscoli	8/ 2/45
2614553	L./Cpl. J. O'Connor	8/ 2/45
2618280	Gdsm. W. Hind	1/ 3/45
2622575	L./Sergt. C. Pacey	1/ 3/45
2620729	Sergt. W. Partridge	1/ 3/45
2619047	Gdsm. C. Knight	1/ 3/45
2617892	L./Sergt. S. Harper	1/ 3/45
2619502	Gdsm. R. Baylis	1/ 3/45
2615597	Sergt. A. Taylor	1/ 3/45
2615984	L./Cpl. C. Jeanes	1/ 3/45
2610974	Sergt. W. Hopkins	1/ 3/45
2622757	L./Sergt. C. Plumb	1/ 3/45
2617007	Gdsm. F. Binns	1/ 3/45
2618494	L./Sergt. H. Lippitt	1/ 3/45
2615131	Sergt. L. Atkins	1/ 3/45
2612551	Sergt. T. Annis	6/ 3/45
2622000	Gdsm. R. Wood	6/ 3/45
2615239	Gdsm. H. Barnes	6/ 3/45
2618660	L./Cpl. H. Dean	20/ 3/45
2618250	Gdsm. E. Stokes	12/ 4/45
2612026	Sergt. G. Hanks	8/ 5/45
2031321	Sergt. A. Mulligan	8/ 5/45
2618617	Sergt. A. Heritage	8/ 5/45
2622834	L./Sergt. H. Chaffer	22/ 5/45
2611872	C.S.M. T. Ford	21/ 6/45
14671940	Gdsm. A. Barber	21/ 6/45
2618476	L./Sergt. T. Ellingham	26/ 6/45
2621474	L./Sergt. W. Brown	26/ 6/45
2615322	Clr.-Sergt. D. Huxley	10/ 7/45
2622726	L./Sergt. A. Mills	10/ 7/45
2613681	L./Cpl. F. Chappell	10/ 7/45
2614374	L./Sergt. G. Dunham	10/ 7/45
2614606	Sergt. C. Ashcroft	10/ 7/45
2611770	L./Sergt. G. Worsfold	10/ 7/45
2625013	L./Cpl. A. Loosely	10/ 7/45
2612929	L./Sergt. J. Marrow	10/ 7/45
2618135	L./Sergt. A. Grimshaw	2/ 8/45
2617512	L./Sergt. F. Cottrell	2/ 8/45
3447690	C.S.M. S. Lowe	23/ 8/45
2622361	L./Sergt. F. Clutton	23/ 8/45
2615283	L./Sergt. H. York	23/ 8/45

		Gazetted
2615730	Sergt. O. Smith	11/10/45
2615950	Sergt. R. Topham	13/12/45
2610382	R.S.M. A. Spratlet	24/ 1/46
2616032	Sergt. A. Dennis	24/ 1/46
2616704	Sergt. R. Sollitt	24/ 1/46
2620780	Gdsm. T. Caswell	24/ 1/46
6284792	Mscn. W. Dixon	19/ 2/46

BAR TO MILITARY MEDAL

2617252	C.S.M. G. Barnes, M.M.	3/11/42
2617725	L./Sergt. G. Rose, M.M.	14/10/45

MENTIONED IN DESPATCHES

2616209	L./Cpl. H. Leagas	20/12/40
2613737	Gdsm. C. Hodgkinson	20/12/40
5184516	Gdsm. R. Jenkins	20/12/40
2615536	Sergt. F. Bell	20/12/40
2615261	L./Cpl. J. Longdon	20/12/40
2613419	L./Cpl. G. Croft	20/12/40
2616108	Gdsm. R. Brammer	20/12/40
2612976	Sergt. R. Banks	20/12/40
2615143	L./Sergt. A. Moon	20/12/40
2613292	Gdsm. W. Hawthorn	20/12/40
2614807	Gdsm. J. Bowers	20/12/40
2614846	Gdsm. P. Nash	26/ 7/41
2610163	C.S.M. M. Young	26/ 7/41
2611910	C.S.M. C. Longbottom	30/12/41
2609951	C.S.M. J. Butler	6/ 3/42
1066403	P.S.M. W. Frewin	6/ 3/42
3448514	L./Cpl. A. Howarth	5/ 1/43
2615284	Sergt. C. Feebery	22/ 6/43
2608517	C.S.M. J. King	3/ 8/43
5109772	Cpl. J. Holder	14/ 9/43
2022288	D./Sergt. G. Armstrong, D.C.M.	21/ 9/43
2041221	C.S.M. C. Fielding	21/ 9/43
2615248	Sergt. E. Boyers	21/ 9/43
2617420	Sergt. A. Roberts	21/ 9/43
2613794	L./Sergt. W. Cottingham	21/ 9/43
2616716	L./Sergt. B. Cooper	21/ 9/43
2620004	L./Sergt. A. Green	21/ 9/43
2617023	L./Sergt. A. Houghton	21/ 9/43
2614899	L./Sergt. H. Pooley	21/ 9/43
2616943	L./Sergt. V. Purdue	21/ 9/43
2620074	L./Sergt. L. Robinson	21/ 9/43
2620860	L./Sergt. C. Ward	21/ 9/43
2613036	L./Cpl. E. Benton	21/ 9/43
2618085	L./Cpl. J. Cockton	21/ 9/43
2613081	L./Cpl. J. Jepson	21/ 9/43
2618395	L./Cpl. D. Spencer	21/ 9/43
2615697	Gdsm. D. Armstrong	21/ 9/43
2619952	Gdsm. E. Danger	21/ 9/43
2612422	Gdsm. J. Owen	21/ 9/43

		Gazetted
3525857	Gdsm. A. Rigby	21/ 9/43
2614947	Sergt. E. Oatridge	21/ 9/43
2615391	Sergt. R. Woodland	21/ 9/43
2620559	L./Sergt. H. Hough	21/ 9/43
2613987	L./Sergt. C. Dodd	21/ 9/43
2619012	L./Sergt. A. Power	21/ 9/43
2617608	L./Sergt. K. Roberts	21/ 9/43
2616052	L./Sergt. A. Whiting	21/ 9/43
2612266	L./Cpl. P. Pearson	21/ 9/43
2618589	L./Cpl. J. Wilkinson	21/ 9/43
2620082	Gdsm. J. Asbury	21/ 9/43
2622267	Gdsm. F. Holt	21/ 9/43
2621560	Gdsm. I. Peerless	21/ 9/43
5334534	Gdsm. J. Westbrooke	21/ 9/43
2618642	Cpl. G. Ollerenshaw	11/ 1/44
2608714	C.S.M. F. Dorley	25/ 4/44
2621940	Sergt. R. Sidlow	25/ 4/44
2612833	R.S.M. F. Dowling	28/ 4/44
2621595	L./Cpl. J. Leese	28/ 4/44
2621410	L./Cpl. H. Giltspur	22/ 8/44
2619119	Gdsm. C. Hyde	22/ 8/44
2616783	Gdsm. A. Mason	22/ 8/44
2621940	Sergt. R. Sidlow	7/11/44
2615590	Gdsm. G. Spence	5/12/44
2613834	D./Sergt. C. Hackett	11/ 1/45
2616329	Gdsm. J. Blasdale	11/ 1/45
2612320	Gdsm. W. Bower	11/ 1/45
2621969	Gdsm. A. Cuthbertson	11/ 1/45
2620979	Gdsm. W. Davies, M.M.	11/ 1/45
2618036	Gdsm. S. Ryan	11/ 1/45
2620246	L./Sergt. T. Crowder	11/ 1/45
2614142	C.S.M. W. Lewis	11/ 1/45
2614321	C.S.M. K. Waters, M.M.	11/ 1/45
2615305	Sergt. J. Goodlad	11/ 1/45
2615237	Sergt. C. Prior	11/ 1/45
2614823	L./Cpl. D. Marshall	11/ 1/45
2616723	C.S.M. J. Bayliss	11/ 1/45
2612633	Sergt. J. Challinor	11/ 1/45
2616967	Sergt. P. Doherty	11/ 1/45
4530416	Sergt. J. Flanagan	11/ 1/45
2618915	Sergt. L. Hampton	11/ 1/45
5048657	Sergt. C. Pankhurst	11/ 1/45
2621515	L./Cpl. L. Tiplady	11/ 1/45
2620181	Gdsm. F. Beaumont	11/ 1/45
2611098	Sergt. E. Ashwin	22/ 3/45
2622425	Sergt. A. Howe	22/ 3/45
2613547	C.S.M. A. Pook	22/ 3/45
2615805	Gdsm. T. Maxfield	22/ 3/45
829263	Clr.-Sergt. J. Blake	8/ 5/45
2613330	Sergt. L. Berresford	8/ 5/45
2613677	L./Sergt. R. Ridler	8/ 5/45
2615520	Gdsm. A. Beech	8/ 5/45
2617725	R.S.M. G. Rose, M.M.	10/ 5/45
2605318	R.Q.M.S. S. Balchin	10/ 5/45
2612464	S.S.M. H. Stockton	10/ 5/45

		Gazetted
2612188	Sergt. R. Gouldstone	10/ 5/45
2615502	Sergt. G. Edmunds	21/ 6/45
2617681	C.S.M. H. Beasely	19/ 7/45
2611981	C.S.M. F. Williams	19/ 7/45
2612954	Sergt. A. Allen	19/ 7/45
2618007	Sergt. J. Mashiter	19/ 7/45
2617683	Sergt. L. Taylor	19/ 7/45
2613143	Sergt. E. Watson	19/ 7/45
2611144	L./Sergt. R. Hurst	19/ 7/45
2623696	L./Cpl. J. Hirst	19/ 7/45
2911298	Gdsm. J. Boddy	19/ 7/45
2616419	Gdsm. C. Legg	19/ 7/45
2622713	Gdsm. K. Pridham	19/ 7/45
2618663	Gdsm. K. Quiney	19/ 7/45
2605518	R.S.M. E. Kay	2/ 8/45
2613636	Sergt. T. Jackson	7/ 8/45
2031321	Sergt. A. Mulligan, M.M.	7/ 8/45
2616747	Sergt. J. Purser	7/ 8/45
2615877	Sergt. A. Kingston	7/ 8/45
2622163	L./Sergt. R. Chapman	7/ 8/45
2616964	L./Sergt. R. Leadbetter	7/ 8/45
2614705	L./Cpl. L. Gwatkin	1/11/45
2607884	R.S.M. Fitzhugh	8/11/45
2612745	W.O.II L. Huggins	8/11/45
2608082	C.Q.M.S. W. Edwards	8/11/45
2614394	Sergt. R. Gilbert	8/11/45
2611856	Sergt. A. Hooh	8/11/45
2615578	Sergt. C. Tester	8/11/45
2613498	Sergt. G. Young	8/11/45
2615263	L./Cpl. R. Warner	8/11/45
2614839	W.O.II E. Weaver	29/11/45
2615788	Sergt. A. Bowley	29/11/45
2612371	Sergt. A. Bruford	29/11/45
2619016	Sergt. J. Clare	29/11/45
2617480	Sergt. R. Griffin	29/11/45
2612663	Sergt. A. Litchfield	29/11/45
2618946	Sergt. W. Ravilious	29/11/45
2618717	L./Sergt. J. Coleman	29/11/45
2621924	L./Sergt. N. Goodley	29/11/45
2621028	L./Sergt. A. Green	29/11/45
2614656	L./Sergt. F. Matthews	29/11/45
2618786	L./Sergt. A. Pique	29/11/45
2614858	L./Sergt. A. Thornley	29/11/45
2624056	L./Sergt. R. Udall	29/11/45
2620413	L./Cpl. V. Francis	29/11/45
2618918	L./Cpl. F. Lance	29/11/45
2621181	L./Cpl. F. Lewington	29/11/45
2621243	L./Cpl. C. Skeet	29/11/45
2622523	Gdsm. K. Barnham	29/11/45
2622627	Gdsm. A. Clements	29/11/45
2622917	Gdsm. K. Dudley	29/11/45
2618254	Gdsm. B. Lakeland	29/11/45
2622646	Gdsm. A. Lane	29/11/45
2621457	Gdsm. W. York	29/11/45
7263018	Sergt. E. Mullineux	21/ 2/46

		Gazetted
2612477	W.O.II A. Bishop	2/ 4/46
2613590	W.O.II A. Burden	2/ 4/46
2612770	W.O.II G. Chapman	2/ 4/46
2613583	W.O.II G. Rousell	2/ 4/46
2611455	W.O.II H. Shipper	2/ 4/46
2612464	W.O.II H. Stockton	2/ 4/46
2609125	C.Q.M.S. F. Huggett	2/ 4/46
2617154	Sergt. R. Harriman	2/ 4/46
2613959	Sergt. W. Littlewood	2/ 4/46
2618539	Sergt. A. Medhurst	2/ 4/46
2615664	Sergt. J. Noble	2/ 4/46
6967879	Gdsm. E. Hutt	2/ 4/46
2614501	Gdsm. S. Read	2/ 4/46
2613709	W.O.II J. Bignell	21/ 5/46
2609205	W.O.II F. Ellender	21/ 5/46
2614844	W.O.II T. Lythgoe	21/ 5/46
5250214	W.O.II C. Workman	21/ 5/46
2617677	Clr.-Sergt. P. Bradley	21/ 5/46
2615802	Clr.-Sergt. R. Pollington	21/ 5/46
2615123	Sergt. G. Baddeley	21/ 5/46
5884629	Sergt. D. Boniface	21/ 5/46
2617870	Sergt. L. Evans	21/ 5/46
2614996	Sergt. D. Lloyd	21/ 5/46
2619862	Sergt. W. Rogers	21/ 5/46
2616842	Sergt. P. Sullivan	21/ 5/46
2616438	Sergt. D. Warren	21/ 5/46
2617095	Sergt. A. Warrington	21/ 5/46
2618006	L./Sergt. J. Mullin	21/ 5/46
2620067	Cpl. J. Wickers	21/ 5/46
2616226	L./Cpl. A. Burgess	21/ 5/46
2621152	Gdsm. G. Chinnery	21/ 5/46
2625553	Gdsm. F. Dodsworth	21/ 5/46
2625525	Gdsm. G. Ness	21/ 5/46
2624366	Gdsm. G. Newton	21/ 5/46

FOREIGN DECORATIONS AND AWARDS

FRENCH

Croix de Guerre avec Etoile en Vermeil

3448514	L./Sergt. A. Howarth, B.E.M.	1944

Croix de Guerre with Bronze Star

2610382	R.S.M. A. Spratlet, M.M.	1945
2609407	C.S.M. E. Foster	1945
2613677	L./Sergt. E. Ridler	1945

BELGIAN

Croix de Guerre, 1940, with Palm

2614898	R.Q.M.S. D. Anderson	1946
2613582	D./Sergt. G. Rousell	1946
2611163	C.S.M. D. Slack	1946

Gazetted

AMERICAN

SILVER STAR

2615210 L./Sergt. R. Clark 1945

BRONZE STAR

2619311 L./Sergt. R. Philpott 1945
6201036 C.S.M. K. Fisher 1945
2621054 L./Cpl. N. Peters 1945

ACTS OF GALLANTRY

For various acts of gallantry, both in the face of the enemy and in the course of ordinary duty, twenty-one other ranks were cited in orders.

CERTIFICATES FOR GOOD SERVICE

One hundred and thirty-eight other ranks were awarded Certificates for Good Service.

APPENDIX VI

COLONELS, LIEUTENANT-COLONELS, COMMANDING OFFICERS AND REGIMENTAL ADJUTANTS, 1939-1945

COLONELS OF THE REGIMENT

H.R.H. Field-Marshal The Duke of Connaught and Strathearn, K.G., etc.	1/ 5/04 to 23/ 2/42
H.R.H. The Princess Elizabeth	24/ 2/42 to

LIEUTENANT-COLONELS OF THE REGIMENT

Colonel C. R. Britten, M.C.	1/ 7/37 to 31/ 8/39
Colonel M. E. Makgill Crichton Maitland, D.S.O.	1/ 9/39 to 10/ 2/41
Colonel J. A. Prescott	11/ 2/41 to 4/ 1/45
Colonel R. B. R. Colvin, D.S.O.	5/ 1/45 to 11/ 1/48

REGIMENTAL ADJUTANTS

Major H. R. H. Davies	17/ 2/38 to 10/ 3/40
Major T. P. M. Bevan, M.C.	11/ 3/40 to 28/ 9/41
Major A. H. Penn, C.V.O., M.C.	29/ 9/41 to 22/ 6/45
Major P. A. S. Robertson	23/ 6/45 to 18/12/47

COMMANDING OFFICERS

1st BATTALION

Lieut.-Colonel J. A. Prescott	22/ 8/38 to 11/ 2/41
Lieut.-Colonel W. H. Goschen	11/ 2/41 to 17/ 3/41
Lieut.-Colonel J. A. Gascoigne, D.S.O.	17/ 3/41 to 20/ 3/42
Lieut.-Colonel E. H. Goulburn, D.S.O.	20/ 3/42 to 27/10/44
Lieut.-Colonel Lord Tryon, D.S.O.	27/10/44 to 6/11/44
Lieut.-Colonel L. S. Starkey	6/11/44 to 21/ 3/45
Lieut.-Colonel P. H. Lort-Phillips, D.S.O.	23/ 3/45 to 21/ 7/47

2nd BATTALION

Lieut.-Colonel G. M. Cornish, O.B.E., M.C.	1/ 8/39 to 20/ 4/40
Lieut.-Colonel J. A. Lloyd	20/ 4/40 to 29/ 5/40
Lieut.-Colonel P. G. S. Gregson-Ellis, C.B., O.B.E.	10/ 6/40 to 9/10/40
Lieut.-Colonel C. M. Dillwyn-Venables-Llewelyn, M.V.O.	14/10/40 to 26/10/42
Lieut.-Colonel R. N. Brinckman, D.S.O., M.C.	26/10/42 to 24/ 1/44
Lieut.-Colonel J. N. R. Moore, D.S.O.	24/ 1/44 to 15/ 7/45
Lieut.-Colonel C. M. F. Deakin	15/ 7/45 to 28/ 2/46

3RD BATTALION

Lieut.-Colonel Sir John R. Aird, Bt., M.V.O., M.C.	22/ 9/37 to 7/ 5/40
Lieut.-Colonel A. H. S. Adair, D.S.O., M.C.	8/ 5/40 to 16/10/40
Lieut.-Colonel R. B. R. Colvin, D.S.O.	24/10/40 to 8/ 4/42
Lieut.-Colonel A. S. Hanning	8/ 4/42 to 20/ 9/42
Lieut.-Colonel A. G. W. Heber-Percy, D.S.O.	20/ 9/42 to 27/ 4/44
Lieut.-Colonel J. A. Goschen, O.B.E.	27/ 4/44 to 30/ 5/44
Lieut.-Colonel E. J. B. Nelson, D.S.O., M.C.	30/ 5/44 to 1/ 3/45
Lieut.-Colonel P. T. Clifton, D.S.O.	1/ 3/45 to 7/ 3/47

4TH BATTALION

Lieut.-Colonel O. W. D. Smith	15/10/40 to 11/ 8/42
Lieut.-Colonel H. R. H. Davies	11/ 8/42 to 6/11/44
Lieut.-Colonel Lord Tryon, D.S.O.	6/11/44 to 21/ 8/45

5TH BATTALION

Lieut.-Colonel Hon. J. B. G. Hennessy	11/10/41 to 6/ 8/42
Lieut.-Colonel R. H. Bushman	11/ 8/42 to 19/ 4/43
Lieut.-Colonel G. C. Gordon-Lennox, D.S.O.	19/ 4/43 to 27/ 1/44
Lieut.-Colonel A. C. Huntington, M.V.O.	2/ 2/44 to 9/ 2/44
Lieut.-Colonel G. C. Gordon-Lennox, D.S.O.	12/ 3/44 to 11/11/44
Lieut.-Colonel P. T. Clifton, D.S.O.	11/11/44 to 1/ 3/45
Lieut.-Colonel E. J. B. Nelson, D.S.O., M.C.	1/ 3/45 to 15/ 5/45

6TH BATTALION

Lieut.-Colonel A. F. L. Clive, D.S.O., M.C.	14/11/41 to 5/ 8/43
Lieut.-Colonel W. H. Kingsmill, D.S.O., M.C.	6/ 8/43 to 29/ 5/44
Lieut -Colonel R. H. Bushman	29/ 5/44 to 4/12/44

TRAINING BATTALION

Lieut.-Colonel W. S. Pilcher, D.S.O.	1/ 9/39 to 23/10/41
Lieut.-Colonel G. M. Cornish, O.B.E., M.C.	18/11/41 to 26/ 9/44
Lieut.-Colonel Sir Hugh J. F. S. Cholmeley, Bt., D.S.O.	26/ 9/44 to 5/12/44
Lieut.-Colonel R. H. Bushman	5/12/44 to disbandment

HOLDING BATTALION

Lieut.-Colonel G. M. Cornish, O.B.E., M.C.	20/ 4/40 to 18/11/41
Lieut.-Colonel Lord Edward Hay	18/11/41 to 2/11/43 (when renamed Westminster Garrison Battalion)

APPENDIX VII

ORGANIZATION OF TYPICAL INFANTRY AND ARMOURED BATTALION

1

INFANTRY BATTALION, 1940

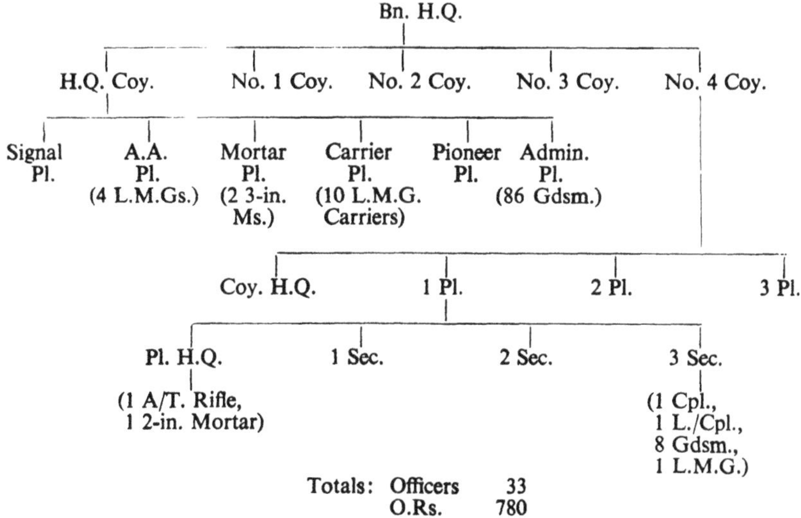

Totals: Officers 33
O.Rs. 780

2

INFANTRY BATTALION, 1943

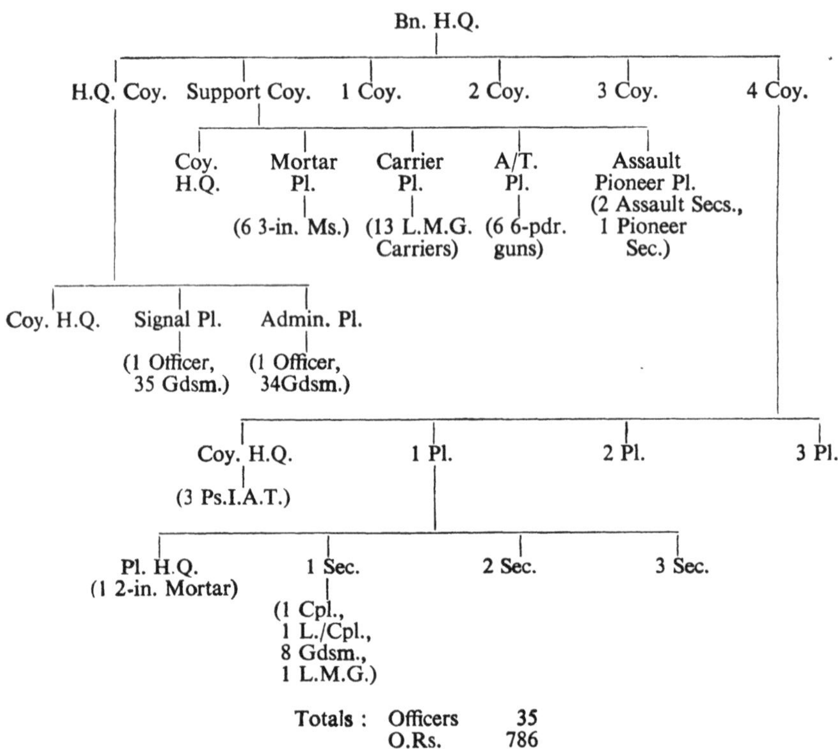

Totals : Officers 35
O.Rs. 786

3

MOTOR BATTALION

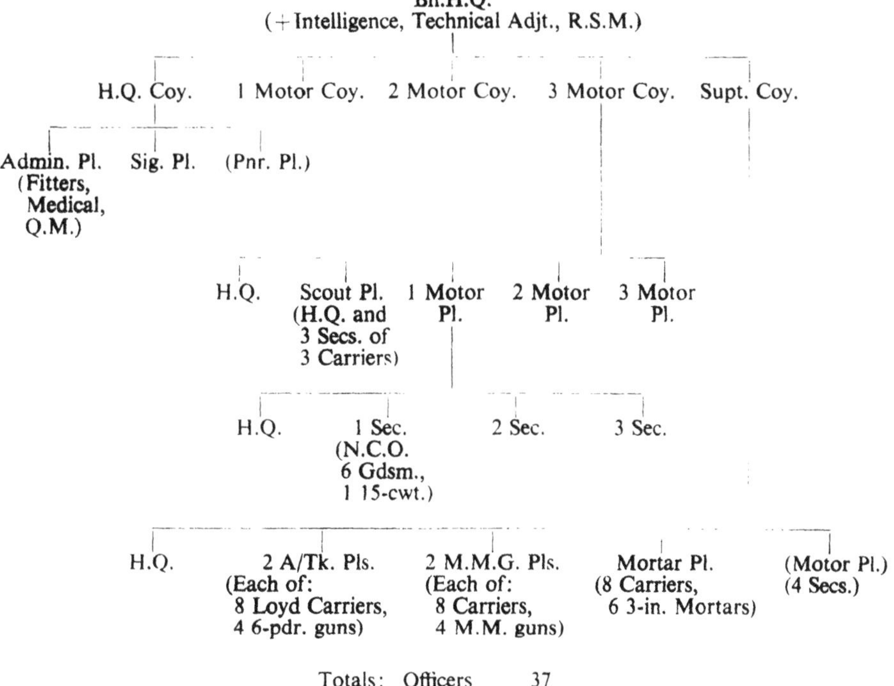

Totals: Officers 37
O.Rs. 782

4

ARMOURED REGIMENT, TYPE "A"

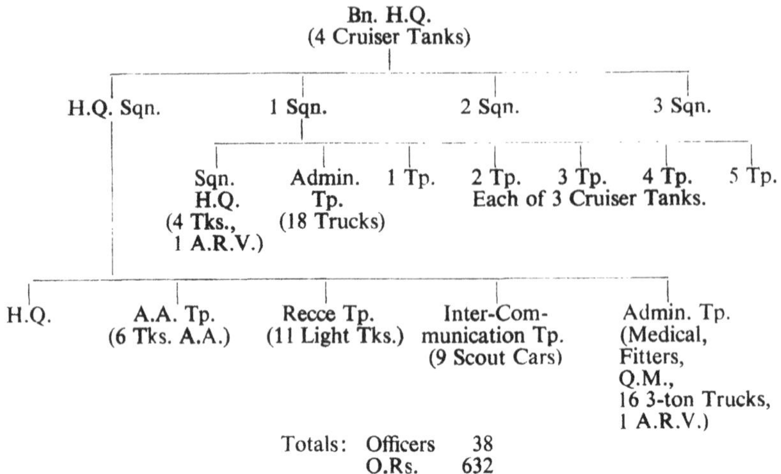

Totals: Officers 38
O.Rs. 632

NOTE.—This type approximates to the 2nd Bn. Grenadier Guards.

5

ARMOURED REGIMENT, TYPE "B"

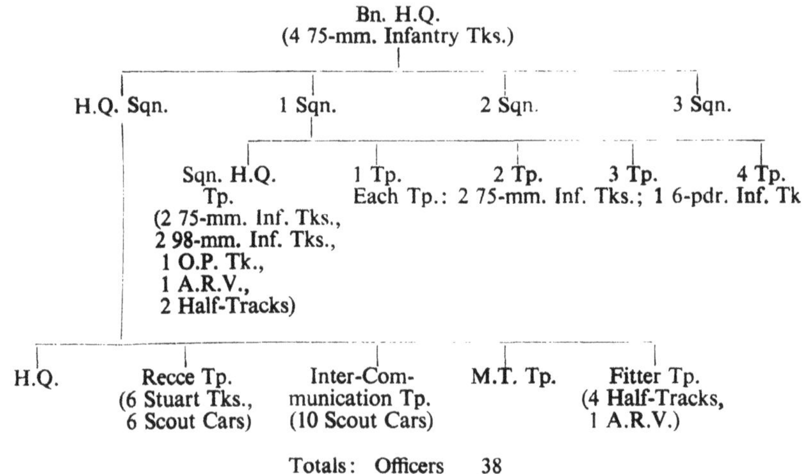

Totals: Officers 38
O.Rs. 632

NOTE.—This was the organization of the 4th Bn. Grenadier Guards, which used Churchill Tanks. The Battalion often had S.P. guns, A.V.R.Es., and Flail and Crocodile Tanks under command. At first, Squadron establishment was for 5 troops of 3 tanks and H.Q. Troop of 3 tanks, but this was reduced owing to lack of replacements.

INDEX

(Pages xii to 256 are to be found in Vol. I; pages 259 to 582 in Vol. II)